The River of Angry Dogs

T0341920

The River of Angry Dogs

A Memoir

Mira Hamermesh

Introduction by Fay Weldon

PLUTO PRESS

First published 2004 by Pluto Press
345 Archway Road, London N6 5AA
This paperback edition published 2019 by Pluto Press

www.plutobooks.com

British Library Cataloguing in Publication Data
A catalogue record for this book is available from the British Library

ISBN 978 0 7453 4029 6 Paperback
ISBN 978 1 84964 232 3 PDF eBook
ISBN 978 1 7868 0539 3 Kindle eBook
ISBN 978 1 7868 0538 6 EPUB eBook

Typeset from disk by Newgen Imaging Systems (P) Ltd, India
Printed and bound by CPI Group (UK) Ltd, Croydon, CR0 4YY

Contents

In memory of my parents.
For my son Jeremy and his family:
Lulu, Benjamin and Anna.
And for all my parents' other grandchildren,
great-grandchildren
and great-great-grandchildren.
Our continuity.

Mira's family together before the war. Inset: Mira before the war.

Acknowledgements

My thanks to my literary friends who devotedly kept an eye on my progress during the writing of the book, reading and rereading, correcting and like 'literary midwives' assisting in the birth of the book.

To Joanna Goldsworthy who had planted the idea of writing the memoir, special thanks. Also to David Elliott, the most patient of readers without whose encouragement the book could never have been completed.

My gratitude to my literary angels who had spread their protective wings: Alan Sillitoe and Ruth Fainlight, Gil Elliot, Naomi Shepherd-Laish, Mai Ghoussoub, Peter Jonson-Smith, Lili Pohlman and Stoddard Martin (Chip).

Thanks to all others whose help made all the difference. Eddie Hamilton, Amanda Sarrant, Tirca Loewenstein, Eugene Wolstoneholme, Frederick Roll, Marie-Ann Lindenstaadt, Anna Macnotchine.

And Keith Meehan who taught me how to build.

Introduction

Fay Weldon

This is a most extraordinary and moving memoir, written by an extraordinary woman. Mira Hamermersh strikes one as being Anne Frank as she could have been, would have been, had things turned out just a little differently. Had Anne Frank, after the manner of so many teenagers, been just a little more unruly and wilful, just a little more enraged by her mother, to the point that she actually ran away from home before the prison walls closed in, what then would have been her future? Much, I imagine, as was Mira's. Mira, by a mixture of delinquency, ingenuity and good luck, as national borders changed around her and Jewishness became ever more dangerous, escaped the fate the Nazis had in mind for her, and lived to face another day, another era, by virtue of a single act of disobedience and apparent ingratitude. In the face of her mother's despair, she left home. She ran away, and so lived to become a wife, a mother, a filmmaker, an artist and writer. Her family, staying behind, perished. It was, for Mira, a bitter irony.

Mira was born and brought up in Lodz in Poland – not an attractive town to all accounts, not in the least like Anne Frank's Amsterdam, with its silvery canals, but industrial, and horribly polluted, even pre-Communism. 'In the Polish city where I was born,' writes Mira, of her early childhood, 'there were no lakes or swans. The only pools of water I was familiar with were discharged from factories and coloured by dyes. Blue, purple, or blood red. I thought the waters of the world were as colourful as the rainbow.' But she came from the same kind of family as the Franks, prosperous, kindly and concerned, thoroughly Jewish by ritual and custom, yet integrated with the community. When she runs, with her elder brother, it is to get to Palestine, where her elder sister has gone before her. It is to be two years before she gets there.

In the meanwhile the family, the friends, the schoolmates, everything she knew and recognised, were to be obliterated. Even her nationality was gone. Mira was as much Polish as she was Jewish, but by the end of the war the Poland she knew did not exist. Part had become Germany, part was annexed by Russia, and the Jews were welcome nowhere. Frontiers shifted and changed. 'In Central

Europe,' writes Mira 'People got used to the fact they go to bed in one country and wake up in another.'

When Mira, at the time barely 15, leaves Lodz with her brother, all Central Europe is crumbling about them. Their ambition is to get to Palestine. Their first destination is smart, cosmopolitan Cracow, only to find the whole country has been crossed off the map of Europe. 'Defeat had a foul smell and stank of blocked lavatories.' They share a compartment on the journey with a genteel woman and her young daughter: the woman dies of a heart attack. It was to be the first of the many deaths, many misadventures, that are to mark their long journey to the Promised Land – already barred to them by British warships. They are without papers in a now hostile land – other than a forged school pass from Mira's school. There is no way back and the only way forward is through a network of friends, Jewish and non-Jewish politicos and casual travelling companions: they are blessed by strange coincidence, and the unexpected kindnesses shown to the very young. Maps are rare and of great significance: letters somehow get through.

They steal across the murderous river of angry dogs to safety, only to find no safety there. Mira's idealistic brother gets converted to Communism, and enrols – no questions asked – as a mine worker in the Soviet Union, in the belief that this is the proper place for a young man in the new world. He is soon to learn differently, is arrested and vanishes into Siberia. In the meanwhile Mira is on her own. She comes to womanhood on the road: on the Soviet-Romanian – once Polish-Romanian – border, attempting another illegal crossing. She wonders what it was like for Joan of Arc, to turn into a woman inside her coat of mail.

The story has as happy an ending as there can be for such a one. Reaching Palestine eventually, Mira's artistic sensibilities and talent for painting become obvious even to the uninitiated: she is taken up, helped, educated, trained. She goes, unsurprisingly, into denial. She puts the past behind her. She goes to Britain, where she has family. She marries an aspiring chartered surveyor who reads poetry, has a child, becomes part of the thriving London art scene of the 1950s and 1960s, studies under Josef Herman (I have her powerful, bold, very black, very white, drawings on my walls). And then, one day, she goes to see a film. It's *Generation*, directed by Andrzej Wajda, a love story set in Poland during the German occupation. The background of the story is the uprising in the Warsaw ghetto, and its terrible end. The film has been processed in Lodz. And Mira's life changes. She makes a pilgrimage to Poland, to face and perhaps regain the past. She joins the Polish Film school – no easy matter, for a British national in a Soviet-ruled country – but she is not to be deterred. She finds true love. She makes films. Thrown out of Poland for being in the wrong place and the wrong time, and having the wrong friends, she comes home and makes dramas and documentaries for the BBC. The world by now is in its flamboyant pre-feminist stage: Mira has another fight to fight, for recognition and independence. She engages boldly. Her subjects, not surprisingly, are conflict, dispossession, death, injustice, lost love between mother and child, the state's cruel intervention into personal lives.

This is not a book about a holocaust survivor, but of what happened to the others, who trailed the edges of death, and were flung out as if by centrifugal force, to places they could never have expected to be. There is no self-pity here, in this inspiring tale of courage and perseverance, honestly and skilfully told. It reads like a novel.

'Write!
For whom?
Write for the dead whom thou didst love in the past.
Will they read me?
Yea, for they return as posterity...'

(Johann Gottfried von Herder)

1
Before the War

Someone said, 'A bullet is too good for the likes of her.'

In 1959, the war caught up with me again. At night, in dreams, I was dragged from the cellar and stood up against a wall, with my hands raised.

When my husband had phoned from his office, proposing we hire a babysitter and go to the cinema that evening, he hadn't known about my recurring nightmares. My son was at the nursery and I was in the studio painting and scraping, frustrated by a problem with pigment: magenta mixed with burnt sienna refused to glow and the canvas was a muddy patch. I welcomed a distraction.

R. had in mind a Polish film at the Academy Cinema in Oxford Street, and read out a glowing review from *The Times* about the film *Generation* by Andrzej Wajda. He was a young director who was little known in England but who had won some major international awards.

My English husband spoke with a cultivated accent. He had a melodious voice and was a perfect mimic. He could imitate a wide range of foreign accents, but not mine, and that annoyed him. No wonder really, as mine was a hybrid that even Professor Higgins could have found a challenge.

His well-modulated voice conveyed satisfaction as the film had offered an occasion to display his sensitivity to my Polish roots. I sensed that he anticipated some expression of pleasure and I tried not to disappoint him. In spite of my undeclared resolve to keep away from anything connected with my birthplace, I wavered. Truthfully, I would have preferred to see a French or an American film. Undecided as to how I could get out of it, I left it to chance. Chance had already saved my life on several occasions.

It was time to collect my son from the nursery. I strapped him into his car seat and drove to do the weekly shopping. He got bored with the familiar supermarket lanes, so we went to Regent's Park to feed the swans and ducks where he could watch the birds engaged in a fight for the breadcrumbs.

'The big ones are getting it all,' my son said, and from his tone of voice I was not sure if this was a complaint against the injustice, or an acknowledgement that he was learning to accept nature's law.

In the Polish city where I was born, there were no lakes and no swans. The only pools of water I was familiar with were discharged from factories and coloured by dyes of blue, purple or blood red. I thought the waters of the world were as colourful as the rainbow.

That evening our babysitting arrangement fell through.

'I'll stay at home,' my husband decided.

'Let's toss a coin,' I suggested. 'Heads goes; tails stays at home.'

R. tossed a coin and Queen Elizabeth's head landed by my feet.

I parked the car in the car park at Selfridges and considered my options. I could tell R. that the film was sold out and go to see another. Despite my resistance, my feet propelled me towards the cinema. At the entrance, the posters showed a montage of young lovers kissing against the background of a German tank. The sight of a Nazi swastika made me panic.

A chatty, young usherette dressed in black, urged me to go in. 'It's really very, very good. Worth seeing.' In her smile there was something of a nurse's concern before administering a painful injection. Not to go in now would seem cowardly.

The cinema was half-empty. The lights faded and the plush red decorations dissolved into darkness.

The film, shot in black and white, was a love story set in Poland during the German occupation. It told of an encounter between Stach, a young factory worker and Dorota, a female, middle-class student. They had joined the resistance and the war had helped them surmount their differences of class. The grim reality of life in Warsaw was the background to their courtship.

In the film, which featured Dorota, the leader of a group of conspirators, and Stach, her recent recruit, love offered hope of being shielded against a hostile world. Gazing into each other's eyes, they exchanged a mute pledge to endure whatever life might bring. Love, their faces proclaimed, would help them resist the German might. Their first kiss, burdened by frustrated desire, was followed by a scene of Jews being led from the sewers of the burning Warsaw ghetto. Jews were jumping from balconies whilst across the road a carousel whirled to a cheerful tune. On other side of the street,

Poles were shutting their windows to keep out the fumes and the stench of burning bodies. Some slept, some were making love, some prayed.

In the safety of the cinema, I was caught in the crossfire of history, Polish history and my own. It triggered a memory of German troops arriving in Lodz, my native city, on 8 September 1939.

Mother and I were standing by the window, peering through the lace curtain, keen to observe the scene in the street below. History was my strong subject at school and the Blitzkrieg offered a chance to see history in the making. I was unashamedly fascinated by the military might rolling through our street, the scene of a victorious army conquering a city. The young weather-beaten faces of the German conquerors, carried along on the wings of victory, looked triumphant.

Mother pulled me away. 'Don't stand there! They shoot at random!'

Her grip on me, both physical and emotional, aroused my resentment. I was well accustomed to Mother's fear of men in uniforms.

Throughout the film I had to push my fist into my mouth to muffle the sobs, overcome with a belated sense of loss. I had to suppress an urge to howl like an injured animal.

Since the Second World War, I had counted the passage of time by using my Mother's measure, adding the number of harvests accumulated in a lifetime. Some were lean, some fertile. The seasons followed one after another; moody autumn skies rolled into winter days. I gorged on life, sweet or bitter. Like most people who had once smelt death, I was hungry for life. I carried it in my teeth like an animal. But in the cinema watching the Polish film it tasted bitter.

When the end-credits rolled, the name of my native city, Lodz, where the film was processed and printed, appeared in large letters that jumped out of the screen like mythical winged horses, galloping towards me. Sliding through the projector's shaft of light was a summons addressed to me. My deferred rendezvous with fate took place in the Academy Cinema. I could not hide.

The lights came on and the cinema emptied.

LOST IN THE CITY

With film everything is possible. Even the dead can be resurrected. Only on the screen, or in dreams, do the dead appear alive without the intervention of miracles. Public figures, long dead, walk and talk. Film stars, long dead, have the power to make us laugh or cry. They face us, talking, singing, kissing, crying or driving fast cars – never ageing. So, perhaps I should not have been surprised at what materialised in the cinema, in the Temple of the Tenth Muse. The screen, like an altar in a church, has the hypnotic power to induce heightened emotions.

Some people court spiritual experiences by venturing out into a desert. Others take up positions on the shores of sacred rivers, recite mantras and wait for the ultimate Enlightenment. Why should I not find my transformation in a cinema?

I think it must have rained. Oxford Street reflected the brightly lit shop windows. Outside a shop filled with male dummies dressed in the latest fashions, I caught my reflection in a mirror, without recognising myself. My father's moustache was superimposed over my own face, his eyes looked through mine. I was the only member of the family who resembled him: high cheekbones, dark hair and blue-grey eyes. My older brother and sister had my mother's fair, Slavonic looks. In a way, I was not surprised to see his apparition materialise in a London street. He loved London, having visited a few times before the war. Although his business took him to other cities, Paris and Brussels for example, London was his favourite. After each visit, he would bring home a new English habit. Jaeger knitwear had become essential in our household. To the disgust of our neighbours, he introduced the custom of drinking tea with milk. Like our family however, they enjoyed his stories. At the entrance to Madame Tussaud's Museum, he mistook a wax policeman for a real one; or his description of the Changing of the Guard at Buckingham Palace as a pantomime performed by men who wore tall and bearskin hats, which would have made the Polish *Chassidim* green with envy. Father also appreciated English politeness in general, and that of the policemen in particular – a sharp contrast to our own brutal Polish variety. He was further impressed by a political system that managed to combine democracy with a monarchy.

Polish culture had been predominantly Francophile for centuries yet my father insisted his children learn English and favoured London over Paris for our future education. Father's particular affection for London contributed to my decision to settle here after the war, a decision strengthened through other ties.

Mother's two sisters and a brother had settled in London after the Great War (1914–18). Though she never visited them, the sisters held reunions in Marienbaad where they travelled to 'take the waters'.

One of them, Rachel (an unmarried aunt), once visited us in Lodz. And it was her presence that increased my interest in the capital of the all-powerful British Empire. England, which looked like a curled-up animal on our school map, took on an additional importance to the girl growing up in a Jewish household. Britain held the mandate over Palestine and was responsible for the implementation of the Balfour Declaration. In our hall stood a white and blue Zionist 'Keren Kayamet' collection box and I understood that the fate of Zionism depended on key political figures residing in London – and that the future of the Jewish settlement in Palestine was in their hands. More important was the knowledge that no Nazi boot made its imprint on English soil.

After the war, I married an English Jew whose family was assimilated. His parents regarded themselves as English first and Jewish second. They never vocalised an awareness of the Holocaust. At the time it suited me. England and my new family provided a shelter from the dead, from the Holocaust itself. My own family simply vanished from my life – without funerals, and with nothing inherited. There was only a void I was afraid to be sucked into.

I arrived in England in 1947 and quickly realised that here was an ideal place for my 'convalescent' needs. One could count on the laissez-faire attitude and be left in peace. The proverbial politeness of English people who refrained from asking questions created for me ample mental space to cope with the awesome losses of war, or so I thought.

The film, *Generation*, had torn open old wounds. My feet carried me through London streets, but my head remained in Poland, unable to part from the characters, and, by association, from my own family. It exploded my defence system, a makeshift survival kit devised to release me from my accountability to the dead.

I was in no condition to face my husband or child; our home was no place to bring back the debris of Poland's war years. My grief was homeless, and I had to shelter them from it.

I walked through dark streets oblivious of time or place. By 2 a.m., I'd strayed into the heart of the City, which at night was like a ghost town. The bright baronial edifices of insurance companies and banks were empty shells.

'Curse these people who design cities where street life dies with the fading of daylight!' The curse could only have come from my mother, who was quick to utter curses. On my lips they felt alien. Was I in danger of becoming her mouthpiece?

In line with my mother's curses, and with the darkness, a black cat darted from a dark alley and crossed my path. As I was in England, not in Poland, it proved to be a good omen. A police car pulled up. Tired, cold and hungry, I was relieved to see it.

'Where am I?' I asked the driver.

One of the two officers in the car started questioning me. What was I doing, a woman all alone wandering at night in the City? He explained that the law permitted them to arrest homeless people, vagrants in need of protection. I had no identification papers; my licence was in the car. I was to be driven to the nearest police station for further questioning.

Once inside the police car, I felt glad to be under the Queen's protection. Her Majesty was already implicated in my misadventure: had she not appeared face up on the floor, I would have been safely tucked up in my bed.

While at the police station I was fortified by tea and biscuits, the latest addition to the nightly crop of detainees. My company included a couple of jaded prostitutes and a middle-aged, Irish drunk with watery blue eyes hiccuping intermittently between cursing England.

A middle-aged officer with thinning hair and bushy dark eyebrows interrogated me. Had I run away? Had I had a fight with my husband? Where was my home?

His assistant, a young officer, was typing with one finger and from time to time, looked up and watched me with a perplexed expression. He had short, cropped hair and pale blond eyelashes that looked as if they had been sprayed with gold dust. My attempts to explain myself must have sounded like a crinkled tape played at the wrong speed.

'...The Academy Cinema...The German invasion of Poland...The war, the Jews, the lovers, the girl shot dead, Mother, Father...Lodz...'

My words made no sense, but my being Polish did. The elder officer had one in the family. His sister, who lived in Scotland, had married a Pole. Adam, his brother-in-law, was a strange character who dissolved into tears when drunk. And a grown man at that, the officer added in disgust. After the censure of the tear-prone Polish brother-in-law, the officers exchanged knowing glances. A smirk added a glint to the younger officer's blushing face.

'Why don't you phone up my husband?' I suggested.

'At 3 o'clock in the morning?'

He looked shocked at my suggestion. It would all be sorted out without having to bother an innocent man in the middle of the night. I appreciated his concern.

They drove me to the car park. After checking my driving licence and, satisfied that I was telling the truth, they trailed behind me all the way to my home. For good measure, they looked on as I let myself into the house.

A HYDRA WITH MANY HEADS

I tiptoed to the nursery trying not to disturb my husband. My son was fast asleep, his cheeks rosy in the glow of the pink night-light. The floor was littered with Dinky cars piled up in a traffic jam. I kissed him and adjusted the covers, desperate to anchor my emotional turmoil in the world of motherhood.

I went to the kitchen to make a cup of tea. Sufficiently anglicised, I found solace in that ritual. Our kitchen, which I had decorated myself, now struck me with its artificiality. The copper pots from Spain and other decorative artefacts hung like a theatrical set waiting to be dismantled. My attempt at an attractive and comfortable kitchen, a hearth of nurture and nourishment, finished in utter futility. Similar homes, including my own in Poland, had been emptied of their inhabitants. My son's paintings of animals, done in bold primary colours, only served to remind me that children similar to him, who perhaps painted similar images, were sent to death camps.

The Academy Cinema had opened a door to ghosts.

R. entered, holding a glass of whisky. Usually a moderate drinker, his breath was saturated with the smell of the spirit. He looked tired but furious.

'Where were you?'

We faced each other across the red Formica table, both distraught. Understandably, he had thought that something terrible had happened to me and had even telephoned several hospitals. My attempts to explain what had happened did not sound convincing.

'Walking alone at night, like some Hemingway character? Who do you take me for? Who is he?'

Controlled as ever, he kept his voice down, but inside was a roar of suppressed rage. I was shocked to discover how quickly he had cast me in the role of a foreign femme fatale, prone to sexual mischief and treachery.

We met in 1951, at a New Year's Eve party held in an elegant flat in Regent's Park. I accompanied Peter, a young academic, who, stood up by his first choice, invited me at the last moment. Peter introduced me to the kind of milieu that I, a Slade art student, living on a five pounds a week scholarship, was not used to; middle-class prosperity showed in every fibre of the thick-pile carpet, the expensive mahogany, and the array of silver ornaments.

Our hostess, an attractive and lively young woman whose parents were away was gracious and tried her best to introduce me to other guests. Peter's good looks were in great demand by the young, well-dressed and well-groomed women. It was a glamorous blonde that finally snatched him up.

Everything about me spoke of my being an outsider. I possessed only one party outfit, which served all occasions in every season – a self-made assembly of odd colours and materials, a curtain brocade purchased at a sale and used as a wrap worn over a long, black skirt with a black velvet, off-the-shoulder top, fastened by safety pins. It was a clumsy attempt to imitate an outfit worn by Arletty in Carne's film *Les Enfants du Paradis*.

Even the accessory, the only one I possessed, was an improvisation: a unique choker comprised of a junk buckle from a Victorian belt and a black velvet ribbon. In those years, when Dior ruled the fashion world, only art students, impelled by necessity, ventured to bend the rules; yet to the well-dressed, fashion-conscious women in my present company the outfit was seen as vulgar in its theatrical effect.

However, secretly, I derived some pleasure from my 'ironmongered' adornment. I had developed an aversion to jewellery since my mother lost hers – our apartment having been raided by Nazis just before my parents were forced into the Lodz ghetto. Rather than surrender her jewellery, Mother flushed most of it down the toilet.

The party was in full swing. Midnight arrived, the lights were dimmed, glasses were filled with champagne and everybody struck a toast in time with Big Ben to celebrate the New Year. A wave of sadness sent me from the celebrating crowd, and I found myself in the kitchen. My entry disturbed a couple sitting side by side on the kitchen table. I was about to withdraw when the man invited me to join them.

One often moves into the future in unpredictable ways. The young man, prematurely bald and with amber-coloured eyes, drew me into their conversation. They were talking, of all things, about *Les Enfants du Paradis*. Had I seen it? Not once, but twice. Hearing my enthusiasm, he let go of the girl's hand. She had only just expressed her irritation with the marriage-wrecker, Garance, the film's heroine; her sympathy lay with Natalie, the long-suffering wife of the mime, Baptiste. Sensing a shift in her partner's interest, the young woman moved on.

He was smitten with Garance, the mysterious and majestic woman who glided across the screen. A child of the slums, Garance graced the palace of her aristocratic lover while still preserving her love for the actor.

Looking into my eyes, he immediately asked if I would like to see the film again. I proposed that we join another New Year's Eve fancy dress party at the Arts Club, where I supposed the bohemian atmosphere would enhance our romancing, and where dancing might generate erotic charges between us. At the Arts Club, my outfit was no longer out of place. R. later confessed that it aided in the transfer of his fascination from Garance to me. Fantasy had paved the way for reality. Arletty, as Garance, was cast in yet another role: that of a matchmaker. We were married six months later.

Several unsuitable past relationships had precluded commitment. R. was a stable, loving, intelligent and honourable man. My friends described him as a true English gentleman, which indeed he was. They thought I had much to be grateful for and so did I. In the space of a few years, our economic situation shifted by serendipity to a modest degree of prosperity. We converted our house in central London, acquired as a wreck, into an attractive home. More, I was allowed to develop my talent and paint full time. I was also now the mother of a healthy and lively toddler. As an aspiring painter, I juggled motherhood and art as best as I could, at times almost succeeding. Life seemed good. I told myself that I was contented and had the good sense to avoid reading about war, post-war Poland or the Holocaust. Cities were being rebuilt, and the renewed world was beckoning. With a British passport I could travel freely, no longer needing to register as an alien with the police. I felt like a caged bird newly released. Artists were flocking to see Picasso and post-Impressionists in Paris. My husband and I went further afield on trips to the museums and churches of France, Spain and Italy.

Our life in London was also stimulating, socially and culturally. Theatres, cinemas and exhibitions – 1950s Soho was the nerve centre of bohemian and cafe life. We would converge with friends in clubs located in dingy cellars where we discussed books, art, films and theatre. We frequented artists' parties, drank cheap wine and danced to the music of cafe accordionists who played for fun. At home we held unconventional dinner parties, ignoring culinary niceties, and argued fiercely about Freud, Marx, existentialism, psychoanalysis and politics. It was a timid prelude to the 1960s. After Stalin's death and Khrushchev's revelations, friends who were 'fellow travellers' or Communists held heated discussions, obsessively examining how they could have been so deluded while somewhere in the distance old empires were cracking, giving birth to new nations that were entering a world of unrest in violent spasms.

Meanwhile, our marriage hit the proverbial seven-year itch, which took us to a Marriage Guidance Clinic. We each had our own individual analysts allotted by a process neither of us understood fully. It was helpful to a degree, but it also created new and invisible barriers between us.

When I arrived in 1947 to study at the Slade, I landed in a country whose war wounds were still visible. I had known in advance of England's suffering and sacrifices. The country had been devastated by the bombs, but had been spared the crippling effects of an invasion: no round-ups, no public executions and no ghettos. It was this that was the most obvious difference. The map of England was free of the characteristic red dots used to mark the concentration camps and death camps that coloured the map of Europe. The density of those red dots on the map of Poland in particular gave it the face of a smallpox epidemic chart.

'For heaven's sake, you're in England!' R. was hugging and shaking me, trying to rid me of whatever had attached itself during my absence from home. 'Nazi boots have not soiled this land,' he was quick to remind me. I did not need to be reminded.

'You sent me to see a Polish film,' I reproached him.

'You are like a hydra with many heads and I never know with which of them I am dealing!'

Poor man. He was never sure which part of me, the Pole or the Jew, would turn up in our touchy partnership, or which aspect of my personality would react with tears, indifference or laughter. The boundaries of my identity were unstable, as fast-shifting as quicksand. Sometimes it would be the Polish/Slav that held sway. At other times my ancestral Jewish heritage dominated. I myself was not clear where the dividing line was, or if in the complexity of the Polish-Jewish cultural dichotomy, it existed at all.

Looking back, I don't understand how I managed to avoid the subject of the Holocaust for so long. I must have performed mental acrobatics to reach this state of oblivion to be protected from the

post-war revelations about the extent of the Nazi crimes, just when
the Nuremberg trials continued to be front-page news. What I tried
to forget was the fact that my entire family, with the exception of
my brother and sister, had been wiped out. A nation was murdered
and I somehow managed to avoid grieving! At the time, I understood little of the symbiotic relationship between the living and the
dead and the cost of ignoring the demands of the latter.

I had turned my back on the country I had once loved. As a child,
I strongly identified with Poland's tragic history that had suffered
300 years of oppression and dismemberment by foreign powers.
Most of its literature and art was saturated with patriotic sorrow.

After the war, the revelations about the degree of Polish indifference
towards the Nazi annihilation of its Jewish neighbours made me feel
betrayed. Although the Germans were the chief executioners, many
Poles, with some honourable exceptions, looked on without protest.
Some even noisily expressed satisfaction with the elimination of Jews:
the Germans were solving the 'Jewish Problem' for them.

That night in our kitchen, R. and I were confronting each other
separated by the shadow of the war, *his* and *mine*.

The war had affected R. in a different way. He had served in the
Intelligence Corps in Iraq and India. His injury was caused not by a
bullet, but by polio. He was sent to India to convalesce and was
exposed to a colonial lifestyle (the experience of the 'Raj' mystique
left a lasting impression on him). Looking at his war photo album
drew my imagination to far away Kashmir. R. would identify the
faces of the people: low-caste Indian servants, long-haired, turbaned
Sikhs and his English Raj brother officers. He survived his war with
a lame leg and a disability pension.

There were more than enough differences in our backgrounds
without having to cope with the added psychoanalytic shockwaves,
yet both of us nursed the emerging fragile growth of our new and
emotionally foreign selves.

'You must talk it out with your analyst,' was all R. could bring
himself to say.

We went to our king-size marital bed in silence, each wrapped in
separate thoughts.

THE ANALYST

Amongst the middle classes living in the northwest part of London
many took to psychoanalysis like to a new faith. We were no

exception and after an initial consultation with both of us, the Marriage Guidance Clinic allocated R. a male Freudian analyst, whilst I landed Mary, a Jungian lay analyst. Initially, I protested that, basically, there was nothing wrong with me. I was born with an excess of tears and, like my mother, I was prone to crying a lot. The attacks of sadness, which my mother's generation knew as melancholia, were part of my Polish-Jewish temperament, definitely not due to any neurosis.

At first, I was not very co-operative but later, I let myself be persuaded that the psyche in crisis needs a talking cure from a soul-doctor. Indeed, why not? I liked talking. At times it was difficult to stop me. I could never understand English couples who silently faced each other in restaurants while consuming the best food and drinking the best wines.

'Why don't they converse?' I would ask my husband.

'The English are not as free with spoken words as you Continentals.'

So much the worse for them, I thought. My mother believed that words could move mountains. Being English, R. had difficulties with spontaneous communication, though in letters, his words took off from the page.

Jungian analysis resembled a baptism of sorts. Instead of immersion in water, I waded into the symbols of growing and healing. Inside my psyche, Mary claimed, lay buried riches waiting to be explored. The analogies between the mental process of a neurotic and the archaic components of primitive people's psyche fascinated me. Mary enticed me into the labyrinth where I would encounter the beasts and demons lurking in my own psyche.

I was always early for my analyst's sessions. In a psychoanalytical context, such promptness might be interpreted as a sign of anxiety or greed, never as an attempt at being punctual. I soon learned that the trained analysts were listening to sensible explanations with an inner ear, detecting various acts of self-betrayal in words. They observe how we trap ourselves, trying to cover up the depth of our confusion as we stumble over words and get lost in spells of inarticulateness. For a talking cure, such linguistic lapses can be regarded as a positive contribution.

The sessions took place in a basement consulting room, leading out into a garden. The walls were hung with a variety of Chinese-inspired mandalas and one large painting representing a forest of black hands trying to reach a white sky. The painting was by an ex-patient.

Mary Williams was a tall elderly English woman. With a straight back and thin limbs, she carried her head high. Her melodious voice sounded younger than her age. A framed photo of her as a girl in a public school uniform playing hockey fixed her in my mind as the embodiment of Englishness. Though childless, I regarded her as a surrogate mother, which helped to foster an illusion of gaining, by proxy, a share of Anglo-Saxon roots.

Mary's chair was covered in black leather. Behind her, propped up on her desk, was a portrait of Jung. Her enthusiasm for him persuaded me that I was lucky to belong to the Jungian fold. I had become a willing neophyte, going through the initiation rites of Jungian psychoanalysis with Jung as an apostle of the new faith. In waking life and in dreams, I was soaking up his ideas like a sponge.

What I longed for, but didn't realise at the time, was to be in touch with the components of my own culture; to be encircled by the elders of my tribe in a ritual of blowing the *shofar*, the ram's horn used on the Day of Atonement. I needed purification rituals as an antidote to the Auschwitz fallout. I had visions of ancient rituals conducted either by a rabbi, a priest or a shaman who would dare to venture into the underworld of the dead. I needed a ritual of a sacred purification ceremony that would bring peace between the living and the dead.

Instead, I made do with the evocative power of Jung's psychoanalytic terms. Introverts/extroverts, symbols of transformation, anima/animus, archetypes and the collective unconscious were magic keys to the doors of a spacecraft and each session was a blast off into the unknown.

From behind Mary's glasses, her eyes signalled she was waiting for me to begin. The session began with an account of my nocturnal adventure after the cinema outing. From the way she shifted in her seat, I gauged the depth of her involvement in my experiences. It used to astonish me how she managed to remember everything I said.

'Any dreams?'

I had begun to keep a diary of my dreams and carried it around like snapshots to be looked at. My attachment to dreams and their significance had a pre-Freudian, pre-psychoanalytic origin. In Poland, dream swapping or dream sharing was as common a way of communicating with people as comments about the weather are in England. I grew up storing remembered dreams, not only my own but also the dreams of others. Even the dreams of my mother stayed fresh, preserved in the formaldehyde of memory. In one dream, wolves in a forest chased her. She tripped and fell, picked herself up and suddenly realised she was floating. 'Not very high,' she said, puzzled by the dream. It made us laugh. It was so funny trying to imagine our corpulent mother floating. Even when stepping off a kerb, she always took extra care, respectful of gravity's pull.

I would offer the crop of my dreams as gifts to Mary. Apparently, my dreams fitted perfectly into Jung's theories. Was it possible that the psyche manufactures dreams to suit the particular schools of psychoanalysis? The abundance of my dream life was evidence of the hard work we had done together.

In my dream, my husband and I were in his Rolls-Royce approaching the walls of the Warsaw ghetto. Buildings were in flames; a man jumped from a window and crashed into the rubble below. At another window, a young woman was trying to lower a painting on a rope, desperate to save it. I recognised it as Rembrandt's *The Woman at the Window*. She was appealing, repeating her cry for help from the crowd below in Yiddish, 'Listen, people, I was once a painter too!'

'Stop!' I begged R. but he drove on accelerating to get away from the ghetto. Turning a corner, I was surprised to see my parents standing in the middle of the road. I hardly recognised them. They were no longer the corpulent parents I had known. They were wearing tattered rags and looked shrivelled, emaciated from hunger. How, I wondered, had my parents managed to escape from the Lodz ghetto and reach the Warsaw ghetto?

'Stop the car!' I shouted, but no voice came out of my mouth. In desperation, I tried to lower the window but it was stuck. I saw my parents running after the car and Father even managed to reach the car window. He pounded on it, begging to be given a lift.

'Take us with you. We weigh so little!'

When Mother reached the car, she echoed Father: 'We will take up very little space.'

My last sight of them was of a forlorn-looking couple standing in the middle of the road. Mary handed me a tissue and waited for my crying to subside.

This dream, Mary decided, was clear and unambiguous in its clues. Rembrandt had stolen into my dream about my parents in the ghetto.

'My parents had never even set eyes on a Rembrandt painting!' I rambled on, connecting words to thoughts, memories to feelings.

'It all adds up,' she continued. 'Your husband's Rolls, the burning ghetto, Rembrandt's painting and your parents.' She reminded me that the Amsterdam Jewish ghetto was familiar to the painter, where he found many of his sitters, including the rabbis in his portraits.

'Why should I care if a Rembrandt painting was endangered when people were trapped in a burning ghetto?'

'Wasn't your mother's grandfather a Rabbi in Poland?'

I nodded. The memory of the ghetto woman frightened me, as did her lament in Yiddish, the language my parents spoke to each other and which I refused to learn. Childish snobbery made me reject it. Hadn't she cried out, 'Listen, people, I was once a painter too!'

Mary's enigmatic smile suggested the woman might well have been me. Never! I was an aspiring painter who shivered with emotion when standing before a Rembrandt painting! I could not conceive of a life without painting! While I protested, a premonition of something with no name yet buzzed in my head.

Mary said nothing. She was waiting for further association and I dredged up memories of the previous summer spent in Spain with my son.

By 1958, the Balearic island Ibiza was a fashionable magnet for artists from many countries. My one-woman exhibition in London was looming on the horizon and the place was ideal for painting. A magnificent landscape, the sea, sunshine, plus cheap rent, food and booze made it the perfect setting for all sorts of artistic, sexual and social experimentation. The presence of visiting artists with newly hatched literary reputations, like Norman Mailer and Gunter Grass, would make any party a magnet. A girl nicknamed 'La Cubana' organised a party that lasted till daybreak and sunrise swims.

It was also a good place for children, the locals were hospitable and the beaches were safe. We used to sail across the bay to Talamanca beach where other mothers used to bring their children. During the short crossing, my son playfully trailed his hand below the smooth surface of the water, fascinated by the mysteries of the green-blue sea. One day, he unexpectedly shot at me a startling question.

'Mum, who would you save first? You or me?'

The sea was calm but inside my son's mind a storm must have been raging in which we were both drowning. Evidently, my protestations about him being the priority did not reassure him. He kept gazing at the rocks overgrown with seaweed, as if searching for the imaginary debris of our sunken boat. I drew him close to me and held him tight.

He persisted, 'Me or a Rembrandt painting?'

His bright eyes, made a shade bluer by the ultramarine colour of the sea, were fixed on me. My son knew the name of Rembrandt. I would often take him to the National Gallery when I needed to absorb the magical glow of Rembrandt's light. He made it plain he did not enjoy these visits. The child's anxiety also carried echoes of a recent marital quarrel between R. and myself, which he may have overheard, R. taking exception to my declaration that my art be given priority over other concerns. The issue of art had become a vehicle for thrashing out marital difficulties. R. attacked the 'personality cult' which many artists use to shield themselves from the demands of everyday cares.

'Artistes!' he would mock some of my painter-friends who affected bohemian lifestyles. He saw them as arrogant and self-centred creatures. Many were known to him because, following a Polish custom, I kept an open house, which meant that friends could turn up unannounced when in need of a meal or shelter after late night pub-crawling.

Marital skirmishes always seek out the opponent's most vulnerable positions. Under the guise of criticising my bohemian friends, R. touched on the more profound issue of the moral bankruptcy of art with a capital A.

A post-war controversy about the validity of art was in the air. The debate about what kind of art was possible after Auschwitz and Hiroshima, reverberated around our household. In Auschwitz, not only the sacredness of human life was demolished, but also the cherished notion of the sacredness of art. Amongst my acquaintances was a musician who, as a member of the Auschwitz orchestra, was forced to play classical music for the inmates as they marched to work or to death. Auschwitz offered a compelling argument about the debasement of art. R.'s accusation was valid and it touched on a raw nerve.

To do justice to R., he was no philistine. He had a keen eye for good painting and a perceptive appreciation of literature. When I first met him, I was impressed by the collection of poetry books on his shelves. It was I who had unwittingly introduced the discordant note into his life. Holocaust particles must have been circulating in my system like a virus that takes its time before attacking. Some mild symptoms were beginning to manifest themselves, affecting our family life. It was upsetting to hear my son echo our discord in the calm of the Mediterranean Sea, in the glare of the midday sun. Unwittingly, the child had plugged into my own anxieties.

Mary blinked and smiled. Her interpretation revealed a clarity to which I was blind. The issue of survival was paramount in this session. My son's deep-seated anxiety about being saved had echoed my own.

'In your dream you are reproaching yourself for having survived leaving your parents to die.' She lit a cigarette, inhaled and took some time before continuing.

'The dream took you back to Poland. Have you considered going back?'

'How can you suggest it! The country's a graveyard.'

The look in her eyes dared me to face the challenge.

'Mira, the war is over.'

'For the English, yes. Not for us! You English...!'

When stirred to anger, the phrase, 'you English,' stood as an insurmountable barrier between us. My affection for England was, and still is, mixed with constant irritation. During the analysis with Mary, my quarrel with 'you English' was muted by admiration for many of the civic qualities of English life. Mary represented for me a proud Englishness, unsullied by the rape of foreign invasions.

The analysis, unexpectedly, had planted me more solidly in my Polish-Jewish roots. Encoded in my psyche were the souvenirs of a different history in which conquests, invasions, pogroms, pillage and rape had tampered with our genes, as hordes of barbarians crossed and re-crossed the land of my ancestors.

No, I had no wish to go back to Lodz, a rogue city that had left a taste of ashes in my mouth. I would never go back to the city belching soot, which even half a century later kept pouring blackness over my life. In abandoning Mother, I let the passing years pile upon me, and in the act of forgetting, was buried with her in a tomb I had never seen. Now a shrub was growing from her breasts and she was feeding life again.

The session flopped into a prolonged silence, minutes ticking away, bells ringing in my ears. Analytical silence draws on you like no other kind – measured in money and psychologically taxing.

The arm supporting Mary's chin changed position and she unfolded the mohair blanket. It was a signal that the session was at an end.

'Your time is up.'

ORDINARY FAMILY

I refused to consider going back to Poland, but in Mary's consulting room my current English home in St John's Wood was beginning to shrink in importance whilst my home in Lodz now stood like a tower.

Mary would be sitting on her plinth-like black easy chair, listening and smoking. References to my childhood home would pull in some of the vanished people like Abraham. He was a poor widower whom Mother used to feed whenever he came to the house. While sipping his tea and munching a cube of sugar, he liked to philosophise.

'*Look at this*,' he said, picking up a piece of coal from the kitchen floor and holding it in his skinny hand.

'*What do you see? A lump, just a shapeless piece of black coal. But with God's grace, after it's lit up, it burns roaring, sending sparks in all directions. It makes you wonder, doesn't it?*'

The loud sigh and his crestfallen face betrayed the depth of his existential angst. Mother would scold him:

'Abraham, she is only a child. Stop philosophising and eat up your soup!'

After his departure Mother would note that he preferred to hang around the women in the kitchen, sipping tea and speculating about life, instead of chasing an honest penny.

My big brother mocked the likes of Abraham, and in a voice that was just breaking and sounded like a puppy's attempt at barking, he called them '*Shtetle* philosophers!'

My son would always notice when I was 'visiting' the past:

'Mum, you look so sad!'

Before I even had a chance to explain that I wasn't sad but introspective, my mother's voice would break in. 'The child is telling the truth!'

I had left home in part to get away from my Cassandra-like Mother and now her spirit had anchored itself firmly to my life.

'You talk often about your mother, what about the rest of the family?' Mary observed.

Children have an uncanny sense about the absence of marital harmony. Very early on in life I understood that my parents were an ill-matched couple. Father was optimistic about the future whilst Mother was gripped by fear. For her, life was an obligation, for him, it was an ongoing challenge, filled with rewards. He was a contented, cheerful man, with an appetite for life and its novelties. I was more comfortable with him than with Mother. To me he was a beacon, his flashes a promise of new opportunities. Very early on, I realised that life was divided into two spheres: Father's domain was out in the world, and the domestic sphere was that of women and children. Without being aware of when or why, I began to construct a mental bridge for crossing these borders. I was not to know that these crossings were rehearsals for future life-saving strategies. On many occasions, as a female and a Jew, the ability to move fast from one side to the other would get me out of some dangerous situations.

Both of my parents came from sizeable families. Father was born in Staszow, a small township verging on the rural. As a youth of 14, he, like thousands of others, drifted from the countryside to the big city to make good. He followed the example of his older brothers. He did not make a great fortune, but he and his brothers made a good living. One or two of them had even become very prosperous.

Father had five brothers and one sister. The youngest brother was an emigrant to Brazil. Assembled at family gatherings, the siblings looked like replicas of each other. The brothers' faces had strong features: identical dark hair cut short, narrow foreheads and deep-set dark blue eyes, shaded by bushy eyebrows. All of them sported butterfly-style moustaches that emphasised their fleshy, sensual lips. Seated together at a table during festive occasions, they resembled the faces found on Byzantine frescoes.

Mother had five sisters and two brothers. After the Great War, two of the sisters and one brother settled in London and one of the brothers had emigrated to America. The sisters who remained in Poland kept in close touch, visiting each other often. Most of the children of the extended families, our cousins, were our constant companions.

My parents' marriage was childless for seven years and the proverbial biblical seven, infertile years, Mother spent praying and making visits to 'Wonder Rabbis'. Her prayers were answered when her first-born, a son, Mordechai, came into the world exactly a year after the end of the Great War. A child of peace, he was treated like a gift from heaven. Within three years my sister, Golda, was conceived, and I was the last, an afterthought. Both girls were born without recourse to rabbinical intervention.

It's not easy to define the social rank of my family. Mother's aristocratic pretensions extended beyond the bounds of class snobbery and would have perplexed any sociologist. Without being specific, she somehow managed to convey a sense of an ancient lineage. No aristocratic title could ever have matched her sense of social elevation. As a child, I was convinced that she was directly descended from the tribe of the Temple High Priests. Within the family, she alone would strictly observe the day-long fast that commemorated the date of the Tisha B'Av, which marked the destruction of Jerusalem's First and Second Temple. Mother shed tears and grieved for the historical catastrophes as if they had happened in her own lifetime. According to the Hebrew calendar my birthday coincided with that date, and every year Mother was weepy.

Ours was a first generation of urbanised lower-middle-class family. Father's economic success was not achieved through the textile industry that was the pride of Lodz (known in the world as the Second Manchester of Europe). It was rubber which offered him the opportunity to make money, first by importing it from England and later, by opening his own small factory.

Father was a thoroughly modern, self-taught man and admired the technological and social advancement of Western Europe. A sucker for modern gadgets, he often fell prey to the latest technological fads. I must admit I have inherited his weakness.

His enthusiasm for new inventions showed in the choice of gifts he would bring back from his foreign travels. Once, he brought back a small wooden box that generated gentle vibrations by inducing a mild current, supposedly beneficial to health. It was claimed to activate the body's own potential magnetism. Each demonstration became an occasion for entertaining friends and relatives. A lead with handles resembling a skipping rope was connected to the current and people linked hands. The vibrations penetrated through the line of hands, inducing a pleasant sensation and much laughter.

For Father and his cronies, teatime in our drawing room was about disputing politics. Squeezing slices of lemon into pale tea and stirring noisily with silver spoons, they were forever discussing the state of the world. The term '*Welt*' (world) was in constant use, as were the names of political leaders. The men would speculate on what Roosevelt, Hitler, Mussolini or Stalin might or might not do. This made the names of world leaders familiar, but no less forbidding as they jostled into our lives like uninvited guests. Tempers would explode as words like socialism, Communism, national-socialism, fascism and Zionism were tossed across the table like missiles. Sometimes one of the men's anger would flare to such a degree that everyone retreated to their homes. Father would help himself to another cup of tea, tinkle the spoon nervously against the glass and shake his head in disapproval, sharing his thoughts with me,

'Politics will be the end of the Jews.'

THE BUSY TRAFFIC OF SOULS

I could still hear the voices from Lodz. After sessions with Mary, my past would hitch a ride even on the London Underground. The faces

I glimpsed in the rush hour would trigger unexpected memories. The bearded Muslim sitting next to me conjured up Salomon, the old '*drozkah*' coachman from Lodz who liked to muse aloud about fate, sickness and death to any chance listener, including me.

'One day you get a generous tip and next day, you are attacked and robbed. I drove the same "*drozkah*" with the same horse and took the same route and look what happened to me...'

Salomon had just come out of the hospital where he was recovering from the injuries he sustained when attacked by vicious hooligans.

Once home I would leave behind the intruders from the past. I had to re-locate myself, much like a traveller who had spent the night in a strange hotel in a foreign city, reminding myself that I lived in a quiet London street where polite neighbours greeted each other with comments about the weather.

'*Only in the hour of need will you learn about your neighbours!*' Perhaps the collective memories of the pogroms coloured Mother's mistrust and Kasia our Catholic maid echoed her mistress's views.

If the voices of the dead needed any encouragement, it was psychoanalysis that must have cleared some of the hidden channels inside my head. I only hoped that Mary possessed the 'shamanistic' authority to seal up the void from where the voices of the dead were flowing.

At the age of five or six, I picked up from Mother and Kasia the idea of possessing a soul and it made me determined to see it with my own eyes, but how? I tried the mirror but all I could see was a reflection of my chubby face framed by a dark fringe cut with geometric precision. The mirror was hiding my soul from myself.

'Don't you worry, your soul sees you. Be good and make sure you don't upset it,' Mother comforted me.

Mother and Kasia dominated the corporeal and spiritual world of my childhood. Both Madam and Maid were uneducated, but rich in another kind of knowledge. And sitting on their laps I learnt about the mysteries of God and creation.

Being the youngest, I hung around Kasia's skirt the longest. She would tell me her dreams, swear and curse when frustrated, kiss and whirl me around when happy, like the occasion when she won a brooch in a church raffle. During the domestic chores, ironing or mending socks, Kasia would often muse aloud about the shape of the earth.

'They say the earth is round but how can it be? People at the bottom would fall off, wouldn't they?'

Her cosmic angst was an obsession and she kept returning to the subject often. Another subject that brought colour to her usually pale cheeks was hell. She feared hell and drunks with equal passion. When she encountered one in the street, she would verbally send him to hell. I was under the impression she might even know its exact address. But on sunny days, she had cheerful thoughts.

'On Saturdays, the Holy Virgin Mary washes Jesus' nappies and spreads them out to dry on clouds.'

I was easily seduced by the allure of Catholic rituals, most of all by the sight of children led by nuns on their way to Holy Communion. The girls, dressed like brides in long white robes and holding candles, looked so glamorous! They were usually paired with boys attired like miniature bridegrooms. I would have given anything to be fitted out like that and be paraded through the streets in front of an admiring crowd.

Kasia kept her collection of card-size New Testament illustrations in a drawer next to a bottle of camphor oil, a remedy for her rheumatism. I did not like the smell, but I was mesmerised by the images. My favourite was of the Infant Jesus surrounded by Angels, resembling fat babies swimming in the sky upside down. With the help of Kasia's pictures, I keenly followed the path of Jesus as he grew from baby to youth – Jesus, a shepherd boy holding a lamb round his neck like a fur collar. Jesus, the grown man, wearing a crown of thorns, blood dripping from his forehead, and his flesh torn revealing a pierced heart inside his chest. The kitsch illustrations, the kind popular amongst the lower classes, provided my first visual rapture.

Above Kasia's bed hung an icon of Mary holding Jesus in her arms. The Holy Mother had rosy cheeks and intense, blue eyes that were focused on the sky. I presumed she was keeping an eye on the celestial nappies drying on the clouds. In fact, she resembled Felusia, the Polish washerwoman who used to come once a month to do the family laundry. Kasia's domesticated heaven encouraged me to dream of becoming an angel. I was often on the lookout for nappy-shaped clouds. I also cherished the thought of catching a glimpse of Mary, the Holy Laundry Woman.

The icon of the Holy Virgin in Kasia's little room lavished radiance on the servant's soul. A sweet melancholy would overwhelm her when she talked about a dream she once had in which she was graced with a divine visitation. She never tired of describing in detail how the Holy Mother came into her room and unceremoniously picked up a pair of socks from the pile, settling down to mend them.

'Just like that,' Kasia said, busy with the task of darning.

Kasia's Christ looked very Polish. Straw-blond hair with watery, blue eyes, gazing transfixed into space. In the palm of his hand he held his own heart that radiated golden rays as sharp as arrows.

I knew what a heart looked like, as I often watched Kasia dismember a chicken and while she struggled with the entrails I was initiated into the Crucifixion story. I don't recall ever hearing the phrase 'Christ killers' from her, but there was no way she could avoid the subject of the supposedly Jewish guilt. She sometimes quoted her parish priest, a supposed biblical authority, who once explained during a sermon the true meaning of the Jewish customs of washing hands and saying grace before meals. 'Why do they do it?' the priest asked. For the likes of him the answer was simple: the Jews were still trying to wash off the blood of the Saviour. It signified an admission of Jewish guilt.

Thus came my first exposure to the demonic image of the Jews. Without being told, I understood that I must never breathe a word of this to Mother or anyone else in the family. I have since discovered that countless other Jewish children in Christian Europe had similar experiences.

Kasia's head was filled with a mixture of Gospel stories, folklore superstitions about hellfire and cauldrons of boiling oil for the sinners.

'That's where sinners end up! Don't you ever forget it, my child!'

She played an important role in bringing home to me the contradictions of Jewish-Christian antagonism. This became apparent when she began to teach me to love Jesus. The man on the cross was God's son. That was easy to accept. I hit a problem with the claim of Jesus' divinity. How could Jesus be the Son of God and God in the same person? Did they run heaven as a family business? At least the Jewish God had the good sense to be unmarried with no children.

Kasia, of course, was familiar with Jewish rituals, customs and the Jewish holiday timetable. She spent most of her life in a thoroughly Jewish environment and was sufficiently 'judeicised' to be able, when necessary, to prattle in Yiddish. She had lived with us since the age of 16. Ours was the only home and security she had known.

My pre-school Catholic indoctrination came to an end when I started school and Jewish history lessons began to fill in the gaps. I was afraid to share my newly acquired knowledge with Kasia in case it made loving her more difficult. I spared her the bitter collective memories of medieval ghettos, the Spanish Inquisition, the expulsions, the forced conversions, centuries of humiliation and widespread pogroms in Europe. I kept from Kasia the trail of misery left by the rift between the two religions, the calamities that stemmed from the violent interlocking of Judaism and Christianity.

I was made to understand that the Jewish God loved words and writing above everything else. The sacred Hebrew books served to this end and the Jewish reverence for books was almost sensual. If a prayer book slipped from Mother's hands, she would pick it up from the floor and kiss it three times and her children had to do the same.

Mother had her own way of making sure that I understood the uniqueness of the Jewish God. 'God is invisible. A Jew must never, never utter his name.' Mother's injunction over God's invisibility, made in quiet tones, did not protect me from visualising him and from committing idolatrous acts. I chose Salomon, Father's ageing coachman, as a model for God. His face was lined with thick folds of skin under rheumy eyes and his long, silver beard gave him dignity. Even his lack of decorum, his worn-out patched-up coat, grimy nails and a chronically runny nose did not disqualify him. What Almighty God made of my choice was an open question. I only hoped that God's love of humble creatures endeared both of us.

Salomon was no match for the young, handsome and tragic-looking Jesus. In the competitive heaven Jesus had star billing.

Mother's version of heaven resembled a busy junction where the traffic of souls circulated in all directions. The sun was like a magnifying glass through which God kept watch on the souls of his righteous creatures. I liked the idea of a celestial sphere where souls were flying like birds or insects.

One hot summer evening, sitting on the balcony with Mother she pointed out a falling star. 'Each time a person dies,' she explained, 'somewhere in the world a star falls.' Since that night, reassured by the warmth of Mother's body and her secure grip, the star-hung firmament has always been a reminder that, at least, I will be mourned. Up there in all weathers, obscured by the clouds, unborn and dying souls were riding on falling stars.

Kasia held the opposite view. 'Each time you see a falling star, Jesus is issuing a new-born baby with a divine soul. A Christian, Catholic soul!' It was all very confusing. We were Jews and I was born with a Jewish soul that, according to my mother's vague but strong insinuation, was superior and older than a Christian soul. Either way, the sky started to resemble a busy thoroughfare, with God in the role of divine policeman, regulating the traffic of souls, the new-born descending and the dead ascending. God was the Supreme Controller of the cycle of birth and death.

Mother's and Kasia's highly original and poetic preoccupation with the mystery of the Universe and God paralleled in time with Einstein's Theory of Relativity. Einstein's famous saying, 'God does not play dice with the Universe', never reached the women's ears, but in their own quaint way they shared with Einstein the longing to understand the divine mystery.

Father, in contrast to Mother, had little time for celestial matters. The sky held no great mystery for him. He had already been up and seen it from an aeroplane on a flight to London. Family and friends regarded this action as a feat of daring as well as a display of extravagance. Travel by air was expensive, mostly used by aristocrats, diplomats or film stars, rarely by middle-class businessmen burdened with an overdraft. By nature a country boy, he had adapted to the adventure of urban life with enthusiasm, while preserving a deep attachment to his village roots.

Had he seen any angels from the plane? He smiled and hoisted me onto his lap, explaining the difference between the sky and heaven. The clouds apparently resembled floating loose pieces of cotton wool racing each other. The losers descended bringing rain or snow, according to the season. He dropped another bombshell. The sky was really black, not blue. Why this was so, he didn't understand himself, but that's what a German scientist, a fellow passenger sitting next to him, had told him. Father was a self-taught man and was keen to learn from everybody, including his better-educated children.

'A black sky indeed!' Mother scoffed. 'Anyone can see it's blue!' A black sky was hardly a place for God or angels of any religious persuasion.

Father's travels made the unknown world feel closer and safer. He took pleasure in telling me about the extraordinary things that women were accomplishing in the '*grosse Welt*', where progress was visible even in the streets of the big cities. In Paris, women drove cars. An English woman flew across the ocean! Out there in the big world, women were becoming involved in global affairs, like Mrs Roosevelt, for instance. Father hoped that by the time I grew up, women in Poland might be doing similar things.

Mother was not impressed with Father's Western ways, the electric gadgets or with his ideas about 'the new woman'. In her view, there was nothing wrong with women the way they were.

Just as Kasia couldn't comprehend how gravity worked and why people at the South Pole didn't fall off, I, better educated, still fail to comprehend the sweep of ideas surrounding modern cosmology – namely, the existence of the black hole or the notion of a left-handed universe. But I am grateful to Mother and Kasia who between them have set my imagination spinning. They were not too bothered with the question of what was or wasn't suitable for a young child.

THE GUTTER KING AND QUEEN

Psychoanalysis regards childhood as the matrix of a neurosis. I was beset by doubts about the ability of clinical textbooks to relate to the legacy of the Holocaust.

In the ordinary run of life, memory serves as a storage space for life's experiences. For survivors of catastrophes, memories can be dangerous incendiaries. Like unexploded bombs, they lie dormant, without ticking a warning sign. I was not convinced that psychotherapists could be trusted to render them safe, or that talking about childhood would not become a dangerous trap for me.

The allure of childhood is capable of transforming even the shallowest sentiments into fierce attachments. It's so easy to rhapsodise about it, or dismiss it as a living hell. Either way, it can hold one hostage to the past and delude one into believing that somehow one can purify it.

Where then could I place my early experiences with Josele? Josele was the son of our next-door neighbours in Lodz. Perhaps typical of a boy of six, he liked to keep spiders in matchboxes. But Josele was boy-savant with a genius for manipulating numbers, and he used to dazzle me with his cleverness. From the age of four he could tell the date of any given day of the week, any given month of the year, in the past or future. But this mathematical genius could not learn how to lace up his shoes.

Pelusia, the housekeeper taking care of Josele, would have to do it for him.

'Tell me pet, last year, the first of May, what day was it?'

'Wednesday,' Josele replied without hesitation.

She rewarded him with a kiss and a sweet. As for myself, I was proud that this genius, three years older than me, consented to be my companion.

From the age of three he was attending a *cheder*, a traditional school for orthodox infants where they were learning by rote to read the Torah. This clever and studious boy had become yet another voice initiating me into his version of 'enlightenment.' For me Josele was an authority and I believed everything he told me.

'Moses possessed the secrets of numbers. The Ten Commandments proved it,' he declared.

In his company, beyond the horizon and the rainbow, the world stretched like a ribbon. One day, with Josele's help, I was going to tie it round my head. I was a queen and he was a king. When, after a heavy rainfall, the foul-smelling drains became blocked and flooded our street, he would sail his paper ships. In the swift currents of the gutter, we watched them shipwreck, peering into the iron grilles of the sewage system, curious to see what was inside the earth itself.

'A huge furnace keeps the earth from becoming ice.' The world, he explained, was composed of water and fire. Luckily for everybody, water eats fire and fire drinks water. My Josele knew everything!

Josele would lead me to his mother's grocery shop storeroom and teach me how to squeeze through the goods chute. Full of mischief, we would slide down and land with a bang in paradise! The basement was filled with riches upon riches, exotic spices, and raisins that resembled beads. We thrust them into our mouths tasting the heat of a sun in the faraway lands that had scorched them black. Munching nuts, we pushed our hands into sacks of polished rice that ran through our fingers like precious pearls. We pressed our hands against the flour's limp substance, delighted by imprints left on the soft, white surface.

'What's whiter? Flour or snow?' Josele asked.

'Flour,' I said.

'Snow,' he corrected.

'Why?'

'Snow comes from heaven so it's touched by God's purity. Flour comes from the earth and is contaminated by the serpent's belly.'

There was no arguing about it. Josele was busy pulling at the strings of a sealed sack, releasing an avalanche of rice. We slid out and ran for our lives.

On the way home, Josele revealed another kind of knowledge when he would alert me to an accident about to happen.

'Watch the sparks caused by the friction of the horseshoes striking against the cobbles.' The street traffic of Lodz consisted mostly of tramways, horse-driven carts and the odd taxi that would create havoc amongst the horses. Next to watching the commotion created by an epileptic fit, we liked best the drama of a horse slipping on the cobbled road surface. Known as the Belgium breed, the workhorses were of a heavy build, and usually had to pull overloaded carts of coal, bricks or sacks of potatoes.

Indeed, before slipping, horses' hooves would send out sparks.

'Horses in harness fall mostly on their left side.'

Only my Josele was likely to know on which side horses fall and how their legs would hit the air, an expert at the ways horses could come to grief.

I am ashamed to admit that I watched, taking in every detail, though I could hardly bear to see the mute expression of terror in the eyes of a fallen horse. The bridle and rings of the harness that were cutting into the horse's mouth exposed its brown gums and yellowed teeth. The worst part of such street incidents would be the coachman's behaviour, invariably furiously using his whip to raise the horse. Instead of releasing the harness, the coachman would rely on the effectiveness of the whip. Whack! Whack! Whack! Blows would rain on the animal's rump covered in sweat. The horse's supreme effort to bring itself to its feet was in vain. It was held captive by the buckled leather straps. Stiff with fright, the horse lay as if dead. The onlookers, children among them, watched without protesting. Eventually, the cursing coachman gave in and released the horse, which sprang to its feet like an acrobat.

Mary, an animal lover, winced. I wondered how she would receive the next story.

One day when Pelusia was drying Josele after his bath, I came into the room unannounced. He stood on a stool, a thin, bony little figure, rather short for his age.

'Come closer,' she urged.

When I was close enough she let the towel drop and invited me to admire him in the nude.

'Come nearer!'

Josele stood immobile like a statue. His boyishness hung on him like a bunch of young purple grapes.

'You may kiss it.'

She pulled me towards him. I touched his prick with my lips. Josele let out a shriek and jumped off the stool. With all his might he pounded Pelusia with his clenched fists while she was seized with spasms of laughter. The more he attacked her, the more she seemed to enjoy it.

'Go on, my lamb, go on, learn to roar like a lion. See little girl, how fierce your fiancé is.' While she was wiping the tears of laughter from her eyes, Josele picked up the towel and ran out of the room. At the door he hissed in my direction.

'I'd sooner be dead than be seen talking to you ever again.'

His exit was regal. Clad in the towel he looked like an emperor. I adored him but also knew he would keep his word. In no time everybody in the building got to hear Pelusia's prediction that the two of us would get married in the future.

Josele shunned me for many years. He was 17 when he spoke to me again but by then our street was bedecked with Nazi flags. It was in September 1939.

ART, KITSCH AND THE MUSE

A fellow artist once asked me what was the most decisive factor in the development of my artistic talent and the style of my painting. Was it family, school or an early exposure to fine art? It was neither home nor art museums, which Lodz lacked. The artistic stimuli reached me from the most unexpected quarters.

At home, neither paintings nor photographs were allowed on the walls, due to Mother's war against bed bugs, which infested our native town. She regarded her choice of colourful wallpaper sufficiently artistic and decorative.

The people amongst whom I grew up regarded the covers of chocolate boxes decorated with smiling Cupids as art. It was kitsch that made me wish to become a painter and it had begun with a painting *Rebecca at the Well*, the first original painting I saw. It was large, framed in a heavy, ornate golden frame and belonged to Mrs B., Josele's mother. Mrs B. had acquired the 'expensive' picture as part of refurbishing improvements to her apartment and it hung in the bedroom above her queen-size bed.

I must have been six or seven years old when seeing it made me conscious of the fact that to *see* was the most wonderful thing, and that looking at a painting was particularly magical! It's hard to describe what impressed me most. Perhaps it was the liquid blue of the sky, which spread like liquorice over the canvas. It was certainly the nearest representation of a heaven fit for Kasia's angels. The 'earthly' areas depicted a desert sprinkled with golden sand where spiky flowers were throwing purple shadows.

I was vaguely familiar with the biblical story of *Rebecca at the Well*, depicting Abraham's young son Isaac encountering Rebecca as she drew water from the well. The soft, silky robes of the young maiden painted in all the colours of the rainbow flowed like clouds. This frozen moment from the biblical story was a revelation to me! To be able to create a world pulsating with so much beauty and mystery on a flat surface seemed magical.

I was only allowed access to the bewitching painting on Saturday mornings reserved for rest in bed. Mrs B. ran her grocery shop assisted by her two daughters of marriageable age. When I would sneak in, all three women would still be in the queen-size bed in their nightwear, propped up high on feather pillows and covered with an eiderdown. In the winter, the room reeked of overheated female bodies mixed with the scent of stale perfume.

My fixation with the painting was a source of great amusement to them and I was teased mercilessly by the oldest daughter. What was I prepared to do, she asked, to be allowed to look at it? What about emptying the piss pot standing under the bed? I said I would do it and I did. As a reward, I was allowed to stand at the foot of the bed and gaze at the painting for as long as I wished. I knew there and then that I would give anything to be able to paint something like it.

Another instance of exposure to art, and this time not kitsch, happened in an attic room of a poor bookbinder where I chanced to see a reproduction of *L'Angelus* by Jean-François Millet (1814–1874). It was an oleograph – an early form reproduction – and I had no idea that it was considered the work of a great artist.

Under Mother's orders, visits to the consumptive girl, and the *L'Angelus*, were strictly forbidden. For the children of the better-off tenants occupying the more elegant part of the building, the attic was a no-go area. Mother regarded the top floor as a 'slum, up in the sky' where, in her own words, 'there is too much poverty and sickness, and too many bed bugs and lice.' She would visit them herself and help any of them, but her children were to be protected from the danger of infections.

Urban life in Poland, as in France, created dwellings that contained a microcosm of all social classes. One learned to co-exist with many strata of society. Our house in which I grew up was like many in our street. Within one building, a large oblong yard was enclosed by four sections, forming one unit. The front, facing the street, was the most expensive, rented by the wealthy. The side buildings housed the 'middle' ranks, and the basement area was occupied by the lower classes. Often, the heads of the poverty-stricken families were unemployed and the families were riddled with sick children. Jewish charities tried to provide some kind of survival net but it was like pouring water into a bottomless bucket. Mother was active in such charities and would be seen on street corners with boxes, collecting money.

Attics, like basements, presented another version of deprivation. They were occupied by poor artisans and their families who lived and worked in one room, with the number of children in many cases approaching ten. The rooms, with low ceilings and slanting eaves were damp and airless, and narrow dormer windows were their only source of daylight. Children like me, curious and cheeky, could not be kept away from any part of a building, and once inside would roam freely from one floor to the next, despite parental prohibition.

The bookbinder was a widower who lived alone with his twelve-year-old consumptive daughter. Most of the time the consumptive girl, in the advanced stages of tuberculosis, was propped up on pillows in her wrought-iron bed, sometimes coughing up blood. She looked very frail, her skin was almost transparent and a delicate blue vein stood out on her forehead making her blue eyes even bluer. *L'Angelus* hung above her bed.

It was not so much the theme of the *L'Angelus* that enthralled me. Peasants bent double, toiling in the fields and taking a break in response to the church bells calling the faithful for the Angelus prayer were not unfamiliar. During the summer visits to the countryside I could see identical scenes of peasant life.

My feeling of elation came from Millet's painting alone and not the recognisable reality. It was the glow of the sunset light, a light that ignited everything in the landscape. The sky and the air seemed to be filled with piety. The picture imposed a mood of solemnity similar to the feeling I used to get when entering a synagogue or Kasia's church. Millet's painting gave me a taste of the sublime in art. It would be years before I would discover that I was looking at a masterpiece!

In life, few things run in a straight line, and it wasn't until many years later that I finally had a chance to stand face to face with the original *L'Angelus* at the Musée d'Orsay in Paris. Splendidly displayed in the spacious marble halls of the converted railway station, I was looking at the painting through three pairs of eyes: my own, the bookbinder's and his consumptive daughter's.

Separated by time and geography, by culture and history, the museum occasioned a meeting in my mind between the great French master and the humble Polish-Jewish bookbinder. Millet, the artist who professed a love for the simple, labouring people, and the Jewish bookbinder in Lodz, who had hung the image of *L'Angelus* in his damp, rain-damaged attic room, seemed to make good company. After all, the Jewish bookbinder and *L'Angelus* had encountered the German war machine. Millet's painting was lucky to survive the Nazi occupation of Paris, the bookbinder perished at Auschwitz.

A converted railway station was an apt place to mourn the fate of the people whose last journey carried them to Auschwitz by train.

THE GYPSIES ARE COMING

The Gypsies were an integral part of the patchwork of childhood memories. The plaintive sound of a violin, echoed by the cheerful tambourine, would always signal that the Gypsies had arrived in our yard. Their seasonal entertainment was only rivalled in importance by visits of a man with a dancing bear from another Gypsy tribe. Both events heralded the end of the long Polish winter and the approach of spring.

I was standing at the window, my heart pounding with a mixture of fear and anticipation. Too small to get a proper view of the events in the courtyard below, I tried to balance on the edge of the skirting to make myself taller. Kasia would come to my aid, flinging the window open, her strong arm gripping me as I leaned over the ledge.

From above, the Gypsies resembled overblown colourful flowers blown by the wind, seemingly growing from the grey concrete yard. Women and young girls' whirling long skirts, their rainbow-coloured scarves and ribbons were flying in the air. The men, wearing embroidered velvet waistcoats over white shirts with puffy sleeves, moved around the yard, their fiddles producing sounds that filled me with strange yearnings.

Soon, one of them, usually a child, would be at the doorbell, waiting for alms or handouts.

'If you don't behave, we will give you back to the Gypsies.' Kasia's warning, given as she went to open the door, would send me rushing to hide in the pantry. Small in stature, but huge in authority, she always held the key to my panic. It started when I had sullied the shiny white tiles of our continental-style stove with soot. I claimed it was a drawing, to Kasia it was plain dirt. She followed her threat to thrash me with a 'revelation' about my origin. I was a foundling! My mother had found me on the doorstep, abandoned by the Gypsies. To make it more plausible, she had even added a few vivid details. The swaddling bundle, wrapped with a red ribbon, was dirty and I was crying and hungry. Lucky for me, I was taken into a good home. I understood that it was a family secret and I was not to breathe a word about it to anybody.

When she pulled me out from the hiding place, the window was shut and the Gypsies were gone. Her hugs and kisses reassured me that the danger had passed. Kasia's mock seriousness changed into an outburst of laughter.

I feared the Gypsies, yet at the same time longed to melt into the colours of the women's colourful outfits. I was torn by conflicting feelings: on the one hand, a desire for contact with them, and on the other, anxiety over the separation from my family.

The Gypsies represented an otherness that was at once threatening and seductive. Since Kasia's disclosure, I had become painfully aware that I was the only dark-haired child in the family. Mother, my older brother and sister were all fair-skinned, fair-haired and blue-eyed. Only Father and I had dark hair and grey-blue eyes. Was he a Gypsy too? A Jewish Gypsy?

On the whole Gypsy habits and customs were held in contempt. They were accused of dark practices and even among my family I often overheard disparaging remarks about the 'filthy, thieving, work-shy Gypsies'.

'They'll nick anything in their path, and worst of all, they even steal children!' In my case, according to Kasia, they did the reverse. What was so wrong with me that even they did not want me? Kasia took much pleasure in my gullible acceptance, though she loved me too much to have intended any deliberate cruelty.

Geographically, Poland lay in the middle of the routes used by the Gypsies making their way from the East to Western Europe. These nomadic people epitomised an Arcadian dream of freedom and wanderlust. Come spring, the call of the Gypsy fiddle would always make me restless.

In 1935, we went on holiday with father to the Tatra Mountains. Growing up in Lodz, a city as flat as a pancake, a vacation in the Tatra Mountains was an exciting prospect. More so as father was going to be in charge of the three of us: brother, sister and myself. Father was physically robust with a keen interest in outdoor activities, and at the same time domesticated; an unusual combination for a middle-class man. We girls admired his competence at working with a needle. To be looked after by him, away from Mother's stern supervision, was always fun. Mother was to travel to Marienbaad for a reunion with her two sisters from England.

This was to be my first visit to the mountains and Kasia, who had never seen mountains in her life, was preparing me for the event. Mountains were God-made steps to heaven, she was telling me. Angels' wings swept the snow but when they quarrelled, an avalanche would roll down from the mountains. Did Kasia really believe that or was she still feeding me yarns, forgetting that I now considered myself to be a *panienka*, a 'Miss'? By this time, I looked down on her both from a position of greater height and my newly acquired sophistication.

Szczawnica was a health resort in the Tatra Mountains, not far from the Czechoslovakian border. My perception of the Tatras differed from Kasia's. I kept seeing fortresses guarded by giant figures with stony faces, cloaked in clouds.

Our days under Father's care were filled with excursions: climbing, and paddling in mountain streams, the icy water cutting like knives into the soles of our feet. One day, Father announced a surprise journey across the Polish-Czechoslovakian border, to visit a Gypsy encampment where many Gypsy tribes were congregating for the election of a king.

We set out early in the morning in the horsedrawn buggy driven by Karol, the owner of the inn where we were staying. He was an elderly *Goral*, a Highlander, with sharp, weatherbeaten features. The mountain people treasured their ethnic traditions and were attired in colourful embroidered outfits. Karol wore his black hat decorated with a feather set at a rakish angle and his jacket was nonchalantly slung over one shoulder. He had a good voice and during the journey he sang songs about bandits and eagles, the guardians of the mountains, who soar over the Tatra peaks.

Father and Karol sat in the front of the buggy; my sister and I were piled into the back. At one stage of the journey our Father took over the reins, keen to show his urban children the skills he had acquired growing up in the country. My brother, driven as always by a competitive urge, asked to have a go. Squeezing himself between Karol and Father, and helped by both, he delighted in his success at controlling the horse.

The winding road ran along the Dunajec, a river squeezed between rocky banks with sheer drops. At one stage of the journey, the road was getting dangerously narrow. The jingling horse bells, decorated with red pompoms, served as a warning for anything approaching from the opposite direction. Karol took back the reins, stopped singing, and instead issued grunts and whistles to control his horse.

As so often happens in the mountains, the weather changed suddenly as we approached a narrow gorge. Black clouds darkened the sky, heralding a storm; the river below was foaming, turning into rapids. Flashes of lightning ripped the sky apart and thunder rolled through the mountains pouring rain in torrents.

Karol sheltered the buggy beneath a thicket of trees. It turned cold and we sat drenched, but he assured us it was bound to be over soon. That's how it was in the mountains.

Lightning, followed by a loud bang, struck a nearby tree. The horse bolted, pulling the buggy dangerously towards the precipice. The torrential rain had washed away part of the road. Karol jumped off, just in time to stop the buggy going over the edge. My father and brother pulled it back, and pushed a rock in front of the wheels. We gaped down at the raging river below and could see the side wheels dangling in the air, suspended over the precipice, still spinning, reminding us how close we had come to disaster. Karol took the harness off the restless horse and tied it to a tree.

The rain stopped as abruptly as it had begun. The sky cleared, the mountain air was intoxicatingly fresh. We inspected the tree that had been struck – a birch, still smouldering. The lightning had singed the foliage of the surrounding trees, leaving untouched an old oak that housed the shrine of a wood-carved Madonna and Child. To Karol, it was a miracle! He fell to his knees, crossed himself and prayed.

The sun came out just as we reached the Polish-Czech border. Formalities for day-trippers were simple. Once in Czechoslovakia, the road widened and we were travelling downhill. This time the horse had to be reined back, the iron brakes screeching in a shower of sparks.

The valley below, washed clean by the rain, sparkled in the sun, the light bouncing off countless caravans and tents of every shape and colour. The Gypsy encampment resounded with the rhythms and melodies of Tziganer music.

We were privileged to witness an event that was to be the last in the history of European Gypsies. Gypsy representatives from all over Europe had gathered in this valley to cast their votes for the choice of a new king. By tradition, this kind of event should take place every five years. Father thought it was highly democratic, everywhere else kingship was hereditary.

'They have no country. What do they want a king for?' Karol mocked, betraying his dislike of the people.

At lunchtime Father went to get food at an open-air cafe and I followed him. To this day, I have no idea how I managed to detach myself from him and get lost. Finally it had happened! The Gypsy world had claimed me and I would never find my way back! I was panic-stricken, though in fact, I was not very far from the restaurant.

Long after the summer vacation, a strange nostalgia for the sound of the Gypsy fiddles made me search out the Bucharest station that used to broadcast Tzigan music.

Later in life I often wondered how our Kasia had come to invent the story of my foundling origin. The key could have been Kasia's own beginnings. She herself, on account of her gender, was rejected at birth. She was rescued from the pigsty where her drunken father, disappointed that his wife had borne him a girl, left her to die.

Kasia's flair for storytelling and her innocent teasing about my origins planted in me a bond with the Gypsies. She may have been responsible for many of my psychological and emotional traits, unwittingly creating an insatiable hunger for drama and mystery, laying the foundations from which my personality would evolve.

Neither my family nor Kasia could have foreseen that in only four years' time the Germans would invade Poland and single out both Gypsies and Jews in their 'Final Solution' project.

LAST SUMMER

At the beginning of August 1939, despite the tension of the 'phoney war', Mother, to my relief, did not object to my going to a summer youth camp.

'You can go, the British Prime Minister Chamberlain has said there will be no war.'

The camp was located on the shores of Lake Troki and the nearest city was Wilno, famous for numerous churches and synagogues. To Jews it was known as the Second Jerusalem.

The weeks of camp life offered an idyllic setting. It was a back-to-nature existence with no electricity, no radio or telephone, and the post was delivered once a week. Each morning the Polish flag was raised and then lowered at sunset as we pledged to obey the Scouts' motto of 'Duty and Honour'.

Close to the shore of the lake was a pine forest and behind it, a village. It was harvest time and in the distant fields the scythes were flashing in the sun. It was the best crop in living memory, the peasants said. They would cut the golden wheat, pile it high onto horse-driven carts, and after sunset make their way back to their village waving and shouting greetings:

'God be with you!'

In the fading light, the silhouettes of the bundles of neatly arranged sheaves looked like neighbours come together for a gossip.

The peasants were keen readers of signs in the sky: an inflamed sky, pulled low by heavy clouds, was a harbinger of disaster. But this August weather was exceptionally fair and dry, which was an auspicious sign for a prosperous year – a good omen.

Something blossomed between the teenage boys and girls splashing about in the lake. As our bodies hardened and feelings softened, our awareness of erotic and romantic attachments was heightened. In the evenings, sitting around the campfire we watched the reflection of the flames licking the surface of the water. We sang sad songs about love and regrets for fleeting time. Our exalted hearts gave in to fits of introspection.

'I would like to keep this evening for ever and ever!' Agnieszka, a girl with whom I shared a tent, exclaimed. I too wanted to catch the moment and to preserve it as one does a plucked flower, pressing between the pages of a diary. If only our memories could be consigned to something as solid and impenetrable as a safe. We were consumed by *Weltschmerz*, the German word for juvenile angst, and badly needed to keep hold of what was precious.

I experienced my first romantic heartache. The object of my adoration was Janek and I entrusted the secret to an ancient oak, carving a heart pierced with an arrow with the initials 'M' and 'J'. The knife was blunt and the misshapen heart resembled a potato.

Janek was 19, a visiting scout leader. When he greeted me, the gold-flecked irises of his brown eyes reduced me to quivers of love sickness. His deep voice invaded my head, giving me the illusion that he existed only for me.

Unfortunately, it was an unrequited love. Janek was much taken with Irka, a 17-year-old redhead endowed with a pair of well-developed breasts. When we went swimming, the lake played a brutal role in making me self-conscious about the inadequate shape of my own breasts. The reflection in the water sadly reminded me that I had very little to show. My breasts, like shy maidens, took time to show up. That summer at the lake marked the beginning of a pubescent girl's dissatisfaction with her body. The cursed condition of harsh self-criticism about the shape of my body lasted well into womanhood.

Janek was the older brother of Fredek, a fat, lazy boy who was regarded as my special boyfriend. I let Fredek be my constant companion in order to have access to his elder brother Janek, who in spite of his youth was already regarded as a heroic figure, and not only by me. Rumours had it that he was a 'wanted man', and that the English had put a price on his head, a fact that added shivers to my calf love. He was involved in the illegal immigration of Jews to Palestine from the age of 17. One day Janek vanished from the camp. His brother Fredek shared with me the secret of his whereabouts. He had been summoned to Istanbul, to assist with the illegal emigration of Young Zionist pioneers from Poland. The political situation had taken a turn for the worse.

The enchanted days were coming to an end. The collective mood in the camp swung from high spirits to sombreness as news of war preparations spread. Poland had declared general mobilisation; trenches were being dug in cities, rehearsals for air raids were taking place everywhere. Under pressure from parents, it was decided to wind up the camp ahead of time and return home immediately.

On the last day, we were marched in crocodile formation for the last swim of the day. We splashed and swam in a lake reflecting the red ball of a sunset about to plunge into the water. We were swimming in a liquid heaven.

During the closing down of the camp some tearful girls were swearing eternal friendships. The boys, busy dismantling the camp, kept their attention on the task in hand as if the sadness of separation had nothing to with them.

'Attention!'

We stood to attention as the red and white flag rolled down without a hitch. We sang the national anthem and from the depths of our healthy lungs proclaimed our love for Poland in the words 'While we live, Poland will never perish...'

The villagers came to watch the ceremony. They looked anxious and dour, searching for reassurance from the camp leaders, who for them represented urban authority.

'Is there really going to be a war?' they asked.

'Who knows? Only God knows...' were the consoling phrases offered by the urbanites. In this part of Poland, generations of peasants had encountered wars, uprisings, reprisals and deportations. Many armies or bands of marauders had overrun their land. Sometimes the battlefield had run through their villages, splitting farmland. Fear of hunger and loss of livestock dominated the peasants' collective memories. Their faces, chiselled by weather, looked at us with bewilderment as we were marched off in formation. An old woman, whose lined face resembled a furrowed field made the sign of the cross and wiped away a tear.

'May the good Lord protect you.'

While waiting at the Wilno railway station for the train to take us to Lodz, my departure home was curtailed by an attack of an inflamed appendix. An hour before boarding the train I doubled up in pain. The doctor who was summoned diagnosed an acute attack of appendicitis in danger of bursting. The blind, obsolete organ took the lead role in the railway station drama. I was rushed to hospital in an ambulance as an emergency case.

At St Jakob's Hospital, in the absence of family or any other authorised adult, I was requested to sign the consent for the operation. The form included the phrase 'in case of death'. I was too young to consider that a possibility; on the contrary, the consent for a surgical knife to cut into my body made me feel I had gained full authority over my own person. My life was in my hands and I was signing a pact with life on new terms.

I floated in the blissful state induced by the anaesthetic. The surgeon later assured me that the operation would leave only a very, very neat scar. Whilst under the anaesthetic, I made the jump into adult status. The operation was a substitute for a rite of passage. I experienced a true awakening.

I relished the hospital experience of being part of an adult ward. A girl alone, far from home, I was the ward's pet. After a week, the woman doctor in charge of my case invited me to her home to convalesce. Frantic phone calls from my parents to get me home met with the doctor's reservations. According to her it was too soon to move me. Besides, this part of Poland, in case of war, was regarded to be safe. Most sensible people in central Poland were making arrangements to move in the eastern or northern direction. My parents disregarded her arguments and insisted that I set out on the journey home. I didn't mind either way.

The travel conditions were already chaotic for civilians as the soldiers had priority. There was no longer a direct connection with my hometown, the only way was via Warsaw. The doctor managed to get me a seat on an express train with a reserved sleeping berth.

It was my first long-distance journey alone in a sleeper, and it thrilled me. I shared it with a high-ranking officer. I forgot his face but never forgot his uniform decorated with brass and stars, a symbol of Polish military might, hanging in the compartment. Having him as my guardian was reassuring.

The train's sharp stops and starts lulled me in and out of dreams. At the railway station in Warsaw I could already smell the acrid air and hear the first air raid alert, which had proved a false alarm. The station was full of jostling civilians and soldiers on their way to join their units.

Father had arranged for a friend to meet the train in Warsaw. Mr Ruven greeted me looking gloomy. Most trains were requisitioned for troop movements; civilians had to wait: the army had priority. Mr Ruven tried frantically to find a seat on the next departing train. With the intervention of my guardian, the Colonel – who himself was having difficulty in joining his unit – I was allowed to get on a train reserved for the military.

We arrived in Lodz four hours late where I was greeted by my anxious-looking parents and my big brother. It was an emotional reunion. I shrank back into being a homesick, bandaged-up girl clinging to mother. My brother carried me all the way to a taxi. I was home – back to my books, my pet dog Puppi, and Kasia fussing over me.

It was the last day of peace.

BLESSINGS

On 5 September 1939, after the Blitzkrieg, Lodz, unlike Warsaw, surrendered without resistance. Within days of the Nazi occupation, the Jews were being singled out for 'special treatment'. In the meantime we were still living in our apartment, learning about the black market and the risks facing Jews when stepping out into the streets.

I was ashamed to admit that I had found the war exhilarating. Everything was in motion; heaven and earth shook with explosions. I was aware that I was a witness to something momentous and I was curious about everything to do with it. The war had released a new kind of vitality.

I watched with excitement as history paraded right outside our windows. Lodz was bedecked with swastikas. The schools were shut and the long curfew hours and the restrictions imposed on the Jews made my friends and me restless. The war had transformed me from a bookish, home-loving teenager into a character from an adventure story. My usual classroom bossiness metamorphosed into a new organisational drive, looking for ways to break the restrictions imposed on us. After the ban on travelling by tram, my friends and I would make a point of riding them aimlessly from morning until the curfew hour. After cinemas were declared out of bounds to Jews, we ignored the prohibition and went early enough to sit through two showings. Even a bellyful of Nazi propaganda and anti-Semitic films like *Jude Suss*, which was showing at most cinemas, did not put us off. We never knew that the historians' term for such impulses was 'resistance'.

Any occasion served our rebellious purposes, like the first public hanging in Liberty Square (Plac Wolnosci), ironically, where the bronze monument dedicated to Kosciuszko, a Polish national hero had been erected. Kosciuszko was famed for his involvement in the American War of Independence, where he uttered the memorable battle cry: *'For our and your Liberty!'*

The hanging was in retaliation for an act of sabotage that had taken place soon after the German troops marched in. A public execution was meant to serve as an example to the rest of the population, and people were rounded up and forced to watch it.

Keen not to miss anything, together with my school friends, I watched the hanging, persuading myself that it was important to witness such events. In truth, it was a case of brute curiosity on my part. Asked by Father what I had seen, I compared it to watching a film without a screen.

The hanging episode revealed that when faced with the barrel of a gun, grown-ups were pathetically helpless. In charge of the execution were only a handful of Germans. Yet it was the same crowd who only weeks earlier boisterously proclaimed their readiness to fight to the last breath.

Soon after the hanging, Kosciuszko himself was blown off his pedestal. Jews were rounded up to clean up the rubble with their bare hands. Somehow my Father was amongst the men picked up in the street. He came home with bleeding fingers, feeling humiliated. Amongst the uniformed Germans supervising the action was an ex-employee from his rubber factory who was particularly mean to him. He, a local *Volksdeutsche* – a group of Poles, of German descent, most of whom were active as the 'Fifth Column' – took pleasure in humiliating Father.

By October, the Jews had been stripped of the right to own a business or be employed by non-Jews and were burdened with countless other prohibitions of a punitive kind.

The Day of Atonement is the most significant date in the Jewish calendar and the Germans, in a calculated blow, proclaimed a prohibition forbidding Jews to congregate in places of worship. Commonality is the key to the spirit of the holiday and throughout the world most Jews fast and flock to synagogues. It's a time of prayer and confession, addressed as much to members of the community for forgiveness as to God.

Like most families, my parents were forced to observe the fast and to pray secluded in their homes. Despite the oppressive atmosphere, my parents dressed festively, the way they had always done when going to the synagogue, and stuck to the yearly ritual of blessing their children. With my older sister away in Palestine, only my brother and I were the recipients of the blessing. We stood in line with our heads bent, each waiting our turn. Even in peacetime, the ritual had always filled me with shivers of anticipation. I may have regarded my parents' hands as an instrument of transmission of some aspect of sacredness.

Father, covered from head to foot in his prayer shawl, acquired a priestly aura. When he raised his hands above my brother's head in a gesture of blessing he was tearful. This was the first time I had seen him cry. He stood like an exile chased from the gates of his sanctum, a phantom of his previous self. At that moment, my father was a bearer of immense spirituality.

When Mother's turn came, she gripped my head hard like a midwife about to pull out a new life. Did she intimate that this would be the last time she would bless me? The impact of that blessing was, and still is, my most deeply felt religious experience.

The next day, in a mood of defiance against a God who let us down, my brother and I did the unthinkable. Without our parents' knowledge, we broke the sanctity of the Day of Atonement by going to work in the bar owned by Mr Grodek. He was Father's Christian acquaintance, who had recently come to lodge with us on Father's initiative. The presence of a Christian Pole, Father hoped, might be a protection against imminent eviction.

Above the entrance of his pub was a sign encased in a glass display, which proclaimed:

> Life is short, joy is scant.
> Enter Bacchus and be merry.

Any misgivings my brother and I had about venturing into an ambience of profanity on the Holiest of Holy days vanished as we entered the bar: God did not strike us dead!

The bar served drinks and snacks and was crowded with German soldiers, currently the publican's most profitable customers. They were mainly from the lower ranks; the high-ranking officers frequented establishments of a better class. Mostly very young, with a few middle-aged faces amongst them, they looked flushed from the consumption of huge amounts of beer.

My brother behind the counter helped to pour drinks while I collected the empty beer mugs. From close proximity, the faces of our enemies seemed friendly and cheerful. They had plenty to be cheerful about. Victorious, they were celebrating their military superiority and the rapid success of the Blitzkrieg.

During the first days of the occupation, many of them behaved like tourists. Individually or in groups, they could be seen in the streets, constantly clicking cameras. The invaders revealed themselves as tireless photographers, indulging in a collective craze to accumulate evidence of their personal share in Hitler's '1,000-Year Reich'. Members of the German army were tireless in collecting souvenirs for posterity. They were not to know that in the future, the evidence of their military triumphs as well as the recorded atrocities they committed, would be used against them.

The bar, with Bacchus as its patron, offered the German soldiers ample opportunity for indulging in their photograph mania. At the entrance of the pub stood a life-size cardboard image of the fat-bellied Bacchus, the Roman god of wine and merriment. It was an ideal background for individual and collective snapshots celebrating the conquest of Lodz.

To the soldiers I was just a *Fraulein* clearing empty mugs. Some would even flirt, but as an example of female attractiveness, a soldier's roving eye could not have found me a very enticing specimen. Untouched by any make-up, in my school outfit, I presented a prim teenager. I wore my long plaits hanging loose in an unfashionable style.

While collecting the empty mugs I was busy eavesdropping on their conversations. Mostly, they swapped experiences of the military campaign complaining about 'dirty Polaks' and the primitive conditions in which the Polish peasants lived. Many references were made to the vast number of 'filthy Jews' found everywhere in Lodz.

At one of the tables, two young soldiers drew me into a conversation, having discovered that I spoke passable German. A fair-skinned youth with an unusually mobile, protruding Adam's apple, insisted that I reminded him of his younger sister. Her name was Beatte.

What was mine? I lied and told him 'Anka', a very Polish name. He said he felt at home in Lodz; in fact, he had a large family here. His Uncle Gustav, a prominent *Volksdeutsche*, was now high-up in the Nazi administration. His uncle was, he proudly declared, one of the new city fathers. On my next round of collecting the empties, the brother of Beatte tried again to engage me in a conversation, this time promising to bring a photo of his sister the following day, to confirm our striking resemblance. The irony of the situation did not escape me. Somewhere in Germany, a girl called Beatte looked like a Jewish girl from Lodz! I imagined she was a faithful member of the Hitler Youth organisation who was racially classified as a member of the superior Aryan race.

When I again appeared at their table to collect more of the empty mugs, he tugged at my sleeve. By now, the blond soldier with the jumping Adam's apple was very drunk. He said he wanted to tell me a secret and whispered in my ear that his Uncle Gustav was going to rid Lodz of the *verfluchter Juden*, the stinking Jews, rendering the city finally *Juden rein*, free of Jews.

His drinking companion, a boy with an olive complexion and dark hair, tried to shut him up. In a very short time my eyes had already become accustomed to picking out the Aryan from the non-Aryan looks, even amongst the 'master race'.

Each time I passed, Beatte's brother tried to stop me and speak to me.

'One prick in the heart, and the *Jude* "kaput"!' He kept repeating the phrase, smiling cheerfully at me. It sent shivers down my spine. He was unsteady on his feet when he got up to go to the lavatory. On the way back, he again sought me out and suggested I visit his hometown, Breslau, and meet his sister Beatte.

His pal steadied him but before disappearing he once more got hold of me. 'Soon,' he said, 'Lodz will be incorporated into Germany proper and you would be able to visit my family.'

Back at the table his companion declared, indulgently, '*Ganz verruckt*', meaning his mate was completely off his head.

On the way home, I told my brother what I had heard.

'We must tell everybody about it!'

'Miss Fantasy, grow up and stop being so gullible!'

'Miss Fantasy' being the name my brother had chosen for me; one that, owing to reputation as a gullible idiot who would accept any story at face value, gained currency in our family. When I protested that I really had heard the words '*prick in the heart*', he nodded, looking at me askance: 'Yes, yes, yes, of course you've heard it.'

Back home, during the curfew hour, as we went through the sham of breaking the Yom Kippur fast with our parents, I repeated what I had overheard – though not where I had heard it. My brother, protective of Mother's fragile state of nerves, ordered me to shut up.

'Don't listen to her. You know your daughter, send her to get a bottle of soda water and she will return with a story about a circus elephant on the rampage!'

To me it was perfectly plausible. Hadn't I myself indulged in outrageous fantasies of revenge against the Germans? These visions, usually conjured at night in bed, took a variety of forms. Only recently I imagined that I invented a gadget that could send rays capable of immobilising any moving object. Before falling asleep, I had triumphantly immobilised the entire German military might. However, I hadn't yet considered annihilating them en masse. My schemes were not so malign: I used my magic rays to put the soldiers into a kind of collective slumber. I was undecided what to do with them next.

Nevertheless, there was no doubt in my mind that if I, in my wishful thinking, could come up with such ideas, scientists could easily invent a quick and painless way of doing away with people.

'Injections in the heart? No, child, injections are for making people better, not to harm them. After the initial excess, the Germans will calm down.'

Father liked to show off his ability to think things through rationally, but aware of his lack of formal education would preface anything he had to say with a protestation about how little he knew of the subject – in this case, war: war and conquests, since time immemorial, were a part of life. Conquerors the world over were always interested in deriving maximum profit from their conquests. Land is requisitioned, and native populations are robbed of property. Exploitation was practised in every possible way, but the conqueror would always be mindful of the fact that people were the most valuable asset. Conquerors gain from exploiting the talents, skills and manpower of the conquered people.

'Wait and see, soon they will make the Jews part of their war machinery!'*

---

*   In gruesome fulfilment of what the soldier had told me, and of my own father's words, the Nazis used concentration camp inmates in medical experiments, which included phenol injections into the heart (instant death results).

Mother gave him a despairing look. Father was undeterred.

'Manpower,' he continued, 'is more important than horsepower. Would the Germans be so foolish as to ignore such advantages? Anyway, a war begins and, sooner or later, comes to an end. It's neither the first nor the last time that the Jewish people have faced adversity in wars. With God's help, we will somehow manage. It's important not to panic,' he concluded.

'Your father is a fool. The last war lasted four years!'

Father let Mother's outburst go unchallenged.

This type of disharmony was nothing new for my parents. What I sensed was different, however, was their present lack of authority over us. Mother repeated what she had been saying since the summer, when rumours of war began.

'I know something terrible is going to happen. I feel it in my heart.'

'Let's leave!'

Mother gave me a sharp look.

'Where to? Who wants us? Go on, tell me, Miss Fantasy!'

'Suppose the Germans are spreading such rumours on purpose?' my father thought aloud, intending to calm Mother's fears.

In years to come, historians would still be wrangling over the question of why the Jews did not leave. Why had they got themselves trapped in ghettos? And, the most painful of all accusations, why had they let themselves be *slaughtered like sheep*? Smarter and better-educated people than my father failed to anticipate Germany's disregard for the rudimentary ethics of war conduct, and my Mother's *crie de coeur* in answer to my plea to leave, her reaction *'Where to? Who wants us?'*, goes some way to explaining why the Jews found themselves trapped.

It is said that throughout the entire globe there are no two faces alike. But I have seen the face of the German soldier with the protruding Adam's apple replicated at different times in many cities. The nameless soldier lives on in my memory. He may have perished on the Russian front, or survived as a prisoner of war. His Uncle Gustav may have protected him from being sent to the Eastern front and given him a post guarding the Jewish ghetto in Lodz. Whatever his ultimate fate, he lives on in my mind as the soldier whose few words, *'One prick in the heart, and* Jude *"kaput"'*, tempered my resolve to leave Lodz.

Mary Williams suggested that the German soldier's words might have saved my life.

THE MANUFACTURE OF IDENTITY

In Mary's consulting room, leaving Mother was a taboo subject. But the sessions revived my memory of our separation.

The door where Mother was standing, trying to stop me from leaving, was a frontier nobody had the right to cross. The echo of her cry, *'I'll never see you again!'*, which chased me down the stairs, often woke me at nights. My husband never asked and I never told. When pressed by Mary, my words were controlled, carrying me through the danger like a boat navigating the rapids.

'Mira, forgetfulness condemns us to emotional imprisonment. Facing the past is the key to release.'

With the passage of time guilt corroded the steel of my self-worth. It was selfish and thoughtless to leave my parents at such a stressful time. There was no doubt in my mind that I was born with a streak of delinquency. Mary tried her best to mitigate the harshness of my self-criticism.

'Even at the best of times, rebellious teenagers can be quite obnoxious,' Mary reminded me. 'If you have no pity for yourself, you'll never be able to pity anyone else.'

My self-image as an adventurous adolescent had become buried under the rubble of a character demolition, all of my own making. There was no meeting point between the teenager who had been carried high by a wave of assertiveness and the adult who so often cried herself to sleep. When eventually I did broach the memory of leaving Mother, the words came out in a deadpan tone of voice, as if a ventriloquist had taken over. I was telling it like a story that had happened to someone else, merely a catalogue of events disconnected from emotions. Mary sat with her head slightly inclined to the right, a position she would adopt when sensitive material would emerge, the deep crease between her eyebrows indicating a silent question mark.

I was on safer ground talking about the war. In those early days of the war, Kasia was still running around the house with a duster, muttering black curses at the 'Fritzes', and I was still writing letters to my sister in Palestine, even though I knew it was no longer possible to post letters from German-occupied Lodz to Palestine, as the latter was under British mandate and was therefore now enemy territory.

'Stop wasting your time,' my brother picked on me.

My sister had become a devoted Zionist in her early teens. Before the war, Polish Jewry was politically splintered into many 'isms': Communism, the *Bund* (Jewish socialism) and Zionism were just a few from the wide spectrum of political parties in existence. My sister had joined a youth organisation called Hanoar Haziyoni (Zionist Youth), a middle-of-the-road branch of the Zionist movement.

She departed for Palestine in the spring of 1938, to attend an agricultural school. Ben-Shemen was a Youth Village run on progressive educational principles. After her departure, I missed her and I only discovered how badly through my compulsion to write to her almost daily. I wrote the letters in the classroom during lessons, hiding them from the eyes of the teachers.

When I announced my wish to join my sister in Palestine, my family and neighbours dismissed it as plain crazy. The consensus was that I was an out-of-control daughter and the victim of an overactive imagination. Everything about me was at variance with commonly accepted wisdom of staying together. Mother wrung her hands and shouted: 'Going to Palestine in the middle of a war! Whoever heard of such madness?'

I was deaf to the long list of obstacles presented to me. Mother complained bitterly about disobedient children and was angry with Father for failing to exercise his authority. The incurable optimist, Father tried to calm her.

'Let her go. She'll soon find out for herself that leaving home is no picnic! Just wait and see how quickly she'll come running back.'

In London, Mary, like a good housekeeper, tried to sort out the facts from my embellishments: for instance, the truth behind how had I arrived at the idea of faking a school ID. After so many years it was not easy to trace the mental process that had led to my becoming a forger.

In pre-war Poland, school IDs played an important role. With affixed photographs, bearing the pupil's name, age, place of birth, we were obliged to carry them at all times. The school uniform with a badge identified the school. The ID *legitymacja* entitled us to concessions for public transport, museums, cinemas and theatres.

I always claimed that a chance encounter in the street with the school caretaker started the ball rolling. It was midday and his breath already smelled of drink. His fondness for vodka was well-known to everybody at the Jaszunska Gymnasium.

'Put a match to his breath and he'll ignite!' my classroom mate once said.

'Shame the gymnasium is shut' he said, rattling a thick bunch of keys. Unexpectedly, without previous forethought, I asked for permission to be allowed to gain access to the school. I claimed that I had left in my locker a few of my possessions. He agreed to unlock the back entrance, and the following day, while retrieving my gym slip and a copy of the Latin grammar book, nostalgia sent me through the empty, ghostly corridors. The notice board on the wall was still filled with last term's announcements, a sad reminder of what had been lost.

The door to the office, the 'sanctum', always so well-guarded by the secretary, was left unlocked. It was a chance to examine what was kept inside the desk drawers. Rummaging, my eyes fell on the school's ID blanks. On impulse, I filled my satchel with a dozen of them.

'Before departing I also spotted a selection of official school seals which I decided to "borrow" as well.'

'Borrow?' Mary censured my adapted use of the word. It never occurred to me that I was stealing something. I may have inherited Father's knack for tricking authorities, I suggested. I was familiar with his tales of the Great War. In my favourite story, he disguised himself as a pregnant peasant in order to smuggle flour across the German–Russian front line. Father's initiative had saved Mother's family from hunger during the war-induced famine.

The blank ID forms were a necessity if I was to join my sister in Palestine. It also occurred to me that it might be prudent to possess alternative school IDs, ones that provided information about alternative places of my birth. I could then obtain a German travel permit by claiming I was a student far from home, trapped by the war in Lodz. Two cities, Wilno in the north and Lwow in the south, were immediately potential destinations. Both cities were outside German-occupied Poland and under Soviet control. In short, the faked school ID could be my 'passport' to freedom!

Mary ascribed to my erratic actions a far greater significance than I was prepared to concede. It fitted in well with her Jungian theories about the unconscious, which supposedly has access to an innate 'sixth sense' as a tool for survival.

'Through this action, you had begun to develop a plot for your own survival.' She compared it to a writer plotting the action of a novel. My war past was put through a Jungian filter and I liked the sound of it.

The faking of the documents became a collective activity carried out with five of my school friends, the same friends with whom I rode on prohibited trams and went to cinemas that were out of bounds to Jews. As prospective partners in the proposed 'trip' to Palestine, each of them was motivated by a personal reason.

We had fun with the forgeries and, like true amateurs, admired the end results. We even remembered to make them look the worse for wear by stamping on them with our boots. The official school seals that I had 'borrowed' gave them an authentic look.

Mary surprised me by her diligence. At the next session she spread out a pre-war map of Central Europe and Poland and she asked me to point out the location of the aforementioned cities. Wilno and Lwow were flung far apart. Lwow in the south was en route to Romania and the Black Sea, from where ships sailed to Palestine. Wilno, located in the North, was closer to the Baltic Sea and to neutral Sweden and had the further distinction of having recently carved itself into me, taking my appendix. My memories of Lwow were happier. I got to know Lwow when father took me with him to meet Mr Silverstein, his business representative. Mr Silverstein would also visit us once a year. As a child I eagerly anticipated his seasonal visits and the gifts he would bring me.

The 'plot', as Mary called our juvenile faking enterprise, involved three girls and two boys. Etka, a girl with a laughing voice and smiling eyes, matched me in cheekiness and was great fun to be with. Andzia, by contrast, was a shy and gentle character with a modest demeanour. Marysia, a splendid gymnast in spite of her big size, was the most surprising candidate. Palestine was of no interest to her as she sympathised with her older brother's Communist leanings. Her aim was to get to the Soviet side, to search for him where he had vanished without trace.

Fredek, the boy whom I allowed to kiss me at the summer camp only because of my infatuation with his older brother Janek, was determined to join Janek in Palestine and take part in the underground activities.

Heniek was a friend with whom I enjoyed a close and uncomplicated relationship. He was a reliable soulmate and my confidant. A regular visitor in our home, he was my mother's favourite. Well-behaved and well-dressed, he often carried a book with him, and Mother trusted a boy with a book in his hand. In my photo album I accumulated a sizeable number of photos of the two of us together. Heniek could never resist the street photographers on the prowl for customers. The photos showed us promenading hand in hand down Piotrkowska, Lodz's main street.

I volunteered to be the first to try out our faked documents at the headquarters of the German command. I joined a long queue outside the Municipality where the section handling German travel permits was housed. When my turn came, my heart was beating fast and so loud that I was sure the German official sitting in front of me could hear it.

The official, a man in his thirties, looked bored when I explained in German that I had been a pupil at the Lodz Gymnasium and that I was separated from my home in Lwow, where my parents resided. He hardly glanced at the document, which made me very nervous.

'My Mother is very ill suffering from a serious heart condition.'

This detail about Mother's attributed failing heart popped up out of the blue. I never meant to say that much. To cover up my nervousness I prattled on, pleading to be allowed to go back to my *heimat*. In German, *heimat* means a place in the heart as well as on the map. I was mistaken in thinking that it would soften his heart. Screwing his eyes into an ironic smile, he muttered half to himself,

'You wish to go to Lwow? Why not America?'

His sarcasm alarmed me. Did he suspect that I was Jewish? To my relief, he picked up a pen and scribbled something, and punched hard a seal with the swastika. I kept my eyes on his hand as he put his signature over the bluish stamp in a handwriting that resembled a rattlesnake on the run. He handed me back the German document together with my faked ID without even glancing in my direction.

'Next,' he called out.

Out in the street I understood the reason for his sarcasm. What I had obtained was not a permit at all. The wording of the German text simply stated that my application for a travel permit was under consideration. Somehow, I decided to trust the power of symbols more than the words. Later on, the potency of the swastika seal proved its worth. Each time it was presented to the German authorities, it was accepted at railway stations and on trains as a bona fide authorisation for travel. I had inadvertently tapped into the secrets of the bureaucrats' passion for official seals. The lesson once learned was never forgotten.

On the eve of the date for our departure, the group disintegrated and my friends, one by one, dropped out. Etka, the girl with the laughing voice and smiling eyes, turned up looking downcast. She could not bring herself to leave her parents and her siblings at such a difficult time. No amount of persuasion could make her change her mind.

Andzia kept away for the same reason without even bothering to explain it in person. Marysia got news that her brother was on the list of soldiers missing in action. She stayed home to look after her drug-addicted mother.

After the war, I saw Marysia's face again, not in person but in a photograph on exhibition at the Kibbutz of the 'Fighters of the Ghettos' in Israel. She had been a courier for the Jewish underground, moving between the various ghettos, carrying information, money and, when available, weapons. Attached to her photograph was the last telegram she had sent before being caught and shot.

I also learned about the fate of the others: Etka's large family perished in Auschwitz. She and her older sister were the only survivors. Members of Andzia's numerous family were caught in the early deportations from Lodz. She herself died of hunger in the ghetto.

Heniek, who had been the heart and soul of the enterprise, turned up at the last minute with a sad expression. He regretted forgoing the chance to depart with me but his father was an emotional wreck and he could not abandon him in view of the fact that his older brother, mobilised for the September campaign, was missing. Heniek apologised for letting me down, at the same time encouraging me to stick to my resolve to leave, confident of my success. (After the hardship of the Lodz ghetto and the deportation to Auschwitz and other camps, Heniek was the sole survivor of his family. When I left home, I took a few of the photographs of us together. These were the only reminders of Heniek's carefree days.)

When Fredek failed to turn up, I went to his home. His mother greeted me with the announcement, 'He is sick!' Positioning herself in front of him, as if trying to render him invisible, she pushed a thermometer into his mouth. In an autocratic voice that made me shrink, she declared that her son would not leave, not now or at any other time.

'This family stays together!'

She drew a line with her hand, encircling her absent family inside a safe haven. Looking down at me she berated my parents for letting a minor like myself make such a momentous decision.

'Outrageous! Children playing at being grown-up!'

Fredek, who was 16, dropped his puppy blue eyes in shame. He took a step towards me indicating that he wished to see me to the door but his mother put herself between us again. We never even kissed.

His mother's insistence that *'If we die, we die together,'* proved futile. She was denied even that wish. Fredek moved to the Warsaw ghetto in the belief that it would be easier for his brother Janek to get him out of Poland via Italy and from there to Palestine. It was not to be. While waiting, he joined the police and during the Warsaw Ghetto Uprising he was trapped in a burning building and never emerged. His parents ended up being deported to Auschwitz.

Janek, who would later be instrumental to my own rescue from war-torn Europe, failed to rescue his own brother.

LAST BREAKFAST

'A weepy day,' Kasia said.

It may have been a Monday or a Tuesday. The dull November morning began with a drizzly rain. There was no frame to that picture of our breakfast table, which later in my life I tried to capture in a painting. The artistic re-creation could never have shown that the bread bought on the black market was mixed with sawdust and flaked when cut, nor that the milk was diluted with water. Neither could it show that my mother, standing at the stove, was cooking the last cupful of porridge oats left in the larder.

The September Blitzkrieg and the subsequent division of Poland between the German and the Soviet armies had turned our lives upside down. Money had lost its value and Father was no longer a provider. Essential foodstuffs were in short supply. The black market flourished and it was dangerous for adults to go outdoors; it was safer for children. Jews, by degrees, were being deprived of civil rights. At the time, we were still in our large flat eating off our fine china and using silver cutlery embossed with the family monogram.

Mother placed an unfamiliar substance on the table: an ersatz German-made coffee substitute that had arrived on the market with the invaders. She inspected the bottle before pouring the brew into our cups. It was bitter in taste and strange in appearance.

'It could be harmful for the kidneys. We don't even know what's in it.' As an afterthought she added, 'A perfect way to poison a whole nation!'

Father tried to soften the effect of her last remark, but the extent of her fear frightened me. Ever since I could remember I had lived riveted to my mother's dread of tomorrow; of next week, next month, next year. Like Cassandra, she was inclined to utter warnings about impending future disasters. There were rivers that might burst their banks, mountains that might slide, cities that might crumble; every minute could be the moment of some terrible loss; every street a potential trap. Anything could happen after one put the telephone down.

'Mark my words, something terrible is going to happen! I feel it in my heart!'

The family regarded Mother's propensity for such utterances of doom as a legacy of her rabbinical ancestry. Luckily for her, Poland, a provincial place, was still remote from the shock-waves of psycho-analytical terms like 'paranoia' and 'persecution mania'.

I used the war as an excuse to cut loose from Mother's dark visions. I tore at the bonds of parental love, snapping attachments with teenage brutality, and in draining off my affection I made place for irritation and hostility.

The kettle was boiling. 'You won't hear such a whistle anywhere,' Kasia stabbed at me, 'You can still change your mind!'

When I said I wanted to go to 'the other side' to reach Palestine, it was a schoolgirl's idea of adventure and liberation and to get away from the storms generated by Mother's sense of doom. In any case I always intended to come back to my dog, Puppi, my friends and my books.

On the map of the new political reality, in which sovereign Poland had been obliterated, 'the other side' was the newly established German–Soviet border to neutral Romania. I was in a hurry to get away.

'Plain crazy!' was my family's and neighbours' view of my behaviour.

Mother had wrung her hands and shouted at me, 'It's insane! We must all stay together. If we die, we die together.' That's exactly what I was not ready for, not yet.

'Listen to your mother!' Kasia admonished me.

Mother was furious with Father for not opposing my scheme. He stuck to his resolve to let me go. He kept reassuring her that it was best to let me find out for myself what was possible. For safety, he had ordered my brother to be my chaperon until the speedy return home of both of us.

The hour of separation struck. Mother stared tearfully at my brother and me, both fully dressed and ready with our backpacks for departure, making her last appeal not to leave. I pretended not to hear. Father comforted Mother in his own way, which irritated her even more.

At the door, Mother's embrace held me rigid, her grip undermining my resolve. Her body was like a magnet, and I knew if I let her hug me one minute more, I would never be able to tear myself away from her. I slid out of her embrace and avoided looking at her face.

'I will never see you again!' Mother's lament was addressed both to me and to heaven. Once out of doors, I ran down the stairs as fast as I could, chased by her sobs.

That scene at the door fixed itself to my peripheral vision, rendering all doors and all separations a descent to Mother's suffering.

Father accompanied us to the railway station. Lodz Fabryczna gave the impression of being under siege by the swelling masses of people, all of whom were trying to get on to the same train. My brother pushed through the crowd, leading the way, with Father behind us. It was like cutting through a human wall that was held together by sheer pressure.

'Remember, whatever happens, never, never separate! Always stay together!'

Father's last-minute instruction was drowned in the roar of the surging crowd. The distance between Father and us grew bigger as we fought to get on the train. My brother, a tall lad, held our baggage above his head with one hand and with the other was pulling me towards the carriage door. Somehow, we managed to board the train and once inside, squeezed ourselves at a window.

We watched Father, like a swimmer steering against the tide, trying to get close. He finally managed to position himself level with the window. My brother leaned out of the window as far as it was possible without falling out, his arm outstretched to touch Father's hand. It was never to be. A sharp whistle blew and the train shuddered, beginning to gather speed. Father ran after it as fast as he could, almost parallel to the window, holding up a small package wrapped in soft tissue and shouted to make himself heard,

'Mother wanted you to have this!'

His attempt to pass us Mother's gift failed. From the moving train, my father's waving arm already seemed cut off from the body of the human mass.

Much later, we learned that the package contained some pieces of Mother's jewellery, which in the chaos he had forgotten to pass on.

We never saw Mother or Father again.

2
Crossing Borders

The first leg of our journey was to Cracow.

Lodz, the city from which I so fervently wished to get away, was receding into the distance. We were travelling in an overcrowded train through a country that had been crossed off the map of Europe. Both the train and the passengers carried the marks of Poland's defeat. Defeat had a foul smell and stank of blocked lavatories. An unfamiliar kind of vandalism signalled the breakdown of social order. Amongst damaged seats and slashed curtains, hordes of unkempt refugees were sleeping on their bundles.

We still thought of ourselves as passengers, not refugees, fleeing from temporary danger, which we hoped might soon blow over and allow us to return home sooner or later. It was an illusion which people share during war and its aftermath.

The train rattled through a landscape of isolated farmsteads, forests and wooden country bridges. It was refreshing to see a part of the countryside where there were no visible marks of the war's destruction.

The importance of home began to grow in proportion to the increasing distance that separated me from it. The clackety-clack of the wheels carried Mother's lament '*I will never see you again!*' To comfort myself I visualised the scene of our triumphant return – a joyous reunion with my parents, Kasia and my pet dog, a permanently shivering brown Chihuahua whose eyes in electric light always shone pink. I was back to my books and photograph albums! My mother would see me again!

A refrain from a song about a brother and sister journeying into a world of wonder no longer fitted the occasion. We were venturing into a hostile world. Since infancy, I had adored my handsome 'big' brother, even though he used to push me around, but in the street or on the ice rink, he had always been my protector. When I started school, we grew apart. He simply ignored me. Girls of my age were a nuisance. Older girls were the focus of his and his friends' fascination. Shortly before the war, he had been transformed from a lanky spotty-faced youth into a young man with pomaded hair, smelling of eau de cologne. He now dressed with care and was always in a hurry, frequenting places that belonged to the enticing world of the grown-ups: the 5 o'clock tea dance and sports clubs. The postman regularly delivered letters in perfumed, mauve-coloured envelopes that were addressed to him. Kasia once spotted a smudge of lipstick on his shirt collar and teased him about being in love. Her name was Salusia. One day he showed me her photograph. She was beautiful, with a spark of sorcery in her dark eyes. My brother's allowing me to see the picture was a privilege, a sign that he could confide in me. The war had brought us closer, and my brother was now my protector again.

The passengers were busy discussing the reasons for Poland's defeat: 'England betrayed Poland,' someone said. Somebody else, in dissecting the reason for the disaster, mentioned 'the pact'.

'Who would have suspected that the Nazis and the Communists, the mortal ideological enemies, would join in a pact of friendship?'

It did not take long before the Jewish bogey was introduced.

'Churchill is a Jew,' a Pole wearing a tattered soldier's uniform said. As evidence, he mentioned Churchill's daughter's name, Sarah. 'Everybody in Poland knows it is a Jewish name,' he added, to prove his point.

'The English and the Rothschilds will profit from this war.'

'The Jews,' another added, 'supported the Soviet invasion.'

I noticed the man was looking at me, the most Semitic-looking person in the compartment. I froze, but my brother squeezed my hand very hard as if to say, 'Ignore him.'

An elderly man with Chekhovian pince-nez and a neatly trimmed, pointed grey beard protested: 'What nonsense! The Poles, Jews and Ukrainians are all in the same boat. If we don't stick together, we will be sunk.'

Already, in the early days of the German invasion, my brother realised that his appearance bestowed on him the advantages of the Nordic race. He carried his racially 'correct' Aryan looks like a badge and looked the enemy straight in the eye. Blond, blue-eyed, tall with a body hardened through sport, the 18-year-old looked like the weather-beaten young conquerors. He closely resembled the archetypal icon of Nazi youth; an image used in German propaganda posters. For the time being, in claiming an imaginary racial kinship with the 'master race', my brother's outrageous chutzpah secured protection, however illusory, for two vulnerable Jewish fugitives.

Like him, I, too, had begun to cultivate a look of steel. When passing a German in the street I learned to meet his or her eyes, hoping it was a signal to the 'master race' that I, too, was of their ilk. The refusal to identify with the defeated people, who walked the streets with hunched shoulders and bent heads, was a dangerous game. It smacked of a false pride and, luckily for both of us, we were not exposed to the German occupation for long enough and were thus saved from the danger of falling for the rewards which collaboration could have offered. We were not put through the moral test that others had to face in the ghettos or death camps. Today, our brief experience of the mental process of 'Aryanisation' adopted by both of us makes me shudder. From the perspective of what we know about such cases, being Jewish was no protection against such a moral downfall.

Among the other passengers in our compartment were a mother and a daughter about my age who drew attention to themselves on account of their exaggerated, genteel manner of speech. The mother looked as if a vampire had drained the blood from her face. The girl addressed her mother in a gamut of endearments – not plain 'Mother' or 'Mama', but 'Mamuska' and 'Mamusienka'. The mother also used a series of embellishments when addressing her daughter 'Wanda', 'Wandeczka'. Their saccharine-coated voices contrasted sharply with the other rough voices heard on the train. Seeing the mother and daughter fused in a loving bond aroused in me pangs of jealousy. My own mother had always been sparing with caresses, both physical and verbal.

My brother pulled a face and winked at me. '*Operetta*,' he whispered. The word was a family code for any pretentious or theatrical behaviour. But I couldn't keep my eyes off them and imagined them sitting in an elegant drawing room with a parquet floor filled with mahogany furniture, dominated by a grand piano. A maid dressed in a white apron would be serving tea in delicate china cups. Wandeczka would be playing the piano, while Mamuska listened in rapture.

I became aware of an ability to visualise aspects of strangers' lives. People could be read like books! It was a thrilling sensation, like being able to dream with one's eyes open.

After a few hours, slumber brought on by fatigue settled over some of the travellers in our compartment, including the mother and daughter. As the girl rested against a maternal shoulder, I used my brother's lap as a cushion. At daybreak, the compartment filled up with the noises people make when dreams depart and restless souls reclaim their bodies.

After Wandeczka awoke, she reached for her mother's handbag, took out some pills and poured a drink from a flask.

'Mamuska, wake up! It's time for your medicine.'

She shook her mother's shoulder, but she just slumped forward. After the commotion of trying to revive her, the elderly passenger with the pince-nez glasses pronounced her dead. The daughter refused to be parted from her dead mother and had to be physically pulled away. The elderly man closed the mother's eyes and others helped him to lay her out on the vacated seats. A cross was placed on her chest and she was covered with her coat. She looked so peaceful as the train rocked her, her hand held by her sobbing daughter. People talked in whispers, the presence of a travelling corpse imposed a funereal sense of decorum. Most of the passengers left the compartment. The soldier in the tattered uniform said in his crass voice, 'A bad omen.'

A long tunnel plunged us into thundering darkness and drew a curtain over the presence of death in the compartment. I wondered about Mamuska's soul. Where would it go? Would it ride back and forth on the train, waiting for its final destination? Or would it depart with the corpse, when the train pulled up at Chorzow where the tearful Wandeczka said they were due to get off and where her uncle, her mother's brother, would be awaiting their arrival.

Her dead mother was for me a testament to my own mother's dread of what might happen when one shuts the door. One may never come back alive! Away from the safety of one's home, disaster awaited. Was this the reason that my mother used to follow her children onto the landing and call after each of us: 'Be careful how you cross the road!' The fragility of life was Mother's chief concern.

At Chorzow, the conductor, with the assistance of passengers, moved the dead woman and the girl off the train. The station-master's whistle and red flag got the train moving again and both of them receded from our view.

We reclaimed our seats and closed ranks, making sure nobody else invaded the compartment.

We were due to reach Cracow soon.

PEASANT ENCOUNTERS

'Don't think of yourselves as smart. You're only greenhorns, so watch out!' were Father's words of caution before our departure. So far, luck had been with us. After Cracow, we travelled in a slow train that stopped frequently at local stations in a monotonous landscape. Beetroot fields and bogs, red earth soaked in peat and peasant cottages sinking in mud were to us an unfamiliar sight.

We shared the compartment with local peasants, most of whom were taciturn, keeping to themselves. Everybody was on his or her guard. Our city attire marked us as outsiders and my brother's ski outfit drew derisive looks. At this time of year the locals were already wrapped in thick sheepskins, fur hats and heavy boots. It was still autumn but in these parts the winter hoar frost glazed over the fields early.

The passengers were mostly Poles or Ukrainians. Jews had lived in this region in great numbers for centuries, but most had now fled across the River Bug to the side occupied by the Soviets. Those who had stayed kept a low profile. At the best of times, the ethnic minorities in Poland co-existed in a state of unease. Since the war, hostilities had resurfaced and the Germans exploited the existing ethnic and national enmities by exercising a 'divide and rule' policy.

Our goal was to get to the River Bug, part of the new demarcation line that divided the German from the Soviet-occupied part of Poland. One of the bridges over the River Bug had been the scene of the historical event in which officers of both armies met, shook hands and saluted each other in the name of the newly forged National Socialist and Communist friendship. The historical handshake had been well documented for posterity in Germany and the Soviet Union and had been shown in cinema newsreels.

That handshake had also driven my cousin Mundek, a sworn Communist, to suicide. As a Communist and as a Polish Jew, the ideological betrayal was a blow beyond endurance. In our family, Mundek was the first victim of the two totalitarian steamrollers crushing Poland.

In planning our route, my brother wisely paid attention to the rumours he picked up from passengers at the various stops along the way. We were warned to avoid the main bridges, congested with hordes of refugees flocking east. They were potential death traps. The refugees were at the mercy of the German and the Soviet guards alike. Sometimes it wasn't even clear from which side the shots were fired. My brother decided we should keep away from the established routes and try our luck by venturing into uncharted territory. The place he selected for our crossing was on the River San, a tributary of the Bug.

The train began to empty slowly, a sign we were getting closer to the border zone. We were left in the compartment with one passenger, a rough-looking peasant. He had a bushy moustache and a few days of growth on his face. Under his fur cap, his hair looked matted, as if it had not seen a comb for a while. His eyes were hooded by heavy lids, which made it difficult to establish if he was watching us or sleeping. We ignored his presence, callow, city-educated youths like us looked down upon eastern peasants. He broke the silence by inquiring where we were heading. His Polish was poor, which made us think he was Ukrainian.

We had several ready-prepared answers for questions about our identity and destination, depending on who was asking. Mostly, my brother was left to handle it, but I was expected to contribute if the situation required raising the emotional heat.

For the benefit of this rough-looking peasant, we were Poles. Our family had been torn apart by the war. Our father, an officer in the Polish army, had crossed with his division into Romania rather than fall into the hands of the Soviets. He and others like him were now interned. Our sick mother was staying with relatives in Lwow. I visualised my sick mother in Lwow and my poor interned father, and felt sorry for our invented family. The peasant, too, seemed affected.

'War is terrible,' he said spitting, as if such vileness had to be spat out. 'May cholera strike the son-of-the-bitch who started this war!'

He was a local and told us he would be getting off at the next station, which was the last before the train entered the 'border zone'. Not getting a reaction from my brother, he asked if we knew about the searches conducted by the German border guards when the trains approached no-man's land. Only residents with special permits were allowed to travel in the prohibited zones, others were always unceremoniously taken off the train. We had not been prepared for such an eventuality. He fixed his eyes on us with a touch of pity for our ignorance.

'Follow me!'

At an obscure little station we got off the train with him in spite of the fact that we had been warned not to trust peasants on trains, who often lured refugees into their homes only to rob them or, worse, deliver them to the Gestapo. There was no alternative but to entrust ourselves to the stranger – anything to avoid a confrontation with the German border guards. Filled with suspicion, we watched his every move.

At the station, another peasant in a horsedrawn cart met our self-appointed protector. My brother looked worried, had he been too rash in accepting help from the stranger? I, too, was unhappy about this peasant who never looked me in the eye. Father used to warn us about such people, they could be shifty. I was flattered that my brother had begun to rely more and more on the mysterious quality of a woman's intuition.

We squeezed into the back of the cart, between sacks of beetroot and potatoes and were driven across a flat, bare countryside. The two peasants sat on a plank that served as the driver's seat and were talking, evidently about us, in Yiddish! Jewish peasants, we wondered? My brother picked up a phrase from their conversation.

'*Amchu?*'

The phrase, of Hebrew origin, amongst Jews stands for a code, meaning '*One of us?*'

'*Nein. Goyim, Polaks.*'

Polish gentiles, the peasant informed his friend. This was an ironic twist of fate. Here we were, desperate to parade ourselves as offspring of the Polish officer caste, landing in the hands of Jewish peasants! I nudged my brother to reveal to them our true identity. He was in no hurry, the situation of mistaken identity began to amuse him. So much for my feminine intuition, I thought.

Our host's house, built of wood in the usual peasant style was a dwelling of a moderately prosperous man. His name was Jacov and when my brother addressed him in Yiddish, he reacted in disbelief. We did not look or act like Jews, he said. It was Friday and he, an observant Jew, was about to light the candles. The ritual of the Sabbath candle blessings offered Jacov the chance to put my brother to the test, inviting him to join in the recitation of the benediction.

Jacov lived alone. His wife and children had gone to stay with his mother-in-law who lived further east in the Soviet zone. Everybody assumed the war would spare the remote parts of Poland. Bogs were no place for tanks, they reasoned. Jacov had stayed behind to look after the business, a modest, beetroot jam factory, which the Germans had requisitioned and appointed a Ukrainian as manager. The Ukrainian, the 'new boss', used to be a worker in Jacov's factory.

Jews were at the mercy of their neighbours who often took advantage of the situation and did as much harm as the Nazis. Like vultures, they were waiting for Jacov's decision to leave and join his family across the border. The house, the factory and his fields could then be theirs for the taking.

Jacov's wedding photo hung in the main room and it showed him as a young man standing stiffly next to his bride, a dark-eyed, beautiful woman. Another smaller framed photograph showed his four children: three girls who resembled their father and the youngest, a boy, looking like his beautiful mother. Many years later, I would see again such photographs hung in museums or used in documentary films about the vanished Jewish life. Faces of buxom matrons or of slim young marriageable girls with porcelain-alabaster complexions. Children dolled up and made to smile. Men, young or old, with bushy beards, and inward looking eyes, were staring at me from the walls of homes doomed to extinction.

The fascination with images made me pay special attention to photographs. I did not know yet that in the future such photographs would play an important role in preventing, in many cases, total oblivion. In what was perhaps a premonitory last-minute decision, I myself removed a stack of photos from my mother's family album without asking her.

Our host observed the Sabbath to the letter, faithfully. Even his horse deserved a rest on the Holy day, he said. The enforced rest was a welcome respite for us as well, allowing us to review our progress. At each step, luck was bringing us closer to our goal. My brother began even to treat my fantasy of reaching the shores of Palestine as a possibility.

Jacov promised to introduce us to his Polish neighbour Piotr, who was a go-between for refugees and Ukrainian smugglers. Smuggling refugees across the river had become a Ukrainian side-business. Piotr's Ukrainian smuggler, he claimed, was not like the others who often robbed or drowned refugees, especially the Jews fleeing from the Nazis, who would easily fall for their promises. The villains would take their money and, instead of taking them across the river, would deliver them to the Gestapo, earning a double reward. On the whole the Ukrainians were a greedy lot, Ivan, Piotr's Ukrainian smuggler, was not at all like them. His description of his choice of smuggler was hardly reassuring and the way he praised the decency and honesty of the Ukrainian guide revealed pitfalls we had never considered. My brother was no longer certain whom to trust. We had little money, Jacov informed Piotr, and assured us that his Polish neighbour didn't expect to be paid for the introduction; he would be doing it as a favour, for the sake of their friendship.

On the Sunday morning, Jacov drove us to a nearby village to meet Piotr, a thin, consumptive-looking man. His isolated timber cottage was sinking in the mud and was surrounded by a crooked wooden fence with missing planks. Indoors, primitive conditions and neglect had made his homestead more like a barn than a home. The rustic reality bore no resemblance to the idealised pictures of peasant cottages that filled Polish calendars, like the one hung in our kitchen.

We were learning about aspects of life in rural Poland, and the conventions of hospitality. Drinking vodka was the welcoming custom as was the exchange of 'calendar wisdom'; politics and miraculous happenings would enliven conversation when tumblers of vodka were knocked back. In the evenings, in the light of smoky oil lamps that left smudges of soot on the glass shade, stories about sickness, ghosts and divine interventions would fill the room. My brother developed a taste for the alcohol and I for the stories.

Piotr was a widower. Of his three sons, the youngest had been killed in action at the age of 19. A photo of the youth dressed in his Polish cavalry recruit's uniform was displayed next to the icon of the Black Madonna of Czestochowa. A faded strip of black crepe paper was pinned to the frame. Two of his older sons had been recruited by a French coal-mining company a year before the outbreak of the war. The lads had sent snaps from France showing strong young men smiling for the camera. This part of Poland was an economically depressed area and provided an easy recruitment market for foreign labour agents. As so often happened with migrant workers, one pulled in another, sometimes leaving whole villages depopulated of their youth.

Jacov introduced us to Piotr as his relatives from central Poland. 'Heaven forbid if any harm befalls them.' Jacov's idiomatic broken Polish sounded almost biblical. He made Piotr swear not to breathe a word about us being Jewish. After wishing us long life and God's blessings, Jacov took his leave.

In the evening, Piotr's hovel, lit by an oil lamp, created a warm cosiness and his generosity in sharing his simple food reinforced our trust. The next day, he refused to take payment for the shelter, but he hinted at how much he admired my brother's ski boots.

What craftsmanship! He had never seen a pair like this. He couldn't keep his covetous eyes off them. Peasant craftiness was in full display.

My brother's ski outfit, including the boots, held a fetishistic importance for him; they symbolised his success as a ski jump champion in a youth competition. The much-admired ski boots would have been too high a price for Piotr's hospitality. Not wishing to part from them in exchange for an old, worn-out pair of peasant boots, he offered to trade instead his sports jacket, which was made of the finest English tweed. They settled the deal with generous helpings of vodka.

We slept in the barn on straw spread on the floor. My brother slept fretfully, with his boots on, distrustful of our benefactor's intentions. In the middle of the night, Piotr woke us. In the light of the oil lamp he resembled a dishevelled apparition, the shadows hardening his features. His sheepskin was thrown over his night-shirt, a sign that he had had no time to dress. He had come, he said, to move us to safety. A neighbour had warned him that a German patrol was prowling in the region raiding farms suspected of hiding livestock. Such nocturnal requisitioning raids gave the Germans a grip over the terrorised peasants. My brother was reluctant to move but Piotr made him understand that he had no choice.

He led us through his field to an underground potato dugout. Our initial euphoria over our lucky progress evaporated. We were, after all, only greenhorns from the city who could be robbed or murdered in this hole and nobody would ever know about it.

We stayed hidden for two or three hours, prepared for the worst. My brother found an iron bar lying on the ground and handed it to me. His weapon was his flick knife.

'In an emergency you aim for the head. Hit hard!'

I often watched Kasia; how in preparation for the Sabbath festive meal, she dealt with a live carp. She used a blunt instrument to hit the wriggling fish on the head. Over the years, she had become an expert at it. My initial squeamishness was overridden by fascination with the fish's vigorous struggle for life, for yet another gasp of breath. Even without its head, the tail still managed to wrench from death a last wriggle.

The idea of hitting someone with the intention to kill alarmed me. Could I do it? I had no doubt that my brother would do it without any compunction. He showed me how to grip the iron and how to swing my arm.

'Make sure you hit hard.'

After a lull, the violent barking of the neighbourhood dogs announced that strangers were indeed moving about in the vicinity. The wind carried scraps of loud German voices, followed by the sound of squealing pigs and the hum of car engines. Piotr had told the truth. They were slaughtering pigs. We ventured out and could see in the distance the headlights of moving vehicles. We gave a sigh of relief and went inside. Piotr found us asleep, curled up against each other.

After the potato dugout, the straw in the barn was almost luxurious by comparison. Feeling secure, my brother took off his boots. Both of us had faced the challenge like seasoned vagabonds.

The following morning, Piotr was as good as his word, the smuggler Ivan turned up and spelled out his terms – half of the payment was to be paid up front before the crossing, and the remainder had to be handed over at the end of the crossing. He would accept dollars, gold or jewellery. German marks were also acceptable. We told them we only had Polish money. Ivan looked disappointed, but Piotr, who was acting the honest broker, took him aside and whispered something into his ear. Ivan, not looking too pleased, agreed to take our zlotys. With the deal finalised, it was sealed with the customary ritual of vodka toasting to the success of the venture. This time, 'the other side' was no longer the figment of a schoolgirl's imagination. It was a concrete territory on the other side of the River San.

THE RIVER BARKS AT NIGHT

We were moved to his house under the cover of the night, in his horsedrawn cart concealed under a bale of hay. Ivan lived on the edge of the riverbank in the fortified no-man's land.

'There she is.'

He pointed in the direction of the turbulent River San, shimmering in the light of the full moon. My nebulous 'other side' had taken on a concrete shape. On the map the new border was a thin twisting line but in reality I was looking at a wide river, with its own caprices and secrets.

His cottage was whitewashed, clean and warm, and a colourful, hand-embroidered wall hanging proclaimed in the Cyrillic alphabet, '*With a guest God enters.*'

A brick stove, a common feature of peasant dwellings, stood in a deep recess, covered with a pile of sheepskins to form a comfortable berth-like space for resting during the day or for sleeping at night.

An icon of Christ, lit by a red light in the shape of a heart, made the recess the cosiest area of the room. Ivan made it clear that the stove area was to be our sleeping quarters for the night. This time my brother baulked at sharing sleeping space with me. Since we had left home, when in danger, we had clung together for safety and warmth. A new confidence in his manhood seemed to remind him of my femininity and he chose to sleep on the floor.

In the early morning, we found Ivan asleep at the table. He must have spent the night like that. As soon as I had vacated the recess, he climbed up and went to sleep.

We had a whole day of waiting ahead of us. We exchanged looks that said, what now?

Part of the room had been screened off with a blanket from where could be heard the sound of people waking. A woman's giggle was followed by a man's prolonged yawn. After a while, the first to appear was a woman in a long, white peasant-embroidered night-dress. Rosy-cheeked with long, dark hair hanging loose, she was the picture of a peasant beauty marred by a pair of highly polished, knee-high officer's boots she carried, her forearms inside the boots. She placed them on the floor and gave them a final shine. Standing on the floor they commanded attention, as if ready for a parade.

A slim, pale-skinned man wearing only long johns followed the plump woman over to a washbasin and splashed his face with water. After his ablutions, the woman once more vanished behind the blanket, emerging the next time with a uniform folded over her arm. While arranging it over the back of the chair, she was careful not to crease it. It was a German officer's uniform!

Our hearts sank: we were trapped. Instead of delivering us to the Gestapo, Ivan had conveniently installed one of their representatives under his roof! The German dressed slowly, assisted by the woman who gazed at him adoringly, anticipating his every wish. Without a word from him, she kneeled down to help with his boots. Fully dressed, the slim, balding man in his early or mid thirties was transformed into a representative of German military might. My brother identified his rank. He was a Captain of the German border unit and he either failed to see us or was just plainly ignoring our presence. Nobody paid any attention to Ivan snoring in his lair, still catching up on sleep. From the woman's looks in his directions we guessed that she was his wife.

My brother's thought centred on the snoring Ivan. Was he sharing his wife with the Captain as well as splitting the profits from his smuggling? Or perhaps, by luring his victims to his cottage, the Germans paid him for delivering Jews? There was a fixed price for each head.

The Captain took his place at the table that had been laid for breakfast and for the first time acknowledged our presence. Between mouthfuls, he inquired if we spoke German. My German was better than my brother's, so I replied that we both understood and spoke German, as we belonged to the *Volksdeutscher*, the German ethnic group in Poland. He gave a sigh of relief.

'Thank God for civilised company!'

Of our many biographical yarns, this one was suitable only for German ears. To patriotic Poles, the *Volksdeutscher* had become anathema, tainted with treacherous Fifth Column activities. Identifying with them would have spelt serious trouble.

We faced the added complication of having to explain why two young *Volksdeutscher* were trying to get across, illegally, to Soviet occupied Lwow. The Captain was offered yet another concocted family saga. Our sick mother was trapped by the war in Lwow where she had suffered a stroke and could not be moved. My brother stepped in and quickly explained that an application had been made via Berlin, but it would take much too long to be processed.

We had already become a good team, our improvisational skills in inventing fictitious family histories were improving all the time. For now I had to get used to living with our imaginary, paralysed mother. I wondered if my brother knew anything about strokes.

The Captain signalled for us to join him and instructed the woman to put more food on the table. Her name was Katarina and she took her place at the corner of the table from where she watched *her* Captain eat. He was generous in his praises of her. His German-Viennese accent made the pronouncing of her name sound as if he was offering liquorice to a child. She washed, ironed and cooked for him. A wink in my brother's direction suggested she had other uses as well, and that there were male secrets from which a girl was excluded. Perversely, the fraternal wink inferred a bond between the German officer and my brother, a young Jew on the run.

Katarina spoke Polish, and we learned from her about the Captain's routine. She always referred to him as '*my* Kapitan', laying, if nothing else, her verbal claim on him. Apparently, he was only on duty in the evenings, which left him free time during the day. He liked riding, but not when it rained. It was just our luck that it was pouring that day and 'her' Captain, bored stiff, was pleased to have company.

A chessboard with finely carved ivory pieces was set up ready for a game, and my brother, a keen chess player, couldn't keep his eyes off it.

'You play chess?' the Captain asked.

The paradox of my brother facing the German Captain across the chessboard mocked everything about Nazism. I watched in amazement the two players intently concentrating on the game as equals, a picture of harmony that would be wrecked in a moment if our true identity were revealed. Both were good players and my brother nevertheless prudently let him take his queen. While setting up the next game, the Captain engaged my brother in a man-to-man talk about women and sex. The older man showed an almost paternalistic interest in the degree of my brother's sexual initiation. He generously offered to share Katarina with him, hinting at the delights that were in store for two men sleeping with the same woman. My brother declined the offer of sexual enlightenment and in his second chess game played more daringly, determined not to lose. The result was checkmate. (I only learned years later the full extent of their 'manly' talk.)

The Captain's boredom and our command of the German language created a risky situation for us – the Captain had taken on the role of a protector. He even tried to persuade us not to go to 'the other side', lecturing about the Soviets, whom he held in contempt. 'Asiatics! You should see the Soviet soldiers. Rifles held up with ropes!'

He openly expressed his critical views about the Nazi-Soviet pact: he suspected that the Führer was making use of it for as long as it suited Germany. But in accordance with the pact, only out of duty did he partner the Soviets in keeping the river border zone free from infiltrators. Personally, he did not mind how many riff-raff succeeded in making it to the other side. Anyway, they were mostly Jews and who needed them, he said, shrugging his shoulders.

He even took my brother for a stroll along the river to give him an opportunity to see, in action, a Soviet patrol on the opposite side of the riverbank. During the walk, he apparently tried to convince him of the great future he and I, both young *Volksdeutscher*, could have in Hitler's Germany. In accordance with the Soviet-German pact, as *Volksdeutscher* we would even be entitled to bring our family from Lwow to Germany proper.

His keen interest in our future was making us anxious about our cover being blown. How much did Ivan know about us? We had been Poles to the Jewish peasant Jacov, Jews to Piotr and now, in the eyes of the Captain, we were *Volksdeutscher*. We were greatly relieved when the Captain vanished behind the curtain to take a nap before his night duty.

'Get up lazy bones!' Katarina nudged Ivan who stirred, stretched himself noisily before jumping off his bedding. His crumpled face with few days of stubble growth made him look as if he had come out of a mangle. He joined us at the table and ordered Katarina to put a bottle of vodka on the table. She did not move, giving him a furious look.

'Do as I say woman! I am still the master here.'

The expression on her face contradicted his claim but she got up reluctantly to fetch a bottle. Ivan took a long sip and passed it to my brother.

'To calm the nerves and warm you up. The river is very cold.' We were to be ready for the crossing as soon as it became dark.

When the Captain reappeared he was dressed for official duty. A pistol holster enhanced his military authority and turned him into a sleek hunter. He soon departed after being seen to the door by Katarina, who received an affectionate slap on her rounded bottom.

Two hours later he returned but not alone. It must have been raining, for his long, black leather overcoat was wet and shiny. Behind him were two German soldiers, who pushed into the room a tall, young albino covered in mud and dripping wet. The Captain sat down opposite him and stared at the captured man with a half-amused and half-intrigued expression.

'Look what we've fished out of the river!' he said.

The shivering man kept his silence and stared defiantly ahead. The Captain ordered Ivan to give the captive a strong dose of schnapps to stop his teeth chattering.

'The Soviets have shot at your friends. Do you still want to cross to the other side?' he asked. The albino nodded.

'You're a Communist?'

'No. I am a Zionist.' His German was a bastardised version of Yiddish. From his accent, he might have been a local lad. My brother and I avoided looking at him. I bit my lips and dug my nails into his hand.

'Were you going to swim all the way to Palestine?' He laughed at his own joke and helped himself to a drink from his hip flask.

'Why waste a bullet? There are other ways of getting rid of the Jews. We'll let him have another try.' After a brief pause he added, addressing us, 'For your benefit!'

The albino kept his eyes on his muddy boots. The Captain ordered the two soldiers who were waiting for his instructions to lead the albino back to the place where they had found him and to wait for him.

Left alone, the Captain congratulated us on our exceptional good luck. He had in mind a perfect diversion for our own crossing by using the albino as a decoy to attract the attention of the Soviets. He gave us the details of the ploy. Once the albino would enter the river and begin his swim, the Captain's men would start shooting, not at the swimmer, but into the air just to alert the Soviets. This would be a signal for Ivan, further down the river, to lead us across.

Ivan looked worried. As for us, we were alarmed at the prospect of this kind of help.

'*Alles gut*! It's bound to work!' our 'friendly' enemy assured us. His outrageous strategy to use the poor albino in order to secure our safe crossing had put us in an impossible situation. We were not prepared for a moral dilemma of such magnitude. One can never know which of the choices fate presents would prove to be the decisive ones. We were too young, morally unprepared to face a situation like this. What was the alternative? To declare our Jewishness would only have increased the number of victims. We went along with the Captain's game and, in our transfer from the chessboard to the game of life and death, we let him win.

My brother realised he was expected to thank him for his desire to help and he muttered something. In the rush of redness spreading to his ears that activated a vein pulsating in his neck, I recognised an onset of rage. At home, we always knew when such a reaction would lead to a fight or a raging quarrel. However, he controlled himself and he shook hands with the German officer before parting from him. Our accidental protector wished us luck and stepped out into the moonless night.

Ivan was fully dressed and ready to lead us towards the place of the Captain's choice. Before setting out, he demanded the first half of the payment, carefully counting the money before putting it into a tin box hidden in a loose brick in the wall.

Ivan led us along the shore through muddy terrain. I felt my brother's firm arm support me as I slipped. A chorus of barking dogs started their canine alarm, breaking the silence Ivan demanded; the river was like an echo chamber. The dogs denounced us in their treacherous tongue until the river itself seemed to be barking. I, who loved dogs, wished them all dead.

At the selected place, Ivan stopped and waited for the prearranged signal from the Captain.

'Once in the water, keep moving, regardless of the shots,' were Ivan's last-minute instructions. As if on cue, shots rang out, accompanied by loud yelling in German.

'*Halt! Halt! Halt!*'

Suddenly, searchlight beams from both sides of the river pierced the blackness of the sky, crossing each other like swords in a fencing duel. When the searchlights hit the surface of the river, they sliced through the water picking up the debris of earlier unsuccessful crossings: discarded suitcases that had spilled their contents and shirts and trousers that floated in the water like inflated dummies. A mile away from us, the albino was being used as quarry. The German stuck to his diversionary tactics.

At first, Ivan led us into the shallowest part of the river. The shock of contact with the freezing river made my teeth chatter. For a while, our progress was made easier by wide planks of wood haphazardly placed over huge boulders. When they came to an abrupt end, the water began to lap round our knees as we began to wade deeper into water. The river kept capriciously rising, one moment reaching up to the men's waists and the next touching their shoulders. I had a problem with my breathing; the freezing water tightened my chest. It was getting deeper, bursting with a violent energy, as if resenting the use made of it. Minutes seemed like hours. I was already dangerously out of my depth and my brother had to keep me afloat by buoying me up. Ivan suddenly stopped.

'From here on, it's getting too deep. I cannot swim.'

'We are not even halfway across the river!' my brother protested. The deal was that he would take us to the other shore, or as near to it as possible. My brother would have throttled Ivan but this was neither the time nor the place to argue with a guide. Besides, we were at his mercy. Before turning back, to show his good will, Ivan volunteered detailed information about the Soviet side. He pointed out two faintly lit houses in the distance that were close to each other. He warned us to avoid the one to the left, which was the headquarters of the Soviet Border Command. To the right was the house of a Polish peasant. He advised us to make our way in her direction.

'Don't let the Russians get you! They turn back refugees.'

We did not believe him, but later we discovered it was true. Abandoned by Ivan and guided by the distant lights, we struggled on. I became paralysed by an attack of fear and was swallowing water. The river washed over me, filling my eyes, nostrils and mouth, reviving my dread of Kasia's Waterman, the one she claimed lived at the bottom of all the rivers. Had he come to claim me? A guardian angel must have tamed the river that had tried to swallow me up.

It seemed like an eternity, but it may have only been 15 or 20 minutes. The shooting had died down, only the searchlights were still zigzagging over the sky uncertain of where to go. When they vanished too, the landscape went pitch black, as if the good night had spread out a protective cover for us. Even the dogs ceased their furious barking. I still remember the sensation of the chill that cut through my flesh and the choking fear that finally rendered me an incurable aquaphobe for the rest of my life. Years later I would inquire as to how my brother had managed to keep me afloat and at the same time hang on to our suitcase. I was and still am a poor swimmer prone to panic.

We had reached terra firma, a slippery, muddy riverbed under our feet. The Soviet shore, unlike the German side, was steep. At each attempt to climb it, we slid back. The earth and mud had formed a slippery clay surface. Finally, my brother groped his way to a weeping willow and managed to hoist himself up. He pulled me up and once our feet were on firm ground, we just collapsed and stayed put for a while to recover. We were exhausted, dripping wet and shivering.

The crossing of the river was a baptism of a kind. Instead of resulting in purification, the immersion had muddied up my perception of myself as a moral human being. With the San waters I had swallowed the sludge of guilt. The albino! How does one remember a person chosen as a sacrifice for one's own safety? Did he get across to the other side safely, or did he end up as a bloated corpse? Whose bullet got him, a German's or a Russian's? In death, the albino would have presented a perfect specimen to satisfy Nazi racist ideology. A Jew, translucently white, staring at eternity through eyes of the palest shades of blue. White eyelashes, white eyebrows, a white soul carried by the current of a river flowing into a black night.

Every time I am near a river, the albino's fate drags me into its vortex. He swims into my sleep and chills my waking life. I am still hoping for a reprieve.

THE SOVIET BORDER ZONE

Which house did Ivan say was the safe one?

My brother realised we had lost our bearings and must have been walking in circles. When Ivan warned us to avoid the Soviet guards' cottage and to aim for the Polish woman's dwelling, there were lights in the windows of both houses. Late into the night, both went out. Desperate to find shelter, we took a risk and approached the nearest house.

A dog on a long chain barking furiously announced the presence of strangers. The silhouette of a woman at the window holding a lighted candle was reassuring, we had reached the right place after all. The door opened slightly and the woman, looking very frightened, crossed herself as if she had seen ghosts. 'Go away,' she pleaded. The candlelight and shadows it cast made the terror in her face accentuated. We didn't move, hoping that our sorry condition and the promise of payment for a night's shelter would make her change her mind. Close to tears, she kept repeating: 'Please, go away.' Her voice lacked authority, more used to taking orders than ordering people around. She would have liked to let us in, she whispered, but it was too dangerous. The Soviet border guards were her immediate neighbours and she, a woman alone with a child, could not take the risk. 'God forgive me!' she muttered, about to shut the door in our faces. Perhaps she was also asking for our forgiveness as well but my brother had wedged the door with his boot. Water dripping from our wet cloths gathered into a puddle around our feet. She just stared at the puddle with intense concentration. Did she see in it a warning about the river's revenge? Rivers have a will of their own. In the past, the San had flooded the land on which her house stood. Whatever it was that she saw in the puddle it made her change her mind and with a sign to be quiet, she let us in and bolted the door behind us.

We learned the reason why she was fearful to let us in. Our presence had put her in a terrible predicament. Her village was in no-man's land and they were forbidden to shelter illegal refugees. Only the previous week in a neighbouring hamlet, a villager had taken in a couple that had crossed the river. When the Soviets discovered them, they drove all of the villagers to an unknown destination.

She got the stove red hot to dry our wet cloths. We sat round the stove wrapped in her bed sheets, while she heated up some milk for us. She was brisk in arranging sleeping places for us. For my brother, she found a pair of her husband's long johns and I was given her best, hand-embroidered nightgown. Her six-year-old son was moved to the other end of the bed to make a place for my brother. The child whimpered his protest in his sleep, but her maternal presence calmed him.

Above the marital bed where she and I were to sleep, hung her wedding photograph. Even as a young woman she was plain looking. The photographer had retouched her face and made her look prettier to do justice to the elaborate bridal outfit. The husband sported a moustache that was curled up at each end in the shape of a question mark. Two years ago he went to France, another of the recruits who had gone to France to work in a coal mine. The money he had sent home made their life easier, but now it had all stopped.

Getting into bed with her under the thick eiderdown was bliss. We were still sound asleep when the Polish woman woke us up. It was before daybreak and we had to leave her house while it was still dark, for her sake as much as for ours. The stove was already lit and the milk was boiling. Thick slices of buttered bread were on the table and she urged us to eat. She refused payment, but asked a favour instead and rummaged in a tin box, from where she pulled out an official-looking envelope with French stamps. It had arrived a few days before the outbreak of the war, but her son's illness had prevented her from travelling to the nearest city to find out what it was about. Her face was filled with expectancy, hoping for good tidings from the messengers who had emerged from the river in the middle of the night. Her son, barefoot, rubbing traces of sleep vigorously from his eyes, came running to his mother who hoisted him on to her lap.

'Mama is waiting for important news from Daddy.'

We took turns reading the letter written in official French while she watched us, her lips also moving as if trying to assist in the reading. The letter from the French Foreign Office included an affidavit sent by her husband and a notification from the French Consulate in Warsaw informing her that a visa for herself and the child was awaiting collection. Before she could even collect them, the war had rendered the visas useless and conspired to rob her of the promise of a reunion with her husband in France. She began to cry, and clasped her son tighter to her bosom.

Taking our leave, my feelings for the Polish peasant went beyond gratitude. I kissed and hugged her at the door where she offered last-minute directions. How much closer can one get to a total stranger who had shared her bed and food in circumstances of risk to herself? To my shame, I forget her name.

'Keep to the edge of the forest, avoid field lanes and open roads.' Apparently the Soviets had extended the no-man's land from the internationally recognised limit of three kilometres to ten.

'God be with you,' she said at the door and crossed herself. The food she prepared for us and the memory of her altruism sustained our hope. There are still some good people left in this chaos-driven world. In later years, when I myself became a mother and my son was the same age as the Polish woman's son, I would often ask myself the disquieting question: how would I have behaved in her position? Nobility of heart is a quality that not everybody is born with, or can attain.

Our passage to the forest was made safe by a thick fog. At times, it seemed that the sky and the earth had fused and we were wading through a space wrapped in gauze. The tree branches, covered with hoar frost, looked as if they were tied together by a giant spider's web.

I recalled Kasia's story about a forest in which rebellious trees, bored with being rooted in one place, went on a stampede. During the walk, I tried to identify the names of trees using the knowledge I had gained from Father, who liked to teach me about trees. He would pluck a leaf and ask, what's that? 'A birch...a chestnut, maple, linden...' Oak was his favourite tree, my recitation satisfied him. Trees and horses were his friends and he would stop to examine them like an inspector.

'Stop counting trees! Measure out steps! It will give us a better idea of the distance we are covering.' My brother urged.

By midday we reached a more populated countryside. It must have been a market day, because in the distance we could see a line of peasant carts. The sound of a train's whistle signalled the proximity of the railway station we were trying to reach.

When a peasant cart came our way we hadn't even tried to avoid it. The driver reined in the horse and assured us we were almost at the end of the limit of the border zone and agreed to drive us to the station, for a fee. We climbed aboard and relaxed, we were close to our goal. It wasn't long before two Soviet soldiers, camouflaged and hiding in a ditch, sprang out, pointing their rifles with fixed bayonets.

'*Ruki na vierch!*'

Without understanding Russian, we obeyed the command ('Hands up!') and scrambled down from the cart with raised hands. After searching us for weapons, they commandeered the same cart and forced the unhappy peasant to drive them and us to the headquarters of the military border guard. We arrived back at the house near the river, the same we had been at such pains to avoid last night. From the window we could see the Polish woman's cottage and the boy playing with the dog.

'KUDA? SUDA?'
('FROM WHERE ARE YOU COMING?
WHERE ARE YOU GOING?')

We were herded into a crowded barn filled with people who, like us, had been picked up in the out-of-bounds border zone. Our first encounter with the Soviets dampened our spirits. Stalin's stern gaze was fixed on us from a huge portrait. A poster was calling for the proletariat of the world to unite in the fight against the parasites and the enemies of the working class. That immediately singled us out. The fact that we were refugees and dispossessed changed little in the Soviet political perception. Inside, people were swapping their experiences and comparing notes about where they had been picked up. The Soviet Union and Communism made no provisions to deal with the hordes of refugees, mostly Polish Jews, who were seen as ideologically troublesome. Even Polish Communists were regarded with suspicion.

My brother was cheered up by a surprise encounter with Jurek, his pal from the Lodz Maccabi tennis club and the cafe Tabarine where they used to go for afternoon-tea dances. Jurek, like my brother, was more devoted to sport and dancing the foxtrot than to politics. But Poland's defeat made him decide that he would rather see Europe under the hammer and sickle than the swastika.

Jurek, too, had crossed the River San, but unlike us, instead of avoiding detection by the Soviets, he was impatient to encounter them. He covered the border zone, walking boldly through country lanes and villages, often singing to attract attention. Yet his boisterous conduct was ignored and most likely he was mistaken for a local drunk. Such was his enthusiasm for the Red Army that he decided to greet the first-seen representative with a fraternal gesture of friendship. Eventually, his wish was fulfilled and he was almost bayoneted when he rushed to greet an approaching Soviet soldier.

In spite of everything, Jurek maintained a cheerful disposition, whistling his favourite tune from a Hollywood musical. He had plans for his future under the Soviets. He would teach fencing or ballroom dancing or anything else to do with leisure sports.

Jurek and my brother put their heads together to consider the situation. Would a bribe do? It was common knowledge that the Russians were crazy about watches. Jurek possessed a Swiss platinum-plated Rolex, as well as some gold dollars sewn into the hem of his coat. The middle-class youths from Lodz with their fashionable haircuts and mastery of tennis, ice hockey and ski sports were at a loss as to how to handle the Soviets, the champions of the oppressed proletariat.

Once again we had to reconsider our identity in the event of interrogation. We decided it would be advantageous to reclaim our Jewishness. We made our mother a widow in order to eliminate the problem of who or where our father was. Our fictional grandmother was erased from our biography. In the event of our having to provide a residential address in Lwow, we decided to provide that of Father's commercial representative, Mr Silverstein.

I was discovering a new side to my brother's hitherto dormant talent for improvisation. He came up with an idea that startled me. He would pretend to be mute, while I would do the talking. His plan made sense, he had an arrogant Polish look about him, and the Soviets were not well-disposed towards Poles of military age.

The interrogation took place the following day. From the window of the room serving as an office we could see the Polish woman's cottage yard and the restless dog on the long chain. Whatever else we would be expected to divulge, we decided never to breathe a word about our presence under her roof.

Our interrogator was a good-looking, young Soviet officer cutting an impressive figure in his uniform trimmed with gold braid and various decorations. His elegance seemed a sharp contrast to the shabby uniform of the soldiers who had arrested us.

A plain wooden table served as a desk. A translator who spoke shaky Polish with a Jewish accent and wore thick-rimmed glasses attended us. His shortsighted eyes were darting back and forth between the officer and me and my 'mute' brother, who had assumed the expression of a village idiot. The officer was addressing the translator as 'tovarisch', 'comrade', and I was 'citizen', 'grazdantka'.

I handed over the faked school IDs and insisted that my brother and I had been born in Lwow. It soon became clear that the authorities' chief concern was how we had reached the border zone and where we were heading. My ears had begun to attune themselves to the repetition of some key Russian words sounding like a nursery rhyme. 'Kuda? Suda?' 'From where are you coming? Where are you going?' The words and their rhythmic variants flowed like a song. I took a liking to the Russian language.

The interrogating officer grew impatient with the muddle between myself and the tovarisch translator. In my rapid, school-slang Polish,

I kept interrupting him in the middle of his translations to correct him. Fuelled by fear, my tongue was like a weapon; words and sentences were my ammunition. I recalled Mother's belief that words could move mountains. I hoped that mine wouldn't turn on me. I must have mentioned Lodz, and Lwow, more than a dozen times, as well as our poor widowed mother, left alone under the German occupation and the Father shot by Nazis, which must have confused the translator. The handsome officer bedecked in red stars was losing patience with his translator and me and, after some more questioning, read out the interrogation report.

The document stated that the two accused had left Lwow and had illegally entered the Soviet border zone with the intention of *leaving* the Soviet Union. The Soviet officer reprimanded us for even attempting to do such a foolish, punishable undertaking. We had committed, he repeated, a very serious offence. The document concluded that the Soviet penal authorities *in Lwow* would deal with our case. The 'confession' required our signature.

The muddle of the *kuda* and *suda* was responsible for the misunderstanding that we planned to *leave* the Soviet Zone. We were so thrilled with the suggestion of being taken to Lwow, the city we were aiming to reach, that we failed to grasp the implication of the ominous threat of being dealt by the 'Soviet penal authorities'.

This time we were herded into open military trucks with other refugees and driven to the nearest railway station, where Soviet guards supervised our transfer to a regular passenger train with two carriages reserved for the prisoners. The windows had been obscured by opaque white paint and the doors were locked behind us to prevent escape. The presence of a Soviet guard in each compartment bearing a rifle with a fixed bayonet made us realise that we were real prisoners!

The one consolation was that we were reunited with Jurek, who was looking less cheerful now. The circumstances of our journey to Lwow destroyed my entire fantasy about getting to the 'other side'. It was no longer a place lodged in my imagination but a territory guarded by Soviet soldiers with bayoneted rifles, not at all welcoming fleeing Jews. It filled me with bitter resentment. The sight of the Soviet guards' rifles held up with ropes, just as the German Captain had so contemptuously described, filled me with silly satisfaction.

The young soldier guarding our compartment had his hair shorn to zero, indicating that he was a new recruit, and each time our eyes met, he looked away with a sheepish expression. Perhaps he felt sorry for us. My brother and Jurek initiated a fraternisation campaign, no doubt encouraged by the guard's open, innocent-looking face. Jurek offered one of his Polish cigarettes, but the soldier proudly refused, proceeding to roll his own brand of Russian *machorka*, a foul-smelling, rough, black tobacco. Jurek's impeccable Polish middle-class manners obliged him to light the Russian's cigarette. The lighter with its adjustable flame aroused the guard's curiosity. Jurek offered the lighter to the guard for inspection, who, like a child delighted with a toy, kept turning the flame up and down. Jurek's gesture that he should keep it was refused. It was the Soviet guard's turn to be generous. He produced a bottle of vodka, from which he took a gulp before passing it round to the men in the compartment. I was offered an apple.

The boys from Lodz were oozing charm, trying to establish some sort of communication with the soldier in spite of the language barrier. Gestures, odd Polish words that resembled Russian and photographs served the purpose. Jurek produced a photo of himself on the tennis court. My brother produced a photo of himself on skis with his arm around his girlfriend, Salusia. I pulled out a photo of our parents. The Russian carried a photo of his extended family; grandmother, grandfather, mother, father and himself with his siblings. We each began to give individual names the faces in the photographs. We learned that the guard's name was Sergiosha and we shook hands, addressing each other by name. We had swapped names and family faces in exchange for a temporary truce. This time Jurek's repeated offer of a cigarette was accepted with a smile. Sergiosha smelled it and turned it around in his fingers, savouring the smoothness of the paper and its delicate aroma. After another round of the vodka bottle he took out a harmonica and began to play.

The opaque windows ensured that we would see nothing of the passing landscape, but the Russian melodies he played conjured up the flowing Volga and Ukrainian fields ripe with gold corn. The Cossack song 'Oj, Danna Oj, Danna' made the guard's eyes light up when I joined in. The arrival of the train in Lwow, however, brought the cosy atmosphere to an end.

The doors were unlocked and we found ourselves surrounded by a cordon of militiamen with red armbands, supervised by Red Army officers. After all the effort we had landed at our intended destination, Lwow, but as prisoners! The frustration was too much to bear and I burst into tears.

The railway station had a festive atmosphere, decorated with red flags and huge portraits of Stalin. Loudspeakers boomed out Soviet military marches. The passers-by pretended not to see us being led under guard.

Sergiosha was escorting our group, and when his eyes met mine they looked to the ground. Jurek manoeuvred himself to walk alongside him and engaged him in a short exchange. 'I have asked him to get us drinks,' he told my brother.

Sergiosha stopped at a kiosk, to make the purchase. That's when my brother and Jurek yanked me across the rail track where we jumped onto a local train that was just about to depart. We locked ourselves in the toilet and held our breath waiting for the train to move. Once moving, we waited. After what seemed like a safe lapse of time and distance, we decided to emerge.

'Sergiosha's kindness saved us,' I said, thinking about the recruit with the trusting blue eyes, who might be punished for our disappearance. He had shown us the true Russian soul! Jurek smiled and pulled up a sleeve to reveal the absence of his Swiss watch. He had used it to bribe Sergiosha. It was not my tears after all, but Jurek's watch that made our escape possible. We got off the train at a suburb of Lwow and took a tram back to town.

It was only a week since we had left home.

RED FLAGS AND PAPRIKA

Father's business associate, Mr Silverstein, greeted us as if he had been expecting our visit. He had a truly golden smile: all of his front teeth were covered with gold crowns. A chubby man with the build of a wrestler that contrasted with his preference for dandy-like attire, he always wore a bow tie and a silk handkerchief in his side pocket. But his most distinguishing feature was his baldness and the pride he took in his suntanned scalp that shone like a Byzantine church dome. He used to boast that, even with a magnifying glass, not a single hair could be found on his naked head. As a child, he would let me touch the smooth skin of his head, which towards the back of his massive neck had baby-like folds.

He was pleased to see us and impressed with the speed of getting there. At Mr Silverstein's apartment, the first thing I noticed was a large, ornate Chinese vase standing in the hall filled with a bunch of peacock feathers. The feathery green eyes stared at me, a reminder of the idyllic past that was behind me. The display of peacock feathers pulled me back home and the prank he had played on me, taking advantage of my reputation of a gullible child.

Once a year he used to visit us in Lodz and I always waited impatiently for his arrival. He used to bring me gifts; mostly dolls dressed in ethnic outfits. Once, he asked what I would like on his next visit. The two things I desired most were as unlikely as could be. The first was a monkey on a chain, like the one I would occasionally glimpse on the balcony of our eccentric neighbour. The second request was for a peacock.

'A peacock it'll be!' he said.

I had never bothered to consider where a bird of this size could be kept in a town apartment. The first peacock I ever saw was an artificial one in a window display of a shop selling silk materials. The arrangements of materials mixed with the splendour of peacock-coloured feathers bewitched me.

When he did arrive, my excitement turned to disappointment. I was handed a single peacock feather.

'Sorry, the peacock flew away during the journey!'

He told me that he tried to grab it by its tail but all that was left in his hand was a single peacock feather. He looked so upset that I believed him.

Silverstein was a born storyteller and would keep the family spellbound by tales of his youth spent in Vienna during the time of Franz Josef, the Austrian Emperor. His reminiscences brought to life the famous cafes, the beautiful promenades along the Danube, operettas, waltzing, a vanished world only seen in films.

Before Poland's short-lived independence, Lwow was part of the Austro-Hungarian Empire, known as Lemberg. Its mix of a multinational population, Poles, Ukrainians, Jews and Armenians, had lent it a cosmopolitan character. The Austrian occupation of Poland was the most liberal and enlightened and Lwow was part of Imperial Vienna's social and cultural life. Mr Silverstein was a typical representative of its charm and manners.

His wife Sarah, daughter Fredka, aged 19, and her sister, aged ten, accepted our unexpected arrival. They occupied a modest-sized apartment of only two bedrooms, a dining room and a sizeable kitchen, which was the centre of family life. The cramped space was no barrier to their hospitality, for invited or uninvited guests. I was given a couch, positioned at the foot of the couple's marital bed. My brother was allotted a folding bed, placed in the corner of the dining room.

On the first day of our arrival, we immediately went to the post office to send a telegram to our parents in Lodz.

'Arrived safely. Staying with the Silversteins.'

My brother had visited Lwow before the war. At every turn he was struck by the transformation of the city. Within a very short time the Soviets had managed to obliterate Lwow's Polish heritage, its new occupiers had 'sovietised' the city.

The loudspeakers in public squares were blaring the 'Internationale' and Soviet military marches creating an artificial mood of public celebration. It was at odds with the grim reality of shortages in shops, long queues, the black market and the presence of masses of refugees. A new iconography reminiscent of Byzantine icons had replaced the old, and the profiles of Marx, Lenin and Stalin, encircled with garlands, were seen in every shop window, mostly empty of merchandise.

Cafes, restaurants and hotel lobbies were the places where the refugees congregated, and immediately after our arrival we went in search of other refugees from Lodz. The Soviet system did not allow for organised centres for refugees. Like everybody else, we were anxious for the latest news from Lodz. Since our departure the situation for the Jews had deteriorated. More and more restrictions were being imposed on the Jews. There were rumours of a ghetto.

Days turned into weeks. We were drifting, spending idle days in cafes and hotel lobbies, obsessed with the need to pick up news from home as if the effort we had made so far had drained our energies. But not our appetites, we could not get enough of the delicious new dishes with the hot red paprika flavours cooked by the Silversteins.

After a few weeks of our stay, our hospitable host grew anxious about his diminishing larder, usually filled with food purchased on the black market. Both husband and wife were devoted to good food, and the war shortages were treated as a challenge to their efforts to satisfy the needs of their stomachs and palettes. At mealtimes, the table was loaded with the kind of food one could no longer find in shops.

The mealtimes had become Mr Silverstein's favourite occasion for raising the issue of our future. Did he begrudge us shelter or food? he would ask. No, he did not. He was acting *in loco parentis* for our own good. It was high time, he reminded my brother of his filial duty, to give a thought to how best to help our parents who had been left to the mercy of the Nazis.

As for me, he was certain that my father would have wished for me to continue with my schooling, and he was right about that. He suggested I should register with a local school, learn Russian, and eventually graduate, and, who knows, become a doctor! In one sentence he had arranged my future. It seemed as simple as eating his wife's dessert of pears conserved in crystallised sugar.

He painted a rosy vision of our future in the Soviet Union, a country that offers free education, free medical service and equality to all people. All this, he said, was awaiting young people like my brother, his own children, and me. He dismissed with a gesture of resignation the future for his own generation. Men like him, he confessed, had already witnessed so many historical changes in their lifetime that it would be too difficult to adjust to the new Soviet reality.

His enthusiasm for the opportunities the Soviet regime offered surprised us. Father knew him as a shrewd businessman and it seemed that the Soviet occupation offered him ample opportunity to make money from the flourishing black market for every kind of commodity. Mr Silverstein's pragmatism was an integral part of the survival instinct. He was dispassionate in his analysis of the political fate of Europe. 'Europe's fate is sealed,' he claimed: Germany and the Soviet Union, by joining in the friendship pact, had outmanoeuvred England and France. Joined together, both dictatorships represented a most formidable military power. As for the Jews, they had no other option but to throw in their lot with the Soviets. At least under the Soviet rule the Jews were spared the vicious Nazi anti-Semitic persecution. He took comfort in the fact that there were many Jews in the Soviet army, as well as many occupying high positions in the Comintern.

The hints that we were beginning to outstay our welcome coincided with the fact that our money was running out and a sense of fatigue had set in. Our host kept up the pressure on my brother by constantly reminding him that he alone could help our parents by volunteering to work in the Soviet Union. Able-bodied men were required to work down the Soviet coalmines! As a worker he could earn privileges connected with the working class, such as being allowed to bring our parents over to the Soviet side. If it was true, it offered a glimmer of hope impossible to ignore.

My brother was not ready for the glorious Soviet future.

'What about the Stalinist treason trials of the years 1935–38? And what sort of country is it that condemns to death veteran revolutionaries and army commanders? But worst of all is the infamous Soviet-Nazi pact,' my brother challenged him.

Nevertheless, Silverstein's enthusiasm for the approaching era of the triumphant '*Homo Sovieticus*' proved infectious.

His daughter's fiancé, Bernard, a dental technician, was the first to respond to Mr Silverstein's vision of the future, and decided to volunteer. Fredka trusted her father's political judgement and hoped that by joining the proletarian fold, Bernard would one day be able to practice his own profession and she would be able to join him within a year or so. Mrs Silverstein was already buying up on the black market lengths of white satin and lace for Fredka's wedding dress.

Prone to indecisiveness, my brother went to discuss the prospect with other young Lodz men who frequented the Cafe Syrena. His friend Jurek was despondent, he neither liked what he saw nor what he heard. People were being arrested at night and deported deep into Russia, just as during the Tsarist times. Red Army soldiers were corrupt drunkards, not averse to robbing innocent citizens; having discovered that most of the things he had planned for his future depended on decisions made in Moscow, he decided that he wasn't cut out for work in a coal mine. A ballroom floor suited him far better. He was seriously considering making his way to Romania.

Another of my brother's acquaintances from Lodz was inclined to volunteer. If this was the only way to rescue his parents, then so be it. He was young and didn't mind hard work, he said. Everywhere miners were regarded as aristocrats of the working class.

One bright morning, Bernard, my brother and the other youth from Lodz went to sign up to become miners in West Ukraine, in Donbass. To celebrate this important event, Mr Silverstein invited everybody to the cinema.

The film *The Circus* was a comedy by Alexandrov (1936), one-time assistant to Eisenstein. The leading lady was Lyubov Orlova, a glamorous platinum blonde, and the film told the simple story of a white American actress who gives birth to a black baby. Finding herself ostracised and humiliated in America, she goes to the Soviet Union. There her life is miraculously transformed into a never-ending feast of social and racial harmony and love.

Soviet ideology informed the context of the film but not the style. The lavish production, in imitation of a Hollywood musical, included extravagant sets, costumes and revue numbers and involved breathtaking acrobatics. The heroes of this sentimental story, in spite of its transparent ideological propaganda slant, radiated an irresistible life-enhancing appeal. The film proclaimed that Marxism, the Communist Party and Stalin were at the helm of the progressive world and only they could steer mankind towards a brighter future.

The circus milieu as a metaphor for life was a perfect place for tricks, physical and ideological. The message about the glory of human solidarity appealed to me, as did the exaltation of the film's style. It satisfied a longing for a world free of racism, oppression and injustice. It made me cry and we all left the cinema feeling elated.

Within a week, the mining volunteers were summoned for interviews and given departure dates.

At the Lwow central railway station, the three volunteers were being seen off. Fredka and her mother were tearful while Mr Silverstein fussed about the supplies of food he had provided for each of the departing young men. My brother and I were looking at each other, holding back tears.

'According to the terms of my contract, I'll have two holidays a year.' He tried to reassure himself and me that the separation was only of a reasonably short duration.

I recalled the pledge given to Father never to separate. My brother had either forgotten or regarded his mission to rescue our parents as a licence to discharge himself from the promise. So far, it had not occurred to me to object to his departure, but now, standing on the snow-covered platform, I felt like saying: 'Don't go! Don't leave me!'

Even now, the scene of our separation is as vivid as a recently seen film. On the freezing, grey December day, we stood close to each other and the frost made each spoken word come out in a steaming breath. Our idle chatter covered up our true emotions. I joked about his ski outfit and the much-cherished ski boots he wore.

'Should you be wearing them?'

'Don't worry.'

'How far is Donbass?'

'I'll write as soon as I arrive.'

The engine garlanded with a festive huge red Soviet star, steamed and hissed, waiting for the stationmaster's whistle and the wave of the red flag. My brother was already inside the train waving and I hardly noticed when the wheels started to move. Within minutes it speeded up and pulled my brother out of my sight.

Back at the Silversteins' apartment, the empty chair where he used to sit made me tearful. I already missed him and knew it was a terrible mistake to let him go. I felt abandoned.

With my brother out of the way, it was now my turn. Mr Silverstein set out to arrange my future. Using persuasive arguments, he reminded me of my foremost obligation to my parents.

I began to take steps about my schooling and presented myself to the secretariat of the nearest gymnasium, hoping that admittance might help me get into a student hostel. During the short interview, I was asked to prove my father's working-class credentials and membership of the Komsomol, the Young Communist Organisation. The absence of both was a barrier to the admittance to schools reserved for the privileged working classes. The headmaster recommended I try the schools for dressmaking or nursing. All the while, Stalin's portrait stared at me from the wall of his office. His omniscient eyes mocked my hopes of getting to where I said I was going – to my sister, to Palestine!

Back at the Silversteins' apartment, I started to pack my belongings.

'Where do you think you're going, young lady?' Mr Silverstein asked, watching me pack.

'To Palestine!'

He shook with laughter, the golden crowns shining in his mouth. After this attack of jollity, he suggested I keep the keys in case I changed my mind. I promised to let them know of my whereabouts, as I was expecting letters from my brother. I kissed them both, thanked them for their hospitality, and leaving the keys on the table I left. I acted on the impulse to leave immediately and not to prolong my stay with them – I might never be able to make a move if I stayed even for another day or night.

On the way out, I pulled a peacock feather from the Chinese vase and took it with me as a talisman. It was not until much later that I discovered they bring bad luck.

JOURNEYS WITH MAPS

In wartime, railway stations tend to become shelters for weary refugees and a place where one can find a bench while waiting for a train that might or might not arrive. Or wait for a chance encounter that might improve one's situation. If one had money, one could still get a hot drink or soup.

At a loss as to where to go, I drifted to the Lwow central railway station. The traffic of people at stations was a perfect metaphor for this phase of my life, a life comprised of instant friendships that dissolved just as quickly, without any sense of loss. My mind, correspondingly, resembled a railway locker where people would deposit bits and pieces of themselves: a face, a voice, a gesture or a story. Without intending it, I became the keeper of stories about the life of total strangers. We exchanged names, addresses and even phone numbers, hurriedly scribbled on scraps of paper, and promised to be in touch. At the time, I never thought that the inventory of people who strayed into my life would permanently stay etched in my memory.

I kept giving out my home address and telephone number, unaware at the time of its symbolic importance. It was a desperate message, an SOS tossed in a bottle into the sea: '*I have a home and a family. The address is Lodz, Kilinskiego—tel.—.*'

It affirmed my status. I was a girl from a home with an address that had the trappings of modernity: a telephone, a radio, a gramophone, and a modern gas cooker. In the winters, I had waltzed on the Traugutta ice rink to the sound of Strauss's music. And in the summers, I would speed on my bicycle through country lanes in Glowno, the summer resort where Father had bought a lodge in the forest. The invitations I extended to casual acquaintances to look me up 'after the war', were a reassuring act of hope. I hung onto the telephone number like a mystic to his mantra. The numbers acquired a magical power and I am ashamed to admit that even today, I try this number when playing the National Lottery.

Occasionally, after the war, a few of the people I encountered strayed into my life again, often through miraculous twists of circumstances, in Israel, the US, Australia, and even once in India. They would listen to me with disbelief after I reminded them about the circumstances of our encounter. 'Did I really say that?'

This time, while sheltering at the Lwow station I was already familiar with the Soviet rules regarding frontiers and the searches for passengers without the proper permits. My goal was the Romanian border, but I had no idea which route to choose without the risk of being picked up. Where exactly would it be safe to get off?

I had no map and the regional maps that were customarily displayed at railway stations had been removed by the Soviets. They showed the Polish pre-war borders and as far as the Kremlin was concerned Poland was crossed off the map. The fact was that I was ignorant of the Polish region that I now needed to explore. The geography lessons that I learned at school were of no help. Knowing the names of capitals of distant countries, of oceans, rivers and the highest mountains in the world was useless.

Looking for a place in the waiting room, I spotted a boy, about my brother's age, consulting a map. The map, which was the centre of my interest, belonged to an attractive young man with a dark mop of unruly hair and dark eyes. I was like a lost dog, seeking to attach myself to any kind master.

The map belonged to Rafael who spoke in a halting, fractured Polish with a foreign accent. He was a Palestinian Jew who had come on a summer visit to meet his ailing grandfather. The war had trapped him in Warsaw while arranging his passage back home, set for the middle of September. Unfortunately, the German Wehrmacht had been faster than he and his uncle with whom he was staying. Rafael was caught in the siege of Warsaw and the heavy bombardments. His uncle's house had been hit and they had lost everything. The loss of his documents had complicated his chances of making his way home. The British Embassy had already been evacuated from Warsaw. In exasperation, he decided to make his way to the Soviet-occupied part of Poland and from there to contact the British Embassy in Moscow. Fed up with the cold climate and the prolonged frustration of waiting in Lwow for news about his application for a new passport, he opted to smuggle himself to Romania, from where it would be easier for him to reach Palestine.

He was the first Palestinian Jew I had met. Everything about him appealed to me. He represented the new breed of pioneering Jew my sister had chosen to become. Meeting Rafael renewed the longing for my sister. In the last photographs she sent home, she was wearing a pair of shorts and a gymshirt revealing her suntanned arms and legs. She had changed beyond recognition. My sister, who used to be so easily frightened by a single chicken, was now feeding a brood of them, learning to milk cows and to handle a gun.

Rafael proved to be a born leader and took charge of organising the route of our expedition. In his backpack, he had other maps as well, including a map of Romania. He could read a map the way musicians read a score. The map's markings and colours led him confidently through unknown territories. He could gauge the distances by the scale and the criss-crossing lines of rivers and roads. I was map-blind and he soon gave up trying to instruct me in the art of map-reading.

The route Rafael chose bypassed Stanislawow, a city I had originally opted for. He pointed his finger to Kolomyja, a smaller town, close enough but not too close to the Romanian border. From there, we were to move in stages towards the Soviet-Romanian frontier, avoiding travel by train.

He knew about the place from a member of his kibbutz, who used to talk with nostalgia about his native town. Rafael was confident that the parents of the kibbutznik would be pleased to welcome their son's friend from Palestine.

We arrived in Kolomyja, a modest sized town, without any mishaps and managed to locate the kibbutznik's parents who were delighted to receive us. Isaac, our host, and the rest of the family fussed over Rafael, an emissary from the Promised Land! Since the arrival of the Soviets, the Jews had been cut off from contact with their Palestinian brethren. During the evening meal, some neighbours also dropped in to hear news about Jewish life in Palestine.

Rafael enthusiastically described the kibbutz where life was organised along the socialist principle of 'To each according to his need.' Everybody was equal and all hard work was equally shared, irrespective of the degree of education or family status. Men and women shared the duties of working in the kitchen and laundry. No private profits were allowed: the kibbutz's wealth belonged to the 'collective'.

In wartime Kolomyja under the shadow of the Soviets, the picture of a socialist Paradise presented by Rafael did not sound inviting. The word 'collective' jarred, and the utopian dream of a just and equal society was tarnished by direct contact with the Soviet model of collectivisation. The women did not like what they heard and shook their heads.

'Collective kitchen and laundry? Does it mean that the men don't even own the shirts on their own backs?'

When Grandma Malka, Isaac's mother, spoke, everybody went quiet. She was dressed in black and wore a lace headcover over her wig. Seated in the armchair, she resembled a monolith carved in granite.

'Collective nurseries? They take the children away? What sort of Jewish parents are they? Who spoils the children?'

Rafael assured the grandmother that the kindergarten infants lived in 'collective' nurseries and were looked after by trained nurses. The older children received education from excellent teachers as well as being taught how to become good farmers.

Grandma Malka shook her head in disapproval. 'Poor children!' Rafael tried to convince her that the children had the best of everything! As an example, he cited the fact that many of the adults in his kibbutz lived under canvas tents, whereas the children had the best brick dwellings. Grandma Malka wasn't convinced.

'I feel sorry for my grandson who has chosen a life like this. May heaven help those ungodly kibbutzes! They are just like the

Bolsheviks!' she muttered on the way to the kitchen. She soon returned with a plate of her homemade cookies.

A knock on the door announced a latecomer and the silence that fell on the room signalled that the man who entered was an unwelcome guest. The red band of the Soviet Militia around his sleeve explained why. Having heard that Isaac had visitors from afar he had come to find out who they were.

Gershon was a renowned Communist with a reputation of someone who had been openly hostile towards Zionism even before the war. When the Russians invaded Kolomyja, Gershon was appointed secretary to the local Soviet Commissar. They could rely on him to detect illegal Zionist activities. Gershon knew that Kolomyja was a stronghold of Zionism and never missed an opportunity to try to convert them to the Soviet style of socialism. Many suspected him of having denounced the local Hebrew teacher and the president of the Zionist Federation, who had been arrested and deported to remote parts of Russia.

Only Grandma Malka was not afraid of him and she made a welcoming gesture by pushing the plate of cookies towards him.

'Gershon, are you still praying to Stalin's idols?' she teased him.

'Mother,' Isaac scolded her.

Gershon laughed, enjoying the description of himself as a faithful Stalinist. His faith in the party and Stalin was absolute. Every action the Great Leader took was inspired by a superior intelligence. Gershon had stopped believing in God a long time ago, his allegiance having turned from God to Stalin when he was a teenager.

'Grandma Malka, you're a wise old woman. You should persuade your son to join the Communist Party. It would be good for him and the whole family.'

Gershon's presence provoked an argument about the future of the Jews. Should it be with the Soviet Union or Palestine?

'Anyone who wants a Jewish State can go to Birobidjan, the Soviet autonomous Jewish Republic,' Gershon proclaimed.

Isaac's wife wasn't happy about Gershon's visit or the discussion and began to collect the dishes. The neighbours, one by one, departed. Isaac took Gershon's visit as a warning. The uninvited guests, for their own safety, should make a move as soon as possible. Isaac waited for Gershon's departure but he ignored the hint and lingered on.

After everybody had left, Gershon, somewhat crestfallen, addressed Rafael in fluent Hebrew. Isaac was dumbstruck and stared at him in disbelief. In all the years he had known him, he had never let on that he knew Hebrew. What secrets he must have gleaned by this deception for the benefit of his party! It turned out he had a request regarding a delicate personal matter. Looking very embarrassed, he produced a photograph showing a handsome young woman with a boy.

'The mother of my son,' he said. In silence the photo went from hand to hand. He confessed that many years ago he had got this girl into trouble, and that she had emigrated to Palestine. 'This is the child I have never seen. My son!' he said, in a voice charged with emotion, and took back the photo, hiding it in his wallet.

'I would like to send her some money. My contribution to the upkeep of my son.' He carefully counted 20 dollars and five pounds sterling and put them on the table. He was counting on Rafael to take the money. In gratitude he shook Rafael's hand and wished us all a safe journey before departing hastily.

'Well I never!' Isaac said as he watched Gershon close the door. 'Who would have believed it of Gershon?'

THE RUSSIAN SPY MANIA

Rafael's plan had worked. We had managed to avoid Soviet patrols and reached a place called Zaleszczyki, which had a reputation for easy, illegal border crossings. Before the war it had been close to the Polish-Romanian frontier but was now Soviet-Romanian. In Central Europe, people got used to the fact that they may go to bed in one country and wake up in another. The same place acquires a different flag and a new language.

We reached the place that Gershon had recommended, an inn run by a Jew with Romanian connections. Janos was a friendly middle-aged man with Zionist leanings, and thus sympathetic to our goal. He was in touch with a reliable smuggler, someone from across the Romanian border who had already accomplished a few previous crossings, mostly of Jews, who, like us, were trying to reach Palestine.

The few days we spent in Janos's inn were a welcome break. Janos's wife was instructing me how to cope with menstruation. My first bleed occurred after we left Kolomyja during the trek to Janos's inn. The flow was unstoppable and was wetting my pants and trousers. I used up all of my handkerchiefs. Rafael must have guessed that I was in trouble for he offered me his as well. We were nowhere near a pharmacy or any other kind of shop. I have no recollection about having been embarrassed but it gave rise to strange thoughts, of all things, about Joan of Arc. What I wanted to know was whether the Maid of

Orleans was already menstruating when she challenged the English? And how had she managed wearing the soldier's chain mail? I have never forgotten the film I saw before the war in a Lodz cinema and the impact of the close-up of her face, lips cracked and terror-stricken eyes choked by the smoke raising from the smouldering stake.

'A young girl like you should be under the protection of her mother!' Janos's wife brought me back to reality by looking at me with a maternal concern. I was in her husband's inn, waiting with Raphael to be helped to cross the border. Rafael was made happy by a map he desired that hung on the wall of the attic room. It was of the Habsburg Empire, circa 1885. In his kibbutz he was known for his map-collecting obsession and had already assembled a modest collection of old maps of the Holy Land. To his delight, Janos offered him the map, saying that it was old and useless to him.

The day before the arranged meeting with the Romanian smuggler was due to take place we became embroiled in the undeclared war between the Soviets and the Polish and Ukrainian nationalists. In this part of Poland, guerrilla activities against the Soviet occupation still continued. The armed skirmishes that took place were never officially acknowledged by the Soviets, who simply saw the guerrillas as bandits. The disorganised armed bands were remnants of the defeated Polish army and rebellious Ukrainian nationalists. They roamed the countryside, operating separately, often turning against each other. But in one aspect of their activities they were united; they all regarded Jews as their bounty. Local Jews, like Janos, feared both groups equally. Under the banner of guerrilla activities against the Soviets, they would often terrorise Jews, in search of money, food and alcohol.

Janos, who had been targeted once before by a Ukrainian gang, had hired an armed night watchman. Last time the gang got away with his cash, his stock of alcohol and his two horses. On this occasion he was well-prepared.

His wife and I hid in the cellar, but for Rafael the shooting was a call to join in the fray. This was a chance to prove to the Diaspora Jews how important it was to be prepared for self-defence. The Jews in Palestine were proud of the chance to revert to the biblical warrior tradition, and he was a good shot.

The gang, having met with armed resistance, retreated in haste leaving one of their injured men behind. Something like this happened only rarely. The rule was you never leave your man behind!

The exchange of fire attracted the local militia, who summoned a member of the NKVD (Soviet secret police). The Soviet authorities were not at all pleased with Janos's Jewish self-defence initiative. The possession of weapons and our presence made his position more compromising, turning the incident into a high-security case.

A preliminary investigation into our individual identities aroused the Soviets' suspicions. In their eyes, Rafael was the most suspect – no documents, no domicile, born in Poland, but left as an infant for Palestine. I had on me only my faked school ID, which gave Lwow as my place of birth, making me out to be a Soviet subject.

Janos was suspected of harbouring spies in addition to the offence of possessing arms. Rafael was accused of being part of a spy ring, and I of being his accomplice. Rafael's maps and the possession of foreign currency were the most incriminating evidence against him.

Unlike my previous experience of arrest by the Soviets, this was the real thing. We were driven back to the Kolomyja prison where we were separated.

This time, it was not an improvised prison in a rural setting but a proper prison, with iron bars in the windows, clinking cell doors with iron locks, and guards treating us as dangerous enemies of the Soviet Union.

I was kept in a cell together with two Polish-speaking prisoners, most likely planted on purpose. I became suspicious when they confided in me their own involvement with the Polish armed resistance against the Soviets.

The winter of 1940 was harsh and the prison was not heated. To this day, when I feel cold, the memory of the dampness and chill of the stone prison walls makes me shiver.

The interrogations were conducted mostly in the late afternoon and in the middle of the night. The walk through the long prison corridors to the interrogation room seemed endless and the fear that accompanied it had the effect of confusing me. I was never sure if I was being led along the same way.

The interrogating officer was dressed in civvies and spoke excellent Polish. He was a heavy smoker and between puffs he fired questions at me about my connection with the Palestinian-Zionist spy ring. Young girls, he suggested, were often used as decoys for spies. He expressed concern for me, conveying the impression that he was inclined to believe that I could have been an innocent victim. Rafael's maps were of great interest to him. All he wished to know, he assured me, was who Rafael and Janos were working for, and who was running the 'espionage' ring in Romania? Were they English or French? Without mentioning my sister in Palestine, I told the truth of how I met Rafael, but to the interrogator the truth sounded like a fanciful fabrication.

By the end of the week spent in the Kolomyja prison I had a taste of the effects of sleep deprivation. During the interrogation the interrogator stepped out of the room for a short while; on his return I was unsure if someone else had taken his place.

Under lock and key in the Kolomyja jail, even my sense of time was arrested. It was inconceivable to think that somewhere in the world, people were celebrating the arrival of the New Year of the 1940. My prison companions had somehow managed to get hold of bottles of vodka and extra sausages, which they shared with me. Encouraged by them, for the first time in my life I drank enough vodka to experience the mixed blessing of a temporary lifting of gloom, followed by a massive hangover that pounded my head with hammer blows. For the first time I discovered that vodka induces tears. I cried and cried in my misery. I wanted my Mother!

What finally saved me was my story about my brother's recruitment to the Donbass colliery, having provided details about his departure and the time when it took place.

Before my release, my inquiries about my companions had been met with friendly assurances. If they were as innocent as they claimed, they too would soon be released. But my request to see them was ignored. Many years after the event, I discovered why I was not allowed to see Rafael or Janos. They were already on the way to Siberia, having been sentenced to 15 years in a penal colony.

The interrogator dismissed me with a fatherly piece of advice. The Soviet Union needed bright young girls like me.

'Go back to Lwow, enrol in a school and stop wasting your time.'

I was put on a train under escort whose duty it was to make sure that I reached Lwow. I soon found myself sitting again in the same waiting room where I had first encountered the young Palestinian Jew with the map. Staring at the baroque features of the massive glass cupola, I took stock of my situation. My brother was in Donbass, digging coal from the bowels of the earth. I was alone and far away from my parents. The demon of self-pity took possession of me.

I knew I would have to swallow my pride, however reluctantly, and show my face to the Silversteins. Mr Silverstein and his wife greeted me with a sigh of relief. My departure had left them feeling unhappy and guilty. How could they ever face my parents if, God forbid, anything had happened to me? Mrs Silverstein noticed that I had lost weight and put a hot meal before me. She was sure

I would come back, she said, she had even kept ready the bedding I had used. I was touched by the degree of their concern over me. Mr Silverstein made his own demonstration of welcome in an almost theatrical gesture of placing the keys on the table.

'Don't you ever leave them again!' he pointed his finger at me accusingly.

I was disappointed not to find letters from my brother. Instead I found a postcard addressed to me from a stranger, send from Pinsk.

Dear Mira,
You don't know me but your letter fell into my hands. The people you addressed it to have moved. You asked how to reach Naomi and your sister? Wilno is the place where they could help you join your sister, which seems to be your goal. Good luck,
Giora B.

I soon recalled that after my brother's departure I had indeed written to Pinsk, to the parents of my sister's friend, who departed for Palestine at the same time as my sister. For a while, her parents had corresponded with mine. In my letter, I had asked if they had any news of their daughter Naomi or my sister. I mentioned that I was keen to join 'Uncle Israel', hoping that the code for Palestine would be understood. I only recalled their family name and an incomplete address in Pinsk. Failing to receive a reply, I had assumed that, without a proper address, my letter had never reached them. The mysterious Giora B., the stranger into whose hands my letter fell, had obviously interpreted my letter correctly.

The message was: *'Change direction and go north to Wilno!'*

A political deal between the Soviet Union and Nazi Germany allowed the Lithuanians to annex the Polish city Wilno, renamed Vilnius. At the time Lithuania was a neutral country and getting there would have enabled me to get in touch with my sister and also my parents.

This time I was determined to keep away from companions with maps.

THE WAY TO WILNO

After the harsh lesson about picking the wrong companions at railway stations, this time I was more cautious when inquiring about how to reach Wilno. The advice was to go first to Grodno, the nearest city to the Soviet-Lithuanian border. Everybody knew that the 'go' meant an illegal crossing.

From school lessons I knew that Grodno was once a royal city, its history rooted in the Polish-Lithuanian Commonwealth. Also that Jews had been settled there for centuries. The journey by train from Lwow to Grodno, from the south to the north of Poland, was long and slow and as a girl travelling alone I attracted more attention than was safe. The onset of menstruation had not changed my self-perception about my identity. In my own eyes I was still 'Daddy's girl' and it had nothing to do with becoming a woman. I remembered well the scene with Mother in the bathroom and her anxious look when she saw me undressed.

'Thank God your breasts are still underdeveloped,' she said. 'In wartime it's dangerous to be a woman.'

The people I encountered on the train journey were more fluent in Russian than in Polish, which put me at a linguistic disadvantage. I was lucky to encounter a Jew who spoke fluent Polish. His name was Aaron and he was a bookkeeper whose profession had been made redundant by Communism.

'No more fiddling of income tax returns,' he lamented. 'Communism and trade don't mix.' Still, a Jew had to feed his family, so he was travelling, picking up odd jobs here and there. He promised to help me.

On arrival in Grodno, he delivered me into the hands of his wealthy uncle, Melczer, a prominent dentist. His wife, Sonia, a plump and cheerful woman, greeted me with her sleeves rolled up; she was in the middle of preparing food for the Sabbath. I had stepped into a home bustling with domestic activity and filled with the delicious smells of traditional Jewish cooking. The atmosphere at Friday night festive dinners, as at home, was dominated by politics. At the core of the discussion was always the issue of which of the competing ideologies – capitalist democracy, socialism or Communism – would cure the ills of the world? And, of course, for the Jews who were squeezed between the Swastika and the Hammer and Sickle, finding an answer was of the utmost importance. The only consolation for the Jews of Gradno was that the Soviet presence had saved them from falling into the hands of the Germans. Melczer perceived the fate of the Jews as a barometer forecasting Europe's political climate.

The household consisted of children of all ages, running in and out of rooms with open doors, and their relatives, all refugees who had fled the Nazis.

'*Biezanice*, like you,' I was told.

As if it were inevitable, I too was finally classed as *biezanice*, a refugee. It was not a desirable status. Like Rafael, we were all at risk of being deported deep into Russia.

People knew about the Soviet deportations of prominent Poles and Jews, but so far Melczer and his family were protected through their connection with a member of the local Belorus Central Committee, and as a dentist, Melczer was in great demand by them. In the Soviet Union gold crowns were commonplace but even gold, in the mouths of strong men with hard-biting jaws, gets bitten through. Melczer was an expert at mending the gold-filled mouths of the Soviet apparatchiks.

In the long, frost-licked evenings of January I was introduced, through Melczer's past, to the pain of an ex-Communist's soul-searching. In the labyrinth of Soviet party politics, familiar and unfamiliar names cropped up: Trotsky, Yagoda, Litvinov, Voroshilov – all of whom were part of Melczer's lament about 'Mother Russia'. Throughout my life I have encountered Russian exiles for whom the 'loss' of their 'Mother Russia' inflicted a state of feverish homesickness. As for Melczer, he was still filled with rancour about the betrayal of Communist ideals.

'I fled Lenin's revolution and now I'm caught in Stalin's iron grip.'

Melczer was the son of a rich timber merchant from Odessa. When his parents decided to flee Russia after the 1917 Revolution, young Melczer, a medical student involved in the revolutionary student movement, chose to stay and attend the monumental task of reforming Russia, and the world. He parted from the Communist Party after the political events of 1920–22, when the first treason trials took place. Amongst the accused were eleven prominent members of the Party's Central Committee and one of them was a relative of Melczer's mother. A virulent strain of spy-paranoia had already attacked the Soviet political body during Lenin's reign; Stalin only extended the scale of it. As a Jew, Melczer, who had relatives in America and Poland, was at risk. The day he sailed from Odessa had been a black day in his life. He and Sonia had themselves once been refugees.

When I first encountered their daughter, Ilonka, she was sitting at the grand piano practising scales. 'Do you like Chopin?' she asked, and without waiting for the answer she played for me a polonaise. The ease with which I became grafted onto the family was due to the irrepressible spirit of Sonia's cheerfulness and my friendship with Ilonka, a girl my age.

Ilonka was a plain, soft-spoken girl, talented, 'the family artist'. Her poetry had won first prize in a school poetry competition. We soon discovered we had a lot in common – mainly a fixation on French films and their leading actors: Jean Gabin, Charles Boyer and Michelle Morgan. We had also read and admired the same authors, some Polish, and some Europeans whose works were in translation. It was a strange mix of classical and popular literature: Sienkiewicz, Gorky, Dickens, Zola, Knut Hamsun and Romain Rolland.

We also shared an admiration for Axel Munthe, the Swedish doctor and the author of *The Story of San Michele*. Before the war it had been a bestseller. The book depicted the life of a fashionable doctor in Paris who became obsessed with excavating a villa in Capri that was built over the buried ruins of Roman Emperor Tiberius's property. His search for a buried ancient past stalked his imagination. Autobiographical, but disguised as fiction, the book was written in an exalted prose, and was of the kind that made me want to combine becoming a doctor and writer. Ilonka herself could not decide if she should become a pianist or a writer.

The friendship between Ilonka and me grew into intimacy, swapping dreams of a life filled with adventure and romance. We planned to meet after the war and argued about the place for our future rendezvous. Should it be in Warsaw, in front of the Syrena statue, the symbol of the Polish capital? Or should it be in Paris near the Arc de Triomphe? We were in total agreement about the time. Our rendezvous should take place definitely on the first Sunday in May 'after the war', a date that was easy to remember. Were we tempting fate?

In Grodno, 'this godforsaken province' as Ilonka's mother disparagingly referred to the city, I found myself in a multilingual ambience with a wide range of culture superior to my own 'big city' background. I was as hungry for books as I was for home-cooked food and their house was brimming with both. The books were kept in heavy mahogany bookcases spread around the rooms and long corridors. The books, cased in elegant leather bindings, were in Polish, Russian, German, Hebrew and Yiddish; they, too, had a history, having migrated like Ilonka's father from Odessa when his family fled the revolution. In my later years, Chekhov's plays would bring back memories of those Grodno evenings, made warm and cosy by the silver samovar, a family heirloom also rescued from Odessa that emitted the gentle hiss of a contented cat.

Ilonka's family treated me like one of the family and I was getting to feel too comfortable. I was afraid I'd never find enough incentive to leave and move on to Wilno. An urge that sprang from some instinct perhaps similar to the kind that guides migratory birds commanded me to leave.

'Child, you are out of your mind! In the middle of our harsh winter!'

'Why not wait until summer?' both Melczer and Sonia argued, but I was impatient, chased by a vision of getting back to Wilno and from there to my sister in Palestine. A restlessness for which I had no name demanded I move, sooner rather than later.

Even Ilonka could not talk me into staying much longer. I still have the photograph of us taken before my departure. The local photographer had arranged our pose, heads inclined towards each other, eyes boldly staring at the camera. We each inscribed on the back of the photos: 'Don't forget our date!'

As a parting gift, Ilonka gave me a short poem she had written in calligraphy, on a page decorated with fanciful coloured butterflies.

> To Mira,
> My friendship rolls like a tear.
> My dreams fly like birds,
> Circling the earth.
> In a heap of words,
> Solid as rocks.
> Listen and look out for them!

ANOTHER FRONTIER

In the first year of the war, three different occupational armies had passed through the Wilno region. Now Lithuania enjoyed a period of neutrality for a limited time.

The shifts of the wartime frontier had split up many families, including Sonia's. Her father and some other members of the family had found themselves within the Lithuanian borders. Of necessity, the illegal traffic of people and goods flourished in spite of the Soviets' rigorous attempts to curb it. The timber business of Sonia's father flourished and he would dispatch his trusted Belorussian retainer across the border to the Soviet side, to keep in touch with the rest of the family and his business partners. The place for such meetings was Radun. Kostia, who had been with the family since boyhood and was regarded as loyal and trustworthy, would bring with him news about the health of Sonia's father, stories of the 'good life' in Lithuania, as well as money.

Sonia's family connections facilitated my departure from Grodno.

I travelled with Sonia to meet Kostia, who was the great-grandson of a serf who had been granted freedom by his aristocratic master. Born in this region, he knew the local people and the countryside 'like his own pocket'. With the help of bribery and friendly contacts on both sides of the border, he had done the illegal crossing many times.

'You'll be safe in his hands,' Sonia said, when the time came to part.

Kostia resembled Harpo Marx. His ash-blond hair sat on his head like a wig, the tangled curls jumping about like corkscrews. His ruddy complexion suggested a liking for vodka, and he looked me up and down with sky-blue eyes that were neither friendly nor hostile.

When he and I set out in a horsedrawn sledge to Saliszki to meet Gregory, his regular 'contact', it was a sunny, frosty day and the winter sky seemed high as if retreating from the vast, snow-covered landscape. The chiming bells of the horses evoked winter scenes I had seen in films shown at the Lodz Apollo Cinema. Greta Garbo, in the role of Anna Karenina, took such rides with her lover, wrapped in thick furs. The sheer beauty of the place and the pleasure of the ride were so intense it almost hurt. I wanted to stand up, raise my arms and shout, 'God, how I love life!'

Kostia showed no interest in me. My attempts at conversation met with grunts and silence. But he did comment on my city boots: 'You're not well shod.' Had I been a horse, he would have led me to a smithy to be re-shod. As it was, he suggested I stuffed bits of newspapers inside my laced up boots for insulation. He was not altogether indifferent and made sure I was not suffering from thirst or hunger.

We reached Gregory, his contact, a Belorussian peasant who lived in an isolated hamlet a safe distance from the Soviet-Lithuanian border. Gregory had serious reservations regarding my presence, questioning the wisdom of taking me along. It was too late for Kostia to change his mind.

Gregory's place had become a trading post for the Soviet guards who would drop in to trade in their army rations for vodka or to obtain goods smuggled from across the Lithuanian border. He had befriended some of the Soviet soldiers, as well as some Lithuanian border guards. He knew the routes used by the Soviet patrols and drew Kostia a map showing the position of the treacherous dugouts.

'Watch out for the son-of-a-bitch holes!'

The Soviet border guards hid in them, usually in twos, camouflaged by the protective white-hooded overalls they wore over their uniforms, rendering themselves almost invisible in the snow. The trouble was that they often changed their observation positions, moving from one dugout to another.

Armed with this information Kostia and I set out on foot towards no-man's land on another moonless night – a sky cleared of the moon is the best protection for people crossing frontiers. We had a distance of about 25 kilometres to cover and it was bitterly cold – below 25 degrees Celsius.

'Not so far,' Kostia said in his laconic way.

'Once over the border, on the Lithuanian side, we'll be close to Ejszyszki, a town with a railway station. And from there to Vilnius, it's one hour.' This was Kostia's only effort to boost my courage. We kept absolutely silent during the trek for safety reasons, as well as to preserve energy. It was too cold even for the dogs to bark.

The sky was black but the surface of the thick layer of snow was shining like a glacier. With each step, a loud crunching noise resonated in the muffled silence. In places we sank knee-deep and it was an effort just to retrieve one's feet.

At first I felt hot and was perspiring, but soon the cold grew teeth and began to penetrate and nibble at my toes and fingers. Even the fur hat that Ilonka had given me and the thick woollen sweater knitted by her mother did not insulate me from the chill gnawing into my bones.

We had reached the forest that marked the beginning of the border zone. This was the kind of territory into which Kasia's imagination had once led me, a forest filled with wolves. Stories of packs of hungry wolves stalking lost travellers were a familiar theme in Polish folklore.

'Don't be afraid, there are no wolves left here,' Kostia assured me, 'they have all been hunted by soldiers who sell their valuable skins for vodka and cigarettes.'

All of a sudden what looked like wolves' shiny eyes of were glaring at us. They were the torches of two Soviet border guards who sprang from their camouflaged dugout almost from under our feet.

'*Ruki na vierch!*' ('Hands up!')

Their camouflage was perfect! In their long, hooded white overalls, they made me think of children in white sheets playing ghosts.

By now the Russian command 'Hands up!' was familiar and a feeling of déjà vu came over me as we were marched to a wooden barn that had been converted into a provisional detention centre. Kostia cursed loudly, mumbling that I had brought him bad luck. We had been only half a kilometre from the Lithuanian border!

THE POLE WITH A FUR COAT

The barn resembled a marketplace where people bartered goods and swapped information. Planks of wood for sleeping or resting ran along the entire length of the barn, just above the level of the rough earth floor. Near the door stood an iron stove with a pipe running into an opening in the roof. This area was the hearth, where people clustered for warmth and the baked potatoes, kept nearby in a sack. This was the only food provided except for hot, watered-down tea.

Whilst this was the second time I had found myself in a barn as a prisoner, it was Kostia's first time and he was indignant about his failure, swearing that he would have managed better on his own. He warned me that during his interrogation he would have to disown me – I was a total stranger he found in the forest wandering all alone upon whom he had taken pity. He would have to do it, he claimed, to protect Sonia's family. I accepted this, as I was also keen to protect Sonia's family. Somehow, I hoped that my alternative faked school ID that gave Wilno as my birthplace would protect me.

Kostia was the first to be called in for interrogation. His papers had proof that he was a resident of Ejszyszki in Lithuania, and his story about me convinced the authorities. As a plausible excuse for his illegal crossing he gave a romantic story about a sweetheart on the Soviet side. To his surprise, he was released with only a caution.

Left alone again, I stared at two dim light bulbs hanging in the barn that were on day and night. In spite of the iron stove and the heat generated by over 100 people, the temperature indoors was close to freezing. The bales of straw, spread on the bare wooden planks, served as mattresses. I found a place between a woman and a man and I burrowed into the straw, like an animal. The cold woke me up.

The piping hot stove was like a beehive, where people gathered, pushing to get as close as possible to warm up. I managed to manoeuvre myself next to a man who offered me a hot, baked potato. Even with the ashes rubbed into the burnt skin, it tasted delicious.

'Where are your parents?' he asked.

'In Lodz.'

Amongst those arrested, I stood out as the youngest and the only one unaccompanied by an adult. There was a Polish boy my age, but he was with his father. Most of those arrested were either attempting to cross the border or were regular smugglers. The man who shared his baked potato had also been picked up in no-man's land.

His name was Pawel Kaminski and the story of his arrest made him laugh at himself. He had simply stepped into one of the dugouts and literally crashed into the guard's shelter, landing on top of the Soviet soldiers who had been caught napping after generous helpings of vodka.

'Jesus, how frightened they looked!'

By the time they realised what had happened, they offered him a hefty helping of vodka in gratitude for making their job so easy. Even the Commandant in charge of the barn rocked with laughter when he heard the story. Pawel's misadventure galled him as he was already so very close to his home! He was a local Pole, who had taught physical fitness at a Wilno gymnasium before the war. After being mobilised he was sent to the front where his cavalry unit was destroyed in battle.

'Imagine,' he said, 'men on horses with lances galloping against tanks!'

He and his horse were both wounded, but both managed to avoid capture by the Soviets. A bullet had pierced his shinbone and a Polish vet, living on a remote estate, had nursed both the man and the horse back to health. On account of his military record, he tried to keep away from any contact with the Soviet militia. His family's estate was on the Lithuanian side and he was keen to get back and out of the clutches of the Soviets. He knew the neighbourhood well; before the war he often went riding in this region.

He was perhaps in his late twenties or early thirties and must have looked very handsome on horseback. Pawel reminded me of a taller and slimmer Charles Boyer, the French film star, his attractiveness enhanced by a fashionable, dark-grey worsted winter coat. The shiny silver fox collar reminded me of Father's winter coat. Even in the barn he managed to maintain an air of elegance, keeping his riding boots immaculately polished. I noticed his limp when he walked, dragging his right foot, but the impediment didn't diminish his imposing bearing.

In the mornings, he washed himself outdoors with snow, stripped to his waist! His displays of hardiness in the face of the severe frost gained him much admiration. Even the Soviet guards were impressed and, as a reward, treated him with a large mug of steaming hot tea, laced with vodka.

During the four days and nights we were thrown together, I developed a dog-like attachment. His concern for me was expressed through his coat which, like a friendly animal, was offered for warmth. On the first night, after the offer of a baked potato, I woke up to find his coat spread over me. During the day he would often put it over my shoulders to keep me warm. I began to develop a crush on him. My eyes followed him everywhere. He treated me like a pupil from his gym class, in need of supervision.

'Be alert!' was his favourite saying.

Altogether, the regime of this 'prison' was like nothing I had experienced before when under arrest. Far from being strict it was ruled by an almost absent-minded slackness.

It transpired that people held in this barn were kept for a short period only. The detainees apparently fell into two categories. The first were local people caught for the first time who could legitimately claim the right of domicile within Lithuanian territory, providing they had the right documents. For some inexplicable reason, the Soviet authorities, contrary to expectations, were lenient towards such individuals who were often released with only a strongly worded caution. The second, the most dreaded category, was for political suspects who would be driven to the city prison in Bialystok.

There was also talk of a 'list'.

In the evenings, the atmosphere in the barn became charged with tension in anticipation of the entry of the Soviet officer with 'the list'. The same routine was followed each evening, the same Soviet officer would enter, perch himself on a box, adjust his glasses and clear his throat before reading out names from the list. If by chance his Russian accent distorted his pronunciation of some Polish or Jewish names, he would repeat and correct them. The names on the list belonged to those individuals granted permission to cross the Soviet-Lithuanian border. The lucky individuals would be gathered to one side. At midnight, the segregated group, under escort, would be led out of the barn. The Soviets attached one condition – don't get caught by the Lithuanian border guards, you'll not be allowed back! The danger of being picked up by the Lithuanians was spelled out. They were known to rob people before forcing them back or worse, kill them first and then rob them of their possessions. Some people in the barn suspected it was a trick. Understandably, the unusual display of Soviet benevolence was viewed with suspicion.

It was a far cry from the usual harsh attitude towards people trying to leave the Soviet Union. Nevertheless, for many, to be included on this list seemed a desirable option.

Pawel's and my interrogation fell on the same day. I had been confident on account of my faked ID claiming I was born in Wilno. In the evening when the list was read, Pawel's name was included but not mine! I dreaded the idea of being transferred to the Bialystok prison, another version of the Kolomyja prison.

Pawel was beaming. He would be home soon! His birth certificate, which he hid inside his riding boot, had helped! I was sad to have to part from his coat as well as from him and I burrowed under the straw, not wishing to see him go. I must have fallen asleep.

Next morning, when I opened my eyes, I found him standing over me, looking furious.

'Damn it! Girls like you should stay home!'

He was angry with me, but more so with himself for not being able to take advantage of the opportunity to be freed. His conscience about leaving me had made him turn back. Determined to get me freed, as much for his own sake as mine, he boldly demanded to see the '*Tovarisch* Commandant'. After all, he was the man who had fallen into the dugout and who had so obligingly delivered himself to the Soviet border unit.

Pawel claimed that I was his relative, under his care, from whom he had got separated in the forest and was lucky enough to have been reunited with me in the barn. If his name appeared on the list so should mine. The '*Tovarisch* Commandant' a round faced, middle-aged man, with front gold teeth, was not at all convinced. What proof could he provide that I was his relative?

He told him about my appendix operation performed in Wilno last summer. How he, and other members of his family, had visited me at St Jakob's Hospital and even provided the name of the surgeon who had operated me.

Pawel made use of the conversations we had had about my home, family, my brother, and the episode at the Wilno hospital. What a yarn-spinner, I thought.

The Commandant looked at him long and hard. Why not verify the truth, Pawel suggested with great panache. To his astonishment, he summoned a nurse to examine me. During the examination, conducted in a screened-off corner that served as a first-aid cubicle, she reported that 'the scar was neat and the stitches were well-healed'. In the evening, both of our names were on the list!

We were led out after the list-reading and ordered to disperse. Pawel knew the Lithuanian side of the territory well and had many friends in the neighbourhood. Not keen to keep walking during the night, he knocked on the door of a friendly gamekeeper. In the heated room, my frost-bitten feet started to burn as if scorched by boiling water. Pawel, who knew how to tend to the delicate legs of horses, applied hot and cold compresses to my burning feet. His friend provided a thick paste that he rubbed into my skin.

Very early next morning, we set out for Ejszyszki. This time, without any guilt, he announced that our ways were about to part. He pointed out the direction I should follow. Before our separation, he lifted my face by the chin and planted a brotherly kiss on my forehead. The idea that I might never see him again made me tearful.

'You have only one more kilometre to cover.'

The route, cutting through the forest in a straight line was safe, he reassured me. The local peasants used it and it led to the railway station.

When I turned to look back, he was already some distance away, his limp making his body sway from side to side. I wanted to call after him, but felt ashamed. He had done more than enough for me.

VILNIUS, A SHORT-LIVED NEUTRALITY

The Ejszyszki railway station was almost deserted except for a man sitting in a corner, watching my every move. He, and the presence of a Lithuanian uniformed policeman, unnerved me. Everything about me betrayed the fact that I was an illegal refugee. To make matters worse, I didn't have any Lithuanian currency with which to purchase a ticket. The man who had his eye on me approached and asked, '*Amchu?*' I nodded. The 'Are you one of us?' confirmed that I was one of the tribe – that of the Wandering Jews.

'Chaim Milsztein,' he introduced himself, vigorously shaking my hand. He had spotted me, he said, because I was looking confused. He belonged to a Zionist organisation, which was part of a network actively assisting illegal arrivals. For this reason he and others like him kept vigil at the station. Nearly everybody working at this railway station had been bribed to make them 'look the other way'. This included the local Lithuanian policeman as well, who indeed was staring through the window, pretending not to see us. Chaim bought the tickets to Wilno, now renamed Vilnius. He was of slight build and his round smiling face betrayed the satisfaction of having found a needy new arrival. A compulsive talker, he was babbling on cheerfully, the corners of his mouth gathering bubbles of saliva, as if his tongue was not quick enough to keep up with the rush of words.

During the short journey, I could hardly keep my eyes open, but his enthusiasm about the favourable conditions for refugees in neutral Lithuania kept me alert. Rumours had been circulating about possible negotiations with Moscow over transit visas for refugees possessing certificates for Palestine. Lots of other rumours were buzzing about which made Vilnius the right place to be, he concluded.

When the train pulled into the station the name 'Vilnius' danced in my eyes. I had reached the city that to the Poles was Wilno, to the Jews Vilna, and Vilnius to the Lithuanians! It was the same station that was the scene of my appendix attack and consequent hospital stay. And from here I took the last train home on the day the war was declared. I had come full circle – escaped, but not from enclosure.

An unspoken, self-congratulatory feeling inflated my sense of triumph. In that instant, I was too puffed up to remember that a momentum not entirely of my own making carried me. I was kept afloat by so many other people's contribution and sacrifice for my sake.

Chaim introduced me to his hostel-kibbutz located in the centre of the city on Pohulanka Street. Inadvertently, he had led me to the very place that the mysterious Giora B. had referred to in his letter from Pinsk, the letter I would have missed had I not swallowed my pride and gone back to the Silversteins'.

Wilno/Vilnius, a beautiful city, when dressed in its winter attire was magical. The gentle flowing River Wilejka stood still locked by ice. In the hours of dusk, the forest of the city's church spires and gold-covered cupolas drew arabesque lines against the sky. The neutrality of Lithuania, which later proved to be short-lived, opened up the whole world to me. For the cost of a postage stamp, I was free to send letters anywhere: to my parents in the Lodz ghetto, to my sister in Palestine, and to the Silversteins in Lwow, informing them of my new address.

The sensation of freedom made me feel drunk. Never again would I experience the fullness of freedom with such sharpness. Just as a prolonged illness makes one acutely aware of good health, the suffocating world of the Nazis and the Soviets enhanced my sense of freedom.

Soon after my arrival in Vilnius, I got myself accepted into a private gymnasium, thus keeping my promise to Father not to neglect my education. Mr Epsztein, the Principal, who tactfully suggested that my father settle the account after the war, resolved the delicate issue of payment. I signed a promissory note, certain that Father would honour the agreement after the war.

At the new gymnasium, I received help from my new schoolmates with maths and Latin, the subjects in which I had fallen far behind.

THE VALUE OF POSTAGE STAMPS

Within a short time of my arrival, a windfall of letters made me walk on air. First to arrive was a postcard from my parents. It was an officially printed postcard, bearing the swastika seal over the Lodz ghetto stamp. The restricted space and German censorship reduced the communication to a short, cryptic style. My parents were happy to hear I had reached Vilnius. Why wasn't my brother with me? Where was he? Our separation made them very anxious.

'In the ghetto life, our only comfort is the fact that none of our children are here with us.'

At first I was too elated to read between the lines, and only after a few re-readings did I grasp the fact of how dreadful the conditions in the ghetto must be. Otherwise, how would parents find their children's absence a consolation?

All sorts of questions piled up in my mind to which I had no answers. What, I wondered, would a twentieth-century ghetto look like, and how would people who were only very recently part of a modern industrial city fare in it? Was it safer for the Jews to be isolated and protected from contact with their hostile Christian neighbours or had the total separation made them more vulnerable?

One day I came across a book in the library, with illustrations about Jews of Venice, confined in the medieval ghetto. For easy recognition, they were attired in cone-shaped hats, and wore yellow cloaks. Whenever I tried to conjure up an image of my parents inside a ghetto, I saw them wearing the ridiculous costume. The failure of my imagination to fit them into a Nazi-type ghetto made it easier to bear.

The next letter to arrive was from my sister in Palestine. Even the envelope with the Palestinian stamp became like a talisman I carried with me everywhere. In her letter she assured me that she would spare no effort to bring me over to Palestine. Soon after, a telegram from my brother made me believe in divine justice – what else could explain such lucky timing? My mother's belief that there was some-body in the beyond protecting her family must have rubbed off on me. In the craziness of war, such irrational thoughts seemed natural. The idea that my parents' Yom Kippur blessing could secure the safety of their children seemed irrefutable.

The telegram from my brother was sent from Lwow and gave the Silversteins' address. He had run away from the Donbass colliery and planned to join me soon! Finally I would be able to deal with Father's anxious request about his disappearance.

At the first opportunity, I passed my brother's name and address to an 'official' Zionist emissary, Joshua Gilboa, who was about to be sent on a mission across the Lithuanian-Soviet frontier with the objective of reaching Jewish communities under Soviet rule. He promised to contact my brother in Lwow and assist him with useful contacts.

My role as a postal go-between soon extended beyond my family. Friends and friends of friends in the Lodz ghetto had begun to send me all sorts of requests. 'Please, write to our relatives abroad and appeal for help on our behalf,' they wrote. They needed affidavits, visas and food parcels. The addresses they provided spanned the globe: America, Canada, Brazil, Mexico, Argentina, Palestine, even Cuba. However slight or distant the connection, people were desperate to establish any contact which offered hope. One unusual request came from a schoolboy stamp-collector who before the war had been in correspondence with a pen friend in Canada. In his letter to the distant stamp-collecting pal, he explained the plight of his family, begging for help. (Years later I discovered that the Canadian stamp-collector's intervention saved his life.) The task of taking care of these requests made me feel useful and important. I was helping others and not just attending to my own family's needs. I was not sure if the occasional Red Cross food parcel would even reach the ghetto.

Desperate to help my parents, I wrote to relatives in the US ask-ing for help. There was no reply. After the war I discovered they had moved. The address on the letter to Mother's English family was incomplete, and never reached them.

In my correspondence with family and friends inside the ghetto, I tried to keep them informed about the military and political events in the world at large. All the radios in the ghetto had been confiscated and the only published news was an official, German-controlled daily bulletin. The war was being conducted on many fronts: Germany had invaded the Low Countries, Denmark and

Norway. The British had suffered defeat at Dunkirk and, with the fall of France, the Battle of Britain began in earnest. Italy declared war and invaded Greece, the British began an offensive against the Italians in the Western desert, and the Rome–Berlin axis was joined from the Far East by Japan.

In my letters, when referring to the military situation, I used improvised codes, in which England was 'Auntie Anka'. America, of course, was 'Uncle Sam'; France, 'Cousin Franka', and Palestine was 'Uncle Israel'. They were either 'unwell', 'losing ground under their feet', or 'bleeding'. Germany was 'Hans Reich', a name which belonged to a *Volksdeutsche* worker in my father's factory. At the beginning of the summer of 1939, he had taken a long leave and returned to Lodz with the invading German army, attired in Wehrmacht uniform. There was little need to write about 'Hans Reich' though, as the Germans themselves were boastful enough about their victories. He was only referred to when I wanted to convey Churchill's spirit of defiance. Mussolini's Rome was represented as 'Romulus', a fictitious puppy, 'whose bark was worse than his bite'. I assigned the name 'Apollo' (again, the name of a Lodz cinema) to Greece.

The idea of writing in codes had come to me out of the blue and I had fun doing it. The war was tearing the world apart and I tried to encompass its convulsions in my own schoolgirl manner. It worked, however, and by return post I was asked for more, which was a confirmation that, somehow, my bizarre 'militaresque' concoctions were being correctly interpreted.

My friend Heniek, who stayed behind in Lodz, used to visit my parents in the ghetto regularly and, after reading my letters, would circulate the news to a wider range of people. This he told me after the war.

The money for my extensive correspondence was provided in part by the secretariat of the hostel-kibbutz, and by the discrete help of the parents of a newly-acquired school friend, Renata. She used to invite me home for tea, ostensibly to do homework together, but in truth it was a charitable gesture intended to feed me and give me a break from the 'collective life'. While there, I would take the opportunity to catch up with the letter writing for which Renata's mother would provide envelopes and stamps.

The hostel-kibbutz, which numbered between 40 and 50 members, was run as an urban-collective. Most of the members belonged to the Zionist Youth movement and had already spent the previous two years on a farm, in preparation for emigration to Palestine.

Even though it was supported by the labour of its members and charitable organisations, the standard of living was frugal. Double bunks solved the problem of overcrowding. I shared the bunk with Sarah, a woman from Warsaw.

Another girl and I were the only members attending schools instead of working and contributing towards the upkeep of the collective, which most members did. This added to the financial burden of the establishment. We made up for it, however, by doing night duty in the communal kitchen, where we peeled bucketfuls of rotting potatoes.

It was an austere but stimulating life. During the week, we would eat at a charity kitchen run for refugees. It was the centre for the dissemination of the latest war news and about the deteriorating conditions of life under the German occupation. Most important, the rumours about the chances of leaving for Sweden or Palestine were passionately discussed.

On Friday nights, to celebrate the Sabbath, candles were lit and the long wooden tables were covered with white paper. The modest collective meal would be followed first with Hebrew pioneering songs, invoking a yearning for the Promised Land. As the evening drew on, the collective mood would swing in the opposite direction, carried by the soulful repertoire of Yiddish songs. The tunes and texts, rooted in the *Shtetle* tradition, expressed sentiments born of centuries-old Diaspora history, at odds with the pioneers' dream of a life in socialist Palestine. None of us knew that in a few years time the Jewish Diaspora in Central and Eastern Europe would be reduced to ashes and only in such songs would its spirit be preserved.

The year I spent at the hostel-kibbutz made me realise that I was an incurable individualist, not made for collective living, however much I admired the people partaking in such an existence.

So far, my situation in Vilnius was satisfactory. I was registered with the Red Cross and was issued with a refugee booklet that entitled me to collect warm underwear as well as a pair of boots. I became used to the sight of shops filled with goods, often passing patisseries displaying my favourite cakes that I could not afford to buy.

I was counting the days waiting for my brother's arrival. Often, on the way back from school I would imagine the scene of our reunion. 'Look who is here!' somebody would call out and lead me towards the bunk, where my brother would be resting.

As the days ran into weeks, I found comfort in the thought that the weather had prevented him from undertaking the crossing. The winter had turned nasty; heavy snowfalls and exceptionally low temperatures had brought everything to a standstill. So far, there had been no word from the emissary Joshua either. I kept my worries from my parents and sister.

The letters from my sister were encouraging. Apparently, negotiations were being conducted with the Soviet Union about transit visas from war-torn Europe for as many youngsters as possible. The American-Jewish organisation, Joint, was dedicated to this rescue action.

During the school's summer break, some of us were sent to the countryside to work on a Lithuanian farm. I was assigned to gather strawberries and made myself sick by eating half of what I had picked. The rustic tranquillity was disturbed by rumours of an imminent Soviet invasion. Stalin had laid a claim to the territories of the three Baltic states that included Lithuania.

My letters to my sister became more frantic. From hers I learned the meaning of the 'White Paper', a document that was relevant to my fate. It had been drawn up under pressure of Arab objections to Jewish immigration to Palestine, designed to curb it severely. The British were in charge of implementing the policies of the White Paper and they observed the imposed terms down to the letter. The restrictions applied to adult Jews only and not to minors. Due to this loophole, the Youth Aliya organisation (Children's Immigration) could bypass the restrictions and the headquarters in Jerusalem would be in charge of preparing a list of candidates from Lithuania.

My sister was in touch with them and was doing her best to make sure that my name would be included on such a list, pulling as many strings as possible to make it happen. Before the war, at home, my sister had the reputation of being a fearful girl, easily frightened. Much as I tried, I found it difficult to recast her into the role of a fighter.

A historic turn of events had altered dramatically the conditions of the hostel-kibbutz. On a cloudless summer morning, on 17 June 1940, the rattle of the Soviet tanks woke us up. The news spread that Vilnius had surrendered to Stalin's ultimatum. Lithuanian sovereignty and neutrality had been cut short. The Soviet regime did not lose much time in making its ideological presence felt. At the beginning of the school year, the curriculum at the Epsztein Gymnasium underwent a drastic change. We no longer had to sweat over the difficult Lithuanian language, but instead Russian had become compulsory. So had the study of Marxism and Stalin's works. The Beloved Leader of the People was apparently a prolific writer and the shelves of the school library were groaning under the weight of the leather-bound volumes of Stalin's works, all in Russian.

Zionism was declared anti-Soviet, and the refugee hostel-kibbutz had to be liquidated. The negotiations with the Soviet Union about transit visas, which had begun before the Russians invaded Lithuania, were put on hold. The situation of those who were registered for emigration to Palestine was unclear.

I moved to a girls' hostel for Polish refugees that housed teenagers. The switch from living in a Jewish environment to a Polish one, where I was the only Jewish girl, was not easy. I was picked on by one of the residents: a bully with strong anti-Semitic tendencies. Her favourite way to harass me was to dump all kinds of rubbish on my bunk. Some of the girls, shamed by the antics of the troublemaker, tried to compensate with a display of over-friendliness.

One evening, after a provocation one too many, in which the ringleader shouted the abusive slogan 'Yids to Palestine!,' I shouted back: 'Palestine, that's exactly where I'll be going shortly,' and gave her a good thrashing. I must have remembered how my brother had used me as a punch-bag when practising his boxing. From then on I never found rubbish on my bunk and a sort of unspoken truce was established. I would have left the hostel but there was nowhere else to go.

The dispersed members of the hostel-kibbutz used to gather daily at lunchtime at a communal kitchen where the chief preoccupation was the question: would Stalin relax the rule and let some of the refugees out? We existed in a state of suspense, waiting for the latest news concerning the negotiations. By now it was no longer a question of transit visas but of exit visas as well. Every now and then unconfirmed news would reach us.

'The negotiations are on!'

'No! They are off!'

Out of the blue, another rumour spread that the Soviets, apparently desperate for dollars, were prepared to grant exit visas for the price of $500 per head. Joint, an American organisation about which I knew little, would have to pay $500 to get youngsters like me out of the Soviet Union! Another period of waiting followed, this time for the Youth Aliya list compiled in Jerusalem – the very list my sister had promised to make sure that my name should be on.

When it finally arrived, I saw that her promise was kept. My name was on it! At the time I had no thought for the person who was perhaps removed from the list in order to make a place for me.

I still had not heard from my brother by the time I was getting ready for my departure from Vilnius. Instead, a short note arrived from Mr Silverstein informing me that he had been arrested trying to cross the Soviet border on skis and had landed in the Stanislawow prison. He had been tried for espionage and sentenced to 15 years' hard labour in a gulag somewhere in Siberia. Mr Silverstein was very sorry about the bad news and finished the letter with the following request: 'It's best if you don't write to us any more. We ourselves may be forced to move.'

The reason behind his request was easily understood. My brother's arrest could lead the NKVD, the dreaded Soviet secret service, to my brother's last address, the Silversteins'. It would be easy to pin 'economic crimes', his black market activities, on him, adding to the charge of abetting my brother's attempted escape. The Soviets were liquidating people for less.

My brother's choice of transport was unfortunate. He was more than proficient as a skier, having won a junior prize in ski jumping. At the time, only the Soviet military ski units who were patrolling on skis were trained skiers. To them it would have been absolute proof that my brother must have belonged to a military organisation.

One sentence from Silverstein's letter kept going around and around my head.

'...He was sentenced to 15 years of hard labour and was deported to a gulag, somewhere in Siberia.'

Siberia held many connotations for Poles. It was a place where, historically, in Tsarist Russia, generation after generation of Poles were deported for any number of patriotic 'crimes'. I decided not to inform my parents about the disaster, at least not yet.

It was a grey, rainy February day in 1941 when we assembled at Vilnius railway station. I was one of 200 youngsters selected to depart for Palestine. We were instructed by the Soviet authorities not to draw attention to our departure, so the farewells were subdued. The friends I left behind were hopeful of joining me.

On 30 June 1941, the Germans attacked the Soviet Union. The surprise action, codenamed 'Barbarossa', cancelled the pact between Hitler and Stalin. The Soviet Union would be engulfed by a rapid occupation of its land that threatened even Moscow.

In Vilnius, the German invasion unleashed a wave of massacres of Jews. Most of the Jewish friends I had left behind perished, first in the massacres, then in the ghettos and deportations to the death camps. Only three months separated me from their fate.

'Once more you managed to get away from mortal danger on time,' Mary observed in her consulting room, looking at the maps of pre-war Europe she had pinned on the wall where the various cities mentioned by me were marked with coloured pins.

'Only three months separated me from annihilation,' I repeated, still baffled by the luck that had kept me from the clutches of death. First, by departing from Lodz, I had avoided the fate of the ghettos and deportation to a death camp. And the second time by getting away from Vilnius.

Mary thought that an extraordinary instinct of self-preservation had guided my steps. Though at this stage of analysis I was full of self-loathing, I was certain I was not worth the $500 the Joint organisation had paid for me.

'Someone, a boy or a girl like me, was excluded from the list that had secured my life.' Suddenly, the idea of the unknown person's sacrifice reduced me to tears.

'It was a *selection*, like the one the Germans practised in death camps!'

Mary knew to what I was referring. The columns of prisoners and the German officer pointing with his hand, 'Right–left, right–left', which the prisoners understood to mean life or death.

Life's lottery, that had protected my own life, would in time exact its price. How do you conduct your life when others have paid for it with theirs?

The historic catastrophe was indeed personal.

3
Reunions

ORGY OF SISTERHOOD

Moscow was the first stop on our journey to Palestine. The British Consulate had to finalise details of our visas. From the hotel window I could see the Kremlin and behind its walls was Stalin, the man in whose hands rested my brother's fate. When I mentioned my brother at the British Consulate, the official's face conveyed to me the necessity of silence, while I was still within the Soviet orbit, regarding my brother's fate.

After Moscow, we travelled to Odessa where we boarded a Russian ship due to sail to Istanbul, via Varna, a port in Bulgaria.

A prolonged stay in Istanbul, nearly four months, left jumbled memories like an interrupted dream. The glory of the ancient city that spread over two continents like a colossus, with one foot in Europe and the other in Asia, was too rich to absorb. I looked at churches that had been converted into mosques, walked by a sea as smooth as a mirror surface. In the souks, the display of endless varieties of exotic spices tickled my nostrils – but my mind was still held captive by war-torn Poland. For reasons I cannot fathom even today, I retained a vivid memory of a cinema outing showing the film *A Night at the Opera* with the Marx brothers. I heard myself laugh heartily and realised that I had forgotten to laugh.

From Istanbul, a train journey took us to Syria where a railway line no longer in existence seemed to float on clouds while turning and twisting over a mountain smelling of jasmine.

In Damascus, we visited more souks filled with stalls displaying gold jewellery and bales of silks, ruffled by the wind. In Aleppo, Jewish beggars dressed like Arabs were amazed to see Jewish youngsters from war-torn Europe. Fragments of insubstantial memories have stayed with me, often attaching themselves to the wrong city or the wrong ruin. From Damascus we travelled to Beirut, and the last leg of the journey was made by taxi to Haifa where I was to be reunited with my sister, the one I missed and who was responsible for the phantasy of going to the 'other side'!

Our reunion in Haifa took place in March 1941. When the taxi deposited me at the entrance of the Haifa hostel for new arrivals, my sister was standing at the entrance. Our eyes met and we fell into each other's arms, crying tears of joy and sadness. The tumultuous embrace vindicated her stubbornness in securing my arrival.

The reunion also inflicted a stinging sorrow. Every time she looked at me she was reminded of the other missing members of our family. She saw clearly the gaps, as if looking at a family photograph from which they were maliciously cut, leaving only black. Later in life, I would discover a sharp divergence in our memories of the event.

In the hostel she helped me to unpack my meagre possessions. I handed her my 'treasure', the postcards and letters from the Lodz ghetto, stamped with the Nazi swastika – her first insight into the awfulness of our parents' ghetto existence. She cried, perhaps recalling her own departure from home and the last time she saw our parents, a year before the war.

That scene was also etched on my memory. Mother looked sad but my sister was excited about the forthcoming journey. She was reading from a list of itemised articles to take, whilst Mother carefully packed. 'The trousseau,' all-new clothing with name tags sewn on by Kasia, was placed into a brand new large suitcase. I pretended not to be interested and kept my nose in a book, but I was jealous of her new wardrobe.

My sister pressed the bundle of the correspondence to her heart and before returning it to me, planted a kiss on the postcard with Father's handwriting, as if it was some sacred relic.

I remember our first walk together. The sun was setting over Haifa Bay, in the sky a huge orange balloon slowly dipping into the ink-blue sea splashing shades of purple and red over the horizon.

'What do you remember of our reunion?' I once asked her.

'Taking you for a walk and showing you the shipwreck of the *Patria* in the Haifa Bay.'

She pointed out the wreck of a rusting ship in the harbour and explained why it was there. The *Patria* had carried illegal immigrants from war-torn Europe and was intercepted by the British when she reached Haifa. The illegal immigrants were to be transported to the island of Mauritius, to specially set up camps. Rather than submit, the Jews blew themselves up with the ship. The tragic loss of so many lives, in full view of the inhabitants of Haifa, sent shock-waves through the entire Jewish community of Palestine. From over 1,800 passengers, only 200 bodies were recovered. My sister obviously felt it was important to present me with another aspect of war. Her war!

'What else do you remember?'

'You looked so outlandish!'

By contrast, my sister looked native – like a suntanned pioneer. The familiar curl over her right eyebrow was no longer there. At home, whenever our brother caught her in front of the mirror, twisting a strand of her forelock, he would tease her mercilessly.

I told her about the fight I had had with the British authorities at the Lebanon–Palestine border checkpoint, on account of the envelopes and postcards from Lodz ghetto stamped with the Nazi swastika. Though the search was conducted with customary English politeness, the package of correspondence in my suitcase was evidence of contact with the enemy. The lot had to be impounded and censored, I was informed. I became hysterical and despite pressure from my group, I refused to get into the taxi and continue with the journey. After much delay and hurried telephone exchanges between the barrack buildings that resembled a fortress, and various huts, the contents of the correspondence were carefully examined and it was decided that I could keep them.

'You used to be such a gullible child!' my sister commented, surprised by my refusal to accept the British authorities' assurances that the letters would be returned after the censor's inspection. She certainly was the one to know about that feature of my character, for she often used it to make me obey her. As children, we were very different. I was a tomboy, a 'Daddy's girl'; she by contrast, a 'Mummy's girl', always neat and well-behaved. When learning to ride a bike, I was daring, even reckless, while she was fearful and cautious. We used to tease her about her fear of live chickens: she was afraid even to touch one. Mother would buy both of us clothes at the same time, and to my dismay, her shoes and dresses would still look new after prolonged wear but mine looked as though they had been pulled through a pig's snout.

From early infancy, everything about my older sister amazed and intrigued me. When she once fainted, I regarded the swoon as something so impressive that I wished to imitate it. Only grown women fainted and my sister had done it as well! While I was still collecting tinsel and paper angels, my sister, though only four years older, was a perfect model of a miniature adult.

Mother often used her as my minder, forcing her to include me in her leisure-time activities, which I imagine she must have resented. Even today, for fun, we occasionally debate what really happened when she lost me during an outing in a park, after Mother entrusted me into her care. Did she abandon me on purpose, or did I get lost in the holiday crowds? Mother never got to the bottom of what really took place. In the midst of the milling crowd, one minute I was nervously clutching her hand, the next we were separated! Was it her revenge for being forced to look after me against her wish? Whatever the truth, it planted a germ of a suspicion that my benevolent sister could hide another side.

The emotional tangle about my sister, who was instrumental in saving my life, also included memories of resentment and score-settling in our undeclared rivalry.

I always admired the strength of her character, which manifested itself early in her life. She could be very obstinate, something I was not incapable of. At the age of ten, offended by Mother about something or other, she went 'on strike', refusing to speak to her for a week. I was too young to know about the thin dividing line between strength of character and obstinacy. Perhaps to be obstinate one needed a strong character, or was it the other way round? At any rate, to save my life, she employed it to full measure.

She described in detail the day when she received the first news from me. On that particular morning she was at the orange grove picking oranges, when Rachel, her Ben-Shemen housemother, came running breathless waving a letter in her hand.

'A letter for you! From Europe!'

The address 'Vilnius/Lithuania' surprised her. Who could it be from? She tore it open and, recognising my handwriting, she sat down on an orange case, devouring every word on the page.

The letter, in which I described the adventures and misadventures of reaching Vilnius, had an electrifying effect on her. The description of the departure from home with my brother reduced her to tears; and our enforced separation in Lwow fixed her resolve to get me out.

In the letters that followed, I continued with the story of stealing through frontiers at night in freezing weather, and the unfortunate encounters with the Soviet border patrols disguised as white ghosts. However much I tried to strike a high note of heroic posturing in my Vilnius letters, they often gave way to spells of self-pity. My desperate loneliness broke through the juvenile bravura.

With single-mindedness remarkable for a girl of her age, she decided that her 'little' sister must be brought out of Europe to Palestine!

She fought indefatigably, ignoring the obstacles that history and geography presented. Her campaign to save me began with writing endless letters to the British Mandate administration in Jerusalem, including letters addressed to the High Commissioner himself. The key to entry to Palestine was the possession of a 'certificate'.

She besieged the Youth Aliya (Children's Immigration) with appeals on my behalf. Miss Henrietta Szold, the founder and the distinguished Director of the organisation, devoted to saving children, had the final say in all matters pertaining to children's immigration certificates. But even for minors, the number of 'certificates' and financial resources were restricted. Having failed to get results from the correspondence and telephone calls, and in spite of her limited financial means, she travelled to Jerusalem. In the corridors of various institutions she soon earned the reputation of someone who, when thrown out through the door, would climb back through the window. The officials learned to avoid the pestering young person who was making a thorough nuisance of herself.

After August of 1940, when the Soviet troops marched in and annexed Lithuania, our contact was cut, but not my sister's resolve to get me out of Vilnius. In desperation, she decided to obtain an interview with Henrietta Szold in person. This was no easy matter as the demands of her job were escalating with the pressures of the war. Failing to gain admittance to her office, she decided to go to her home! Her inborn streak of obstinacy made her daring.

Once there, she kept up a vigil on the doorstep of her Jerusalem residence and waited. The unsuspecting elderly lady was pounced on, just as she was making her way to her apartment. My sister's 'secret weapon' was the bundle of my letters. While pleading for her intervention on my behalf she forced them on her. Perhaps Miss Henrietta Szold was feeling worn out after a heavy day's work, or was touched by this girl's devotion to her sister. Her resistance to the intruder weakened and in a magnanimous gesture she invited her in, where my sister read one of my letters that described my despair and the old lady shed a tear. Soon after, I was put on the Youth Aliya list!

After the war ended, my sister took on a self-appointed role of family matriarch, driven by a vision of piecing together what had remained of the decimated family, often reaching out to scattered branches of the family in places as far apart as England, Mexico, Brazil and America.

With maturity, she began to resemble Mother. In her Slavonic-looking face and grey eyes I could detect Mother's replicated state of anxiety. Even her body has become a repository for Mother's ailments, and I often teased her that she lived in her own body like a troublesome subtenant about to be evicted.

Her capacity for worry grew with age and, like mother, she is gripped by a permanent dread of catastrophe. She worries about everybody in the family, about the situation in the Middle East and the safety of the rest of the world.

During one of her visits to London, a theatre outing took us to Sophocles's *Antigone*. Antigone and Ismene, the mythological sisters, made me reflect about my sister and myself: the devoted and dutiful, and the kind the fails in filial duty, like myself.

In retribution for the crimes of their father, Oedipus, the two sisters are flung into a political and familial conflict by King Creon. Creon, their uncle, demands absolute loyalty from the sisters and their two brothers, Eteoles and Polynices. Eteoles complies, and when he dies in battle is buried with full honours. But when Polynices, who challenges his uncle, is killed in battle, Creon forbids him a proper burial. Antigone cannot bear the idea of her beloved brother's dishonour and approaches Ismene for help to bury him. Ismene fails to act, too weak or confused about where her loyalty belongs. Antigone disobeys Creon, and buries her brother Polynices, facing a punishment worse than death.

I mentally transposed the action of the play from ancient Thebes to ghetto Lodz. The war had virtually turned the hermetically sealed ghetto into a caricature of a city-state at the mercy of tyrannical decrees from the Nazi authorities, mouthed by Chaim Rumkowski, the puppet leader appointed by them. If fate had played it differently, my sister and I might have shared the ghetto experience and faced dreadful, unimaginable choices. In Lodz, the heart of the drama was not burials but the periodic demands to surrender the living – thousands of children, the old and the sick – for deportation.

I used the mythological sisters as a yardstick by which to measure our own differences and I suspected that my sister would have acted more like Antigone, ready for the self-sacrifice in the name of family honour. I, on the other hand, feared that I might have acted more like Ismene who so tragically let Antigone down.

I am often tormented by such dark thoughts. How would I have behaved in a ghetto, a concentration camp? What kind of betrayals would I have been capable of for the sake of a crust of bread? When I shared my self-incriminating thoughts with my sister, her comment was short and wise.

'You can never be too sure.'

My sister, I discovered, had left a strong mark on another woman's life as well. Some years ago on a visit to New York, one of her school classmates, Lilka, who had survived the Lodz ghetto and Auschwitz, related the following tale.

'As you know,' Lilka said, 'we lived only a few houses away from each other and habitually walked home from the school together. On one occasion, your sister, the ardent Zionist, tried to recruit me to join her Zionist organisation. I was not interested but she persisted and we became engaged in a fierce argument. To score a point, in a dramatic gesture of exasperation, she grabbed my arm, and pointing towards the gutter exclaimed:

"Can't you see? Jewish blood will flow in these gutters!"'

Startled by her histrionics, Lilka retorted:

'You go to your Palestine, my future is in Poland!'

She also recalled the exact time when it took place. It was after the Passover festivities and she was wearing new shoes that my sister greatly admired. Another detail about that spring day in Lodz had stayed etched in Lilka's memory.

'The gutter, that your sister saw filled with blood, was freshly whitewashed with lime.'

Each spring the concierges would be seen with a bucket filled with lime for painting the gutter, a practice ordained by the municipality as a precaution against health hazards.

'And you know what?' she continued. 'Every day, literally every day inside the ghetto and later in Auschwitz, your sister's words kept beating inside my head.' She knew that my sister was safe in Palestine, having been among the school friends who had seen her off at Lodz railway station in April 1938.

After my encounter with Lilka, on a subsequent visit to Tel Aviv I repeated her story. A look, bordering on the incredulous, registered on my sister's face. She had entirely forgotten the episode, but vehemently denied any profound meaning attached to her words. 'I simply mouthed what I must have heard from various Palestinian Zionist emissaries visiting Poland.'

'Perhaps like our mother, you are something of a Cassandra.' This, too, she dismissed with a gesture of impatience.

THE WRONG PARADISE

Shortly after my arrival in Palestine, in late March, my sister accompanied me on the bus to my new school, keen to describe the attractions awaiting me.

'Ben-Shemen is a children's paradise! Just wait and see.'

The entrance to the Ben-Shemen school was garlanded with the 'Welcome!' signs hung over the gate. Naively, I took it to be a welcome for new arrivals like myself. No, it was for Dr Siegfried Lehman, founder and Principal of the school, who was expected home after his release from prison. He had been arrested in 1940, when the British during a raid found in his office a sizeable arsenal of arms hidden under the floor.

My sister provided the background to his arrest. Unbeknown to him, Haganna, the illegal Jewish self-defence organisation, operating under his very nose, chose his office as a safe place precisely on account of his well-publicised political views about a shared Jewish-Arab state. His seven-year prison sentence, after the intervention by Albert Einstein amongst others, was suspended. The circumstances of his arrest added an ironic twist to his educational and political creed.

Dr Lehman was German-born and had originally trained as a physician, but under the influence of Martin Buber's philosophy had become a teacher instead. He pioneered a progressive curriculum that included the idea of student self-government, a programme of education for peace, tolerance and international understanding, *especially with the Arabs*.

I had difficulties settling into the idyllic Ben-Shemen school life. The swimming pool, the horses, the regular meals and the sacks of oranges placed at the entrance to the dining room were too much of a good thing. I moved in a haze through a landscape of red-tiled roof cottages surrounded with trimmed lawns and flowerbeds guarded by avenues of tall eucalyptus trees. The blinding brightness of the white-painted rooms with white-tiled floors leading out to spacious verandas had the reverse effect. It dimmed my ability to appreciate its aesthetic appeal.

My situation was made worse by my sister's reputation as an exemplary student that invited comparisons. At the time I was not familiar with the saying 'Beware of dreams coming true!'

A crisis of sorts occurred on the first Saturday, during a morning outdoor concert played by the school orchestra. Mozart sent me into a spiral of emotions that had me running for cover, sobbing my heart out. My new housemother tried to cheer me up.

'Look at the beautiful clear blue sky and the bright sun!'

I longed for grey, angry clouds breaking into thunder that would echo the storms inside me. In the children's Ben-Shemen paradise, there was no place for the Hebrew word '*depressia*'; and the term 'war trauma' had yet to make its way into the psychological lexicon.

Educationally, the school's timetable was divided into two: four hours of lessons and a similar amount of time allotted for work on the land. New students were offered a choice of where they would like to work. Given the option of the orange groves, the flower garden, the chicken coops or the cowshed, without a moment's hesitation I opted for the cowshed. The committee members were somewhat surprised. Why would a city girl choose for her new life the most demanding branch of agricultural labour?

'Because cows have beautiful, Madonna-like eyes.'

They kindly restrained from openly laughing at me, but not so my peers, after the story of the 'Madonna-like eyes' had spilled out of the confines of the office. Needless to say it earned me collective derision. My reputation did not improve after someone once spotted me in the cowshed crying, with my arms wrapped round a cow's neck. I missed my mother.

In the classroom my progress at learning Hebrew was slow. The words that went into my ears and came out of my mouth refused to lodge in my brain. The Hebrew letters and words remained abstractions, refusing to mould into meaning. My mind was filled with the ripple of Polish words, which, like a stream, carried me elsewhere. The copybooks provided for Hebrew words and phrases were filled instead with letters written in Polish to my family and friends left in Poland, never to be sent. An unexpected outburst of creativity roared through me compelling me to fill up any scrap of paper with writing and drawings, even trying my hand at sculpture.

I shared the doll-like white-tiled room with two Polish-speaking girls. Tirca, from Drohobycz, and Irka, from Cracow, had arrived earlier, via Romania, and had already acquired a smattering of Hebrew. I was lucky that they were protective of me, forgiving my erratic behaviour and the artistic mess I created. I started to collect stones resembling sculptures and pieces of dead wood with intriguing forms. Irka and Tirca's tolerance must have been stretched to the limits. They liked to keep the room tidy and beautiful with arrangements of flowers and decorative embroidery.

A reproduction of Kathe Kolwitz's dramatic drawing *Hunger* that hung in the room was the only object that connected me to the world I had left. Perhaps my roommates' indulgence was due to the fact that I was the first arrival from war-torn Poland since the outbreak of the war. Later, others would arrive from Romania, Serbia and Bulgaria. From Irka, I learned an important Hebrew word: *'oman'* ('artist'). Both girls were proud to have an *oman* for a room-mate, and my latest fascination was modelling heads in clay, in all sizes. I had already assembled a crowd of them, kept under the bed.

'Mira, our artist,' my roommates would say, sometimes with irony when they had to tidy up the room before the housemother's inspection. I made an effort to adjust, but without success.

My work at the cowshed, in the initial stage, consisted of cleaning out shit-covered straw and replacing it with fresh layers. I liked the smell of cows and the fact that they had names. The one I favoured was Rebecca, a yellow-patched cow with lots of spots on her bristle, some even covering her milk-filled udder. When no one was present, I would lean against her to soak up the warmth of her body. Rebecca's steady, moist eyes fringed by blonde lashes encouraged me to pour out my woes. Rebecca was patient and would stand still, giving notice when she lost her patience by thrashing her dirt- and shit-coated tail.

I was ashamed to feel so unhappy and letting my sister down. But I was more concerned about letting down Father by failing to keep up with my academic studies. The school soon realised they had a 'problem' pupil and summoned my sister in the hope that her intervention would help. Instead of discussing my difficulties in adjusting, we reminisced nostalgically about our home in Lodz and our brother who had vanished into the frozen limbo of Siberia. My sister must have sensed that she had managed to get me out of Europe safe, but not all of me had arrived; a vital part was left behind.

On one occasion, during one of my cowshed tête-à-têtes with Rebecca, I was startled to discover that Dr Blaukopf, the resident veterinarian, on his usual health inspections of the herd, was watching me. Behind his metal-rimmed glasses, his kind eyes looked at me with a questioning expression. He approached Rebecca, and gave her an affectionate slap on the rump.

'She is a very special cow!' he said, 'A new breed of Dutch-Syrian ancestry, a result of an experiment in cross-breeding that I was involved in.' His voice was gentle and I was grateful he made no comment about my crying.

Dr Blaukopf was a stout man of average height with a round face and a receding hairline. Originally from Galicia, in southern Poland, his Polish was halting with a strong Jewish accent.

He wondered why, of all the cows, I chose Rebecca. Did the name resonate in any way?

This pulled me sharply back to Lodz and the painting of *Rebecca at the Well*; the kitsch painting that had impressed me in childhood and gave me a desire to become a painter.

'Aha, did you know what happened to her after she became Isaac's wife?'

I was vague about biblical stories and their complicated genealogies.

'If you ask me,' he said, 'the biblical Rebecca was a cow, no insult intended towards our Ben-Shemen Rebecca!' His laughter was infectious. 'Your demure maiden proved to have the character of a scheming bitch. As a mother she committed the worst maternal offence imaginable! Favouring Jacob over Esau, she used a trick to rob Esau of his rightful paternal blessing.'

His description of Rebecca's married life sounded like gossip about a neighbour. Effortlessly, he managed to pull together the biblical world with present-day reality. So reading the biblical stories as prototypes of living characters could be fun, not a chore!

He invited me back to his cottage. His modest-sized study was filled with many books, and amongst them art books. An art-loving vet was a revelation to me! He visibly derived pleasure from the sight of my excitement when I picked out Rembrandt and he extended an open invitation. Any time I wished to come and look at them, I would be welcome.

'Our doors are never locked,' he said. He lit a cigarette and finally broached the subject of my tears.

I told him about the pledge I gave Father not to neglect my studies and that I found it difficult to give up my dream about emulating my idol, Axel Munthe, the doctor/writer. I expected to hear what I had heard from others: 'One must learn to compromise in life.' But he was listening attentively, nodding in agreement to my unreasonable expectations.

'Did you know there is a Polish gymnasium in Tel Aviv?'

I was stunned. He suggested I should go to Tel Aviv and inquire about the chances of taking the matriculation exam *in-externo*. He even offered to lend me the money for the trip.

In Tel Aviv, the director of the Polish Gymnasium, Mme Bartoszewska, a matronly elderly woman, was most sympathetic and promised to accept me as an 'external' student. She would provide me with the textbooks and I would only be required to turn up for tutorials, from time to time.

Back in Ben-Shemen, I first ran to the cowshed and nearly choked Rebecca from excess of joy. Dr Blaukopf was pleased with the result

of my Tel Aviv trip and immediately turned my attention to practical
matters. To make my studies possible I would have to be released
from certain school tasks and clarify my position vis-à-vis Youth
Aliya. I was a ward of Ben-Shemen and had to obtain formal permission from Youth Aliya. He warned me that neither would take
kindly to the idea that one of their charges was linking up with
the Polish Gymnasium. He promised to pull a few strings to win
their approval and briefed me on what to say in order to sway any
opposition from the collegiate.

'Solemnly promise that after obtaining the matriculation you'll
endeavour to become a good agricultural student.'

After one month, in spite of trying hard, I found it too difficult to
study in isolation. I was massively behind with mathematics,
physics and Latin and I felt defeated.

'Don't give up!' Dr Blaukopf advised. 'The solution is simple, you
should move to Tel Aviv.'

'They would never agree to that!' I despaired. I was running out
of time. It was only a few months before the final matriculation
exams.

'He who says "a" must say "b, c, d" etc.', he consoled me. This
home truth was new to me, but he was right. The Ben-Shemen
authorities were already compromised and had to agree to give me
leave of absence, albeit reluctantly.

'Do you have anywhere to stay?' he inquired.

I hoped to be put up by a woman I had met soon after my arrival
in Palestine. She was the sister of one of our neighbours who, it
seemed, had taken seriously my plan of 'going to Palestine' and,
unbelievably, delivered a note that he actually expected me to hand
over to his sister in Tel Aviv! His unquestioning trust in my success
made Father pronounce the man to be a complete idiot.

Stenia was a tiny woman with a large heart and she offered to put
me up in her small, one-bedroom apartment. The only place for me
to sleep was the marital bed, which we shared. Her husband was
away, enlisted in the British Army, and she was working in a cigarette
factory.

At night, we often had to run to the shelter during the air raids
when Mussolini's planes were dropping bombs on Tel Aviv.
Notwithstanding the nightly alarms and Tel Aviv's steaming heat, I
attended the Polish Gymnasium in Allenby Street daily, benefiting
from the auxiliary help offered by some teachers and pupils. On the
way to and from the school, I would look with envy at the houses

where people were leading normal, urban lives. The sound of a telephone ringing would make me think of my lost world.

The examinations lasted a whole week. In assessing my results the teachers must have been very lenient towards me to let me pass. The ceremony of collecting the much-coveted matriculation certificate, rolled and tied with a red and white ribbon, the colour of the Polish flag, was a modest affair. We each got a red rose as well. I felt lonely and sad that for this important occasion nobody from my family was with me.

On my return to Ben-Shemen, Tirca and Irka received me with worried faces. A storm was brewing, with me at its centre, after an article published in the Hebrew press had voiced protest against a handful of Jewish pupils who studied at the Polish Gymnasium. I was not mentioned by name, but the article did cite the case of a Youth Aliya charge from Ben-Shemen, currently studying for her matriculation. The affair had turned into a political-cultural scandal! Apparently the relationship between the Tel Aviv Jewish municipality and the Polish Gymnasium was strained. The published article added heat to an already inflamed Zionist public opinion.

The article created ripples in Ben-Shemen. The self-governing student body called for a general meeting to discuss my conduct and whether there was a place for someone like me in their midst. Dr Blaukopf calmly declared that it was a storm in a teacup best ignored. This was the time he chose to tell me why he had stuck out his neck to help me.

As a young man he made his way from his small hometown in Ukraine to Palestine to join a kibbutz. He got married, had children, and worked hard at all sorts of jobs, including road building. He soon realised that his main interest was in livestock breeding and, at the age of 25, decided to become a veterinary surgeon. In the late 1920s Germany was the only country suitable for someone like him, without formal education. When he set out penniless from Port Said to sail to Hamburg, the only languages he knew were Yiddish, Hebrew and a smattering of Russian. It was a hard struggle and after five years, about the time he was close to obtaining his doctorate, he realised he had to obtain a matriculation certificate as well!

'After that experience I vowed to do my utmost to help anyone keen to study,' he said with the smile of a contented man.

'One day, it will be your turn to do the same for somebody else.'

After I left Ben-Shemen, the wrong 'paradise' for me, I heard from him that Rebbeca had produced a calf and he had named her Mira.

ADRIFT IN JERUSALEM

I moved to Jerusalem the city both ancient and modern, and found myself adrift. Never becoming a proper tourist, without a guidebook or map and free to absorb and observe life, I would let my eyes to guide me. I often got lost in the Old City narrow streets; some filled with pools of light, others shaded and as dark as tunnels.

I was oblivious to the fact that solitary young females should not enter cafes where Arab men in white *gallabiyahs* (long tunics) were smoking *nargilas* (water pipes) laced with hashish, idling their time away. Sitting on an ancient rock, I would sketch scenes evoking biblical times, Bedouin shepherds and their flocks of sheep grazing in the valley stretching below the walls of the Old City. The valley was known by a string of frightening names including the Hill of Evil Counsel.

After a while, urged by my sister, I applied to and was accepted by Bezalel, the Jerusalem Art School – at the time, strongly dominated by the Munich School of painting, noted for its sombre brown palette. I found the routine of painting and drawing casts of classical statues oppressive. After a term, the director of the school decided I lacked both talent and application and I was asked to leave. So soon after the Ben-Shemen school debacle, yet another school had assessed correctly my inability to fit in.

The Jerusalem of 1941–42 was a place less important for its religious significance than for its strategic importance. For the Allies it was strategically a tense time. Field Marshal Rommel's army was in Egypt and Jerusalem had become the Middle Eastern nerve centre of manifold activities: military, diplomatic, cultural and, less obvious, espionage. Day and night, large numbers of military jeeps and army lorries rolled through the streets. Faces of soldiers from every part of the British Empire revealed their presence. The streets were filled with men and women in military uniforms, also seen in cafes and restaurants, or touring ancient sites. The various kinds of uniforms of the British, South African, Australian and New Zealand contingents mingled with the uniforms representing Europe, marked 'Free French', 'Free Polish', 'Free Czech' and 'Free Yugoslavia'.

The Anzacs' playfulness and generosity had earned the affection of local children, especially the Arab urchins, who followed them in droves.

The feverish military activities couldn't hide the fact that the war situation was precarious, the Germans held the upper hand on most fronts and the Jewish community in Palestine had reasons to worry. Rommel, who himself was involved in the Blitzkrieg that had defeated Poland, was now in charge of German troops in Egypt, threatening Palestine and other Middle Eastern countries.

At the most critical time, when the future of Western civilisation hung in the balance, I hid away in a capsule, set on a voyage of self-discovery through books and art. I must have been successful in blocking out the awareness of the proximity of the war.

In the absence of an externally imposed discipline, I devised in a haphazard way an alternative system to take care of my cultural/educational programme. My artistic stimuli were derived from the 'street life' impressions. The library at the Jerusalem University on Mount Scopus was well-equipped with a sizeable collection of Polish books, which helped to fill in the gaps of my knowledge. I read, in an unstructured way, Russian and French classical literature, and bits of philosophy.

Bookshops were another source for my erratic education. Never buying any, I would browse through art books, the reproductions serving as museums without walls.

Once, I found on a skip outside a hospital some glass plates of X-ray negatives, which gave a new direction to my painting. I took them home and realised that by scratching on the black surface, I could paint over them, obtaining a stained-glass window effect. I painted landscapes, figures, flower pieces and decorative still lives. Once framed, my icon-like paintings began to sell. I would hawk them to English and French officers, accosting them outside their clubs. This was my first taste of earning money through art, competing with other street hawkers selling cigarettes, matches or religious souvenirs carved in olive wood. One day, an art dealer picked up the lot.

By chance, a drawing shown in a street display case outside a gallery caught my eye. The seated figure, with a face both young and ancient, was held in place by fluent, delicate lines. The drawing led me to the one-man exhibition held by a Polish painter on leave from the army in Egypt. Impressed by Edward Matuszczak's work, I approached him about becoming my teacher. I introduced myself as an artist, without mentioning that I was untutored. At his studio, looking at samples of my work, he found merit in the spontaneity of my use of colour and line, which he thought was influenced by Matisse, a painter about whom I knew nothing.

For the first time in my life, I had access to a proper easel, good brushes, oil paints and canvasses. The act of squeezing tubes of paint onto a palette gave me a sensuous pleasure. I could have licked them like liquorice!

Matuszczak, before the war, had studied in Paris and I was introduced to the French School of Impressionism. He was the right teacher at the right time, and encouraged my style of self-expression. I began to flourish as an artist and regarded myself as very lucky.

In hindsight, perhaps I should have anticipated the complications; what began as a master–pupil relationship became an emotionally charged situation. The artist was in love with his pupil, which was a reversal of the more customary configuration. In itself it was not an unusual situation, almost predictable, but the snag was that he was 38 years old and I was just turning 17, not interested or ready for sex, at least with him. I admired him greatly as an artist and teacher but did not wish to become his 'fiancé'.

His years spent in Paris and the attractions of sexual freedom in bohemian circles had not prepared him for someone like me. So bold in other ways, I stayed a confirmed virgin. He regarded my sexual reserve and my virginity as an impediment best to be rid of, the sooner the better. Feeling rejected and hurt, he foretold for me a grim future: 'Nobody will ever love you the way I do.' It was a kind of emotional blackmail that I would encounter more than once when breaking up a relationship. It was a lesson about the amorous wrestling that takes place between men and women.

I carried on painting on my own and I held my first exhibition in Jerusalem in February 1943, at the Cabinet of Arts gallery owned by M. Z. Schlosser and a Mr Glasberg. The reviews of my paintings and drawings were encouraging and fair, praising some qualities and criticising others. More important, the exhibition also earned me contact with a number of established Jewish painters.

Schlosser was an eccentric Jew from Vienna whose profile resembled medieval portraits. His brown eyes matched his neatly trimmed brown-red pointed beard and the reddish-brown hair he kept longer than fashion prescribed. Brown was his colour and everything he wore was brown, including decorative rings set with huge, dark-brown amber stones. His two fully-grown, brown-haired giant schnauzer dogs, bearded like their master, repeated the colour motive.

The gallery was located in an old Arab house in Princess Mary Street; and its ribbed ceilings, stone walls and small windows gave the gallery an atmosphere of coolness and oriental mystery. Schlosser was prodigiously hospitable and he would make sure that his parties evoked the spirit of the *Arabian Nights*. Bunches of grapes, figs, apricots and oranges were hung in baskets from the ceiling, tempting the revellers with appetising delights of every kind – the ones displayed and others kept out of sight.

In the middle of the war, the middle-aged Vienna-born aesthete tried hard to provide distractions for his guests. His gallery had earned a reputation of mixing art with social and political intrigue. For Schlosser, any occasion was a good reason to throw a party, bringing together English officers with their Jewish mistresses, and Greek and Armenian local society. His gallery provided an opportunity to practice my shaky English.

Not entirely oblivious to the Jewish-Arab conflict, I had rendered myself almost blind and deaf to the highly charged political reality around me. Painting and reading were my escape and I would apply the same ostrich strategy at the end of the war, when the images of newsreels in cinemas started showing the heaps of corpses and death-camp survivors resembling walking skeletons.

One day, a survivor of the Lodz ghetto turned up at my sister's with firsthand information of when and how Mother died in the ghetto and about Father's deportation to Auschwitz. My sister wept but I listened to the story dry-eyed. I felt nothing. On that same afternoon I went to the cinema and watched a Hitchcock film. Later I would recall details about the cinema where I saw it, but nothing of the film. The cinema's darkness with the flickering screen was a welcome pool of neutrality that helped to maintain the 'nothing' feeling. Years later, I would question my sister about that period of my life.

'What a monster I was,' I said in self-disgust. As always, her answer was laconic and to the point.

'You had your own way of grieving.'

THE SOLDIERS ARRIVING FROM THE DESERT

My sister brooded about the fate of our missing brother.

'If he was alive, he would have got in touch with me!' He knew her Palestine address, she argued. What made his silence worse was the constant stream of Polish soldiers, recently released from Soviet gulags, many of whom were reaching Palestine via Persia and Iraq.

'He is dead.' My sister's grief truncated my fantasy of our happy reunion. She shed tears, and reproached me for having let him go off on his own.

'If he died in Siberia we will never know where he is buried,' she carried on.

I could not envisage my brother dead. The presence of the Polish soldiers recently arrived in Palestine was due to the German invasion of the Soviet Union in June 1941, and the consequent signing of the pact between General Sikorski, who was heading the Polish government in exile in London, with Molotov, the Soviet Foreign Minister. This pact helped to liberate from prisons and gulags over 1 million Polish citizens, victims of Stalin's anti-Polish policies. The treaty also included the right to form a Polish army and 25,000 recruits were allowed to leave the Soviet Union for the Middle East. I hoped that our brother would be among them.

Weeks turned into months and another year went by without any news about our brother. To ease the pain, we kept him alive by delving into our memories. We recalled Mother's anxiety about her first-born son. The child conceived after the upheavals of the Great War, who was to be the child of peace, turned out to be just the opposite, a fearless boy with an aggressive streak.

Even as a toddler, he showed no fear and would climb any scaffolding in sight, often leading other children into mischief. Mother's adored son grew up with an obsession for sports and boxing. Worse, his itchy fists kept getting him into trouble with our neighbours' children, and once even with the police. Mother, who abhorred violence of any kind, feared that his impulsive temper would bode ill for his future.

'Hooligan! I don't want a *pogromtchik* [the perpetrator of a pogrom] in my family!'

Her admonition would be followed by a recitation of the things that a decent Jew didn't do. 'Jews don't get blind drunk and make pogroms! They don't smash neighbours' homes! They don't rape and don't kill!'

For his future, she modelled her expectations on a relative, a chaplain in the Polish army with the grand title of 'Doctor-Rabbiner'. For Mother, herself the proud granddaughter of the Zgierz rabbi, such a title combined a secular, academic education with the position of a trained rabbi.

Unlike Mother, we, his sisters, appreciated the protection his bellicose stance gave us. In the street or on the ice rink our 'big' brother was our defender, ready to beat up anyone who threatened us. His role as my protector was reconfirmed when Father appointed him my chaperon. The shared experience of the illegal border crossing and our stay with the Silversteins had created even a stronger bond. My secret magic belief in being instrumental in keeping him alive in the frozen north survived my relocation to Palestine.

Jerusalem was the right place for keeping alive the hope of finding him. Most of the Polish soldiers, arriving from Persia and Iraq, sooner or later would pass through Jerusalem. Not far from the Jaffa Gate was a huge parking lot where military trucks would disgorge soldiers. I would often go there on the look out for the arrival of new transports. Holding up his photograph I would randomly question Polish soldiers for information about Siberian gulags or military camps in Iraq or Persia. I firmly believed that one of these days I would find him amongst the red-necked Polish soldiers, scorched by the Middle Eastern sun. Often, prompted by erratic sightings in the streets, I would rush up to a soldier who I thought resembled him.

The *Farbarov* restaurant in Jaffa Street was the place where my new 'arty' friends and I would meet regularly. But they were accustomed to my sudden departures from the table whenever I would notice Polish soldiers enter in groups or on their own. They were familiar with the phrase '*One of these days one of them will be my brother*'.

On that particular day, Jerusalem was sweltering and enveloped in a desert sandstorm, a *chamsin*, and the restaurant was an oasis of coolness and shade. Our table was at the far end, offering a good view of the main door. Each time the door opened, the harsh light would tear into the shaded interior, framing the newcomers.

The soldier who entered stood blinking, adjusting to the murky dimness of the restaurant. I was watching him approach the bar and order a beer.

'Watch her, here he comes. Another of her victims!' I didn't mind their teasing.

The restaurant was crowded and the Polish soldier was looking for a place. Something in his piercing blue eyes drew my attention, though he did not resemble my brother. His sunken cheeks and the short, dark bristles of his hair gave him the air of a convict. In contrast to my brother's peach complexion, the soldier I was looking at had skin covered in pealing blisters. Nevertheless, I moved closer and our eyes locked. The soldier's icy, blue gaze melted into tears, his mouth moved as if trying to say something, revealing missing front teeth. Both of us were rendered mute. We fell into each other's arms and stood frozen like this for a while just weeping. People watched us, guessing what was taking place, and cried with us.

It took my brother some time before he recovered from the shock. Since our separation he had been tormented by guilt about leaving me alone in Lwow and feared that he would never see me again.

Later, we often pondered over our chance reunion in the Jerusalem restaurant. He almost did not enter Farbarov's, considering a more modest, cheaper place next door. The bar next door was suffocatingly hot and the rowdy crowd of Australian soldiers chased him out. The coolness of the more elegant and spacious restaurant decided for him.

Jerusalem was indeed a city of miracles!

It turned out that our surprise encounter took place on the last day of his three-day compassionate leave when he was at the end of his futile search, not for me, but for his sister in Ben-Shemen!

We had only a few hours together and on our first walk through Jerusalem we held hands like children. The sun was setting and Jerusalem's pink-stoned houses glowed in the heat and the city's breath was hot, like a patient's in fever. We, too, were in a feverish state of excitement. I wanted to stop the traffic and shout: 'Look we are together again!'

There was a long wait for the army truck travelling to his military camp in Serafand. We both remembered our chilling separation at the Lwow railway station and could not stop hugging. The onlookers must have taken us for lovers.

My sister fainted on hearing of our encounter, passed out. The reunion with the brother she was already mourning was for her like witnessing a resurrection. It was the summer of 1943.

THREE BULLETS

I couldn't get used to my brother's new name, Ryszard. At home, he was Mietek and now he was Rysiek short for Ryszard. Later, an additional Hebrew name Mordechai would further add to the list of his aliases! Even our shared wartime history of invented identities had not prepared me for his string of names.

Not the greatest of talkers, it took time to extract the story of how he was arrested and his experiences in Siberia. He had to be in the right mood, and even then I'd learn only some details as if what he held in his memories was too vast to share.

One day I showed him the crumpled telegram I had received from him in Vilnius. He stared for a while at the piece of paper, which predated his downfall. Between sips of vodka, he described the arrival at the Donbass colliery. The 'Silverstein boys' as they called themselves, in no time at all realised that the place was a disaster. The food was inadequate and the penalties for not delivering the required quotas reduced their pay. Most important, the safety provisions in the mines were inadequate, and an accident in a nearby mine that had left over 30 miners killed and many injured was the signal to leave.

They had begun to plot their escape. Against the background of Soviet controls over the movements of its own citizens, for foreigners to escape was near impossible. Eventually they set out without any identity documents or travel permits, more risky for young men like themselves. When the militia picked them up, they had already managed to cover half of the distance.

Amazingly, reminiscences about the Russians always made him sentimental. 'Ah, the *Russkies*,' he would sigh, and sip his vodka.

'One day I was set upon by a gang of women who nearly raped me.'

'Women miners?'

'Devil only knows what their function was!'

'How did you manage to get away?'

'From the women?' A smile revealed his amusement at the memory.

'No, from the Soviet militia!'

'You'll laugh, my diarrhoea saved me. I was shitting hidden in a thicket.' I wasn't laughing, but he was.

'The others, poor guys, were picked up.'

By the time he had managed to reach the Silversteins in Lwow he was a very sick man, only the news that I was safe in Vilnius kept up his spirit. After his recovery, he made preparations to join me. It was winter and the snow-covered flat territory offered ideal conditions for cross-country skiing. As an experienced skier, he hoped to make the illegal Soviet-Lithuanian border crossing on skis. Unbeknownst to him, in the Soviet Union, only the army had highly skilled skiers.

'When they caught me the Swiss-made skis aroused their suspicion that they had caught an important spy. My protestations that I was a Polish Jew on the run from the Nazis were of little help.'

He was transferred to Bialystock prison and held in solitary confinement. At first he refused to sign a confession that he was part of a spy ring. He held out in solitary confinement for as long as he could bear it in the damp dungeon-like cell. After being interrogated day and night, with occasional beatings that had knocked out his front teeth, and broken in health and spirit, he finally signed.

Yes, he confessed, he did try to get to neutral Lithuania in order to reach Sweden. Yes, he was under instructions to report about the Soviet troop movements to the English. He was sentenced to 15 years' hard labour in a Siberian gulag in Vorkuta.

I pulled out a map and asked him to show me where Vorkuta in the Archangielsk region was.

He and his fellow prisoners, mostly Poles, including Polish Jews, made the nightmare journey in an overcrowded train that lasted three weeks. The main part of their diet was salted herrings, which kept them tormented by thirst. At the journey's end, the prisoners were made to disembark and given tools for cutting down trees to build their own shelters. After the first night spent in the hastily constructed hut, my brother woke up next to a frozen corpse. The elderly Pole's death had turned his fully dressed body into an ice-mummy with eyes like frogs popped from their sockets. His frozen hair had turned into icicle spikes that nailed his head to the rough wooden planks. To release him, his mates had to chop them off, with scraps of frozen flesh left on.

Every morning, winter or summer, it was the same routine. The prisoners were marched from their camp to the forest to chop the trees, the wood was required for laying rail tracks. In winter it was hell, 40 or more degrees below zero. The trick was to move as far as possible from the overseer, just pretend to be working and preserve energy. One day, doing just that, he came across a cluster of frozen blueberries. He dared eat only a few at the time, the rest he planned to preserve for a later date. He was suffering from scurvy and his body was crying out for vitamin C. Like a squirrel, he carefully dug a hole and hid some berries deep under the snow. He marked the location by making incisions on the surrounding trees. When the first opportunity presented itself to return to the same place, he could not find his secret 'larder'. Another working gang had chopped down all the trees in the vicinity.

'Imagine,' he said. 'I broke down crying.'

'What did you wear?' I asked.

'The most important was the thick, hip-length padded jacket worn over padded trousers, and that in turn was worn over layers of any article of clothing that one could lay my hands on, including thick paper sacks. There were fights over boots and clothing taken from a dead prisoner. We all looked like wooden manikins.'

'What happened to your ski boots?' I asked, recalling how much they meant to him. For a while he managed to protect them, for practical as well as for sentimental reasons. They enhanced his chances of survival. He did not reckon with the gangs of Russian criminals who held the dominant position in the camp's hierarchy. One day my brother received an ultimatum: give them up and you'll earn our protection. He tried to bargain by offering other items of his wardrobe.

'I was not going to surrender and it nearly cost me my life.'

It was a female doctor who saved his life. His good looks had always made him a favourite with women. The gang leader later took pleasure in parading around in the ski boots, making sure my brother could see them.

At no time was there any rancour in his recollections. Where had his rage gone, I wondered? In spite of the brutality of the political system and the vicious individuals he had encountered, he showed a surprising indulgence towards his oppressors. He would shrug his shoulders, saying with a bittersweet smile: 'Ah, the *Russkies*, the *Russkies*!'

After his release from the Siberian gulag he was roaming through some of the Asiatic republics, riding on trains, selling and buying goods that were in short supply. Everywhere, my young good-looking brother met women who looked after him, loved him and wished to keep him. But he had a goal that helped to sustain him through the two years of the gulag: to find his family. The guilt of having left me, in spite of the pledge given to Father, was eating him up.

'I don't think I could have faced our parents without finding you alive,' he confessed.

On another occasion, he told the story of the three bullets. We were sitting in an outdoor cafe and the cool evening breeze carried a whiff of jasmine scent. With a tumbler of vodka in his hand, he was reminiscing about his time in Iraq.

'Have I mentioned Franciszek to you?'

'Yes, he was your mate in the gulag.'

The friendship with Franciszek had begun on the train to Siberia. They became the best of buddies and a relationship developed that would survive many severe tests. On one occasion Franciszek protected my brother at the risk of his own life.

'We stuck together and arrived with our unit in Iraq, in a training camp in Mosul. There both of us were selected for the officers' course and passed with flying colours.'

After the graduation ceremony, to celebrate, he and Franciszek went 'on the town'. In the summer heat of Mosul, the two friends were getting drunk in a clip joint, drinking beer mixed with whisky, a drink they were not used to. In high spirits they started spinning dreams about the end of the war. The 'after the war' fantasies resembled an epic film in which they played the heroic liberators of Poland, arriving in Warsaw seated high on top of a tank. The girls would be lining the streets, welcoming the victorious liberators with flowers and kisses. They drank to victory and glory, to eternal friendship and to love.

At some stage in the celebrations, Franciszek pulled out his pistol, released the safety catch and removed three bullets, carefully lining them up on the table. He picked up the first one and, twisting it between his fingers, announced:

'The first bullet is reserved for the first German soldier I encounter.'

Both he and my brother clicked their glasses and drank with enthusiasm to the liquidation of the enemy. Franciszek picked the second bullet.

'The second is for the first Bolshevik to cross my path.'

My brother hesitated a bit, the Soviet Army was being bled as they spoke, but for the sake of their friendship, he raised his mug.

'And the third bullet,' Franciszek continued, 'is reserved for the first Yid: those bastards sold our Motherland to the Bolsheviks!'

In the family we all knew the signs of an impending rage. Poor Franciszek failed to notice the change in my brother's complexion, which had quickly turned a choleric purple. He had no idea that my brother was a Jew.

There was a reason why my brother had kept his Jewish origin a secret, and was parading as a practising Catholic. After his release from the Siberian gulag he made his way south, where the newly formed General Anders' Polish army had set up recruiting centres. In the first centre, after filling in the form that included a question about religion, the authorities rejected his application. He tried his luck at another centre with the same result. He could have enlisted to serve with a parallel, Soviet-dominated, army in formation, an alternative option he adamantly refused to consider. At his third attempt, he declared himself a Roman Catholic and was accepted!

My brother picked up the bullet that Franciszek had reserved for the first Jew he encountered and, holding it up between his fingers just as Franciszek had done, asked in a voice choked with rage.

'Who did you say this was for?'

Franciszek was only too happy to repeat it and raised his beer mug to drink to the prospect of fulfilling his wish. My brother pulled his pistol from the holster and, pointing it at Franciszek, pulled the trigger. Luckily for him, the pistol jammed and in frustration, he used it as a blunt weapon. Franciszek, severely injured and blinded in one eye, was rushed to the field hospital. My brother was arrested, court-martialled, stripped of his officer's rank, and sentenced to serve a year in prison that was later reduced to six months for good behaviour.

The painful irony of my brother's situation would have been beyond Franciszek's ability to comprehend. As a Polish patriot, an able-bodied young Jew had to resort to the use of subterfuge to be accepted as a suitable candidate to fight, and perhaps die, for his country's liberation.

At the end of the story he helped himself to another vodka and mumbled, half to himself:

'I wonder what happened to the son of a bitch? I was very fond of Franciszek!'

AT THE TEL AVIV BUS STOP

True to form, it did not take long for my brother to become involved in a Tel Aviv street brawl. When it happened he was no longer a soldier of General Anders' Polish army. He had terminated his stormy relationship with Poland's military establishment by demonstratively burning his Polish uniform. Partly, it was his private protest against the difficulties that he had encountered as a Jew when trying to enlist, but the decisive factor was Franciszek's vituperative example of the 'three bullets'.

His impulsive action had put him in a precarious situation. Before the war had ended, he had become a de facto deserter from one army while trying to enlist in another, the British Jewish Brigade. A friendly lawyer advised him to lie low for a while before his position could be legalised.

My sister found him a temporary job as a night watchman at the Tel Aviv harbour, a marine designation in name only, as it lacked facilities for ships to dock. The British Army was using it for storage purposes and his duty was to guard military hardware. It allowed him to think that he was still making a vital contribution to the war effort.

The night watchman's job suited him. The night sky filled with stars and the sound of lapping sea waves soothed his jumpy nerves. His fear of hunger and of being frozen to death was never far away.

He was still compulsively hoarding bread and wore thick sweaters even in the Mediterranean heat. For company he had a dog, a Dobermann he had named Sobaka – Russian for 'dog' – for even here Siberia still held him in its grip.

My visits to his hut, which he had arranged into a cosy place, deepened the bond between us, which in some respects even excluded our sister. For a man not particularly disposed towards introspection, he would occasionally betray signs of a troubled inner life. A name, a place, an object would be sufficient to bring back some incident of past life. In spite of the alcohol-induced cheerfulness, his sorrow about life's tribulations would unexpectedly break through. Over a meal, with the help of the vodka to which he had become partial, the chaos of war reverberated in his thoughts.

'The albino. Do you think he made it?'

No more needed to be said. Both he and I would be thinking about the crossing of the River San, the 'good' German officer, the young Jew drained of colour and the cost of our own survival. That's how it was between us.

Accompanying him on his rounds with Sobaka held on the leash, I would get to hear more snippets about his life in Russia. I never knew which of the Asiatic Soviet Republics would be mentioned, as he had roamed through many of them, taking advantage of the lax movement restrictions due to the wartime chaos.

In Kazakhstan he nearly died from typhus fever. He had collapsed at a roadside and when he regained consciousness, he found himself under the roof of a mud dwelling with a large Muslim family, being nursed by a bearded man with a turban. He was the local healer and in a corner, his wife was milking their goat to provide fresh milk for the sick stranger. The whole village seemed to be involved in nursing him back to health. Every day somebody else would turn up with items of food, refusing payment. He regained his health, and before his departure his host provided him with a locally made and foul-smelling tincture to rid him of lice.

'Such good people!' His voice was troubled when he was dealing with the weighty matter of the monster of evil and the angel of mercy as he met them in their many forms. As a young prisoner, he had the chance to observe all kinds of brutality, wanton cruelty, meanness, greed and avarice of spirit. He had met so many people who had hardened their hearts. The occasional goodness explained little; on the contrary, it had added to his confusion. For people like him, the moral issue of the human potential for good and evil was no abstract philosophical dilemma.

Loosened up with more helpings of vodka, his tale carried me along the way to Tiflis, the capital of Georgia. Somewhere halfway to his destination, he calculated that the Jewish High Holidays were probably due. Overcome with a strong need to mark the Day of Atonement and in the absence of a synagogue, he entered an almost deserted village church. The gift of prayer deserted him but the memory of the parental blessings received before leaving home made him tearful. He lit a candle and placed it at the foot of the Jew hung on the Cross and wept.

Such rare confessional moments from my brother were precious. On another occasion I questioned him about the scuffle at the Tel Aviv bus stop.

'What provoked it?'

'The Jew was pushing himself to the head of the queue. He stepped on my toe and didn't say sorry.'

'Since when have you become a stickler for drawing-room etiquette?'

He claimed he was very nervous, he was on the way to the lawyer to sign some documents that would pave the way to his joining the British Army. In my brother's version, the middle-aged man standing behind him in the bus queue provoked him.

'I grabbed him and unceremoniously lifted him off the bus. It was meant as a lesson in good manners,' he said.

The man, amongst other invectives, called him 'Hooligan'! 'Hooligan' was a term our mother used to equate with '*pogromtchik*'. Before he knew how, his fist landed on the man's nose, causing a massive nosebleed. At the sight of blood on his white shirt the man became hysterical. Other passengers and the driver stepped into the brawl and the scuffle attracted the attention of the police who escorted both of them to the nearby police station.

My brother addressed the policeman in a mixture of Yiddish and Polish. The policeman, a Moroccan Jew, didn't understand.

'Don't listen to him, he is a liar!' the injured man declared in Hebrew, nursing his nose.

At the Police station, a Polish-speaking policeman was assigned to the case. My brother was the first to give his testimony.

After giving his name and place of birth, the victim of his aggression took a step closer to him. A policeman quickly stepped between them, to prevent another brawl breaking out.

My brother's surname seemed to galvanise his accuser who took off his glasses and, giving them a good wipe, stared at him as if he had seen him properly only now.

'Hamermesh from Lodz? Where did you live?'

'Kilinskiego Street.'

'What was your father's name?

'Josef Meir.'

'My God!' he exclaimed. The policemen observed them, perplexed.

'Can you imagine? I knew his parents well! I am also from Lodz!' He was telling the policeman, hardly able to contain his excitement when he embraced the 'hooligan', his attacker.

'Dr Lewinski,' he introduced himself.

The investigating policeman, realising that no charges would be lodged, dismissed them.

My brother already deeply regretted his appalling behaviour towards a 'landsman'. His apologies met with a nod and they left the station together.

At a nearby cafe, Dr Lewinski questioned him further.

'Are you the only survivor?' His voice was cultivated and he spoke beautiful Polish as well as fluent Hebrew. He was astounded to hear that all of their three offspring had survived.

'I remember your parents had three children.'

The Prudential insurance company, which had a branch in Poland, employed him as a doctor. In 1935 he personally examined both Mother and Father.

'I could tell you, your parents were fit. There was nothing wrong with your father's lungs, it was just a nervous cough. Mother was a bit overweight. I told her she should stop eating her delicious cakes.'

My brother had no idea that they had taken out a life policy.

'Your father, who believed everything English was superior, chose the Prudential.'

During the war, the Polish branch of the Prudential had its offices in the Bristol Hotel. After the German invasion it was taken over by the Gestapo who had confiscated all the assets and removed the files to an unknown location. That much was known. Dr Lewinski offered to introduce him to a lawyer who could advise on how to go about making a claim.

'It may take a long time,' he warned. 'I will be your witness!' he declared. 'With a bit of luck, they should have a record of your father's insurance in London.'

Soon after, my sister and I met Dr Lewinski who felt duty-bound to befriend us. He was a religious Jew and regarded the encounter with my brother, albeit in circumstances unpleasant for him, nothing less than an act of divine justice. God's will! Without the extraordinary twist of circumstances, we would never have learned about the Prudential insurance policy.

'It was your parents' intention to provide for their children.' Indeed, it was thrilling to be able to fulfil their wish.

Years later, when I settled in London, I discovered that the Prudential did indeed possess Father's insurance file. Apparently, before the war he had tried to take out a loan and this was the reason why Warsaw had transferred the documents to its London headquarters. Of their Polish clients, the 'Hamermesh file' was one of the very few records that had survived.

My brother's extraordinary 'encounter' with the pre-war official of the Prudential seemed indeed an act of 'divine' justice. However, insurance companies have little traffic with divine or any other kind of justice. Where claimants' payments were concerned, the Prudential's accountants made sure that our rightful inheritance was reduced to a minimal sum. We badly mishandled the claims procedure, being too ignorant about the pitfalls of confronting a company as powerful as the Prudential, and regretfully settled for a paltry sum.

For my brother, the astonishing array of coincidences brought a transformation of character. Mysteriously, something had come full circle. The nasty bus episode and the consequent friendship with Dr Lewinski were a turning point in his life. In recognition of his obligation towards the parental blessing, his fists learned to loosen up. Purged of their volatile unpredictability, his hands had become what they should have always been, loving hands caressing his children, later his grandchildren, and the women who loved him.

A SURPRISE VISIT

At the end of the war, reunions with Holocaust survivors, however joyous, would leave a feeling of unease. Whatever one said in their presence was always inadequate. And, if this or that one had survived, they were thinking, surely others may still turn up? Some did, like my school friend Heniek – or Etka, the girl with the smiling eyes. Occasionally, a survivor would unexpectedly appear at my sister's Friday evening Sabbath meal. On this occasion my brother prepared the way for the surprise.

'Guess who'll join us later?' The question was addressed to me. I was given a clue: 'peacock feathers.' I let out a scream: 'Silverstein is alive!'

'Not he, but his daughter Fredka.' She had recently arrived in Israel, the sole survivor of the family.

I recalled Fredka, the attractive young woman whose fiancé, the dental technician, had volunteered for work in the Donbass coal mines at the same time as my brother. The scene in which her mother came home with lengths of silk and taffeta materials for Fredka's wedding dress, flashed through my mind. The silk was tea-rose coloured and the taffeta had the sheen of morning dew.

The snub-nosed, blonde, curly-haired girl of my memory was now a round, barrel-shaped women. Only her shapely legs, of which she used to be proud, stayed unchanged. The twinkle in her honey-coloured eyes survived, as did the rippling giggles puncturing her speech, which used to irritate her father.

We toasted her lucky survival and looked with admiration at the snaps of her three children: two girls born in Poland during the war and a son born in Israel.

'You must come and meet my Israeli husband.' Fredka urged. They now lived in Acco, a city she described as the most beautiful place on this earth.

'Even Napoleon tried to capture it!'

She radiated happiness. Fredka's smile reminded me of her father's that revealed the display of gold crowns in his mouth.

'Come to us for a Friday night meal,' she pressed an invitation on us. 'Jakov [her husband] has already learned to cook with paprika!'

The mention of paprika made us laugh. My sister, who had never met her before, was happy to hear anecdotes about her parents' cooking talents. She had already heard from me about the paprika saga.

We were soon to discover that behind Fredka's irrepressible contentment with her new life in Acco was another story involving directly my brother's failure to make his way to Vilno with dire consequences for the Silvestein family.

After he was caught crossing the frontier on skis, the Soviets came looking for Fredka's father. Being resourceful, he and his family went into hiding. He found a comfortable lodge in the heart of the forest, owned by Stanislaw, a Polish gamekeeper who lived there with his family. To make room for the Silversteins, the gamekeeper had moved his wife, a daughter almost Fredka's age and a son aged 15 to the nearby village, where his in-laws lived. The arrangement was to the advantage of both families.

The forest lodge was a comfortable rural retreat while waiting for the war to end. He had enough gold coins and other valuables not to worry about the foreseeable future. Rabbits and wild fowl were plentiful in the forest – enough to allow the parents to indulge in their culinary passion of cooking appetising dishes with paprika.

All this changed with the German invasion of the Soviet Union in May 1941. The German occupation of Lwow had begun with a massacre of the Jews, in which the local Ukrainian population took an active part.

The Silversteins were lucky. Stanislaw was sympathetic to the plight of his likeable and generous Jewish guests, who from now on had to depend on him for everything: for news, for contacts with the city and for food supplies. Soon, the relationship changed drastically. The family was no longer welcomed, despite being paying guests – they were Jews in hiding; and if it was good business for some, it was also dangerous. Anyone who was discovered hiding Jews risked his or her life; often, whole families were punished

The gamekeeper had begun to grumble about the rising cost of living.

'What price for each sheltered life?' he mused aloud, when negotiating the amount of money he needed.

'It makes no difference, one gets a bullet regardless of the number of people.'

Their lives were now in Stanislaw's hands. The demands for payments for their protection kept going up. The gamekeeper would bring them stories about people in their neighbourhood, who had sheltered Jews and paid with their own lives – most likely true, but they had no way of finding out.

After the first year, Fredka's father ran out of gold coins. It was time to dig into the family 'heirloom' which Silverstein had buried in the Jewish cemetery, a place he believed to be safe. Who would dare to desecrate the graves?

Fredka knew the hiding place. After deliberation, her parents decided that she, who did not look Jewish, should undertake the journey to Lwow. She got there safely, and with the help of the gravedigger, dug up the buried Chinese vase, into which her father had stuffed the family valuables, having sealed it hermetically. Fredka had to break the vase to get to her father's collection of Austrian Empire gold coins with Empress Theresa's profile.

Fredka stuffed the family treasures into a body belt her mother had sewn especially for this purpose. By the time she left the cemetery she appeared to be in the advanced stages of pregnancy. At the end of her mission, Fredka had reason to be pleased with herself.

She walked through the streets of Lwow, her native city, without being recognised by anyone. The journey on the suburban train passed without her being molested by the Ukrainian auxiliary police.

The station was nearly empty and she felt conspicuous, being loaded with the family fortune. Stanislaw should have been waiting for her with his horsedrawn buggy, and she became anxious. He arrived two hours late and told her the reasons for his delay.

Just before his departure, he was warned about the presence of a German patrol searching for Jews in hiding in the vicinity. The information made her shiver with fear.

'Don't worry!' he calmed her, 'I have moved your family to a safe place.' As if the dread of the German patrol was not enough, he mentioned that on the way to pick her up, he had the misfortune to run into a band of armed Ukrainians who had searched his buggy. He was lucky they did not take his horse away.

On the way to the lodge he was chatty, which helped her to relax. They reached the lodge plunged in darkness.

'I'll go and fetch them,' he said.

She went inside to light the oil lamps and stoke the fire in the stove, deciding that all of them could do with a hot drink. Suddenly she heard Stanislaw's screams.

'Jesus, sweet Jesus, have mercy upon my soul!' He returned crying, repeating the same phrase over and over: 'Slaughtered like pigs! Jesus, sweet Jesus, have mercy upon my soul.'

She rushed out into the forest calling out 'Mame! Tato! Erika!' but he pulled her back.

'It's best you don't look. It's a bloody mess!'

Fredka's story of how her mother, father and her younger sister were murdered was related in a flat voice. No mention of emotions, only of what she'd done: how she pulled her mother's tablecloth off the dining table and wrapped it over her, curling up in a corner of the floor, making herself invisible. She had no idea what made her do it. She wanted to die and refused food and drink but Stanislaw was very caring and forced her to accept the nourishment he prepared.

The burial arrangements had to be done in secret. Under the cover of darkness, she watched Stanislaw dig three deep holes in the ground for the three wooden boxes serving as coffins. She did not wish to see the bodies of her dead parents or her sister, 'slaughtered like pigs'. He nailed the lids of the makeshift coffins and lowered them.

'Say a Jewish prayer,' he suggested as they stood near the fresh mounds of earth marked with temporary wooden plaques, identifying them by their first names only: her father Ruben, her mother, Rutka, and Erika, her little sister.

After the burial, Fredka decided to leave the lodge and make her way back to Lwow.

'Even a girl like you with "good" non-Jewish looks wouldn't last longer than a few days!' Stanislaw declared that he now felt responsible for her safety.

'It's a madhouse out there! Hunting Jews like rabbits has become a sport for the Germans and the Ukranians,' he told her. He never mentioned whether the Poles had joined in this sport and she did not ask.

He provided a safe hiding place in the forest, an ingenious underground bunker he had dug out that was well-camouflaged from the outside. He arranged it into a comfortable cabin, with a bunk for sleeping, a shelf and a hole for a bucket for relieving herself.

'In a way, I was pleased to be holed up in the bowels of Mother Earth. I had no wish to see the sky or nature's relentless cycle of forest life.'

The forest, smelling of rotting moss, scary and hunted by darkness, was no place for a girl alone. Even in fairytales forests were places where people would vanish without a trace.

But Fredka was a prisoner of her rescuer. The routine that the gamekeeper established gave her a sense of the days and nights that were passing. Once a week, after dark, he would appear with food, water and other life necessities. Her needs were basic. During the summer he would take her out for walks at night. In the winter, she spent most of her time curled up on the bunk, reading the same books over and over or the backdated German newspapers, which Stanislaw provided.

Sometimes he stayed for a chat and she would learn about the progress of the war. Most of the time the Germans were winning. She was safe and was grateful, aware how much it must have cost Stanislaw to keep her hidden. She tried to reward him for the risk to himself and his family but he declined payment, claiming he did it from his heart. Eventually, she forced him to accept some of her father's gold coins. She never thought he was greedy. If he so chose, he could have taken from her everything she had brought back from the cemetery.

'Keep it! You'll need it for after the war,' he told her repeatedly.

It made her think about the time after the war. What kind of world would she find after creeping out from her lair? Her father's world lay in ruins, her fiancé was snapped away from her. She was 19 and stuck in a bunker – for how much longer she had no idea. When she looked into the hand mirror a strange faced looked back at her.

One day, he informed her that he had encountered a problem. His son had followed him and he now knew about her hiding place. So far he had taken great care to keep it from his family, for her sake as well as for and theirs. And now his brother in-law had begun to talk about the reward the Germans were offering for each delivered Jew. In short, the brother-in-law expected to be paid for his silence. Fredka gave him more of her father's gold coins.

Soon after, Stanislaw failed to appear for his usual fixed visit. By the second week, Fredka was prepared for the worst. She was more than relieved to see him after the suspense of waiting.

'I had to stay away,' he told her. 'It would have been too dangerous to come,' was all he cared to explain. She understood that he must have been trailed. With the usual food supplies he also brought news of the Stalingrad battle.

'Good news, the besieged city is holding out!' he said.

Fredka wondered if she would live to see the defeat of Germany. For a time his usual routine was again resumed, indicating that the immediate danger was over.

'Where is your son?

'He was sent away.'

It was best for his family to be ignorant about the exact location and he always took care when visiting, choosing a roundabout way and making sure that nobody was following.

One Sunday he surprised her by turning up at a different time. He was clean-shaven and smelt of scented soap but his breath was saturated with the vapours of alcohol.

'The Russians have broken the Siege of Stalingrad and have trapped the German army!' The besieger had become besieged. It was winter, January 1943. She realised she had been living hidden underground for over two years!

Stanislaw produced a bottle of her father's favourite Hungarian Tokay wine to celebrate Germany's first great defeat. When he began to fondle and kiss her, her resistance proved in vain. After raping her, he cried, proclaiming how much she meant to him. He was just four years younger than her father.

This went on until she was too big with child. When the time came, he helped to deliver the baby. It was a girl. Fredka's breasts swelled with milk but the baby was a sluggish sucker and slept a lot. She rarely cried, as if she knew from the moment she was born that it was best not make too much noise. After the child's birth he moved them to a new hiding place. He must have worked hard, and in great secrecy, to provide an even more comfortable place.

Fredka knew something was seriously wrong with the baby but there was nothing she could do except try and love her, which to her shame she found difficult. Stanislaw displayed a great deal more affection for the baby than she did. She hoped that in naming her Rutka, after her mother, her affection for the infant she did not want in the first place would grow. Stanislaw, when possible, took on the responsibilities of a father and 'husband', taking care of mother and child.

One day, a youth aged 16 turned up and said his father would not be coming any more. From now on, he would look after her and the 'Jewish bastard'. Aloisi, Stanislaw's son, unbuttoned his fly and presented his erect penis.

'The son of a bitch has had his fill, now it's my turn!' he said, getting on top of her.

She never saw Stanislaw again. When asked what had happened to him, the youth simply mumbled that his father had suffered a stroke. The son, unlike the father, began to demand payment, claiming that he and his mother needed money for Stanislaw's doctors. She gave him everything she possessed.

By the time she discovered she was pregnant again the Soviet army was on the offensive, chasing the retreating Germans. The Soviets had already reached the Wistula River and Lwow had been liberated by the Soviets. When her confinement was due, she was no longer in her bunker but back in the lodge. This time Aloisi's mother was the midwife. She was a tall, prematurely aged peasant, who always wore black, as widows should. Fredka neither liked nor disliked the woman who had entered her life as a blood relation. 'You'd better tell them we looked after you well,' she said. The 'them' were the returned Soviets and the local Communist apparatchiks. Aloisi vanished, apparently to live with his married sister. And where was the supposedly paralysed gamekeeper, her husband?

'The sinner is dead and buried,' she said shrugging her shoulders as if there was nothing else to add.

Fredka was delivered of her second baby, a girl whom she named after her dead sister, Erika. The woman who until now had been a shadowy, absent figure, was now central in taking care of Fredka and both of her children. She tried to work out the complicated kin relationships with the woman in black, who was her blood relation, twice over, through the widow's husband and her son!

Rutka, her first-born, sired by the widow's husband, was Aloisi's stepsister. Erika, fathered by Aloisi, was the widow's granddaughter. Aloisi was also an uncle to Erika! Fredka found comfort in the fact that both girls resembled her mother's family; both had curly red hair.

Erika, unlike her older sister, was a lively, enchanting infant, and Fredka doted on her. One day, trying to retrieve a ball dropped by her, she pushed herself under the widow's bed. Fredka was surprised to find her mother's hatbox. Looking inside, to her horror, she found in it the full set of her father's golden dental crowns, twisted and broken in places. Whoever forced them out of his mouth must have done so after his death. She also found her father's golden watch on a chain, the kind with triple lids that would snap open when pressed. Also in the box was her mother's wedding ring, about which she used to joke that to remove it she would have to cut off her finger first. The horror of her parents' tragic death stared at her.

She now regretted that she had not looked inside the boxes that Stanislaw had constructed before he buried them. The words 'slaughtered like pigs' had kept her away.

'I knew I had to flee from that cursed place.'

By that time, April 1945, the Soviets had hoisted the Red Flag over the ruins of Berlin's Reichstag.

Fredka put her two daughters in a makeshift pram and made her way back to Lwow. Not finding anybody of her extended family, she moved to Austria and eventually reached Italy. Her intention was to get to Palestine, where she had a cousin.

She spent some time in a Jewish refugee centre in Rome where a doctor diagnosed Rutka, her first-born daughter, as brain damaged. The younger one, Erika, suffered from a neglected inner ear infection that damaged her hearing; otherwise, she was assessed to be a bright, well-developed child.

Like many others, Fredka was waiting for illegal transport to Palestine. The Jews had perfected the art of slipping in arrivals, often at night at various points along the coast where British vigilance was at its weakest.

In the spring of 1946, she and the children arrived by train in Naples with a group of refugees to board a Greek vessel, the *Aurora*. The groups of refugees, including Fredka, were ferried to the ship in a rowboat. The sailor who was helping people over the narrow plank, took from Fredka first crying Erika and then the older Rutka. When her own turn came, he lifted her from the rowing boat and, holding her up by the waist, teasingly swung her over the water, before placing her safely on the gangplank. She screamed and laughed, as she hadn't done for years, feeling safe in the sailor's strong arms.

It was a rough crossing. The lingering smell of stale fish on the lower deck made her sick. All through the journey, the sailor, Jakov, took care of her two children. For Jakov it was love at first sight. To Fredka, the man who had hoisted her over the deep blue sea had helped to lift her from the blackness of the forest bunker.

Jakov was a Polish-born Jew who had emigrated to Palestine before the war. The sea was his passion and before the war he had worked on ships, often making the transatlantic crossings. During the war he was a sailor with the British merchant navy and after his discharge, became involved with the illegal traffic of Jews to Palestine.

They got married, and a year later Fredka gave birth to a boy whom she named after her father, Ruben. Jakov gave up sailing and devoted himself to Fredka and their children – his *and* hers. Rutka was severely retarded and was eventually institutionalised.

Fredka ended her story with a surprise reflection: 'Do you think my children will be able to make sense of a life like mine?'

She looked at each of us as if waiting for an answer. My sister blew her nose and wiped tears and my brother's face was drained of colour. He had just been hit by the full scope of the disasters that his actions had brought upon the Silverstein family.

I, too, was pondering about the savage interlocking of our destinies. Were the events that had ended so tragically for the Silversteins in essence the result of my juvenile idea of getting to the 'other side'? Fredka's story lent further weight to the burden of guilt.

My brother regained his composure and turned to his most reliable remedy for sadness: a bottle of chilled vodka. He raised his tumbler for a toast.

'To Fredka and her new life!' We were clicking tumblers for '*L'chaim*! (the traditional celebratory toast)'.

'Let me know when you will come to Acco,' she said. 'Jakov's paprika dishes are as good as Father's.' Fredka was again smiling, looking cheerful. The mention of paprika made us laugh.

A NEW MEMBER OF THE FAMILY

The end of the war came and I was watching at the Jerusalem Zion Cinema how people had greeted it in London. In Piccadilly Circus, under the statue of Eros, crowds were dancing and strangers were kissing. The Royal Family, assembled on the Buckingham Palace balcony, was waving to rapturous crowds. The cinema newsreels also showed the devastation the Blitz had inflicted on the capital of the Empire.

In Poland, the end of the war was received differently. The devastation was total and the political defeat inflicted by the Yalta Agreement reached between Churchill, Roosevelt and Stalin – to Poland's disadvantage – had again redrawn the map of Poland.

Some Polish anti-Semites found consolation that Poland was 'Juden frei', free of Jews. In my own family, except for my brother, my sister, myself and two cousins, nobody from our large extended family had survived. I managed to cope with the losses by the well-tried strategy of escaping into an imaginary world of miraculous reunions.

By February of 1946, all my energies were directed towards the preparation of my second exhibition of oil paintings, watercolours and drawings, sponsored by the British Council that was part of a scholarship recommendation to study art in London.

On the day of the opening, Jerusalem woke up to find a thick blanket of snow covering the city. The Holy City resembled a Swiss skiing resort. Jerusalem winters can be cold and wet but snowfalls occur rarely and the city was brought to a total standstill. To people who had never seen snow in their lives, particularly children, it was a fun time, and a regiment of snowmen appeared standing in the middle of roads free of traffic.

It spelled disaster for my exhibition, held in the main hall of the British Council premises on Princess Mary Street. The official in charge of preparing the reception commiserated with me. It was obvious that neither the guests nor the press would turn up for the occasion. He was wrong: as soon as the doors opened, the first visitor appeared though, as it turned out, he would be the only one. In his raincoat and trilby hat, he looked like an English civil servant.

It soon transpired that the eager visitor was not interested in my art, though he made polite noises about it, but more in my name.

'I have just arrived from Germany,' he said, 'and my attention was drawn to the posters on the billboards displaying the name Hamermesh. Is Helena Hamermesh a relation of yours?'

'Not that I know of.'

He looked disappointed for he had hoped to renew contact with the woman he had met at the trial of the Nazis in Luneburg.

The visitor was Professor Norman Bentwitch, about whom I knew next to nothing. But the secretary of the British Council, an elderly Englishwoman who had lived most of her life in Jerusalem, knew of him and his reputation as an international jurist. He had been one of the judges at the Bergen-Belsen trial in Luneburg. As I avoided reading about such matters, I was ignorant about the trial and his part in it.

'Helena Hamermesh was an important witness at the trial.'

She had struck him as an impressive young woman whose story of survival was just as remarkable. Helena had survived Auschwitz, Bergen-Belsen and the infamous 'death march' that finished off so many of the remaining prisoners. When the British liberated Bergen-Belsen, she was in poor health, suffering from tuberculosis. Yet her indomitable spirit survived intact, as was evident in the contribution she made as a witness at the trial. Against all odds, she had managed to preserve a list of the names and events that implicated the Germans who had perpetrated acts of brutality. She claimed that her desire to see justice done had kept her alive.

After the liberation she learned that her husband, also deported to Auschwitz, was declared dead. She was left all alone having lost her husband and a child.

'I have come to the exhibition on the off chance of finding a family connection,' Professor Bentwitch admitted. He was looking at me through his wire-rimmed glasses with anticipation.

'Helena Hamermesh,' he repeated her name, as if offering me a tool for digging up my memories.

'Personally, I have no recollection of a Helena in the family, but I'll ask my sister who is a reliable chronicler of the family connections.' I promised to let him know.

My sister was struck by the providential timing of my inquiry. By coincidence, the previous day she had received from the Red Cross a communication about our cousin, Dr Mumek Hamermesh, an Auschwitz survivor, who was recuperating in Italy. Other details about him included a reference to a dead wife and a missing child, without mentioning the wife's name.

'Helena Hamermesh could well be his wife!' she declared.

Our cousin in Italy was contacted and he confirmed that indeed his wife's name was Helena. The information about her death was a case of a mistaken identity and the visit of Professor Bentwich to my exhibition had resurrected her.

Mumek and Helena met and married during the war when he was on the run from the Germans in the Soviet-occupied part of Poland. After the German invasion of the Soviet Union they were again on the run and had managed to entrust their baby boy to a local peasant family. Soon after, they were caught and deported to Auschwitz where they became separated and lost sight of each other. At the end of the war, while Mumek was searching for his wife he was informed that Helena was on the list of women sent to the crematorium.

As soon as his health permitted, our cousin set out in search of his son. The peasant couple they had entrusted their son to had themselves vanished in the mêlée of shifting fronts, either having fled or been deported. After trekking from village to village, visiting various monasteries and orphanages, the search for his son proved futile. He eventually made his way to Italy, awaiting a chance to join his uncle in Palestine.

My British Council exhibition, after the initial weather setback, was well-attended and received some favourable reviews. However, nothing in my life as a painter would ever match the gratification I experienced from the fact that my art was instrumental in reuniting two displaced persons, husband and wife, both given up for dead.

For the reunited couple, the war would not end for another two years. After their reunion in Italy, they set out for Palestine on a ship packed with survivors like themselves. The British Royal Navy, dutifully carrying out the White Paper policy, intercepted the ship with its illegal human cargo and transported them to specially set-up camps in Cyprus. The British, who had liberated people like Helena in Bergen-Belsen, now kept them prisoners behind barbed wire, in camps guarded by British soldiers with machine-guns.

A year after the couple's arrival in sunny Cyprus, the birthplace of Aphrodite, Helena gave birth to a daughter. Israel's declaration of independence brought them freedom and they settled in Israel in 1948.

The birth of the second child, a son, reopened the wound of the missing first-born, Jakub. Neither dead nor alive, like a phantom, he would hover over the daily lives of the parents and their two growing children. Contrary to psychological predictions, time was not a healer and his shadowy presence grew with the passage of time. In a way they never gave up hope of tracing him, one way or another.

The experience of the Holocaust affected husband and wife differently. The trauma of the war eventually crushed the husband's spirit, whereas Helena's was fortified. As well as devoting herself to the demands of family life she was energised by a sense of mission, driven by the idea of Christian-Jewish reconciliation. She preached that no healing could take place, either for the Jews or for the Germans, without facing up to the grim facts about places like Auschwitz and Bergen-Belsen.

She became a public speaker and in this capacity she would often be invited by various organisations to Germany for meetings with school children, university students, teachers and clergymen.

She happened to be invited to address a congregation in a church in Dresden, a city familiar to her from the time she was led through its ruins during the 'death march'. She included an amazing detail relating to the procession of the emaciated prisoners, led through Dresden already in ruins, shuffling past the dour, indifferent passers-by staring at them. At a certain moment, Helena looked up and noticed a woman at a window busy sketching a procession resembling living skeletons.

'I even tried to imagine how she saw us and what she felt,' Helena said, proud to remember her thought process, in spite of having been reduced to such a pitiful condition.

At the end of her address, a tearful woman got up and informed the audience that the person sketching at the window was her mother, an artist, and that after her death, she had inherited the drawing depicting the scene Helena had just described. The audience was startled, and so was Helena.

'I would like to offer it to the Speaker as a gift.'

In capturing the Dresden street scene, the artist had immortalised the death march, 'the sorry spectacle' under her window. A clue to what the artist felt while executing the sketch is contained in the inscription she included at the bottom of the drawing:

'*Der letzte Gang, Jahr 45*' ('The last walk').

It was too good a story to be missed by the media, and a reproduction of the drawing was publicised in many German newspapers. The scrap of yellowing paper is preserved in a museum. Helena, now in her mid eighties, still travels and gives talks about Christian-Jewish reconciliation.

Helena became a much-loved member of the Hamermesh family.

'DEAR SCOTLAND YARD'

My departure from Palestine in 1947 to become an art student in London signalled a new beginning. In the past, departures meant mostly dramatic separations. This time, the separation from my sister and brother was free of pain, balanced by the fact that I would be visiting them during the summer breaks. Another important factor was the anticipated reunion in London with my mother's relatives.

Officially I was still a stateless person issued with an international travel document. Even so, I no longer thought of myself as the refugee who used to smuggle herself through frontiers.

I travelled by train from Jerusalem to Egypt, and in the Port Said harbour I boarded the SS *Andes*. The Royal Mail liner decorated with the Royal Crest, a floating extension of British territory, offered an inkling of the mystique of the Empire's maritime power. Even as a third-class passenger, the ship represented glamour and luxury that I had only seen in films. For a week, the surroundings of this floating 'hotel' were a source of enchantment. The ship was also a suitable ground for meeting new people.

Two Polish officers, the purser and the doctor, who had served during the war on Polish submarines that patrolled the Mediterranean Sea, took me under their wings. They represented the part of Poland that had little to do with the likes of Franciszek's three bullets story. The Polish crew members arranged to transfer me to the Captain's table, a great privilege, they assured me.

The Captain of the SS *Andes* was proud of the ship's war history. She was launched in 1939 as a modern luxury passenger ship but was 'mobilised' and converted into a troop carrier. Ships like the *Andes* had their share of near-disastrous encounters with German U-boats. By the time I boarded her she was restored and once more put into the service of passenger traffic.

The carefree time included an encounter with a girl about my age, who unbeknown to her had made an impact on me once before, while she was boarding a bus in Tel Aviv. Even then, during the short bus ride, I was mesmerised by her looks. She was the most beautiful and graceful young person I had seen outside the glamour of a cinema screen. There was an aura of crispness about her striking good looks. I could not keep my eyes off her and took in every detail about her appearance: the silver choker round her long neck, the crisp, off-the-shoulder white cotton blouse edged with black velvet, the Roman sandals and the leather, bucket-shaped shoulder bag. Soon after setting eyes on the stranger, I strove to imitate her and began to wear chokers and asked my brother to get me a bag like hers.

I spotted her promenading on the upper deck, looking fresh and well-groomed when most of the other passengers looked wind-blown or seasick. Her poise and melodious voice won adoring looks from other passengers as well, particularly from the men. Her attractiveness had less to do with her striking good looks than with her personality. The qualities that had sparked admiration at the bus sighting were still operative on the ship and the sea journey facilitated the opportunity to get to know her.

Her name was Assia Gutman. Assia's father was a Jew and her mother was a German Christian. With the advent of Hitler's racial laws, the family fled Germany and had settled in Palestine, not as part of the Jewish rebuilding of the Promised Land, but living in an enclave of German-speaking settlers. Assia grew up on the margins of the Zionist enterprise, from which she was kept at a distance. Her mother tongue was German, the same language used by the people who had declared war unto death against the Jews. This linguistic quagmire made Assia determined to learn Hebrew in addition to English, a language she was educated in.

We were conversing in a mixture of English and Hebrew. Like everything else about her, Assia's perfect command of English was the object of my admiration and envy. I was eager to impress her and won her over with my Scotland Yard story.

With the approach of my departure date to London I was determined to trace the English branch of our family. Finding my relatives in London, Mother's two sisters and a brother, had taken on a great importance. I had to find them! My sister's sensible advice was to wait and start the search after arriving in London. That however, clashed with my fantasy, which included a scene of being greeted by a member of my family on arrival. The imaginary scene included details of emotional embraces. Any blood relation would turn the arrival at the London railway station into a special occasion. Knotting together reality and fantasy had already become a fixed character trait that called for action.

My sister knew the married name of one of my aunts, and my brother recalled 'Mile End' as part of an address, but he wasn't sure if it was the name of a street or of something else. The scant information was insufficient for the Red Cross to assist with the search.

One restless evening, on impulse, I composed a letter to Scotland Yard, an organisation known to me only from detective stories and some English films. Within the confines of my imagination, Scotland Yard was an organisation in control of all the secrets of the world, including the whereabouts of my mother's family. In the letter, I explained the family circumstances and asked for help. The envelope bore a streamlined address: 'SCOTLAND YARD, ENGLAND'. Anybody else in my place would have taken the trouble to find an English-speaking person with a typewriter and at least try to get hold of Scotland Yard's proper address! My letter, with its appalling spelling mistakes, would have amused a Scotland Yard official, if, against the odds, it had landed on an official's desk and not in the rubbish bin.

I never mentioned the letter to either of my siblings and, not getting any reply, I put it out of my mind. To my surprise, shortly before my departure, a letter arrived bearing the markings of His Majesty's Scotland Yard office in London. The form of address, 'Dear Miss', gave me a warm feeling: Scotland Yard liked me! In Polish letter-writing etiquette, a formal address would be 'Esteemed So & So'. 'Dear' was reserved only for emotional exchanges.

The letter wished to inform me that they had indeed managed to locate the whereabouts of my relatives. Unfortunately, the law prohibited them from divulging information of any kind, without the prior consent of the individuals concerned. However, they could forward a letter written directly to them.

I was thrilled by the success of my intervention. My brother and sister were impressed and handled the letter gingerly.

I showed the Scotland Yard letter to Assia and she read it out aloud, imitating to perfection an upper-class English accent. She even found my simplistic approach to dealing with officialdom endearing. Next to her sophistication, my provincialism made me feel wanting and for the second time in my life I wished to be like her. I even began to comb my hair in imitation of her hairstyle, letting it fall over my left eye.

Sunning ourselves on the upper deck, we talked about our plans for the future: mine as an artist, hers as a linguist. For both of us, the surge towards a new beginning was an escape from a wounding past.

We reached Liverpool on a foggy autumn morning and stood on the deck watching the activities of the ship docking. The row of red-brick houses and the cranes standing like giraffes on the edge of the quayside, was the first introduction to the urban English landscape. The screaming seagulls were flying overhead and would dive into the water to scoop up food from the discharged refuse.

Assia and I shared the train journey to London, where both of us hoped to be met at the station.

During the carefree time that we shared on the ship, it was inconceivable to think that the same assets that won her so much admiration would cut her life short. Her beauty and poise, which I so envied, proved to be a gift with a fatal sting.

In the distant future, Assia would find herself entwined in a love triangle in which she would be cast in the role of the 'other woman'. The couple into whose marital web fate had lured her were the poets Ted Hughes and Sylvia Plath. By the time Ted Hughes encountered Assia, she was already married to another poet. Hughes, like many others, found Assia's attractiveness fatally irresistible. The romantic story took on its tragic dimension with the suicide of his wife Sylvia, then of Assia who, disappointed that he would not marry her, gassed herself together with their four-year-old daughter, Shura.

On the SS *Andes*, ploughing through the stormy Atlantic, there was no hint of Assia's forthcoming tragic fate. At the time of her death we were close friends, but unfortunately I was away from London at the time of crisis. The news of her death was a blow to all of her friends.

BLOOD IS THICKER THAN WATER

Getting off the train in London, I spotted a man standing on the platform, holding up a board with my name on it.

'I am your cousin Mot,' he said when I approached him, and we fell into each other's arms. My fantasy had become a reality! I was his cousin from Poland, the daughter of his Polish uncle, whose life ended in Auschwitz. As a teenager, Mot got to know my father well, acting as his guide on his frequent visits to London. He would accompany him to business meetings as his translator.

On the way to his apartment I learned facts relating to the English branch of our family. His mother, my aunt, had died during the war. His father was an ageing, sick man. My mother's other sister, who had once visited Lodz, was also dead: an unhappy romance with a German drove her to suicide. Mother's youngest brother enlisted and was killed in the war. His widow and two surviving sons were estranged from the rest of the family and nobody knew their whereabouts.

Mot was married and had two children: a boy aged four and a baby girl. Sam, Mot's younger brother, was also married and had one son. When I met Sam, in contrast to Mot who was a fast-talking, highly emotional man, I found that his English reserve and manner of speech – the stiff-upper-lip version – fitted the image of him in the photograph showing him in the uniform of a British Army officer. Numerically, my newly found family was small. All the same, they were my blood relations!

'Blood is thicker than water,' Mot joked about our emotional reactions.

Mot's wife, Cipy, was a quiet, soft-spoken woman, of the type of beauty seen in Italian paintings. Her milky complexion contrasted sharply with her dark eyes and brown hair. Her dimpled smile made me nickname her 'Madonna'. She was the personification of gentleness and kindness and I was welcomed by both of them in spite of the fact that they had no extra room to accommodate me. In their sitting room, an improvised easy chair and a footstool served as my bed.

In their house I found photographs of my own family, showing my parents with their children dressed up for the occasion. The visits to the photographer for the yearly photo sessions were a routine. Prints of the same photographs were also dispatched to the family members in New York and Brazil. It was a strange sensation to see pictures of my family intact, in London! I decided there and then that photography was the greatest invention of all time! They were the guardians of the past, which even when half faded, help to save the dead from oblivion.

At the family gathering arranged for my arrival, I got to hear Mot's version of the Scotland Yard inquiry story. One day, the neighbours informed Mot's widowed father that while he was out a policeman came looking for him. The visit alarmed the old man, who thought the reason for the policeman's unwelcome interest in him was his dealings with the black market! He was still living in Mile End above his modest shop selling lengths of women's materials and other utility goods. The thriving black market helped him in his wheeling and dealing. Panic-stricken, he went into hiding hoping the threat would soon blow over. But the police did not let up. Day after day a different policeman would turn up and, not finding him, would wait outside his shop. Scotland Yard was also making inquiries amongst the next-door neighbours regarding his whereabouts. This went on for more than a week. His sons, feeling sorry for their father, finally went to inquire about what sort of charges their father was facing. They were greatly relieved to hear about the letter sent to Scotland Yard from Palestine!

Their father returned home and the story spread through the neighbourhood. My poor uncle became the subject of merciless teasing. When he finally met me, the author of his troubles, he fixed me with a critical look and, wagging his finger at me, said:

'You and your Scotland Yard nearly gave me a heart attack!'

THE SLADE SCHOOL OF FINE ARTS

The London that my father had so admired was no more. I was walking through streets scarred by the Blitz with the open spaces of the bomb sites overgrown with shrubs and accumulating rubbish. I was getting used to a different London.

My life in London entered a relatively relaxed phase. I had family, lived in a city filled with art treasures, and was a scholarship student at the Slade School of Fine Arts. No more drifting, as I had done in Jerusalem.

I moved out of my cousin's apartment that offered a safety buffer while finding my bearings in London. I rented a small attic room in Swiss Cottage and was learning to cope with a nosy landlady; an elderly retired actress who behaved as if her house were a stage where she was playing a leading role.

My room was dingy and the mattress on the bed had as many humps as a camel. The bathroom was heated by a system connected to a voracious meter that needed frequent feeding with sixpences or shillings. The ancient boiler, like the landlady, would make threatening noises and then explode.

The exterior of the Slade in Gower Street was impressive; a spacious forecourt enclosed the buildings imitating a Greek temple. But the interior was a let-down. Due to the war the building was in a state of neglect. The studios, the staircases and the long corridors, where the work of past luminaries was on display, were covered with dust. The space where artistic inspiration should have glowed was dimly lit and unheated.

After a while, I moved from painting to the sculpture department, under Professor Gerrard, a friendly tutor with an elongated horsy face. In his office he used to keep boxes of apples grown on his farm and he encouraged his students to help themselves. I liked the feel of clay under my fingers, it recalled the time in Ben-Shemen when I was modelling heads and figures that formed an illusionary world.

I also enrolled to do a stage design course, run by Vladimir Polunin, a dapper-looking elderly Russian with a grey goatee and piercing blue eyes. Theatre-going, as well as being a school obligation, became my passion. It was an exciting time for London theatre-goers. New and innovative plays by young English playwrights were filling the theatres, and the London repertoire also included Sartre, Cocteau and other continental playwrights introducing the theatre-going public to the intellectual jolts of existentialism.

The winter of 1946/47 was unusually severe and people looked pinched by the cold. Rationing and shortages made life difficult. After the Middle East, I was ill-prepared for the dampness and chill of the English climate. Sulphurous fogs would often engulf whole neighbourhoods, blotting out the faint gas lighting, reminiscent of films about Victorian London.

By contrast, the student body added a touch of exoticism. African and Asian faces, a mix of diverse nationalities and races from the colonies, livened up the scene and so did their colourful saris and African cotton prints.

The first year of studies provided a degree of stability I had not experienced since I left home. But it was not to last. The peace, won at the cost of so many sacrifices and so much bloodshed, rested on fragile foundations. The British Empire, like a badly stitched-up quilt, was coming apart.

'A case of wear and tear applied to history,' one of the more cynical tutors commented. The effects of the partition of India, and the creation of Pakistan that unleashed a wave of massacres, was seen in the anxious faces of the students from the Asian countries.

Bishaka, a fellow student from India, one day stopped coming to the college. We had become friends and I was missing her and the exquisite silk saris she wore that made her silhouette resemble a butterfly. With her sudden disappearance, the wet cloth that was wrapped round the clay figure she was modelling began to dry out. Students took turns in keeping it wet. After a time her absence was explained by the story of what had happened to her family.

For generations, Bishaka's Hindu family had lived in Lahore which came under Pakistan rule. In the chaos of the frantic population exchanges, which took place after partition, the lawlessness that led to massacres on both side of the border had claimed the lives of Bishaka's family as well. Her fleeing family was on a train that was attacked and her parents and her two brothers were killed.

After a while, most of the students stopped taking interest in the tragedy of her family. For me it was an extension of the scenes familiar from the recent Jewish history in Poland. The atrocities of Europe had spilled out into another continent.

The majority of the male students were recently demobilised, veterans of many theatres of war. They had served on ships that were torpedoed, participated in air battles, dug trenches in Africa's desert sands or in snow-covered Europe. Some had been liberated from jungle prison camps, one even from an infamous German prison camp. The hardened ex-warriors were older than the usual student intake, presenting an unusual crop of budding artists for the Muse to nurture. They were creating, if not things of beauty, at least original objets d'art.

The pubs in the vicinity of Euston Road were meeting places for students from the neighbouring colleges, the Drama School, the Architecture School and the Medicine department. As they drained mugs of beer, the men enjoyed lively conversations with each other, but the moment we, the long-haired, sandal-wearing Slade girls, joined them, their conversations would falter. The subjects of war and sport created a bond that excluded women. The men were too full of themselves to bother to discover what kind of war some of the girls might have had.

Some of the tutors held views that women were inclined to take up art in order to find a husband or be a muse to a budding genius. A talented but angry college professor would taunt us: 'Either make babies or art!' He may even have meant it.

The Slade provided the background to my first intimate relationship with an Englishman, which I hoped to be the right step towards integration into the host society. I soon learned of my error, however. Peter was no Englishman; he was from Scotland.

'Don't ever mix me up with the English lot!' he warned, rolling the 'R's around his tongue. In fact, he looked like the archetypal highlander in the advert for porridge oats. He had flaming-red curly hair, a red beard, which set off his blue eyes, and lips of such a girlish red that I used to tease him about using lipstick. In the college he was known as 'Scot', which at first I took to be his surname. It was he who first alerted me to the invisible fault lines rumbling quietly under the political reality of the United Kingdom. Hidden under the nuances of 'Englishness' were the Northern Irish, the

Scots and the Welsh, who never stopped clamouring for autonomy or independence.

Peter, a war veteran, never asked me about my war. I, on the other hand, was insatiably curious about his. At first he was reluctant to talk about it, his art was now his battlefield and his line of attack was to gain control of pigment on canvas.

Peter lived in Kentish Town, in a dark and unheated basement room, which smelled of stale beer and pipe tobacco. As my own landlady did not allow male visitors to stay after dark, I would stay at Peter's place at weekends. Our affair lacked the spark of passion, yet the intimacy was comforting to both of us. We would spend Sunday afternoons visiting the British Museum or the National Gallery. Occasionally we would go to the Everyman Cinema in Hampstead to see the latest French films.

Both of us were often short of money. The scholarship of five pounds a week did not cover all the living expenses or the cost of art materials. When we ran out of small change to feed his gas meter, we had to huddle together under his army blankets. When absolutely broke, we took turns posing for each other. The sitter had to stay close to the gas fire or risk catching pneumonia. In the nude Peter resembled a marble statue, his flesh so white that the markings of his veins seemed like marble blemishes. We saw in each other statues of flesh, and our lovemaking was stony. The aesthetics of art had obscured our emotions and we treated our bodies like objets d'art.

Peter once formulated the proportions of my body thus: 'A Gothic top above a Byzantine base,' and he went out of his way to prove that I resembled Maillol's nude sculptures. Once, he even tried to measure Maillol's *Three Graces*, at the time displayed in the entrance hall of the Tate Gallery.

We each had our own art patron. Rembrandt was mine and Vincent Van Gogh was his. The two great masters were responsible for our intimacy surviving as long as it did, almost a year.

Above Peter's bed, he had pinned copies of Vincent's letters to his brother Theo. He had created a collage interspersed with reproductions of Van Gogh's self-portraits, including the one with his ear cut off. On the margins he added his own gloomy thoughts about life, art and love, which spoke of his identification with Vincent's own frustrations and mental sufferings. The display resembled a medieval scroll.

One cannot always tell what it is that keeps us shut in, confines us, seems to bury us, but still one feels certain barriers, certain gates, certain walls. Is all this imagination or fantasy? Do you know what frees one from captivity? It is a very deep, serious affection. Being friends, being brothers, love, that is what opens the prison by supreme power, by some magic force. But without this one remains in prison.*

Peter's own paintings were muddy and dark, held together with thick black contours. They expressed his emotional turmoil, which was made more incoherent by his poor sense for painterly space. The canvas simply resisted his energetic efforts to create satisfactory paintings. He was talented, sensitive and terribly frustrated. I suspected that his talent would have been better placed in writing.

Rembrandt was my icon and reproductions of his self-portraits were pinned on the walls of my attic room. Eventually, I got Peter to join me in my Rembrandt reverence. I knew I had succeeded when, once during our frequent visits to Kenwood House where Rembrandt's self-portrait hangs, Peter read out to me Van Gogh's comment on Rembrandt:

> Alone or almost alone amongst painters, Rembrandt has that heartbroken tenderness, that glimpse into a superhuman infinitude that seems so natural there; you come upon it in many places in Shakespeare as well.**

Peter's stories about his childhood and life in a Glasgow slum corresponded to what I knew about the conditions in Polish slums: drunken men; hard-working and long-suffering women coping with large families; children playing in the streets which resembled dark tunnels enclosed by overcrowded tenement houses. His mother died when he was a small boy and his stepmother made his life hell. For his father he had nothing but angry words.

The relationship with Peter made me realise that for some people the war offered the chance of a lifetime. It had rescued him from the Glasgow slum and its deprivation. To me it was incomprehensible that the Second World War, which had turned Europe and other continents into a slaughterhouse, could have been an enriching experience. Peter was an example of the British serviceman for whom the bloody battlefields had served as some kind of a military 'Grand Tour' of the world, courtesy of His Majesty's government.

He volunteered young, ahead of being called up, and served in the Middle East. The scorching desert sun in Libya and Egypt exposed his

---

* *Letters of Vincent Van Gogh*, edited by Mark Roskill, (London: Flamingo, 1983).

** Ibid.

white skin to peeling. His Celtic genes were ill-suited to desert warfare and life under canvas. And yet, in his tales about his war experiences, I sensed a longing for that time when clad in His Majesty's uniform, he lived like a nomad, his warrior 'tribe' constantly on the move.

Coming from a deprived background in a class-ridden society, the exposure to new social and cultural opportunities widened his horizon. The war, he claimed, had turned him into a fully conscious human being, when he had learned about different cultures and people, about books and music. But most importantly, it had made him an artist. After the war, Peter took full advantage of the generous educational opportunities that the newly installed Labour government offered to ex-servicemen.

Like his idol Van Gogh, Peter suffered frequent bouts of severe depression. One of them took place towards the end of our relationship. He dropped out of his Slade studies and I lost sight of him.

THE BATTLE FOR ENGLISH

My English was adequate for my social and cultural activities, or so I thought, oblivious to the fact of how insubstantial it really was. Occasionally my English-born, well-educated friends would politely correct my faulty pronunciation of difficult words. I tended to use highbrow words in conversation, not yet fully aware how presumptuous it was and that only a foreigner would choose to use them in colloquial speech.

Reading had become an important part of my student life. I began to devour English literature, both classical and modern. Cheap paperback editions even made it possible to assemble a small library of my own. On buses or the Underground, my ears were soaking up the sound of colloquial speech and I would regurgitate any new idiom from scraps of overheard conversation. It was mimicry, a foreigner's attempt to penetrate the intimate aspect of a language. The radio saga of the time was *Mrs Dale's Diary* that allowed me to peep into the private lives of the 'ordinary' English people.

Theatre-going was another source of enriching my English. But following Shakespearean English in the theatre was more difficult and it forced me to read the plays, overcoming the resistance the text offered.

I kept invoking my English teacher in Jerusalem who had worked so hard to teach me. Miss Joffe had the reputation of being the best amongst English teachers and in great demand; indeed at the time she was coaching many of the elders of the Jewish Agency, preparing them for their future roles of statesmen.

Originally from South Africa, Miss Joffe was a frail woman, looking older than her middle age, unmarried and utterly devoted to her profession. She took me on free of charge and turned her act of charity into an honourable deal for both of us, tactfully resolving to postpone the issue of payment until such time as I'd be earning money. Miss Joffe became my linguistic godmother and I was very diligent, keen to please her. Affection made learning easy.

Her method of teaching foreigners the correct pronunciation of the tricky 'th's' involved placing flimsy pieces of paper on the palm of ones hand, and while holding it up at the mouth level, she watched how the pieces moved. If they flew off, she would reward the accomplishment with a broad smile. When failing to achieve the expected result, she would shake her head in disapproval and make me try again.

At first, the foreign-sounding words strained my vocal chords. Acquiring a proficient command of English meant switching from the swishing sounds of the Polish to a language with restricted lip movement. English, Miss Joffe declared, was a man's language with no place for the feminine frills of the Slavonic languages. Like the Polish malleable diminutives, a way of verbally caressing objects. A chair can be a plain chair, or have a choice of at least four diminutives to convey one's emotional relationship to it.

I loved the idea of being an English-speaking person. The attempt to learn the language had begun in pre-war Poland. At school, the choice of foreign language was French or German, but my Father nursed a hope that in the future at least one of his children would assist him with his commercial dealings with England. He hired a neighbour's son, a student of English, to give us lessons. The young man was timid and would blush at the slightest provocation. Predictably, my brother dropped out, my sister was lukewarm about it and I was the one who tried to memorise sentences, which included 'The cat sat on the mat'.

Hitler's invasion had put a stop to the English lessons. The war had brought linguistic chaos into my life. Within a short period of time (1940–45), in quick succession, I was exposed to four language changes: Russian, Lithuanian, Hebrew and English. The crossings of linguistic boundaries paralleled my border crossings.

The first switch was into Russian, after my brother and I reached the Soviet part of occupied Poland. Next was Lithuanian, a difficult language rooted in Sanskrit, taught at the Vilnius school. After the Soviets marched into Lithuania, Russian had become compulsory in schools. My second exposure to the Russian language was short-lived, never progressing beyond learning the Cyrillic alphabet and a few basic conversational phrases. Nowadays, I regret missing the chance to learn the language of Dostoevsky and Chekhov.

Once in Palestine, Hebrew was the third language to be absorbed. By that time, a linguistic fatigue must have set in. I just couldn't apply myself to study the language of my forefathers, therefore depriving myself of great linguistic rewards. Instead, I made do with a smattering of colloquial Hebrew, picking up bits here and there.

I was a linguistic exile and my displacement happened just at a time when my passion for books and writing paralleled my absorption in visual arts. The urge to write was nothing new. Already at the Jaszunska Gymnasium I collected prizes for writing short stories and essays. Inspired by Axel Munthe's *The Story of San Michele*, I dreamt of combining a career as a writer with that of medicine.

In Jerusalem, trapped in linguistic limbo, I renewed my effort to learn English. By this time, I already knew that my parents had not survived. The pledge given to Father, that I would learn English, was an even more potent incentive.

The route to English was filled with obstacles, but the effort was worthwhile. As well as giving access to the St James's version of the Bible, Shakespeare and other linguistic treasures, to become an English-speaking person was regarded everywhere in the world as a privilege, offering many advantages in life. The British Empire may have been shrinking territorially, but linguistically it was victorious. English was becoming a universal language and the British Council, the 'language missionaries', had paved the way for this unparalleled conquest. A road sweeper in Holland, Denmark or Sweden was likely to give directions in faultless English. In Bombay, taxi drivers managed a fractured kind of Indo-English. In the Middle East and the Far East, many people read and spoke English.

My linguistic transition to English was not without trepidation. After all, one was taking on a literary legacy of tremendous status. Would I ever dare write in this language the stories that were crawling like insects inside my skull? When I first timidly put pen to paper, I would hide the results in a drawer to which nobody had access. The term writing 'for the drawer', used to describe the case of Russian dissidents hiding from the secret police, was an apt description in my own case. I was hiding not from the KGB but from an internal harsh taskmaster hissing into my ear, 'How dare you use the language of Shakespeare?' I was afraid that English, my borrowed language, would find my alien spirit uncongenial. I had before me an image of a bouncer who kept guard at the gates leading to the English heritage fortress. Surely, anyone could see at a glance that I was a gatecrasher!

After a few years of secretive writing, my psyche began to feel linguistically more relaxed. But if a word that I was after would slip from my grasp, or be replaced with a word from another language blotting out the original English, I would be reduced to a state of panic. It was a reminder that an eviction from my new linguistic residence could be served on me at any time. The anxiety about losing a grip on the only language I now possessed for self-expression was real, however unreasonable. The self-consciousness about being engaged in a charade would imperceptibly creep up on me: I was and was not entirely at home with the English language.

Many years later, an encounter with an elderly patient in a hospital where I was undergoing a neurosurgical spinal operation epitomised, par excellence, my linguistic nightmare. We shared the same ward, and I watched a woman who was an accomplished translator of four languages lose them all! Her command of Italian, French, Spanish and Russian was reduced to gibberish. An accidental severance of a nerve during her neck operation had deprived her of all of her linguistic skills. Since the failed operation she could still use words, but what came out was an incoherent mix of words which nobody could understand.

In spite of my fears about English being snatched from me, my spirit was flourishing in the English culture. Miss Joffe would have been proud of her pupil. Soon after my arrival in London I even managed to see some modest pieces of my writing in print: some reviews about exhibitions and a few stories about Jerusalem with my own illustrations.

English had turned out to be a magnanimous verbal stepmother, keen to make up for the loss of my mother tongue. The metaphorical gatekeeper was after so many years now a paralytic old man and the gates were wide open. True, I was an outsider, still insecure, still liable to mess up tenses or the syntax, or to put commas in the wrong place, but on the whole I no longer felt like a gatecrasher. When I hear English-born people massacre their own language through indifference or ignorance, I feel like shouting at them: 'For heaven's

sake, think about us, we who had to struggle so hard to master it!'
It hurts to hear it maltreated.

Miss Joffe, I think, would turn in her grave.

WAR STALKS THE MUSE

Swiss Cottage had become a marker for my life in London and the
choice of residence in this area turned out to be just right. Its cosmopolitan character due to the presence of German-Jewish refugees
and other foreigners made me feel one of the crowd. The neighbourhood had a number of cheap restaurants and cafes that were
a magnet for students and artists. Among them, Cosmo offered
not only a socially and culturally stimulating ambience but also a
well-heated shelter during the winter.

I soon got to know a bunch of English-born regulars, talented
young people, a few of whom in later years would earn a permanent
place in English cultural life. Amongst them was the poet Danny
Abse, still in the middle of his medical studies, and Joan, his future
wife, by now a distinguished art historian; Emanuel Litvinoff, a poet
who established himself as a novelist, and Rudi Nassauer, a German-
born writer and wine merchant married to Bernice Rubens, who at
the time was trying her hand at writing. Another Cosmo friendship
of importance was with Gil Elliot. His book *The Twentieth Century
Book of the Dead*, dealing with the culture of mass violence and the
impact of the dead on the living, contributed to my own reflections
on the subject. Of the friendships formed at Cosmo some survived
and some went sour.

At the centre of this literary flock was the writer Elias Canetti.
He liked writing in noisy places and was a regular at Cosmo. His
reputation as a writer of importance was at first intimidating and it
took a few years before I dared to join his 'inner circle' of admirers.

In 1947 the newspaper headlines, if they did not scream about
some catastrophic defeat on the cricket or football grounds, carried
news of the simmering Jewish-Arab conflict in Palestine, on the
verge of exploding. Facing a no-win situation regarding its manda-
tory obligation, England passed on the problem to the UN, which
announced plans for partition, consequently rejected by the Arabs.

The prospect of another calamity facing Jews jolted me out of the
tranquillity that the English people radiated. It never ceased to amaze
me how soft-spoken and polite they were. Nobody pushed when
standing in long queues. Children, too, struck me as excessively quiet

and well-behaved. Even the dogs seemed too lethargic to bark. The threat of war in Palestine woke me up.

As far as my new Swiss Cottage friends were concerned, my Palestine connection had obscured my Polish background and its Holocaust shadow. Hearing me speak Hebrew with Palestinian Jews helped to reinforce that impression. They couldn't have known that my grasp of the language was shaky. The false assumptions about my identity saved me from having to explain the fate of my family in Poland. Passing references to my sister and brother in Palestine and to my English family helped to keep the subject of the Holocaust at bay.

Frankly, I liked being taken for a Palestinian Jew. The native-born were known as *sabras*, a nickname borrowed from the prickly cactus pear that is soft and sweet on the inside and prickly on the outside, and which fitted their character. They had earned a reputation of being tough and fearless. The record of the Jewish Brigade's heroism during the war reinforced the collective pride. Their existence seemed to redeem the ill-famed reputation of European Jews who had been blamed 'for going like sheep to their slaughter', a view that condemned the victims of the Nazi atrocities to a double ignominy.

In London there were protest marches, public meetings and discussions about being a Jew in the 'post-Auschwitz' world. The term had become a universal measure of the moral chaos left by the rupture of Western civilisation.

I began to frequent the Anglo-Palestine club, near Piccadilly Circus. It was a meeting place for students with close personal links with Palestine and for members of the Jewish community, including some prominent Anglo-Saxon Zionists.

The club's popularity was enhanced by the presence of young unattached women and the visits of Jewish members of His Majesty's Armed Forces, still in military uniforms. It was whispered that the young military visitors were involved with the recruitment of volunteers and the acquisition of weapons in case of war.

One of the visitors engaged in such a clandestine mission was Janek, the same who was my first juvenile heart-throb at the summer camp in Troki before the outbreak of the war. The bond was deepened by my friendship with his younger brother Fredek, the fat boy who should have joined in the planned departure from Lodz but stayed behind, forced by his mother's assertion that they 'die together'.

To Janek, who had a hand in my survival by actively supporting my sister's actions, I must have presented a painful reminder of his failure to rescue his own brother. Whenever we would get together he would invariably lead the conversation to the time in Lodz when I last visited his home, as if by reliving that moment he could alter his brother's fate.

So far, the escalating tension in Palestine had not affected my close friendship with another Slade School student, an Iraqi. The friendship of the Polish-Jew and the young Muslim from Baghdad was consolidated by a shared passion for the theatre and cinema. Our relationship developed effortlessly, without any erotic under-tones; more like that of a brother and sister.

Hazim was a lively, talented sculptor with a whimsical sense of humour. In the basement studio where we worked, and where vari-ous pieces of sculptures done by previous generations of students were displayed, he had daubed a patch of oil on a life-size stone carving of a female nude. The stony Eve had acquired an oily growth in place of pubic hair. The added erotic dimension to the statue unleashed amongst the male students a wave of prurient innuendoes and rude jokes.

Whenever Hazim visited me, my landlady used to give him sharp looks. Of short stature, he hardly presented an image of a romantic son of the desert. He was dark skinned, his face was framed by black curly hair and his brown eyes were made darker by being deep-set.

I learned about his close-knit, well-to-do family in Baghdad who blended harmoniously oriental and Western lifestyles. He regarded me with awe, at a loss to understand how a young female could have managed to travel through war-torn Europe without the pro-tection of a male relative.

These were pre-feminist times and his ideas about progress and equality were derived from his exposure to Communism. He was a born rebel and his Communist sympathies made him critical of the glaring contrasts between the rich and poor in his country. This made him express curiosity about kibbutz life run on Marxist prin-ciples. We assumed that one day I might visit him in Baghdad and he would come to Palestine to see for himself how the kibbutz egal-itarian principle worked in practice.

He was a caring and loyal friend and when I was taken ill and hos-pitalised with pneumonia, he would visit me frequently, bringing oranges and bananas which were luxuries beyond most students' means. He also picked me up after my discharge from the hospital.

Within an hour of settling in my Swiss Cottage attic room, I was surprised by an unannounced visit of two CID men. Both were very tall and in my small attic room had to be careful not to hit the low ceiling. They were polite but not friendly, and made me think of masculine dummies displayed in shop windows.

Hazim was the first to attract their attention and was questioned about his identity; they had mistakenly taken him for an oriental, Palestinian Jew! Inadvertently he got mixed up in an unpleasant episode caused by my alien status and Palestinian connection. Some Palestinian Jews in London were under surveillance in connection with the activities of Etzel, an extreme right-wing resistance organisation responsible for terrorist outrages against the British.

It soon transpired that the reason for the CID visit was an offence I had apparently committed, serious enough to have me deported.

'What have I done?' I asked, alarmed.

'You have broken a Home Office law regulating the conditions of residence of aliens in the UK. You failed to notify the authorities about the change of address.'

'I have not changed my address!' I protested, nevertheless beginning to feel weak at the knees. The past experiences of interrogations made me overreact.

They asked to see my alien's registration book, my current identity document. One of them read out the relevant instruction printed in very small print at the back of the booklet. It stated clearly that any absence from one's residence lasting longer than 48 hours had to be notified to the authorities immediately.

'I was sick in hospital! Surely that did not constitute a change of address? What's more, during the period of my hospitalisation, I was paying my rent.'

They nodded and confirmed that the authorities indeed *knew* where I was and for how long.

At the end of the visit, because this was my first offence, they decided that they would be lenient. But I had been warned!

After their departure, both of us were left shaken by the incident. We were puzzled as to who were the informers providing information about the whereabouts of foreign residents in this democratic and free England. The CID men knew the *exact* time of my return from the hospital! Who were they? The landlady or the cheerful and friendly milkman? Perhaps the hospital authorities?

The experience invited dark thoughts on the theme of *what if*. What if the Germans had ever managed to invade England? Would the same kind of people have denounced their Jewish neighbours to the Gestapo?

The final stress on our relationship came in 1947 when Iraq joined seven other Arab countries that had declared war on the nascent Jewish state. Hazim was summoned home and was mobilised in the war effort.

Before his departure, we met for dinner in a Soho restaurant. I tried to imagine him in a military uniform, fully armed.

'They may use me for something else,' he joked. 'For instance, to clean the latrines.'

It was a sad occasion for both of us. We were a case of close friends now officially declared 'enemies'. I waited towards the end of the dinner before telling him that I had volunteered to be mobilised. The prospect of either of us aiming guns at each other reduced Hazim to a fit of laughter. In reality my mobilisation papers allotted me to another task: that of looking after refugee youngsters at a camp set up near Marseilles.

In that war I never got near a battlefield. As for Hazim, though we never communicated directly with each other, I know that he carried on with his artistic endeavours.

THE BIRTH OF A NEW STATE

At the Marseilles youth transit camp I was taking care of orphans from many European countries, survivors of the various camps. They spoke a babel of languages and if my Polish, German and a smattering of school French failed, drawings and paintings came in handy when trying to communicate. Their drawings evoked longed-for villages where giant flowers grew in front of their homes, or scenes of executions and deportations. The youngsters rarely cried, as if their sorrows had dried up their tear ducts.

In the spring of 1949 we sailed from Marseilles to Haifa. I was returning to a country which was Palestine when I left and was now renamed Israel.

The crossing was rough and the ship was not up to the journey. The Mediterranean was whipped up by the winds and the ship was tossed by high waves that flooded the lower decks. The vessel had been bought from a naval scrapyard and she, like other similar boats, formed the foundation of the first Israeli shipping company. The crew consisted of motley international seafaring volunteers. The frantic improvisations used by the Jews to consolidate their newly won statehood were truly amazing.

The bulk of the passengers were survivors who were brought from German refugee camps. In between spells of being seasick, the passengers were jubilant, the blue and white flag with the Star of David fluttered above their heads, the same star that the Germans had forced them to wear as a badge of humiliation. When the weather permitted, somebody with an accordion would appear on the deck, rousing people to dance the hora, their feet energetically stomping forward and backward. The remnants of the various concentration and death camps were proclaiming the triumph of survival, and were sailing to their homeland after 2,000 years of dispersion!

At the Haifa harbour I was greeted by my brother who looked transformed; his front teeth knocked out in the Soviet prison had been fixed and he was again serving in the army, this time as a military policeman with the Israeli Defence Forces. The trappings of authority restored his self-confidence and the army jeep at his disposal enhanced his new status.

The drive from Haifa to Tel Aviv revealed a drastically changed landscape. The messy and painful birth of the Jewish state had left visible scars on the land and its people, the Jews and the Arabs. The armistice borders, dividing Israel from its neighbours, Jordan, Syria and Egypt, ran along twisting lines at odd angles. There was no peace, only an uneasy suspension of hostilities.

Irrespective of the political situation, feverish activities were in progress to meet the challenge of the flood of Jewish refugees. The 'in-gathering' process made the country resemble an ant heap, its workers and soldiers energetically scurrying about on various tasks of repairing the nest. A mixture of triumph and sorrow fuelled the outburst of collective energy for the losses suffered in Europe and on Israel's battlefields.

In the streets and cafes there was a babel of languages. Day and night, military vehicles pounded the roads and country lanes. The soldiers – often unshaven and wearing sloppy uniforms; a veritable people's army unlike any other military force – dispensed with the customary army rituals of saluting higher ranks.

By contrast the Arab population, numerically reduced by the flight of so many, were watching the Jewish vigour from the sidelines with aching hearts. They were a people in shock. The local Arabs had another description for their situation: 'catastrophe'. The vanquished watched the victors with fear, feeling humiliated and impotent. Arab villages and the cities from where so many had fled, or were forced to leave, appeared as if suspended in a time capsule. In the countryside, women and young girls in traditional Arab dress were still making their way to fetch water from wells, gracefully balancing the pitchers on their heads. Men and boys on donkeys were trying to avoid being hit by traffic. The exotic, peaceful scenes were deceptive.

After the departure of the British, the Jewish administration had taken over and the Arabs found themselves under military rule. They were now dependent on Jewish bureaucracy for everything: the right to travel, to build, to open shops, which severely curtailed their lives. The harshness they often experienced was obscured or denied by the Israelis who believed in a 'benevolent occupation', but the pain in the eyes of the defeated Arabs spoke volumes.

For the majority of Jews, the plight of the Palestinian Arabs was too close to their own losses to be a serious consideration. 'They've brought it upon themselves,' was the popular view. The memory of the Arab leaders' threat to 'drive the Jews into the sea' was fresh and so was the knowledge that during the Second World War, the Mufti of Jerusalem resided in Berlin and was Hitler's ally. All this did not help to evince compassion; yet, in spite of that, brave voices were raised expressing anxiety and moral unease about the situation.

Traumatised by the Holocaust, the Jews – already yesterday's victims – denied any moral responsibility for the Arabs' suffering. There is no truth to the claim that suffering ennobles. For the majority of Israelis the outcome of the war of independence was seen as a miracle. Biblical similes had begun to creep into the language. The story of David and Goliath was often invoked. The plight of the Palestinian Arabs had not yet become a moral issue to lacerate the consciousness of the Israelis and the Diaspora Jews.

Upon my return, my family and friends were eager to tell me stories about how uncertain the outcome of the war was and how, by all accounts, it was a very close-run thing.

My sister's Ben-Shemen pals, for instance, in a kibbutz named Nitzanim, were besieged by the Egyptian army and eventually overrun. Women and children were evacuated in time but the men who stayed behind were killed. In this war the Arabs took no prisoners.

During my previous stay in Palestine I was too confused about life and how I fitted into it to get involved in the activities aimed at laying the foundations for a future State of Israel. This time, from the moment I got off the boat the mood of collective euphoria carried me along. In a burst of enthusiasm I, too, wanted to be part of the digging, building and planting. To fight and to make peace, all at the same time! But in reality the only thing I was capable of doing was to wander with a sketchbook, or sit in front of a canvas and paint. It did not seem an adequate answer to the demands made by the historic moment.

I went back to Jerusalem but it was no longer the city I knew. The Holy City was divided into two parts. Gone were the Bedouins with their flocks of sheep. It was a divided, mutilated city with a frontier running along a narrow strip of no-man's land filled with thistles, barbed wire and rubbish. The Jewish part of Jerusalem, cut off from the Old City, occupied by the Jordanian Hashemite Kingdom, had lost some of the flavour that used to make it such an exciting place.

The highest observation point within Jewish Jerusalem was from the Notre Dame church steeple, from there one could watch the Jordanian sentries on guard, strategically placed along the city walls, pointing their guns, and from time to time occasional exchanges of fire could be heard.

I moved from Jerusalem to Arab Jaffa 'colonised' by artists of every kind, who had moved to the abandoned Arab properties, converting them into artists' studios. Artists were always attracted to 'Orientalism' and the Jewish artistic 'colonisers' were no exception.

I shared a studio in a condemned property with two other artists. The roof was leaking and the floor was unstable but the window offered a perfect view of the Mediterranean Sea. For me, the attraction was the proximity of the fishing harbour and the view of the Andromeda rocks: sharp-edged, huge boulders sticking out from the foamy sea mouth like sharks' teeth.

Amos, a native-born Israeli was reputed to know every inch of the Holy Land and often used the Bible and ancient myths as a guide in his wanderings. He introduced me to the Greek myth of Andromeda and its connection to Jaffa. Andromeda, in punishment for her boastfulness about being more beautiful than the Nereids, had mortally offended Poseidon; the supreme ruler of the sea. Poseidon was married to a Nereid. In punishment he had Andromeda chained to a rock, from where the mighty Perseus rescued her and carried her off on his winged horse.

Both the landscapes and legends that accompanied them exercised a powerful pull on my imagination.

While I was preoccupied with Jaffa's Andromeda rock, Jews were settling in Arab Jaffa. Houses that once belonged to prosperous families were now divided between new immigrant families, many of them refugees from Arab countries. For hundreds of years the Jews had lived in harmony with their Arab neighbours but now they became victims of anti-Jewish riots as a result of the establishment of the State of Israel. Nationalistic passions had turned neighbours into deadly enemies. Jews from Arab countries were arriving as

refugees to Israel, and Palestinian Arabs became refugees in Arab
countries. Sadly, one wave of refugees had created another.

Moral chaos pervaded in the perceptions of the rights and wrongs
regarding the Palestinian-Jewish issue. It was a subject most people
avoided, including myself when I accompanied my sister to view
a flat she was offered in Jaffa. The apartment was once the home of
a middle-class Arab family. Everywhere were visible signs that the
previous owners had fled in panic. The most upsetting was the
room with children's toys scattered on the floor.

My sister retreated, jolted by the scene. 'That's how our parents'
flat must have looked when they were chased out,' she said. Mother's
spirit hovered around us; for her there could be no equivocation
where justice was concerned. Something was either right or wrong.

It was nearly 20 years before I was ready to grapple actively with
the Arab-Jewish conflict, after I became a filmmaker. But that had to
wait for another unpredictable twist in the route my life would take,
again involving Poland.

NATIVITY IN FLUORESCENT LIGHT

R.'s parents were not too pleased about his choice of future wife.
A refugee, of no esteemed family, and with no passport and no
dowry; a long haired, sandal-wearing Slade School bohemian was
not the right candidate for their only son. R.'s parents were wealthy.
Before the war their household consisted of a cook, a parlourmaid
and a driver. They were the kind of people who lived by life-long
certainties, solidified by daily and strictly observed routines.

'Mother, she's Jewish!' their son tried to console them.

'It doesn't matter! She's not English, she's a refugee!' the mother
replied.

'She is an artist!'

To make sure that he had not fallen for a fortune hunter,
his father warned him that he was not prepared to assist him in
any way.

As a chartered surveyor R. was earning five pounds a week and my
scholarship amounted to the same. Though his bachelor flat was
located in an elegant block, with a lift and a porter who looked like
a general from a banana republic, the truth was we could hardly
make ends meet.

We were an odd couple, the reserved English gentleman and the
extrovert artist. It took a while before my new husband could get
used to the 'open house' hospitality, and my habit of greeting our

many unexpected visitors with a warm, welcoming 'Come in, come in!' In our tiny flat, if the occasion arose, the floor would be cleared and a sleeping place improvised for yet another uninvited visitor. I could not rid myself of the 'once a refugee, always a refugee' attitude towards needy people. With time, I tried to protect him from the discomfort that the exposure to my *Middle European* (German–Polish–Austrian) ways imposed on him.

We were slowly learning about each other's ways. I was surprised to discover that my English-born husband had fewer friends compared to my own already broad circle. For a foreigner it was hard to understand how anyone who had attended school in London and had spent the war years in the army would have so few close friends. Later, I observed this anomaly when meeting other Englishmen married to foreign women.

After our Italian honeymoon nuptials, I became pregnant but suffered a spontaneous miscarriage. When we settled into married life, the issue of having children was never discussed. My pregnancy was not planned, it just happened, but after the miscarriage the loss made us realise how much both of us wanted a baby.

I was lucky with the second pregnancy and loved everything to do with the burgeoning physiological changes taking place in my body. I developed a narcissistic fascination with the constant changes, which affected my senses and choices of food. Contrary to the anticipated discomforts, the only kind I was exposed to was an aversion towards raw meat, and nausea when exposed to the smell of Virginia tobacco or strong perfumes. I was relieved to see that pregnancy did not interfere with artistic and intellectual activities. I was attending art history lectures at the Courtauld Institute and the colours of my painting were becoming more lush and sensuous, as was my pleasure in sex.

The prospect of becoming a mother made me recall with alarm the Slade professor's disparaging comment about his female students: 'Either make babies or art.' Like many other women before and after, I was out to prove him wrong.

The National Gallery had become a refuge from the demands of my pregnant body. I was seeking out paintings dealing with the theme of the Nativity and Madonna and Child. Would they engage me on a different level now that I was nurturing a new life?

I was drawn to Giovanni Bellini's *The Virgin and Child*, also known as *Madonna with the Pomegranate*. The posture of his Madonna appealed to me. That is how peasants sit – with legs comfortably spread, their garments resting across their knees, in readiness to support any weight, be it child, potatoes to be peeled, or a chicken to be plucked. Her broad, fleshy face invoked my childhood memories of Polish peasants. A wholesome, earthy Holy Mother was gazing at her round-faced infant greedy for the nipple. Even the woolly clouds floating behind the green shield failed to render her celestial. She was firmly terrestrial and helped me to brood on the miracle of procreation.

At the pre-natal clinic, the white-coated gynaecologist, the guardian of my growing foetus, was engrossed in the medical routine of measuring my blood pressure and the baby's position in the womb. He was listening to its heartbeat through the stethoscope and was satisfied that everything was clinically sound. Did he hear anything else?, I wondered. He was deaf to the urgent signals of my own heart.

My body knew things which I didn't dare reveal to the doctor. At times I felt like a giantess, a dynamo charged with an extraordinary power. The earth was circling on its orbit, atoms were crushing into each other forming and reforming during the millions of years and my body was like a station picking up signals from the past, present and the future.

'Doctor,' I tried to engage him. The doctor, pencil at the ready, waited.

'Doctor, what do you know about the ways the dead spirits can burrow inside a pregnant woman's growing life?'

The white-coated doctor smiled absent-mindedly. In his clinic there was no place for the meeting of history and biology, he was responsible for his patients' bodies. It was not his concern that my uterus was also a rendezvous point of ghosts from the past and not only the organ of genetic fusion.

Looking at his notes, not at me, he said: 'Pregnancy should be a happy event, tell your husband to take you out to a cheerful show.'

An Irish nurse, who handed out sterilised jars and pills, led me to an office to fix the date for my next visit.

I joined a pre-natal exercise class and in the company of women in the last stages of pregnancy, thrashing on the floor like stranded whales, I learnt to control the abdominal muscles through breathing.

'It's a perfect pregnancy,' the doctor at the clinic was expressing satisfaction with my condition. 'I expect a normal delivery. If anything worries you, just phone and tell my secretary. Otherwise I will see you in the hospital, in the delivery room.'

'Doctor, what do you know about the fallout effect of Auschwitz on growing foetuses?'

Looking puzzled, he cast a sideways glance at me.

'Cheer up, there is nothing to worry about. Tell your husband to come and see me.' He sat down and busied himself with a note, a letter for a psychiatrist.

I ignored his recommendation and waited for the time of confinement.

On a wet, grey March day, I arrived at the Hospital of St John and St Elizabeth. Lured by the false promise of spring, buds on the trees had unfolded prematurely. Outside, the building displayed a huge billboard appealing for donations for its upkeep.

The delivery room resembled an industrial plant. Chrome instruments and hissing pipes circled the floor and the fluorescent lights were draining the colour from the ceiling and walls painted green.

When labour started the highly paid Harley Street specialist who should have been with me was busy elsewhere. I was left alone and waited for the contractions to begin.

A faded reproduction of Titian's *Madonna and Child* hung on the wall, facing the delivery trolley. The Madonna's eyebrows raised slightly as she gave a sigh, just like my mother used to. She looked positively Jewish. Why not? After all, Jesus' mother was Jewish!

Sister Hilary, who kept coming in to monitor the frequency of the contractions, tapped my tummy with her fingers, as if sending signals in Morse code to the impatient foetus. Each time she bent over me, her starched white wimple, resembling wings, made me think of birds.

I must have started to hallucinate, breathing in the gas provided for pain relief. The Madonna was looking at me again, this time with a critical eye. Was she going to tell me off? I wanted her to speak to me about birth, not the celestial but the messy terrestrial kind, but she kept her mouth shut.

'Push, push!' Sister Hilary hoisted my legs over her shoulders and urged me to push harder still. I was panting and pushing, contracting and relaxing in the way I had learned to control pain. I was floating, and was about to fly off into Titian's blue sky.

'Good girl! Now stop! You're doing very well.'

Sister Hilary, Christ's betrothed bride, who had never known sex with a man but was Jesus' bride, worked hard to bring my baby into the world. She praised my labour control and I, like a schoolgirl, was keen to obey her instructions and pleased to be praised.

Waves of massive pain were crushing my body, each contraction accompanied by a noise inside my head resembling an engine revving up. I was pushing and the eyes of Titian's Madonna stayed unmoved. Her tight-lipped mouth was a trap of silence. She was not the kind of mother one could confide in about the first sex experience with a man clumsy in such matters. I didn't understand the reasons why I said yes to one man and no to another and now I was about to give birth to a child of my perplexed feelings.

The pain was shouting in its own language, 'Mama! Mama!' I was calling out in Polish, my mother tongue. I wanted my Jewish mother, not the white-clad, antiseptic hospital staff. With each contraction, I was calling for my mother with renewed longing. How was I to know that in between the contractions of labour, while pushing out a new life, the movement would stir the spirit of my dead mother? The pain of labour was uniting us again.

'Please Mother, protect me.' I prayed to my flesh-and-blood mother, and the painted one fixed to the wall. 'Please, let the baby be born with one head, five fingers on each hand, sound limbs, neither dumb, deaf nor blind...'

'The baby's head is engaged!' Sister Hilary exclaimed with excitement. 'Bear down!' Sister Hilary commanded.

Summoned by my cries, my mother materialised by my bedside. She appeared a tormented spirit who, like Demeter the Earth Goddess, wept and raged over her forced separation from her own children. As they cut my son's umbilical chord I felt my mother's eyes and the eyes of history fixed upon us with an unblinking gaze. Holding my son in my arms for the first time I felt elation. 'Your grandson!' I said to my dead mother, but she was gone, carried off by the black wings of her sorrow.

How was I to know that the delirium of war would flare up beneath me in, of all places, the delivery room? In that instant, I understood how victories, defeats, birth and death were tied to women's umbilical cords.

Sister Hilary wiped my face before my husband was allowed into the room.

'Clever girl!' He kissed me. 'You gave me a son!'

The National Gallery became intimately connected to my life as an artist and my early motherhood. During the frequent visits to the National Gallery, my toddler son would follow me, albeit reluctantly. He learned to ignore the paintings on the wall and I learned to ignore his calculated indifference as I traversed the various rooms, sampling a choice of Dutch, Spanish or Italian rooms. His Dinky toys and people were his chief distractions.

Once, at the age of five, while passing Titian's *Madonna and Child*, he pulled his little hand from my grip and unexpectedly stopped in front of the painting, lost in concentration. Finally, pointing a finger at the Madonna, he exclaimed: 'Look mum, a babysitter!' I did not know whether to laugh or be upset by the child's startling utterance. The Madonna, symbol of sacredness, reduced to the role of a nanny.

A VALID PASSPORT

Nobody prepared me for the paradox that motherhood presented. Having become a parent myself, I was overcome with an overwhelming longing for my own parents. However much I tried to suppress it, my body became vocal in expressing the aching need. Various psychosomatic ailments began to plague me. Attacks of stiffness of limbs or neck would immobilise me. Other chronic disorders, like frequent inflammation of the larynx would render me voiceless. To be reduced to whispering was the ultimate symptom of regression. I lived in my own body like a prisoner under house arrest. The feeling of being ill-at-ease was responsible for the decision to go into psychoanalysis.

During the two years of regular attendance, guided by Mary, the mental journey into the past had reached the safety of England. What a sigh of relief she must have given when the girl from Lodz had finally reached London. Mary's consulting room and her plinth-like black leather armchair had become like a welcome oasis where she, in the role of mother-confessor and a Jungian priestess figure, provided safety. She listened to my stories about people dead and alive, heard me rage or sink into prolonged silences. She never let drop her original suggestion about visiting Poland.

'In your unwillingness to set foot in Poland again, you are preventing the missing parts of the story of coming together. Don't be afraid to close the circle!'

I shook my head, 'No'.

Unexpectedly, one day over breakfast, my husband suggested 'Let's go to Poland this summer.' He had in mind a family holiday. He liked to plan summer holidays in winter, and winter holidays in summer.

'Well, what do you say?'

For him, an Englishman, the geographical distance from London to Lodz was a straightforward journey. For me, it would be a convoluted emotional route that, if undertaken at all, would have to be done alone.

The following day I called up the Polish Consulate and was surprised to hear that the procedure to obtain a visa was quite simple. Unlike Russia, which was hermetically sealed to individual Western visitors, Poland, after the recent political events, had managed to loosen a few chinks in the Iron Curtain.

I was informed that a visa to Poland would require a valid passport, a set of three passport photos, and application forms completed in triplicate. Unless the applicant was known as an enemy of the Polish People's Republic or hiding a criminal record, a visa could be issued in a matter of days. I couldn't believe my ears – in a matter of days?

In the winter of 1960 I drove myself to the Polish Consulate to pick up the application forms. I stepped into a slice of Poland marooned off Great Portland Street that offered a peep into the post-war Polish Diaspora in England. The congested waiting room was filled mostly with Poles who had settled in England after the war – Poles who had taken part in the Battle of Britain and others who had arrived as part of General Anders' demobilised army. Their middle-aged faces showed the endured hardships, active military service, prisoner of war camps, refugeehood and deportations to Siberia. Many of them fought battles on many fronts, Rommel in Africa, and shed blood in Italy at Monte Casino.

Some had English wives: the best kind any foreigner could wish for, as one of them informed me. Loyal and easygoing about their English-born children being initiated into Polish ways, these Church of England wives looked on tolerantly at their Catholic-raised children learning to speak Polish with their fathers. The English-born wives were active in preserving Polish culture in exile and watched with maternal pride as their children dressed in Polish regional costumes danced mazurkas and polkas.

Standing in the queue, the faces around me resembled my own family portraits: round faces, high cheekbones, eyes all shades of blue as if dipped in watercolour washes. A woman standing in front of me in the queue reminded me of Kasia.

Filling in the visa application was not a simple matter after all. I was uncertain how to answer some questions: my nationality, for instance. Not English, British then? The purpose of my visit...Sightseeing? Visiting relatives? Yes, all of them, and all dead. A visit to the Lodz cemetery, and to Auschwitz.

The trickiest question was, when had I left Poland? Was it in November 1939, the date I departed from Lodz with my brother? Or would it be more precise to give the year 1941? Of course I knew the exact date! I was not at all clear which Poland was implied, the one before the war, during the war, or after. Its borders had shifted with each phase of the war. It could be said that I left the country of my birth not once, but twice, the second time from Wilno/Vilnius in the spring of 1941.

The question about one's father's name, and the omission of one's mother's sorely irked me. Even though I knew that it was customary for a visa application to inquire about the paternal line, on this occasion it upset me. It was a pre-feminist irritation provoked by the need to assert my mother's place in Polish-Jewish history. Once again, she was consigned to oblivion by a bureaucratic lapse. I had an urge to fill in reams of paper with an account of the life and death of both my parents. The names of ordinary people like my parents were the pegs on which hung the history of the war against the Jews.

At home, over dinner, I informed my husband about the visit to the Polish Consulate.

'Good,' he said, 'So there will be no problem about us going in the summer.'

'Not *us*, I'll go alone. And not in summer but now.' I needed to mourn alone and in my mother tongue. In a Poland covered under a shroud of white snow.

R. listened in silence, but a frown on his face showed disapproval. At coffee time, he reached for the file marked 'Family' where he kept my naturalisation documents and removed the folder containing the correspondence with the Home Office.

'Read it. Refresh your memory!'

The letter from the Home Office explicitly stated that in the event of my ever going back to Poland, Her Majesty's government regrets to inform that it would be unable to offer protection of any sort.

'Well?' My husband was adamant that under no condition was he going to be party to such a reckless step and refused to give me the money for the trip.

4
Tearing Through the Iron Curtain

TEARING THROUGH THE IRON CURTAIN

The friend who had lent me the money for the journey saw me off at Victoria station. He was the right companion, himself a man in soulful torment. We were both tearful, as though my departure signified a finality of something as yet unknown. In a way it was farewell, for when I came home I was not the same person to whom he had waved goodbye.

The dictionary definition of a pilgrim is of one who journeys to a sacred place as an act of religious devotion and, as far as I was concerned, the Holocaust victims had bestowed a kind of sacredness on Polish soil. Being a secular person, the decision to go on this pilgrimage was a need to placate the dead. If the prerequisite for such an undertaking is a difficult passage, the journey across a Europe divided by an Iron Curtain fulfilled that condition.

What seemed like an ordinary passenger train turned out to be a geopolitical theatre on wheels in which armed train guards acted out the drama of the Cold War. The irony was that the confrontation was taking place between two kinds of German people, the Westerners and Easterners, who not so long ago had shared the Fatherland of Hitler's ravings.

First, the train cut through a slice of West Germany ablaze with wealth and light, a result of the economic miracle made possible by American dollars. At the approach of East Germany, the train was transformed into a fortress on wheels, signalled by a change of guard. The Western guards replaced by their Eastern opposite numbers immediately locked the doors. Fully armed, they were accompanied by Alsatian dogs held on short leashes. The association with the Nazis was made easy by the fact that they were wearing similar olive green uniforms! They searched the luggage rigorously for stowaways and contraband. A special hostility was reserved for passengers with Western passports. One West German passenger was pulled off the train because he possessed a few marks of East German currency, a serious offence. Their menacing presence was a conversation stopper.

The dog-eat-dog scenario was the sort of punishment my mother would have wished for all Germans. I remember her looking through our kitchen window as formations of Luftwaffe bombers headed for besieged Warsaw in September 1939.

'Mark my words. Their day of reckoning will come. They will pay dearly for this!' And they did. Hitler's '1,000 Year Reich' came rapidly to a devastating end – but still too late for the likes of my parents.

The train was again slicing through another frontier, another part of East German territory, and in the middle of the night, at a final border control, I was woken by torchlight shining in my eyes, too reminiscent of the dreaded Gestapo interrogation scenes that I had seen in countless films. I regretted my decision to travel by train.

When my turn came to be searched, the presence of the uniformed German made my heart pound. Many strands of thought ran simultaneously through my head while he scrutinised my passport long enough to have noticed that I was born in Lodz. An East German would know that during the war it was incorporated into Germany proper and renamed Litzmanstadt. Perhaps he himself might have been a son of the Nazis who had helped to herd the Lodz Jews into the trains destined for Auschwitz. No doubt he would protest that his parents and uncles or their friends knew nothing about what had gone on in the Lodz ghetto. As a faithful Soviet satellite, East Germany had escaped the de-Nazification process. As once they had obeyed their Führer, they embraced Communism with equal zeal.

'Danke schön,' the guard said politely, saluted and returned my stamped passport. I wanted to shout after him: 'Please note that I have cheated the death sentence decreed by your Führer!'

By midnight, West Berlin had come into view. It swam past the train windows like an ocean-going luxury liner, its prosperity advertised in a blaze of neon lights. A little later, approaching the East Berlin zone, the train seemed to collide with a wall of darkness.

I was looking at the landscape through my mother's eyes. The blanket of darkness over East Berlin would have satisfied her. Mother believed implacably in divine justice and the power of curses. Like an oracle, she predicted a terrible punishment for Germany: invoking the curses put on the Egyptians when the Children of Israel were making their exodus. The biblical darkness she had wished on the enemy corresponded with the reality of East Berlin. Her curses seemed to possess a posthumous potency. Germany was punished, torn into two halves: one part too prosperous and the other, a subservient client state, pulled into the Soviet orbit, was plunged into a grey zone of austerity.

Whilst passing through East Germany, conversation in our compartment was reduced to the minimum. However, tongues loosened at the approach of the Polish border. It was a great relief when the Polish railway personnel took over from the East Germans. Even the shabbiness of their navy blue uniforms was reassuring. The sight of their peaked caps decorated with the eagle, the Polish national emblem, brought tears to my eyes. I was saddened to see that the eagle had lost its gold crown. The Communist regime had dethroned the king of the skies and stripped it of its glory.

In London, Mary would have reminded me that the eagle, with or without a crown, was a symbol of spiritual regeneration, majesty and power. Her presence shadowed the journey – after all, it was she who had embroiled me in the emotional tangle with my past and cleared the pathways for the voices of the dead to reach me.

'Hearing voices was too close to the clinical definitions of schizophrenia and paranoia.' I mocked her esoteric method of dealing with my sorrow.

'Don't take it literally,' her voice advised, 'The dead use the living as their mouthpiece.'

Mary was right. My parents' voices lived inside my head. Father's voice was raucous coughing in the mornings, as he cleared his throat. Mother's voice was measured, her words carefully allotted, as though she sensed that she would only have a limited amount of them at her disposal.

As the train ploughed into Poland, the voices of the living took over. I happened to be sharing a dining table with two young Poles who were returning from a recent West Berlin film festival. Their impressions, a mixture of admiration and resentment, were tempered with bitterness.

'Look at us Poles! Paupers!' one of them said, pointing at the shabbiness of the train. By contrast, West Germany, pampered by Western democracies, was rich and enjoyed prosperity and freedom, whereas Poland had ended up losing both.

Passport control drew attention to my British passport, which provoked a lively exchange about passports, a painful issue for people behind the Iron Curtain. How long does it take to obtain a passport in England?, I was asked.

'A week or two, maximum a month.'

The Pole put his Polish passport on the table and asked me to guess how long it took him to get his.

Other passengers exchanged knowing smiles.

'Two years!' He said. 'Two bloody years!'

The information revealed the extent of my ignorance about the reality of life behind the Iron Curtain. I, who now took my British passport for granted, was learning that the possession of such a document was not a citizen's right, but a privilege, to be earned through ideologically correct behaviour. Gaining control over the freedom of movement of its citizens was and is the ultimate weapon used by every oppressive regime.

'We're well-guarded, like women in a harem!' his companion joked.

The reason it had taken so long was the political black marks against his father's family who were classified as 'class enemies'. His uncle had been a pilot in the Battle of Britain and was politically active in the London exile circles: reason enough.

Poor Poland! In the passage of history, it had fallen apart like a badly wrapped parcel. The territory defined on post-war maps as the 'new' Poland didn't correspond to the maps that had hung in my school. At the end of the war, Poland lost a chunk of her eastern territory to the Russians, who in turn 'rewarded' the Poles by allotting them a part of East Germany, a *gift* that the Poles feared would turn out to be a Trojan Horse. An uninvited tenderness stole into my heart and a gnarling sensation twisted my stomach. The train was speeding through a country I had sworn never to set foot in again but my eyes feasted on the landscape I had so longed for. The snow-covered fields were as smooth and flat as a well-ironed sheet and the isolated peasant cottages, weighed down by snow, jutted out of the whiteness. The telegraph poles were rushing by as were clusters of trees clad in snow standing grouped like bridesmaids.

English winters, with their mildness and evergreen foliage, used to make me nostalgic for the sharper changes of season. I loved my childhood winters in Poland, when the earth hid beneath a white eiderdown, and winter's end was signalled by perforations in the melting snow, revealing the presence of the first shoots.

A rabbit ran across the snow leaving footprints as regular as sewing machine stitches.

WARSAW, POLISH AND JEWISH

On arrival in Warsaw, I watched with envy the emotional reunions taking place on the platform, a reminder that I did not know a soul in the country my family inhabited for centuries.

Soon after unpacking at the hotel, I panicked. I lay curled up on the bed crying, unable to leave the room. Time was passing, and I stared at the window: in the morning it snowed, at midday the sun came out, and at about 4 o'clock in the afternoon the light vanished as though a shutter had been dropped from the sky. Night fell and my panic increased. After two days like this, I decided to leave Poland. My husband was right, it was a mistake to have come alone.

A total stranger, a contact provided by Josef Herman, the Polish-born painter, came to my rescue. Josef had been my tutor for a number of years and had become a close friend. Being his pupil was a rewarding experience. 'Drawing is action and painting meditation.' He would repeat, having noticed I was short of the meditative quality but was strong when investing my emotions in bold, large drawings.

Amazingly, we hardly ever spoke about Poland and the Holocaust that had consumed so many of both our families. His erudition and wide reading provided enough fodder for interesting conversation. Josef was for me the proverbial wise man to whom I would turn in times of trouble. Although he was adamant about his decision never to return to Poland, when I told him about my intended 'pilgrimage', he did not try to dissuade me. He sucked his pipe in silence and in a characteristic sign of concentration, placed his hand on his brow.

'You must have at least one person you can turn to when in need,' he said, searching in his address book. Staszek, he explained, was a young man from Warsaw who had recently visited him. He was an aspiring young actor who had impressed him as a cultured and sensitive man.

Josef, in anticipating my crisis in Poland, was true to form. He was equally perceptive in relation to his pupils' work in progress.

Staszek had no telephone so I sent a note with a taxi. Suppose he was away touring in the provinces, or had moved to another address? Worst of all, what if he ignored my note? And if he would turn up, what kind of help could he offer?

He turned up an hour later. Tall and handsome, he looked older than his 25 years, with an uncanny resemblance to the young Laurence Olivier. He soon guessed the nature of my distress from the condition of the room, the trays of uneaten food and my swollen eyes. Our exchange was conducted in a kind of shorthand, immediately touching on the core of my distress.

His girlfriend was half Jewish and he himself had Jewish ancestors. Due to the present political climate in Poland, he hinted, nobody was keen to advertise such connections. In a subtle way he alerted me to a new brand of Communist Party-influenced anti-Semitism. To my shame, I was ignorant of the recent troubles Polish Jews had faced in Poland. The handful of survivors, Communist and non-Communist alike, were being singled out as the enemies of socialism and forced to leave the country in droves. I might not have undertaken the journey had I known more about the situation.

Staszek was in a hurry, he was due at the radio station for a recording, he explained, but would be available in the evening. In the meantime, he promised to send up a book to my room, which might offer some comfort. Soon after, the hotel porter delivered a book: *The Living and the Dead Stones* by Adolf Rudnicki. It also contained a wartime map and I realised that the borders of the Warsaw ghetto had run through the street where the hotel was located.

The book was a collection of stories about wartime Poland, specifically about the Jews of Warsaw inside and outside the ghetto. It described the conditions of hunger inside the ghetto and how children, as young as my son, were trying to smuggle in food at the risk of their own lives. That alone brought every page to life and made me identify closely with the characters.

Rudnicki was a well-known writer in Poland and when I was later introduced to him I confessed how much his book had helped to sustain me when I re-entered Poland, the land of the living and the dead. 'Nothing can be more rewarding to a writer,' he said and kissed my hand.

As promised, Staszek turned up in the evening with his girlfriend and they took me to the Bristol Hotel restaurant, which was a popular hotspot for Warsaw's smart set and foreigners.

'The Gestapo set up their headquarters in this hotel,' Staszek mentioned. The shadow of the legacy of the war crept in through the revolving door. I would soon learn that in Poland, the trails left by the war were everywhere.

The interior, on the other hand, belonged to another age. The mock baroque style, with its high gilded ceilings and the gold-painted angels nesting like birds in the cornices, were sheltering under a false sky.

A female band in long black Victorian dresses, were playing sentimental tangos, foxtrots and waltzes on a small stage. Couples, mostly portly middle-aged men and women, moved gracefully on the dance floor despite their bulk.

This was not a suitable setting for my mood and I wanted to leave, but Staszek restrained me. 'Don't be deceived by appearances,' he said. As if reading my thoughts, he added: 'The mayhem of war is present even in this dining room.'

The mood changed after their friends joined our table and I was slowly drawn into the vodka-soaked world of Warsaw's intellectual-artistic life. Steaming dishes appeared on the table, followed by bottles of vodka in silver containers, chilled like champagne and served by waiters dressed in tuxedos. The reality of the new socialist society had obviously failed to banish the leftovers of some bourgeois customs. In the midst of the general bonhomie, people were keen to tell me *their* stories, about *their* losses and sufferings during the war.

Zosia's Christian father had perished in a concentration camp for the 'crime' of sheltering his Jewish wife and family. Jerzy, a fast-talking, fast-drinking journalist, had lost his father in a round-up as part of a reprisal action. It was a random street raid, which claimed the lives of 15 Poles. The street where they had been shot, Jerzy said, was round the corner from the hotel and he offered to take me there later. A memorial plaque fixed to the wall listed the names of the executed men.

'My mother often goes there to pray. For her, the execution site serves as her chapel and the sidewalk is an altar. She brings candles with her that she lights; and prays, completely oblivious to the traffic around her. She's very practical – always carries a piece of plastic to spread on the pavement before kneeling down.' His mother was not alone. Many others observed such rituals of remembrance. He delivered the story in a matter-of-fact way. The topic of the aftermath of the war would trip me at every junction, like the Warsaw potholes left by bombs.

Someone else mentioned that before the war the Prudential insurance company had had its offices in the Bristol Hotel. With time, the various elements of the evening's tales, like scattered parts of a broken mosaic, began to merge into a cohesive picture connecting the place to my parents' Prudential life insurance policy. So it was here that my father came to arrange a loan, the deed that required the relevant files to be transferred to London!

Seated around the table in the Bristol Hotel dining room, men with chivalrous gestures kissed my hand and engaged me in the ritual of *brüderschaft*, downing vodka with locked arms. In the middle of the bonhomie, Staszek drew my attention to a corner table.

'Look over there. The blond man is Andrzej Wajda. Do you want to meet him?'

The director of the film *Generation*, which had pulled me back to Poland, was sitting only a few tables away. I glanced at him from a distance, regarding his presence as an act of providence. In the unsteadiness of the vodka-induced haze, something wiser than me said 'No'.

LODZ, A ROGUE CITY

In a gesture rooted in Polish pre-war etiquette, Staszek turned up with red carnations at the railway station where I was waiting for the train that would take me to my native town.

While we were chatting idly to keep my nerves under control, Staszek spotted friends and, after a brief exchange, he returned with two young men in tow. The pair stood out in the crowd, everything about them had a theatrical touch: both wore long coats in a cavalier fashion, thrown loosely over their shoulders, and their movements seemed to be co-ordinated as if performing a duet. They also contrasted physically: Cezary was lean and tall, while Andrzej was short and round. Cezary was blond and had delicate, fine-chiselled features and Andrzej was dark and had a round, fleshy face. They greeted me with the traditional Polish hand-kissing and heel-clicking ritual. This chivalrous custom, inherited from the gentry, was another remnant of bygone times.

When the train arrived, Staszek hugged me and whispered, 'I've asked them to look after you.'

Flanked by the two of them, we elbowed our way onto the overcrowded train. During the journey they refrained from engaging me in small talk, for which I was grateful. I was encapsulated in a world of my own.

Lodz, the city where I was born and grew up, was the only Polish city without a significant historical past. No rivers or hills enlivened the drab urban landscape. A rogue city, built on the prosperity of industrialisation, it had grown over the last three centuries from an obscure village into a thriving industrial centre. Its main wealth came from the cotton industry, hence the much-exaggerated claim of its being the 'Second Manchester' of Europe.

It was an El Dorado of opportunities where fortunes were made or lost for some industrial magnates like the Poznanskis, the Schreibers or the Kohns. A narrow band of the middle classes managed to generate a surprising amount of intellectual and artistic vigour. For the majority, the working class, life was a hard struggle to survive. The worst off were the flotsam of the working classes, the lumpenproletariat that lived in slums.

The city had a mixed population: Poles, Jews and Polish-born Germans who, during the war, demonstratively identified themselves as *Volksdeutschers*. Even before the war Lodz had earned a reputation for political unrest. The political climate of the 1930s created favourable conditions for Communist and fascist agitation to flourish. As schoolchildren, we would often find Communist or other political propaganda leaflets stuffed in our coat pockets in the school cloakroom.

Most of the inhabitants of Lodz were newcomers, like my father and his four brothers, who as teenagers flocked from their province to the 'big city', each with a bundle over his shoulder and hope in his heart. The drift from the countryside to the big town was unstoppable.

The crash of the 1920s had hit Lodz hard and was often mentioned in Father's stories about the plague of suicides that had swept through Central Europe. In Lodz, not bankruptcy but suicide was the last refuge for ruined merchants. Father survived the hard times thanks to his entrepreneurial flair, and a little bit of luck. He had learned early in life how to think on his feet and be bold when taking risks.

His first break came after the Great War, initially through buying and selling scrap metal from the defunct German navy. But it was through rubber that he got a chance to better himself. At home I used to treat samples of miniaturised models of rubber as toys; for example, the Michelin Man – he was my favourite rubber idol.

By Polish standards, our middle-class household was comfortably off, and we children, like most, took it for granted. We lived in a large flat in a fashionable part of the city, which Mother filled with stylish furniture, expensive lace curtains and fine carpets. We enjoyed the trappings of good living: a servant, a telephone, a radio and trips abroad. There was even a summer lodge in Glowno, a property set in the forest not far from Lodz. But most importantly, we were sent to private schools to receive a good education.

Father had a great affection for his adopted city. On his walks with his children, he would show off with proprietorial pride the main street, Piotrkowska, rich in decorative mock Gothic or art nouveau features. He never tired of repeating the 'rags to riches' stories about the owners of the most impressive buildings. The legends of how the city fathers made their fortunes and built magnificent palaces adjoining their factories exemplified for him the opportunities that Lodz offered. Father eulogised the vigour represented by these red-brick factories and occasionally he would take me to a factory to appreciate the importance of the machines that pumped wealth into our city.

It had the reverse effect and I felt sorry for anyone who had to work in such conditions. I hated the industrial ugliness of Father's chosen city: the urban landscape dominated by red-brick factories and chimneys belching clouds of soot; the cotton-clogged machines tearing and spinning and the pale, bloodless faces of the workers with fluff stuck to their eyebrows and eyelashes.

And yet what a paradox to be homesick for a place I did not even like! It's a mystery how children, untutored in aesthetics, develop their own sense of beauty and ugliness. To me, the walls of factories darkened by soot looked bruised; their iron-grilled windows made me think of prisons. I longed for far-away cities with graceful bridges thrown across rivers, like the ones depicted on the postcards Father used to send home from his trips abroad. I took it for granted that after matriculation I would be sent to study in either Paris or London, and waited impatiently for such a time.

I hardly noticed how quickly the two hours of the journey had passed. My two companions signalled the approach of the Lodz Fabryczna station. This was the station from which our family used to leave on summer holidays or where we would wait for Father's return from his foreign travels. This same station was the scene of my departure with my brother, then already bedecked with swastikas, and where when Father failed to pass on the gift from Mother.

When the train pulled in it was dark and snowing.

THE GRAND HOTEL

The receptionist of the Grand Hotel, once truly 'grand' and now run down and in need of paint and repair, was scrutinising my passport.

'So you were born here,' she said and in the same breath added, 'Hitler stayed in this hotel when he came to Lodz for the victory parade.' I winced.

'So did my father,' I told her. 'He was a regular here.'

On Sundays, the family would come for special treats that included cakes named Napoleonki, in honour of Napoleon's sympathy for the Polish struggle for independence. The Frenchman's romance with Mme Walewska had endeared him to the nation.

Everything about the hotel irritated me: the old-fashioned servant's buzzers that would summon no one; the radio that crackled as if broadcasting from the moon. I found myself thinking about dogs. Not about my own dog, Puppi, but about the kind that inspired films like *Lassie Come Home* – dogs equipped with an extraordinary homing instinct, always guiding them back home no matter what the distance. Was I born with such a 'doggish' nature?

Homesick people are creatures possessed of an armour-plated memory that neither time nor distance can pierce. The globe is saturated with millions of people driven from their homes and suffering from homesickness, a condition often passed on to a future generation. We live in a world filled with millions of refugees torn by the drive to leave and to return. For many there is no hope of returning home. Perhaps not surprisingly, 'homesickness' takes up less space in medical journals than 'lovesickness.'

For me, 'home' was the people left behind. Mary's advice before leaving London came to my mind.

'Let them gather round you.'

I knew whom she meant. My ghosts, unlike Hamlet's, were the homely kind, requiring neither battlements nor the thunder and clutter of armour. All they needed was someone to welcome them.

I let them gather round me. Mother is putting the white, starched tablecloth on the table in preparation for the Friday night dinner. Kasia is polishing the silver candlesticks in readiness. In the evening, Mother will light them and say the blessings. In the bulges of the silver I see the reflection of the room upside down, and Mother's hands drawing circles of piousness over the flames.

Suddenly the lights in the hotel room went out. The chambermaid appeared with lit candles. 'Fixing the fuses will take a bit of time,' she announced.

Next morning, Cezary and Andrzej unexpectedly turned up and offered to drive me to the Jewish cemetery. They were dressed as if for a Polar expedition, wrapped up to their noses in woollen scarves and Soviet-style headgear with floppy earmuffs. I had indeed mentioned my intention to go there and was touched by their gesture. 'Such caring young men,' I thought, thanking them.

'Its important for me to go there on my own.'

'Wouldn't you like a record of your visit, for yourself and relatives abroad? We have a good camera.'

This was a persuasive argument. Planning my pilgrimage, I neglected to make provisions for taking photographs. I hesitated, but eventually agreed on the condition that they kept a distance from me. Wisely, having obtained consent, they knew they had won and said no more.

In front of the hotel a van was waiting marked 'PWSF'. The logo was painted in large letters.

'What does it stand for?'

'Hadn't Staszek told you? We are Film School students. Despite short notice, we managed to commandeer the Film School van for a whole day.'

They withheld from me the fact that they had also managed to acquire equipment and enough film stock to make a short film. I knew little about the manipulative nature of filmmakers, especially when they get hooked onto a promising story.

'It's a brilliant day. The light is perfect for outdoor shooting!'

Their presumption made me indignant. Andrzej became the main negotiator:

'Don't worry, just a few quick impressions of you in the cemetery.'

Why not?, I decided. Perhaps being challenged by the unexpected was part of going on a pilgrimage.

The students could hardly contain their excitement. They were searching for a suitable subject for a documentary assignment and regarded our encounter as a godsend. Without disclosing it to me, they already had the title: *A Woman in Search of Her Mother's Grave*.

The drive through the city that I described to my husband as the 'ugliest in Europe' was surprisingly enchanting owing to the thick layer of snow.

In the van I was introduced to Celina, a fellow student, who was their sound recordist and continuity girl. Celina said she needed a sample of my voice.

'Say something into the microphone!'

Being told to say anything that came into my head immediately emptied it of any thought. My intimidation surprised me and I had to make a conscious effort to force out a few meaningless sentences.

Andrzej's hands vanished inside a strange-looking black bag with holes for sleeves. As he fumbled with something or other, his face looked strained and his eyes were half shut. It made me think of my gynaecologist when he probed inside me with his surgical-gloved fingers. I burst out laughing.

'I am rewinding the negative,' Andrzej explained.

The approach to the Jewish cemetery ran parallel to the neighbouring Gothic Catholic cemetery. A funeral procession led by a priest was making its way towards the chapel. I envied the mourners the chance to participate in the rite that laid the dead to rest. I had been deprived of the opportunity to perform the basic mourning rituals for my own family – one day I had parted from them, and five years later I discovered they were gone. Vanished! Nothing but a void.

Driving alongside the high brick wall that surrounded the consecrated ground of the Jewish cemetery confirmed its reputation of being the largest in Europe. I never knew how immense it was. When we reached the main gate we found it locked and not a sign of a living soul.

'Had you warned the keeper about your visit?' Andrzej asked.

Somehow it had never occurred to me that a cemetery might be locked during the day. Andrzej saved the day. He knew the keeper and was familiar with his habits. Many of the Film School students, including him, were frequent visitors to this place.

'It's a fantastic place for camera exercises!'

I resented the fact that, for these young people, the Jewish cemetery had become an area in which they could sharpen their professional skills. The Lodz cemetery was doomed, and like many others in Central Europe was facing the prospect of dying through neglect. With the burial of the last Lodz survivor, there would be no one left to care for it, and the rupture between the living and the dead would be final.

Andrzej, despite his rounded shape, had managed to squeeze through the gap in the wall. While waiting in the unheated van for his return, Cezary pulled out a sailor's sack from under the seat with an oversized pair of peasant boots stuffed with two pairs of thick hand-knitted woollen socks.

'That's for you,' he said, 'to protect you from frostbite.' Celina pressed on me a sleeveless jerkin that smelled of goat hide and was sizes too large. She also produced a sailor's rope meant to keep the layers of clothing secure. Little by little, the degree of the students' preparation for the cemetery shoot was becoming obvious.

Andrzej returned with the keeper, who unlocked the gate and got into the van with us. Karol, a man in his sixties, was grey-haired, with a weather-beaten face. He was eyeing me with a sly kind of curiosity.

'She is from the school?' he addressed Cezary.

'She has come from England to search for her mother's grave.'

'In this weather! *She* might as well be looking for a needle in a haystack,' he said. Let *her* come back in summer. In their exchange my presence was ignored.

'I speak Polish.' Once more his sly look settled on me.

'In which part of the ghetto section was your mother buried?'

I only knew the date of her death: May 1942. After the war had ended, a friend of the family had put up a proper tombstone. The good woman who had done this sent a photograph of the grave and no other information. She had since died.

He scratched his matted hair.

'I warn you, finding unmarked graves is problematic.'

'I would like to try.'

He invited us to his living quarters, a room that was part of the cottage adjoining a morgue, heated by the iron stove. It resembled a storage shed, filled with rusty gardening equipment, spare bicycle wheels and a pile of bric-a-brac. On the windowsill lay old and torn Hebrew prayer books. We sat on his bed covered with a stained military blanket.

'What is the family name?' On hearing my name he inquired which of the Hamermeshes was my father. He knew their names from the tombstone inscriptions. When told Father's name his eyes widened to take a better look at me.

'You're the daughter of Josef Meir!' To him, my presence was nothing short of a miracle. He well knew how the lottery of survival was stacked against the Lodz Jews. Karol shook his head in disbelief when told that all three of Father's children were alive. How was it possible, in the midst of so much carnage?, his eyes seemed to say. The occasion called for a celebration, he said, filling some tumblers with vodka. I had come to Lodz to lay my mother to rest and had instead found a man who had known my father personally.

Before the war he used to make his living as a driver of a horse-drawn *droshka*, a popular means of transport for people who could not afford taxis. In fact, there were more horsedrawn buggies in Lodz than taxis. And Father, who was a commercial representative of the Dunlop company, was trying to modernise the wheels used by the *droshka* owners. It was not easy to persuade them to replace the commonly used solid rubber bands for the more advanced system of pneumatic tyres.

After the war, on account of his smattering of Yiddish and familiarity with the layout of the cemetery, Karol landed the job as its keeper.

'To life!' Karol toasted, and drained the vodka by tossing his head back.

I was in the presence of a witness to my father's past life, and was soaking up his vivid recollections.

'He would offer credit for six months, or even a year.' He said it with chuckle. 'Among the drivers your father had the reputation of being a soft touch.'

I vividly remembered Mother's moans about Father's habit of lending money without security. She feared he was squandering his children's inheritance with his cavalier attitude towards money.

'When your father would visit the Baluty, the slum neighbourhood where most of us lived, he always kept in his pockets sugar cubes for the horses, and sweets for the street urchins.'

I still associate sugar cubes with the horses' hot breath smelling of hay. Father would place a cube on the palm of my outstretched hand and guide it towards the horse's mouth, reassuring me that it would not bite or kick. The frothing saliva at the corners of its mouth, where the harness pressed into its flesh, alarmed me. So did its curled lips and the large, yellowed teeth. Father's affection and trust in the animals helped me to dare to look into the horse's eyes.

Totally absorbed in the keeper's reminiscences, I missed the commotion in the room. The students had set up the lights and mounted the movie camera on a tripod. While Andrzej was fiddling with the focus, Cezary was looking for a socket in the wall. The loose-hanging socket blew a fuse.

A strange instrument was held up against the keeper's face and mine – to the uninitiated it seemed a bizarre ritual, but Andrzej explained that he was using a light meter to gauge the light level.

'Not enough light,' he announced, looking glum.

After the second fuse, Andrzej cursed Cezary with a string of juicy expletives.

'Idiot! We missed a marvellous scene!'

The students decided to abandon the interior location for outdoors.

Gusts of wind were scooping up snow from the ground. It was a photogenic scene but the students were beset with another crisis. The camera motor had frozen. Andrzej took off his sheepskin coat and wrapped it round the camera, in the hope that it would thaw out. By this time it was too dark for filming. No exposure!

Just as well, I thought, and informed Karol that I would return next summer, this time without a film crew.

Mother would have to wait a while longer.

THE FILM SCHOOL

It was dark when we departed and the thick snowflakes whirled in front of the van's headlights like frosty white moths. My head was splitting from an excess of impressions and vodka. I was keen to get back to the hotel.

The snag was that the van and the equipment had to be returned before the school's storeroom was locked up. Worried about being late, the students asked if I would mind a detour before being driven back to the hotel. It would have been churlish not to agree.

Arriving at the gates of the Film School, I realised that we entered what had been once the property of Baron Oscar Kon, an industrial magnate whose residence was considered a palace. It was a place that Father liked to take me for walks – for him it was a showcase for middle-class aspirations. The marble colonnades and the well-kept gardens, visible through the massive wrought-iron gates, were responsible for my acquired taste for pretentious architectural grandeur.

'Child,' Father once said, 'when you grow up, with God's help, you too may live in a place like this.' For him, nothing was beyond the realms of possibility, and all that was needed in life was determination and luck. And Lodz provided enough examples of the rags-to-riches stories to sustain such hopes.

Baron Kon and family were dead and the marble mausoleum at the Jewish cemetery he had provided for his descendants lay in ruins. But his residence, the 'palace', by becoming the home of the Film School, was buzzing with life. My coming to Baron Kon's pre-war property seemed providential.

Wide-open doors led into a spacious room with highly polished parquet floors. An impressive chandelier was alight for the special evening event, the premiere of a student's graduation film.

Everyone was talking about Roman Polanski, whose diploma film *Two Men With a Wardrobe* was to be presented. Anecdotes about his outrageous behaviour in general, and in particular during the shooting of this film, were recounted with indulgence. '*Roman did this...Roman did that...'* Obviously a colourful character, he had made his mark on the life of the school. He was of short stature and his urchin's looks harmonised with the *enfant terrible* reputation he had earned.

'Would you like to stay? Or we could drive you back now?' My companions were waiting for my decision.

In the corridor were displayed posters of films made by the graduates of the school, amongst them Andrzej Wajda's. What had begun in London at the Academy Cinema with his film, *Generation*, had led me back to Kon's palace, where Father promised that one day fate would make a 'palace' like this accessible to me. The bewildering coincidences that I had encountered since my arrival were unsettling. I felt as if invisible hands had guided my steps.

I now regarded Andrzej and Cezary with a different eye. So this was the place where students like them, men and women, were actually taught how to make such inspiring films. I decided to stay.

Two Men With a Wardrobe started with an unforgettable image: two tramps, staggering under the weight of a large mirrored wardrobe, surfaced from the waves of sea. The wet mirror, reflecting the sky and the racing clouds, added a celestial weight to their burden. The two men and their cumbersome, waterlogged wardrobe make their way towards the town. The interaction of the men with the wardrobe and the townsfolk takes the story into the realms of the absurd. The images on the screen suggested a marine version of a Golgotha; instead of the Cross, the tramps were carrying the debris of a shipwrecked life.

When the lights came on, I took another look at the author of the film, trying to reconcile the contrast between his reputed extrovert character and what had come out from the depths of his imagination.

After the projection the students had gathered in groups discussing the film. Some thought it was too anarchic: the authorities would never permit the film to be sent to an international festival. Others complained about its lack of recognisable realism. Cezary liked it for its allegorical quality. Andrzej pointed out that I was bound to miss political allusions to Poland's present-day regime.

The school's atmosphere was relaxed and nobody was overtly anxious about who might be listening, and could possibly denounce them. Apparently the Lodz film school had a reputation for taking political liberties.

My thoughts went on a high-wire walk, and an inner voice was warning me not to look down, only ahead. The powerful desire to make films was staring at me! The idea had spread warmth, perhaps induced by the effect of the vodka or the light dancing across the chandelier. I wondered if it would it be possible to relocate my Muse from painting to the screen?

'How do you become a student here?' I asked, feeling as if somebody else was using my voice. Andrzej and Cesary exchanged amused looks.

'Speak to the Dean in English. He's a snobbish Anglophile.' They laughed, and I was not sure whether it was their reply they found funny or my question.

Worried that I might have received an adverse impression of the head of the film school, they took turns to assured me that Professor Teoplitz was an accomplished film historian who had done a lot for the reputation of Polish films worldwide.

After more toasts to the glory of films, I was too drunk to remember how I got back to the hotel.

LUNCH ON SUNDAY

It was Sunday. The maid came into the room and announced in a dramatic voice: 'A frost colder than any in living memory has hit the country. It's even split some trees!' It was an exaggeration; a winter of similar severity was recorded during the war.

The weather had interfered with my plans to leave Lodz. Power cables had snapped and trains were immobilised by snow blizzards. It was tempting to stay in the warm bed, a refuge not only from the biting frost but also from the turmoil in my mind. An interminable monologue kept up the speculations of 'What if?'

What if my brother and I hadn't left home and instead went into the ghetto with our parents? Could we have protected them better from the ravages of the ghetto hunger?

'Don't hide in the bed!' Mary's voice urged me.

Where else if not in bed? It is the place where birth and death collide, where life enters through the birth portals and exits in a shroud.

'Don't intellectualise! You have come this far, don't stop now.'

Eventually I ventured out and made my way to the street where we had lived. The balcony of our apartment was gone and the raw marks of the amputation were still visible. What had once been a well-maintained apartment house was now in a state of decay. The raw, chipped bricks showed under the grey, peeling plaster, and the lopped-off balconies were not the result of the war's destruction but of the class warfare against the bourgeoisie. The wreckage had been inflicted not by the war but by socialist neglect that makes no provision for maintenance.

Amazingly, the fragile thermometer that Father had affixed to the window five years before the war was still there. This delicate instrument had survived whilst my parents, along with most of the other Jewish inhabitants of the building, had perished.

Anyone home? I'd come home! If I ran up the stairs, sticking to the fate-appeasing formula of two steps up and one step back, and pressed the buzzer...

Kasia, the maid, rushes from the kitchen to open the door and gathers me into her arms. In the excitement, the single pin made of tortoiseshell that holds up her mousy bun drops to the floor.

My older brother might be home. The smell of cigarettes, smoked secretly in the toilet, betrays his presence. When he emerges and we meet in the corridor, he grabs me under my chin, knowing that this brings on spasms of giggles.

My father, hidden behind a newspaper, with only the top of his head visible, looks up and announces: 'My child, what interesting things are going on in the world!'

Mother is bent over the kitchen table. The bulges of flesh visible under her dress show where her corset has been laced up too tightly. She scrutinises me to make sure if I've come home in one piece – rusty nails often left marks on my clothing or flesh.

Puppi, my brown-coated chihuahua dog with pink eyes, permanently shivering, emerges lazily from her box. She scratches under her ear and runs out to greet me, licking my face all over.

My reveries were interrupted by the approach of a man whose speech identified him as a Jew. Otherwise his face, with watery-blue eyes, sunken flesh hanging on his high cheekbones, as if on hinges, made him indistinguishable from other Poles.

'Excuse me, are you looking for someone? I have been watching you just standing there.'

He could tell at a glance, he said, that I was a stranger and wouldn't be surprised if everyone else in the street wasn't watching me too. In Poland, he went on, people like me often provoke hostility.

'The Poles get nervous when they see people from abroad. They fear they have come back to claim their property.' I followed his anxious look to a small group of Poles commenting on my presence.

'I once lived here.'

'Sieradzki,' he introduced himself, rubbing his red hands vigorously. 'You'd better make a move. Come with me and meet Mrs Kutz. It's lunchtime, her hot soup will warm you up.'

He led me to an apartment in a nearby house. The staircase smelled of Jewish cooking and stepping into Mrs Kutz's apartment was like being yanked into the past. Everything was familiar – the dark mahogany furniture, the huge, German-style sideboard displaying crystal vases and silverware. Even the two kitsch oil paintings, one depicting an old Jew praying and the other a winter forest landscape with wolves chasing a horsedrawn sleigh, rendered the wall they hung on an uncharted territory inhabited by ghosts.

'That's Mrs Kutz,' he said, pushing me forwards. Without his heavy winter coat, Sieradzki looked taller and skinnier.

She was a short, plump, middle-aged woman whose round face showed traces of her faded beauty. Green, cat-like eyes shone with the confidence of one who has been used to male attention.

'Take off your coat and eat with us.' While setting a place for me at the table, she talked about how the service was terrible in the state-run restaurants where the food was neither fresh nor clean. She pointed to the five diners sat at the table. 'I cater for their special diets, they all have such delicate digestions.'

The five elderly men made room for me at the table, listening to Sieradzki's story of our encounter, assisted by vivid gestures.

'She was standing on such a cold day, with her head stuck up, staring at a window, as if glued to the spot. It started to snow and still she made no move. I said to myself...'

Mrs Kutz interrupted his flow. 'We haven't got all day to listen to your stories. Let her eat!' She inquired about my culinary preferences. 'Do you like sweet carrots with raisins?'

Sieradzki felt impelled to continue. 'Excuse me, I said...' Mrs Kutz interrupted again, reminding them that on Sundays the cook had to leave at five.

Sieradzki was not going to be deprived of a chance to display his narrative skills and took up the story again.

'She was tearful. It was not my business, but I said, "Excuse me Miss, but why are you crying?" "I lived here before the war," she said, and said that nothing was left of her home but that thermometer.'

A plate of steaming boiled beef, served with boiled potatoes drenched in gravy was put before me. Mrs Kutz was facing me across the table with her arms folded on her stomach.

'What have you got to cry about? You should be happy! You were not here.' Was it a reproach or a plea? She threw up her arms in a gesture of impatience, and I noticed the faint blue concentration camp number tattooed on her wrist. Mrs Kutz's green eyes studied me. My presence in Lodz intrigued her.

'Now my dear, let's hear what really brought you here.'

Sieradzki was on the point of saying something but she ordered him to keep quiet.

'She has a tongue, let her use it!'

'I think its guilt,' I mumbled.

'What do you have to be guilty about? You should be grateful to be alive. Such talk is sheer nonsense.'

'I've come to find peace of mind.'

'Peace of mind,' she repeated sarcastically, 'you settle inside your own head, or you get it from a doctor's prescription.' She herself took pink pills for nerves, along with others for high blood pressure, and some for sleep. No one in their right mind would spend good money on a journey across the Iron Curtain to find *peace of mind*.

'Unlike you, Sieradzki, I'm no fool. Nobody can fob me off so easily.'

'Now let's hear the truth. You need not fear, we're one big family.' She held no secrets from the other diners. They all help one another. Was it about property or a currency transaction? Had I brought dollars or pounds? She winked at the men. Evidently some of them were partners in her black market currency dealings.

Among these people my own heartache made no sense. My denial about any monetary interest created consternation. Finally, I said, 'My parents were in the ghetto and my mother died there. I have come to find her grave.'

Mrs Kutz's eyes lit up and she repeated in a voice hushed with reverence: 'A mother's grave is a mother's grave!'

She immediately took command of the situation. First, I would have to meet Mr Lubitch, an old Jew who remembered a lot about the burials during the war. Secondly, I must consult the files of the ghetto burials in the Jewish community office. And very important, the keeper of the cemetery should be well-tipped. If anyone knows their way about the cemetery it's him.

'Don't mislead the girl. It's not so simple,' a grey-haired man cautioned.

'Abrahams, did we not find the grave for the American last year?'

'That was summer, now it's winter.'

Mrs Kutz was not having any of it. 'Where there's a will there's a way,' she quoted the proverb. She promised to do all in her power to help me find my mother's grave.

After she left the room everybody started to talk at once. What was my name? Whose daughter was I? Someone else knew of a Hamermesh who had owned a large felt store. 'That was my Uncle Bernard.'

The heat inside the room made my nose and eyes run. I felt like a parcel being unwrapped: strings had been snipped and the contents were spilling out. I was looking for my home and instead Sieradzki had found me staring at a rusty thermometer. He caught me watching the place I had stolen into a million times, the home I had hauled on my back, like a snail.

A man who until then was quiet, recalled that he knew my mother and her two sisters in the ghetto.

'A proud-looking woman,' he said, 'who kept herself to herself.'

He had worked in a bakery where she would come begging for bread, not for herself but for one of her sick sisters. The last time he had seen her was in Zawisza Street, shortly before her death. She was so emaciated that the dress she wore seemed to hang on her like a tent.

I clung to his every word. Which aunt could it have been? Rozia? She had a beautiful voice and was my favourite. Tyla? She was childless and would 'borrow' me for weekends and spoil me rotten. In any case, I had to know more. Was it winter, spring, summer or autumn? I tried to imagine my plump, heavily built mother starved, walking through ghetto streets wearing a yellow star pinned to a dress that hung on her like a tent. Miriam, her 'little dressmaker', made all of her dresses from the fabrics she selected with great care. Every detail about Mother inside the ghetto brought her to life.

Until now, any recollection of my mother always ceased abruptly with the scene of our separation, and of her despairing cry 'I'll never see you again!' as I broke free.

Somehow, I mentioned the name of Chaim Rumkowski. He was the uncle of a young man I got to know in Jerusalem. This caused uproar.

'Who have you brought to my house?!' Mrs Kutz reproached Sieradzki. 'Let no one mention that name in my presence. Curses on his memory! Children he murdered!'

At Mrs Kutz's I discovered that Rumkowski's name was anathema to Lodz survivors. But Rumkowski's reputation as a murderer of children conflicted with my own memories of the tall, handsome man with prematurely white hair who would affectionately pinch my fat cheeks whenever he encountered me with Father. He loved children, and the Jewish orphanage that he administered was the pride of his life. His marriage was childless and Father thought that in caring for orphans his frustrated paternal feelings found an outlet.

Rumkowski was adroit in squeezing contributions from well-to-do Jews like my father. The Grand Hotel was one of the places where he would approach potential donors.

At Mrs Kutz's dining table I was forced to replace the elderly, attractive and charming gentleman of my childhood memories with a murderer of children, of the sick and the old.

'GIVE ME YOUR CHILDREN!'

The Merchant of Lodz is the title of the book written by Adolf Rudnicki, the same writer whose earlier book was offered to me by Staszek as an introduction to the drama of the Warsaw ghetto. The title, suggestive of Shakespeare's tragic Jewish merchant of Venice, was apt, for only the bard could have done full justice to the tragic character of Chaim Rumkowski.

In the ghetto, where over 200,000 people were squeezed into an area consisting of a few slum streets, his official title in German was *'Der Alterste der Jude'*, or 'The Elder of the Jews'. The Germans had selected him randomly, without anything particular recommending him for the job. When he accepted the appointment, he couldn't have foreseen that the Germans, his taskmasters, had chosen him to perform the thankless task of exercising the power of life and death over his fellow Jews trapped in the ghetto.

He proved himself up to the task. An energetic, first-rate organiser, he ruled the ghetto like a mini-state with a fully functioning administration, a police force, a prison, a court of justice, municipal kitchens, food rationing, hospitals and an 'industry'. The ghetto was run on the principle of 'Those who don't work, don't eat!' Chaim Rumkowski passionately believed that his approach could save the population from annihilation by making the Jews indispensable to the German war effort, and to this end he was prepared to use force if need be. He mobilised a large labour force, which included even small children. The virtual slave labour was terrorised by the Germans and the harsh rules of the ghetto administration. And then the deportations began, by which time nobody believed in the deception that it was 'resettlement for work'. Each German decree increased the demand for a higher number of people to be surrendered.

The countless books I would read and the films I would see about these events could never compare with the impact of Mrs Kutz's story of what took place on 4 September 1942. Mother was then still alive and Father would certainly have witnessed it.

'The morning was sunny, as if the summer refused to depart.' Mrs Kutz recalled the date of the public meeting outdoors when Rumkowski made the following announcement in person.

'A grievous blow has struck the ghetto. *They* are asking us to give up the best we possess, our children and our elders. Fathers and mothers, give me your children! Fathers and mothers, I understand you and see your tears...All children below the age of ten, old men over 65, and the sick, are to be surrendered for resettlement.'

'Like hell he did! The scoundrel was childless!' Mrs Kutz's rage was as fresh now as it must have been then. She took a deep breath, the memory of that day left her breathless.

After the meeting, panic-stricken people tried to find ways to win a reprieve for their children and elders. The streets were filled with crazed parents besieging every kind of registration office. Any scrap of paper, false birth certificates or newly signed health certificates that could prevent their children's deportations would do.

Next day, a total curfew was imposed and a commission consisting of Jewish policemen and medical personnel searched each house. Mrs Kutz had hidden her five-year-old son Josele in a place she believed to be safe. From her window she could see screaming children carried out to vans parked in the street, followed by weeping mothers. In the raging madness mothers were attacking the ghetto police whose duty it was to check that no one was missed.

Mrs Kutz's room was 'visited' by two doctors and two nurses, and a policeman who knew Mrs Kutz personally. She felt confident about the safety of her son but not of her aged father. Her father's condition condemned him. Not yet sixty, he was suffering from a bad skin condition and was prematurely aged from hunger. When her turn came, one of the two doctors who examined her noted her swollen ankles.

'I can tell you, we were all swollen from hunger. The idiots went about their business as if at a Marienbaad clinic.'

She was beside herself with grief when they took her father who went quietly, too weak to protest. Just then her sister burst in with the news that her little girl, hidden in a drawer, had been discovered and taken to the van outside the house. Mrs Kutz and her sister ran to the lorry that was already loaded with children and old people. They pushed, determined to get close to the lorry, but a cordon of militiamen held them back. Their father was consoling his weeping daughters, promising to take care of his grandchild.

Then, ominously, the arrival of the Gestapo added to the chaos. The parents who had managed to hide their children in closets, toilet seats, boxes and cellars, scattered at the sight of the Germans. Mrs Kutz rushed back to her room, determined not to give up her Josele. When all went quiet and the lorries departed, she went to her son's hideout. He lay so quiet, so peaceful. The search had lasted too long and he had suffocated in the cramped space.

'My Josele was dead.'

Mrs Kutz rocked herself in the chair, her grief as fresh now as it was then. Some months earlier she had buried her husband. 'I carried Josele to his grave in my arms.' She held out her arms, which were still aching from the emptiness.

After the liquidation of the ghetto, fanciful rumours were circulating about Rumkowski's lust for power and status. 'The Caesar of the Ghetto', as the people mocked him, was by then a man in his sixties, who had remarried a much younger woman. The rumours told that 'The King of Jews' was parading in a carriage pulled by four white horses, that he and his courtiers indulged in orgiastic feasts where champagne and caviar were served while the rest of the ghetto population was dying of hunger. Apparently the Germans dispatched him to Auschwitz in style, in a first-class passenger train. Rumours claim that on arrival, he was beaten to a pulp before he reached the gas chamber.

Rumours were rumours, but the truth, if there was an element of truth in them, tells another story. History is still undecided in its verdict about his role in saving lives.

A merciful darkness had spread outside the double-glazed windows of Mrs Kutz's dining room. Mr Abrahams went over to comfort Mrs Kutz.

'Enough memories for one day. What about another glass of lemon tea?' She stopped rocking and sprang up from the chair, soon returning from the kitchen with a tray of aromatic tea laced with cherry juice.

A bold, moon-faced man, who had kept quiet throughout the afternoon, timidly inquired, 'Tell me, have you seen the Queen of England? What a fine woman, bless her.' His question made everybody laugh.

'Is it true that Prince Charles was circumcised by a *Mohel* [a Jew who performs circumcision]?'

Once again, the Royal Family inadvertently interceded. The coin my husband had tossed that landed with the Queen's face up had decided who stayed at home and who went to see the Polish film at the Academy Cinema. It seemed an appropriate ending to my Sunday lunch at Mrs Kutz's privately run enterprise in socialist Poland. It was time to leave.

HONORATKA

On the way to the hotel, I passed a dark street with a brightly lit window of a cafe with the appealing name of Honoratka. After Mrs Kutz's dining room, the neutrality of a cafe crowd promised a respite. I opened the door and a gust of frosty air shook the chandelier, producing a chime. 'Shut the door!' the waitress's voice called out.

It was small, but the large mirrors fixed to the walls made it appear larger. The hot air was filled with clouds of cigarette smoke and an odour of melting snow brought in by customers' coats and boots.

I was pleased to find the familiar faces of Andrzej and Cezary. They, too, were relieved to see me, as they feared I had given them the slip. Instinct warned me not to mention Mrs Kutz or her customers. Film students in search of suitable subject matter would have fallen upon them like hungry wolves.

Cezary and Andrzej's friends joined our table and it soon became obvious to me that news of their 'scoop' had already spread. I was identified as the subject of their forthcoming film.

Honoratka, I discovered, held an important place in the intellectual and artistic life of post-war Lodz. It was a place where writers, journalists, the theatre and filmmaking crowd gathered. Warsaw had been devastated and Lodz, being the nearest big city left intact by the war, had become the base of Poland's post-war film industry.

In this close-knit artistic community my presence had created a stir. Honoratka served as a second home for the film school students, where they rubbed shoulders with their tutors as well as with established filmmakers. It was also the place where they hatched many of their film ideas and sharpened their critical faculties. A gust of wind brought in an elderly Gypsy fortune-teller. Like many of Honoratka's customers, she, too, was a regular, although not very welcome. The waitress gave her an unfriendly look while others just ignored her intrusive offer to read their future. Doing the rounds, she reached the table where I was sitting. The Gypsy's kohl-painted dark eyes drilled into mine with great concentration.

'I haven't seen you here before,' she observed. She was wearing a colourful woollen wrap over her shabby black coat. A florid scarf with fringes was tied round her head and a strand of loose, greying, frizzy hair obscured one of her eyes. Huge earrings, the size of curtain rings, hung from her ears.

Cezary and the others at our table were loudly deriding the Gypsy's fortune-telling tricks.

'She is smarter than any of us. By now everybody in Honoratka knows where you come from.' Cezary resented her intrusion, but Andrzej scolded him.

'Leave her alone!'

My own mother was not averse to consulting fortune-tellers. Anything to do with the future was preferable to digging into the past. The Gypsy and I moved to a separate table.

She took my hand into hers and shifted her attention to the fate lines etched on my palm. She assured me that everything she was about to tell me was the truth.

'*A Guardian Angel looked after you when you were in danger. The Angel of Death has been close to you twice. A huge sadness clouds your soul,*' she said, looking up. There were also three lines for children, she said. She waited for confirmation. I had had three pregnancies, but had given birth to only one child. It was uncanny.

'*Your success line,*' she said, '*is thin but gets thicker. A surprise triumph is in store. I see a public event, chandeliers, princes.*'

From time to time her eyes searched mine for clues. '*I see no husband next to you.*'

She looked at me questioningly, but I let it pass. Why spoil it for her? I was not going to tell her that she was wrong.

A big change awaited me, she said, no longer looking at my hand. Her own hand was trembling from the effort of holding up mine, and, as she adjusted her position, the sleeve of her coat moved up to reveal a concentration camp number. The blue tattoo was a six-digit number, unevenly etched on her skin. The veins bursting under her skin made them look knotted together.

She noticed my reaction and her eyes misted over. '*Gypsy woman was in Auschwitz. All family dead.*'

'If Gypsy fortune-tellers are so smart, why didn't any of them foretell the catastrophe awaiting them in the war?' an irritated Cezary challenged. She pretended not to hear his comment.

'You'll come back here many, many times,' she continued, unperturbed, lingering on in the hope of getting a generous tip. Satisfied with what she got, she mumbled a Gypsy blessing and moved on to try her luck with other customers.

The Gypsy woman took me back in time. She could have been a member of the tribe that used to pour into our courtyard during the spring seasons of my childhood.

In the years 1941–42, for a short while, the Jews and Gypsies encountered each other in the Lodz ghetto. Within the cramped boundaries of the Lodz ghetto, the Germans set up a Gypsy mini-camp, a ghetto within a ghetto, a provisional enclosure, separated by barbed wire. The Gypsies, a few thousand of them, families with children, were kept in total isolation from the Jews with the exception of two Jewish doctors that were sent in to monitor them during a typhoid epidemic.

Before the war, my father, through his business contacts, got to know a branch of a distinguished Gypsy family who had been settled in Poland for generations. The Kwiek dynasty left an imprint in the annals of Lodz more than once. Scenes of score-settling between rival claimants to the Gypsy throne were reported in the local press.

Since Poland's independence, in 1918, there were three chief claimants from the Kwiek family to the 'royal' title. Of the three brothers, Michal Kwiek II was the most enterprising. In the early 1930s, he included in his vote-catching pre-election promises a startlingly original idea: the formation of a Gypsy state in the land of Gypsy origin somewhere in India, near the holy Ganges river. He even petitioned Mussolini for an audience. Could he have been influenced by the Zionist dream of return to the Zion?

Michal Kwiek II travelled extensively in Europe courting the attention of the press, aware of the importance of newspaper coverage. Unfortunately, he attracted the unwelcome attention of Polish police, who kept an eye on his less legitimate dealings. His two brothers, both of them rivals to the throne and the royal title, were eliminated through foul play – Roman, by profession a *droshka* driver, landed in hospital, badly injured, and Elemer, a street vendor by profession, lost an eye. My father would have known some of the gossip concerning the 'court' intrigues, spread by the *droshka* fraternity in Lodz.

Having disposed of them, 'His Royal Highness' Michal Kwiek was crowned with great pomp near Lodz, in a forest glade, in 1935.

About the coronation, the press in Lodz reported:

The throne was covered with purple cloth and the crown was of gold, set with diamonds. This was a departure from tradition, in which a gold imitation crown decorated with glittering pieces of glass was used.

The article ended with a question:

How did Kwiek manage to amass so much gold?

The glittering aspirations of the Kwiek clan symbolised by the gold-plated crown and the crimson cloak did little to benefit the community at large. The bulk of the Gypsies were poor, exploited and persecuted by the host population.

With the German invasion, the Polish Gypsies, like the Jews, were routinely rounded up for deportation to Auschwitz and other death camps.

At first, when the Gypsy camp was set up at the Lodz ghetto, the Jews could hear Tzigan music, but it soon stopped. They were forbidden to play and their instruments were confiscated. Some surviving photographs, taken by the Germans, show hollow-cheeked Gypsy faces with feverish black eyes, children's emaciated hands pushing through the barbed wire, begging for water and bread.

A typhoid epidemic speeded up the liquidation of the encampment. The Gypsies were simply killed off and buried in a designated small plot within the ghetto section of the Jewish cemetery. The Jewish gravediggers were the only witnesses to the brutal manner of their death. They reported that the bodies showed signs of hanging; some of the corpses still had ropes round their necks. Many had limbs crushed as well. Perhaps they had resisted. Rumour had it that the Germans forced them to hang each other in order to save bullets.

Abram Roseberg, one of the Jewish gravediggers who survived, reported the following episode:*

One morning, in autumn 1941, the van with the boxes of dead Gypsies arrived for burial. A child's whimper could be heard from one of the boxes. The gravediggers opened the box and pulled out a girl aged three or four, half-naked with a rope still around her neck, showing signs of breathing. They revived her and she soon regained

* Jerzy Ficowski, *Cyganie na polskich drogach*, Kracow, 1985.

consciousness. The child tried to tell them what happened but none of them understood her language. Deliberating on what to do with her, their supervisor took the decision to send her to the ghetto hospital. Unfortunately, the Germans heard about it and removed her from the hospital, threatening to punish the gravediggers. The following day, the same child turned up at the cemetery for burial, this time definitely dead.

When I think about Father in the ghetto, I like to imagine that when he chanced to hear the sounds of the Tziganer fiddlers, he remembered the valley in the Tatra Mountains where he and his three children savoured the robust spirit of Gypsy life.

VISITING HOME

Before my final departure from Lodz I was overcome with an irresistible urge to step inside our home, to pass once more through the door that had witnessed my separation from Mother. My guilt required a symbolic crossing of the threshold where mother and daughter would make peace. In my mind, the scene unfolded with clarity. The door would open and I would present a bunch of flowers with apologies for daring to disturb the present tenants. Surely there was no harm in inviting myself in for a brief visit? And when leaving I would use Mother's phrase, 'May God bless you.'

I chose six red roses which the florist tied into an elaborate bow with white ribbon. When I rang the bell, my heart was racing.

The door opened slightly, secured by a chain. An angry voice called out, 'What do you want?' An elderly woman was looking at me with suspicion through the gap. I mumbled something to the effect that I had once lived here. Before I even had time to hand the flowers to her, the door shut in my face. From behind the closed door, the woman launched into a loud tirade, addressed to a collective *them*.

'Who do they think they are? Turning up as if they had rights here. They sucked the blood of poor Poles, amassed fortunes and now come back to upset God-fearing people!'

The hostile reference to the 'they' cut through me. I felt murder in my heart! I banged and kicked at that door, charged with enormous strength. I could have wrenched that door off its hinges.

Attracted by the noise the concierge appeared, whose menacing stance was enough to make me retreat. This dishevelled man, who stank of drink, addressed me in the purest gutter language: 'Woman, move your arse from here! If you don't go this instant, I'll kick you so hard you'll fly all the way back to where your ancestors come! Hoplah, be gone, you cholera!'

Had I possessed a gun, the concierge would have been a dead man as well.

Inside my head, I heard my husband's mocking voice, 'Charming! So this is the Poland you longed for? To encounter barbarians like this? For heaven's sake, Mira, was your journey really necessary?'

I needed help, and turned to the journalist I had met at the Honoratka, who had given me his card. I found him at the offices of his newspaper. He was sympathetic to my determination to gain excess to my old home.

'Poles dread such visits. It reminds them in whose homes they live.'

His intervention was effective, official arrangements had been made 'through the right channels' for me to gain access. Soon after, two militiamen turned up to escort me back.

The concierge, now tidier and almost sober, greeted the representatives of law with ingratiating bows. It had been a terrible misunderstanding, he said. Neither the woman nor he had any idea who I was, or why I wished to visit the apartment. The militiamen brushed past him, ignoring his explanation.

The door, which only a short time ago protected an enemy fortress, was held wide open. The woman, standing at the door, greeted me with a pained smile.

'Come in, come in,' she pushed aside a child who looked at me with curiosity. One of the militiamen entered first and waited for me to follow, the other stood behind me.

I could not make a move, overcome by a feeling of disgust with myself and shamed by my own capacity for murder. The door with its peeling paint and the loose buzzer had turned me into a violent person, even if only in thought. Given the opportunity I would have attacked the woman. This was not the kind of daughter my mother would have welcomed across the threshold into what had once been her domain.

I remembered how Mother used to bemoan the fact that her children's moral standards were slipping. 'God forgive me! I don't want to see the day when my own children become like *them, pogrom-czyks!*' She both feared and abhorred the Polish rabble that so often harassed their law-abiding Jewish neighbours.

'I've changed my mind and no longer wish to enter.' I thanked the militia for their help. The two representatives of socialist law and order exchanged puzzled looks. What the hell was going on?

They had orders to escort me to the apartment, and orders were orders! One of them mumbled under his breath, 'Women! Why can't they make up their minds?'

For the woman who had cleaned up the flat, and had probably removed items that had belonged to my family, my refusal to enter rang alarm bells. She burst into tears, begging me to enter. She feared that, from now on, the authorities would be at her heels and would make life very difficult for her.

Nothing would make me change my mind.

The next morning I was packed and ready to leave Lodz. To my annoyance, the woman turned up at the hotel and stalked me to my breakfast table. She had something very important to tell me, she said. I did not invite her to sit down.

She and her husband had lived for years with the suspicion that somewhere inside the apartment was hidden a 'Jewish treasure'. A fortune-teller whom she had consulted had read it in her cards. Her husband had searched for any telltale signs of a hiding place and even went as far as lifting sections of the parquet floor. It stood to reason, she carried on, that Jews who had lived in spacious apartments like ours were rich. Dollars, gold and jewellery were always the things people tried to hide. Many Poles redecorating or converting their homes often found buried treasures in walls, under floorboards, in pipes and in loft rafters.

'Now you've come to retrieve it.' It was not a question, but rather a statement. My visit had confirmed their suspicions.

'Madam,' she said, 'according to Polish law, such findings must be declared and passed over to the state.' She watched for my reaction and quickly added, 'It's best not to involve the militia. They'd only let you keep a pittance.' She would be satisfied with a small share, let's say one-third? After all, she and her husband deserved it, having kept it safe for me for so many years. Why not come to a satisfactory arrangement?

This farcical scene was hardly a fitting component for a pilgrim's experience. I looked with pity at the woman whose husband turned into a treasure hunter of Jewish caches of gold and other valuables. My old dislike of my native city was revived. I could not wait to leave and ordered a taxi to take me to the station.

A VIP IN HELL

Auschwitz was a short distance from Cracow (once the seat of Polish kings). At the Saski Hotel where I was staying, the receptionist was most helpful about ways of getting there. I was in luck, a visiting French VIP, a guest of Cracow University, would be picked up the following day by a car from the Ministry of Culture. She was sure that neither the official guide nor the VIP would object to my joining them.

The VIP was a Professor of Contemporary Military History, currently researching the subject of French prisoners of war who were assigned to an ammunition factory adjoining the Auschwitz death camp. He was middle-aged and stocky, a sad-looking man with dark, hooded eyes hidden behind dark glasses.

The car, a Volga, was a showpiece used for official functions in most Soviet satellite countries. It was a comfortable limousine, I was seated next to the driver and the VIP was sitting at the back, with his official guide, a chatty young woman who spoke fluent French. Next to her was her ten-year-old son who had been brought along 'for the ride'. When I challenged her about the wisdom of exposing a young child to the horror of the death camp, she protested: *'Everybody should be made to see it! Children should learn about it as early as possible!'* The guide's voice betrayed a fierce determination about the importance of seeing 'it'.

I thought about our family visit to Poland with my husband and son. I certainly wouldn't bring my child at such a tender age to Auschwitz. When he was older, yes; but how much older? What is the right age to confront the kind of horror that Auschwitz represents? Thirteen? Fifteen? Or twenty? Is there an age ripe enough to equip the heart and intellect to cope with it?

In truth I had already failed to protect my son from the full impact of what happened to his Polish grandparents. I had no idea of when or how an idea about the gas chambers had seeped into his consciousness until one particular episode drew my attention to it.

When my son was five I had taken him on a summer holiday in Spain. We had stayed on the outskirts of Ibiza in a house close to a farm, and on hot days we were plagued by swarms of flies. In the mornings, before departing for the beach with him, I would shut the windows and spray fly-killer in all the rooms. When we returned, I would throw the windows open and sweep up the dead flies.

Once, I noticed my son standing at the door, watching intently as I scooped up the mess. One or two flies were still thrashing on the floor in a death dance. Suddenly he asked, 'Was this what the Germans did to your parents?'

His question made me flee from that house the very next day. I rented an apartment overlooking the harbour, hoping that the view of the Mediterranean Sea and the harbour with boats would banish his thoughts about the dying insects.

At the time of giving birth to him, I myself had no idea to what extent I had been psychologically contaminated by the Zyklon B knowledge. Was it at all possible that the invisible toxins of the 'Auschwitz fallout' infected even me, who had been spared the horrors of the Nazi atrocities? Had I unwittingly passed it on to my son?

The guide was still going on about the subject of the beneficial effects of confronting Auschwitz. *'Reading about it can never prepare anyone for the beastliness of the Nazis and their fascist helpers.'*

In the official Communist version, all the victims were 'martyrs of anti-fascist resistance'. The Jews and Gypsies who were singled out for the Final Solution were mentioned only in passing. I presumed that it was her job as a government 'minder' assigned to foreign visitors to toe the Communist Party line. Most of her phraseology was derived from official party jargon: 'the ongoing war against fascism', 'West German capitalist warmongering' and 'the American capitalist exploiters'.

The road from Cracow was hilly and the thick snow gave the landscape a touch of pristine cleanness. It would have looked different to the crowds squashed inside the speeding cattle trains, peering through the gaps of the blocked-out windows.

While travelling in the comfortable Volga, my thoughts turned to my father's ride to Auschwitz. Given his age, middle forties, it was a remarkable feat to have survived the ongoing selection in the ghetto. The fact that he was amongst the last Jews to be deported from the Lodz ghetto, just one month before the end of the war, galled me!

He must have felt very much alone in the cattle train he shared with a crowd. My mother was already dead, as were his brothers and my mother's relatives. Perhaps some of my cousins were with him?

Facing death he would have still been worried about his missing son in Siberia. Perhaps true to his optimistic character, he retained the hope that his son would survive.

The Volga reached a gate bearing the inscription '*ARBEIT MACHT FREI*' ('work liberates'). The meaning of the words cast in black iron letters and fixed to a decorative frame had become over-familiar due to the impact of photos and films. For those who entered through it as inmates, it would have had the power to confuse and muddle the mind.

I had anticipated that powerful emotions would overtake me, but nothing of the sort happened. I felt hollow; no emotions stirred in my heart. The air above me felt light, the winter sky was crystal clear and the sun was shining! I was deaf to the murmur of agony left by those who had passed through these gates.

What sense could an artist make of this place? My painter's eyes, trained to observe contrasts of light and shade and the harmony or disharmony of colours, were of no use here. No canvas was large enough, no wall high enough to accommodate the theme of Auschwitz. Chimneys, smoke, ashes, crematoria, barracks, roll calls, selections, left–right, right–left, corpses, mountains of shoes, women's hair, artificial limbs, discarded spectacle frames, all of which could only add up to a surreal montage. Ironically, during my visit the thick layer of snow had made the place obscenely beautiful.

Films about concentration/death camps create an illusion of 'seeing' with one's own eyes. The unblinking eye of the camera faithfully recorded the skeletal men and women wearing bizarre striped 'pyjamas', moving like zombies among heaps of dead naked bodies. What the cameras failed to capture were the dreams, the prayers and the thoughts of the victims, alive or dead.

In my need to explore the camp through my father's eyes, I detached myself from the VIP's tourist itinerary. I shut my eyes and tried to imagine the doors of the cattle train unlatched. What greeted the starved and thirsty Jews from Lodz upon arrival? What did their eyes perceive; what did their ears hear, their nostrils smell? Later I realised that it was a fraudulent attempt; it was beyond the capacity of one's imagination, however vivid.

Some books about Auschwitz that were written by talented eyewitnesses who were themselves inmates can help one to enter this mad world run on a bookkeeper's logic. Tadeusz Borowski's *This Way for the Gas Chamber, Please* offers a ferocious description of what greeted the stunned and half-dead Jews, who had to step over the companions who had died during the journey. Primo Levi is another example of a helpful hand offered to people like me, whose eyes are open but who suffer from a metaphysical cataract that blurs the view.

As Father tumbled out onto the sidings, he would have been greeted with blows, and the *Kapo*'s (a Nazi-appointed orderly in a concentration or death camp, usually chosen from amongst the detainees) shouts of '*Schnell! Schnell! Schnell!*' The Germans were in a desperate hurry, for it was dangerous to give the victims time to realise where they were. Every trick in the book was used to confuse their sense of reality, including the practice of deception. To force them to hurry they were pushed and beaten or shot at. At all costs the Germans had to prevent resistance. Even enfeebled they could still use the last bit of their strength to resist or spit in the faces of their tormentors. '*Schnell! Schnell! Schnell!*' In the absence of proper industrial efficiency, the chaotic death machine demanded speed.

I had come as the daughter of a father whose shadow was trapped in this hell, in the hope of getting closer to his spirit and of picking up a handful of ashes. In the end it wasn't my head or my heart but my feet that were picking up the horror of the place. My feet were stepping over the lanes sprinkled with the ashes of the victims.

The snow crunched under my boots. Feeling warm in my cosy fur coat, fur hat and fur-lined boots, I thought about the inmates who wore only thin cotton garments and wooden clogs and who had had to stand in line for long hours during the interminable roll calls. They were always conducted before daybreak, and in winter it was still pitch dark. In summer they were exposed to extreme heat and frequently got sunstroke. I marvelled at the capacity of starved, maltreated bodies to adapt and survive against such terrible odds.

I made my way to the only surviving gas chamber 'shower room' and discovered I was not alone. The French Professor was staring at the ceiling and the fake shower fixtures from which, instead of water, the Zyklon B poison used to flow. To my surprise, he pulled from his pocket a folded skullcap and covered his head. In an almost inaudible voice, his lips hardly moving, he began to recite the Kadish, the Hebrew prayer for the dead.

I moved close to him. The Professor cried for his wife and his two young children; I, for my father and other members of my extended family. A wounding grief united the two Jewish mourners who were sharing the space where members of our families might have choked to death. His prayer turned this concrete chamber into a sacred space and filled me with a tranquil piety necessary to bring me close to Father's last choking breath. It held at bay a demon-driven scream for revenge.

The anxious guide interrupted our shared 'service'. She had come to collect her lost VIP, as she was not supposed to let her charges out of her sight.

I stayed on and tried to imagine the chamber after the doors had been sealed. When the showerheads began to hiss, panic would have broken out and the choking, coughing and spitting would have begun...

This ceiling and the walls of the gas chamber retained scratch marks left by people's nails, evidence of crazed desperation. Some victims must have climbed over each other, hoping to reach an area where there was still some air left to breathe.

I shall never know what my father's last thoughts were. Perhaps he uttered '*Shamah Israel*', or maybe he cursed his struggle to stay alive for so long in the ghetto. One thing was certain: he would have been comforted by the absence of his children in this place.

THE MAN WHO GAVE ME POLAND

Zakopane is a popular winter resort located in the Tatra Mountains. In the past, it used to attract winter sports holiday-makers and people sent by doctors for a change of air. Like my Father, who visited Zakopane regularly on a doctor's recommendation, I, too, found myself here on the doctor's advice.

In my case it had begun with a nosebleed inside the Auschwitz 'shower room'. Nothing unusual, I thought; I sometimes had them, and I knew what to do. I sat down on the concrete floor and leaned my head against the wall. The remedy, which in the past had always been effective, on this occasion failed me. In addition to the nosebleed, I became aware of a wet sensation between my legs. At first, I thought I had unexpectedly started to menstruate. But the bleeding was stronger than my usual flow, soaking through my tights and pants. I was bleeding from both orifices, yet I felt no pain! I was sitting on the same floor, where my naked father might have walked.

Back in Cracow the hotel doctor suspected a haemorrhage and recommended a gynaecologist who after the examination seemed intrigued by my condition.

He wanted to know if I had heard or read about the phenomenon of spontaneous vaginal bleeding, which had been a regular occurrence in the gas chambers. I knew nothing about it. The doctor, having done some research about the effect of Zyklon B poison on women's reproductive organs, filled me in. The teams of *Kapos* in charge of removing the corpses and cleaning up the mess in readiness for the next batch of victims observed that the floors of the gas chambers were covered in blood, and congealed with faeces and urine. Even women, whose menstruation had ceased as a result of hunger and stress, would spontaneously start to bleed during the few minutes it took to die. It was as if, just when the women were choking to death, the uterus squirted blood in its last affirmation of life.

The gynaecologist was of the opinion that, in shock, my body had mimicked this condition: a case of psychosomatic identification. He prescribed the old-fashioned treatment: rest, the sun and mountain air, the best of all healers.

'Before you go home to your family in England. Give yourself time to recover.'

A medical referral made it easier to obtain a hotel room during the high season. It was the time when anybody who counted in Polish society was likely to be seen in Zakopane. In the People's Socialist Republic, Zakopane had acquired a reputation of being frequented by the crème de la crème of Polish society. What counted now was not the wealth of the 'rotten capitalists', but party privileges. For Poles it was a time for hedonistic pursuits: sport, drinking, dancing and sexual dalliances.

The doctor's remedy proved effective. The mountains, the rarefied air, the sun and the effect of the high altitude acted like a tranquilliser. The landscape offered an affirmation of nature's majesty, helping to pulverise the images of Auschwitz. Every morning I would take the ski lift to the top of the mountain, hire a deckchair and keep away from the neatly arranged rows of suntan enthusiasts. I would change the position of the chair to avoid the loudspeakers of the nearby restaurant, blasting out old-fashioned, Polish popular tunes.

The puffs of clouds drifting idly between the snow-covered mountain peaks carried my imagination to a plateau where everything was possible. In the imaginary meeting between my parents and my English family, their voices bounced and echoed.

'Say hello to your Polish-born grandparents!'

I nudged my son to approach them, but he recoiled in shyness. At the sight of her grandson, my mother's eyes glazed over in tenderness. With no common language to break the barrier, she might have said the first thing that came into her head. 'My grandson, bless his soul!'

My father, on the other hand, would have managed to establish an immediate rapport with his grandson. An uncritical admirer of everything English, from tweeds to the insipid tea drunk with milk, he would smile adoringly at his English-born grandson, and his son-in-law, a real English gentleman!

A spray of snow hitting my sunglasses ruined my reverie. As well as being a shield to screen my eyes from the glare of the sun, the glasses were also a way of hiding. I became aware of a skier wearing a black and red anorak. Leaning on the ski poles, he said 'Hello,' and waited. I pretended to be asleep. I must have resembled an Egyptian mummy, wrapped up in layers covered with a blanket up to my chin. He glided away and I tried to retrieve the imaginary reunion of my family. They refused to reappear.

The following day, with the skier's next appearance, my self-imposed seclusion was shattered. Whatever remote place I chose for my deckchair, there was no hiding from him. He circled my deckchair performing pirouettes on skis, like a bird flaunting its plumage. My unresponsiveness to his repeated attempts to strike up a conversation did not deter him. It seemed to encourage him. The skier would break his rapid, sudden descent by halting within inches of my deckchair, apparently in order to demonstrate his mastery.

At the end of the day, watching the sunset, at the point when the swollen red disc just missed touching the jutted peak before vanishing, I heard him say, 'If you don't hurry, you'll miss the last ski lift.' He was next to my deckchair, without his goggles. Before I could say thank you he sped away. At the ski lift, the skier's black and red anorak stood out, he was standing at the entrance of the lift, having kept it from departing. As I entered, he gave me a quizzical look.

We were descending through a sky being drained of daylight. The valley below was filling with a liquid greyness, as if molten lead had been poured into its crevices.

In the evenings the hotel would shake to the sounds of vigorous dance music and rowdy activities. I avoided the dining room and had food brought to my room, engrossed in reading the books about wartime Poland and the Holocaust. I welcomed overcast days that kept me indoors. In my post-Auschwitz existential crisis there seemed nothing strange about the fact that I conversed with the God of Mother's ancestral rabbis. I had turned my back on God, having lost Mother's faith.

'Daughter, don't grant a victory to Hitler's vision of a world without Jews. Remember you owe a debt to the people who saved your life!'

Secularism had not shielded me from the question of how to deliver oneself from the horrors of the gas chambers and how not to succumb to the command of revenge. How to forgive without forgetting?

The skier's attempts to make contact progressed to written messages delivered to my room. The first message was an invitation to dinner in which he promised to distract me from whatever troubled me. I politely declined, not wishing to be distracted. The next message delivered with flowers accused me of being an English snob set on ignoring the 'natives'. I ignored this note too, but how could he know I came from England?

I was ready to go home, and booked my return to Warsaw from where I intended to fly to London. No more crossing borders by train! No more Germans!

On entering the train compartment, I was annoyed to find the skier already installed next to my own reserved seat. No longer in his ski outfit, and without the goggles and earmuffs, wearing a dark grey suit, he reminded me of a demobilised soldier going home in civvies. In response to my grimace of displeasure, he stood up and offered his card as a formal introduction. The spidery lettering gave his name and academic title: 'Zb. C. Lecturer at the Anthropological Faculty at Warsaw University.' A forced smile failed to hide his unease, volunteering an explanation of the 'coincidence' of sharing the same compartment.

'The receptionist arranged it.'

Intrigued by my aloofness and driven by curiosity, he had bribed the hotel receptionist, who was not impartial to a gift of her favourite brand of chocolates. She was most helpful with information about me. I was neither deaf nor dumb, but avoided contact with people, she informed him. He learned that I was born in Poland and lived in England. Another gift, of an even larger box of chocolates, contrived a seat on the train next to mine.

'That's how things are done in Poland.'

There was a tinge of irony and self-mockery in his conclusion. The journey was long enough to enable him to find out the reason for my unfriendliness, which he suspected was due to my contempt for Poles. Whatever his original impulse, he also desired a chance to practise his rusty English.

Angry over the trick he played on me, I opted for the 'on your head be it' attitude. The train was leaving the mountains behind and riding into the greyness of the dusk hour, when I began to unpick the tangle of thoughts provoked by my pilgrimage to Poland. Doing it, I realised how much I was in need of letting go. The transient nature of relationships forged during train journeys made it surprisingly easy to unburden myself.

I was grateful for his attention. His eyes served as a kind of sanctuary for my heartbreak. Eye contact, so troublesome to the English, for Poles is an invitation to cross the bridge of separateness.

'Poland! Nothing left but ashes and bitterness.' I lamented.

While I was rejecting my connection to Poland, was he already saving the discarded bits for future repair?

It was now his turn and he described his life in a dry, almost academic style. His father was an officer in the Polish army and was captured by the invading Soviet army and never returned, vanishing along with countless other Soviet prisoners of war.

During the German occupation, he and his mother, a doctor, stayed on in Warsaw. Life was hard for her struggling to bring up her only son. After the war, just when things should have begun to look up, the Cold War politics stepped in, when his father's brother, who fought with General Anders' army in the Middle East and then went to England, decided, against his friends' advice, to return to Poland. Uncle Edek was simply homesick and had had more than enough of wandering. Besides, he felt a responsibility towards his sister-in-law and young nephew.

Six months after his return, Uncle Edek was arrested as an agent for the Polish government in exile. His mother also spent three years in prison, accused of being an accomplice of Uncle Edek and his 'treasonable intentions'.

'It was not easy,' was all he was prepared to say. Information about his personal life was reduced to a few laconic sentences. He had been married, but was now divorced with two children, a girl and a boy. His ex-wife was a doctor and she had remarried. His academic life was in better shape, he said with a smile. He was lucky that his mother's political 'black marks' had not interfered with his chance to study. Except for the imposed limit of 'no field trips abroad', his career had not suffered. His application for a passport had already been refused twice.

His views about the socialist state were amusing and astute.

'The party resembled the proverbial bad mother who never lets go of her charges.' He said. The state's control over its subjects was all-embracing. Luckily, in Poland, unlike Russia, such rigours were more difficult to enforce. The people were too anarchic and too individualistic. It was impossible to keep them as isolated from the rest of the world as the Russian people were. The Polish Diaspora was scattered in every corner of the world and thus economic necessity had loosened some chinks in the Iron Curtain. Poland was desperately short of foreign currency and the Poles abroad were sending dollars to their relatives.

None of this was familiar to me; I was only beginning to learn of Poland's post-war problems.

The train was approaching Warsaw and we began to say goodbye. The skier, who in Zakopane had found my detachment so irritating, hoped that, in spite of everything, I would visit Poland again. And next time not for a reunion with ghosts, but to find pleasure in rediscovering the new Poland.

The hand-kissing ritual marked the end of our shared journey in which a casual meeting had been transformed into a meaningful encounter. We were no longer strangers; each had learned something about each other's pain. I gave him my London address, in case his academic work ever brought him there. At the Warsaw station, the bustle of porters and luggage and passengers trying to manoeuvre skis through the carriage windows, had separated us.

There was a long queue for taxis and my travel companion reappeared, coming to my aid. After being pushed and jostled, within minutes, he displayed another useful skill: that of commandeering taxis from under other people's noses and holding his ground in spite of the noisy protests. Seeing how difficult it was to get hold of a taxi, I invited him to share mine.

At the hotel where I had a reservation, he gallantly helped with the luggage. Once inside, he insisted I check at the reception about my reservation. We said goodbye for the second time.

While I was filling in the registration form, he again reappeared, this time holding out a bunch of keys and, looking ill at ease, he said, 'Please, let me give you back Poland. With those keys...'

He felt that a hotel was not the right place for someone like me.

Was this another of his talents: winning women's favour, as he had done with the receptionist in Zakopane? He must have read my mind, for he immediately added, 'Don't misunderstand the offer. The keys are to my apartment but I'll be staying with my mother. Please don't say no...' He would like me to have the experience of staying in a *home*.

The receptionist was watching the scene 'Is this man bothering you?'

I caught the eyes of the man who wanted to give me back Poland! Some gift! A country fought over by three major powers in the last three centuries! For Jews, Poland was a graveyard.

Without a word I reached out for the keys. He was right. A hotel was not the place for me, a pilgrim coming towards the end of a spiritual journey.

On the way to his apartment I learnt that he lived on Dluga Street, which had played a role in the Warsaw ghetto uprising.

Before the war it had been a vibrant Jewish neighbourhood. Under the foundations of the newly developed estate lay buried the debris of Jewish life.

His apartment was in a block of flats and had all the hallmarks of a bachelor pad. It was small but compact and tastefully arranged. While he briskly went about the task of changing bed sheets and putting fresh towels in the bathroom, I cast a quick glance around the place. Books, records, and on the walls were hung enlarged photographs of South American Indians' faces. They were a welcome presence, as they, too, were a decimated people to whom he had given a home.

He instructed me on how to make a long-distance phone call to London and left his mother's phone number, 'Just in case.'

'In case of what?'

'A police raid, for instance.'

I thought he was joking. But no: in principle, as a foreigner I had no right to stay anywhere privately without being registered with the police. Was it risky for him, I inquired? He shrugged his shoulders and added: 'They no longer send us to Siberia.'

Before leaving he asked if I would like him to show me Warsaw the way a regular tourist should see it. We agreed to meet for lunch and he offered to pick me up.

I phoned London and my husband was delighted to hear about my plans to fly home soon. In a few days time I would be back in London with my son, husband, friends and my paintings.

Curiosity got the better of me, in spite of being aware that I was trespassing on my host's privacy. I examined his life by looking at the things displayed on his desk, such as the photographs of his smiling children, son and daughter, who, like their father, were flaxen-haired. The books and photograph albums gave me a glimpse into my host's intellectual life. A whole shelf was filled with books about primitive warfare in English, French and Polish, and the Polish anthropologist Malinowski had the place of honour. I browsed through his books of Polish poetry and leather-bound editions of Russian classics, possibly a family heirloom.

In the magazine rack amongst some Polish magazines was an outdated, much-thumbed copy of *Men Only*. I was sure this was not meant for my eyes.

His flat was on the fourth floor. I leaned my head against the window pane, and waited to pick up some vibrations from the ground below, just like children do when they listen to telegraph poles, mistaking the faint buzz of whispering wires for echoes of people's conversations. Warsaw had risen from its ruins, and the windows of the new high-rise buildings resembled honeycomb patterns of shimmering lights. It stirred a deep emotion in me. So I did care after all!

I could hear sounds of neighbours' activities. A baby was crying. The lift went up and down and from the floor above I could hear someone pulling the toilet chain. The ordinary sounds took on a special significance. The walls were not groaning, the people behind these walls were breathing, snoring, shitting or fucking. The sounds were reassuring. This was life! His bachelor flat made me feel 'at home'!

In the past, I had managed to persuade myself that I was capable of feeling at home anywhere and everywhere. Mary Williams had called my bluff. It was the desperate bravura of someone who felt permanently homeless! My sense of homelessness permeated everything I touched. I couldn't even give a stable home to my own creativity. I kept losing track of my own paintings, drawings and pieces of writing left scattered at various addresses. I would simply abandon them without much bother or care. My homelessness had become second nature.

The phone rang. At first I hesitated to pick it up in case it was a call for my host, perhaps from a woman friend, impatient to talk to him after his return. It rang persistently, until I finally picked it up. His mother, in a way of welcome, wished to invite me for lunch the following day. Was there anything special that I liked? A Polish mother was going to cook for me! A mother for heaven's sake! The church bells struck midnight. Under the skier's roof, it was the hour of friendly ghosts.

ANIA

Zb.'s mother, Dr Krystyna, was a tall, dignified-looking woman in her mid sixties. An old-fashioned high-piled coiffure made her look older, as did her clothing in all shades of dark grey and black. She represented the archetypal, continental widow in perpetual mourning. By contrast, her sparkling blue eyes preserved a remarkably youthful and cheerful expression. Like her son's when engaged in a conversation, they were attentive and expressive.

She lived in a pre-war apartment. The house had miraculously been spared the bombardment and luckily had escaped the plunder of the retreating Germans.

When I tripped over her frayed carpet she was apologetic about the condition of the furniture and fixtures, worn out from the years of use.

'In socialist Poland maintenance is a real problem.' Her complaint was uttered in a forgiving tone.

A gynaecologist by profession, she had earned distinction in her branch of medicine. Before the war, she had got herself into trouble with the Catholic Church by trying to propagate birth control clinics, a rarity in Poland. This was an aspect of pre-war Polish life about which I knew nothing. In an ironic twist of fate, after the war, Dr Krystyna again landed in trouble with the authorities, this time with the socialist regime. She strongly objected to the wanton use of abortions as an accepted, or even recommended, means of birth control.

'Instead of providing proper birth control they scrape women's wombs like parsnips.'

Dr Krystyna, who had spent a lifetime championing birth control clinics, faced defeat in a country that, for economic reasons, favoured abortions. Now retired, the issue still made her 'blood boil'.

'Go into any pharmacy and what do you see? Official leaflets urging women to contact the nearest abortion clinics about unwanted pregnancies!'

'My mother is a fighter.' Zb. beamed admiration for his mother's fighting spirit.

Even in prison his mother gave them hell fighting for the privileges rightfully due to political prisoners.

'And would you believe it, she made a point of learning, article by article, about the principles of the Communist judicial system. Even today she could recite them in her sleep! In Russia she wouldn't have come out alive!'

'My son is making too much of it,' she said, twisting her wedding ring in embarrassment. The skin on her hands was almost transparent, showing up the protruding blue veins. Looking at them made me think of the scores of new-born babies these hands brought into the world – a world which had turned out to be a death trap for millions of them. And even now, the world with its grandiose claims for a bright Communist future was still not a fit place for masses of women.

The dinner table was set festively: the best silver and china, a crisp starched tablecloth and pre-war serviettes with the family monograms on them, were elegantly displayed. Preparing lunch, she was mindful not to include pork in the cooking, which was her way of showing respect for the Jewish dietary laws. I was not an observant Jew, but I appreciated her concern. Her hospitality was in keeping with the best of Polish traditions.

From the moment the three of us sat down to eat, I became aware of an absent person. *Our Ania* was the name of the young girl in the framed photograph standing on the sideboard.

'My sister,' Zb. explained.

'Not a blood sister,' Dr Krystyna corrected him. 'All the same, much loved by us,' she added.

I was looking at the door, half-expecting the girl from the photograph to join us at any minute. Ania was a blonde, blue-eyed girl of ten, self-consciously posing for the camera.

'Our Ania was full of mischief'; 'Our Ania was the best pupil at school. She played the piano like an angel.' Dr Krystyna's references to the girl exhibited a fierce possessiveness.

'And what a skier!' Zb. quickly added to the list of her accomplishments. He must have instructed her, I thought, having witnessed a display of his own excellence as a skier. Mother and son breathed life into Ania, their monologues creating space for Ania's own unspoken lines. The absent girl lived on the margin of their lives, coming out whenever summoned. On this occasion, for my benefit, more black and white snapshots were put on the table that showed her as a beautiful girl, from infancy to the age of 14. Ania dead, and was I listening to a private service of composed eulogies?

Ania was about three years old when, in the autumn of 1942, she had come into their lives. Dr Krystyna was a member of Zegota, an underground network of Christian Poles involved in the rescue of Jewish children from the ghetto. The help consisted of finding safe hiding places for the children smuggled out, either in monasteries, convents and orphanages or in private homes. The organisation also provided false identity papers. The stakes for this kind of charity work were high: anyone who was discovered to be aiding or hiding Jews, irrespective of sex or age, was under the threat of death.

Ania was smuggled in a horse cart transporting used bricks from the Warsaw ghetto, hidden under bricks in a concealed box. The box had holes for air and the child was given a sleeping pill to keep her from crying. Poles who were engaged in trafficking people did it for profit, with the exception of the Underground members.

Any transaction involving the smuggling of Jews from the ghetto involved large amounts of money changing hands.

Ania's parents must have rewarded the go-between, who in turn would have rewarded the cart driver handsomely. A large share would also have ended up with the Germans guarding the ghetto gates. Bribery was the essential condition of such a deal.

The cart driver, who was transporting the goods with the box of the hidden child, met his first whiff of trouble at the ghetto gate. To his horror he discovered that the regular guard with whom he had an existing arrangement had taken sick and his replacement was dissatisfied with the permit he produced. The German guard was about to begin his search, but the arrival of a party of Gestapo high officials, who had priority, saved him. He gave a sigh of relief when signalled to move out of the way.

Once safely on the Polish side, due to the delay at the checkpoint, the child woke up and began to whimper. The driver was still some distance from his destination and feared that the noise would attract the attention of the Polish police. Alarmed, the coachman, as a precaution, got rid of the child's documents entrusted to him. There was still the danger from the roaming Polish 'Greasers' who knew that any vehicle arriving from the ghetto might be hiding a Jew and that there was a reward offered for each Jew delivered to the Gestapo.

A sudden downpour emptied the streets. The coachman invoked Jesus' name in thanks for such divine intervention from the sky.

'Even the heavens favoured Ania's survival!' Dr Krystyna beamed.

The box was delivered to her apartment without any identification documents. It was covered with a reddish brick dust when the box was opened. She found next to the whimpering child a silver baby spoon embossed with the girl's first name, Anabela. It was wrapped in a man's monogrammed silk handkerchief.

'Our Ania [Dr Krystyna's preferred name for Anabela] was born with the proverbial silver spoon in her mouth,' Dr. Krystyna commented. Her son nodded in agreement. The child's placement with Dr Krystyna was meant to be only temporary. Originally, she had been earmarked for a younger foster mother, but the woman in question was discovered to be suffering from TB. Dr Krystyna was asked to look after her until a new 'safe' house could be found. When assessing her age, she had to take into consideration that ghetto children were often physically stunted. With the help of a paediatrician, the child's age was determined to be about three or four.

'The dear little heart was such a bundle of joy. Imagine, at my age, I wanted to mother her!'

She was a woman past 40, her body bombarded with menopausal flushes. For all she knew, she might have been a widow, if she believed the rumours about the fate of Polish officers taken prisoner of war by the Soviets.

'It wasn't an easy decision. At the time, my son was twelve years old.' A tender smile livened up Dr Krystyna's lined face as she told about the miracle of her love for the undernourished, sickly child.

In spite of her efforts, Dr Krystyna never managed to find out anything about the girl's family – not their name, nor whether the child's parents were still alive, or if they had already been deported.

The timing of Ania's arrival had acquired an almost mystical meaning. Prior to the event, she had had a dream in which she was walking in a forest with a girl aged five. They were passing a wrecked shrine and found on the ground a damaged statue of the Madonna with a missing arm and the infant Jesus with a chipped off nose. The girl had picked up the damaged effigies to play with them. 'Don't!' Dr Krystyna called out. 'They are not dolls.'

'Please, can we take them home?' the child pleaded.

The dream troubled her. She was a professed agnostic and regarded the intrusion of the symbols of the Catholic Church as unwelcome – even in her dreams.

A week later, Ania was 'delivered' to her.

'Do you believe in dreams?' She looked at me with an expression that said, well what do you make of that? I assured her that I certainly did.

'The dream must have been some kind of an omen,' she concluded.

The fact that Ania was Jewish made her even more determined to keep her. Before the war Dr Krystyna had had many Jewish patients and had delivered scores of their babies. For all she knew, the girl's mother might have been one of her own patients. From the moment she bathed the child for the first time she felt a symbiotic kinship with her. Saving Ania's precious life from the Nazis would be her victory over the enemy.

'There was my son to consider. When I asked for his opinion do you know what he said?'

'Mother, enough about me!'

'He said, she can stay – on the condition that she be kept away from his collection of tin soldiers.' This was the first time I heard her laugh. Her son left the room in search of a bottle opener, complaining it had been moved from its usual place.

'At twelve, did he understand the gravity of the situation?'

'He certainly did. Children mature early in wartime.'

Dr Krystyna was aware that, by keeping Ania, she was risking not only her own life, but also his. Neither of them would be spared if Ania's origin were to be discovered. He accepted the new rival for his mother's affection without much resentment. In no time, Ania had captured his heart as well. Mother and son shared the infatuation with Ania who had emerged from the box like a miniature Aphrodite to enchant them.

A flirtatious glint lit up in Zb.'s eyes.

'Ania was a born ravisher. Everybody adored her and she knew it!'

Such an extreme example of altruism made me think how would I have behaved if placed in a similar situation. Would I have put my only son at risk in order to save the life of a stranger's child? It brought into the open the uncertainties I harboured about my own generosity of heart.

Love was not enough. Precautions had to be taken to protect Ania and themselves. Dr Krystyna invented a suitably fictitious family connection. Ania became the daughter of a married niece who lived in the country. The 'fictitious' mother from the country made frequent visits, ostentatiously displaying her maternal concern for 'her' daughter. One had to be watchful about the neighbours and particularly the concierge who was known to take an excessive interest in the affairs of the tenants. Dr Krystyna made Ania's 'health problems' a constant topic of her conversation in the neighbourhood. The child needed medical attention, which she could only get in the big city. She even got a colleague from her clinic to backdate a file with details of Ania's intestine problems.

It was her son, a smart lad obsessed with detective stories, who thought up the idea to arrange a photographic session with all the members of the family, including Ania – an undeniable proof of her 'belonging'. Luckily, Ania was fair and could pass for a gentile. With the right looks and right family roots, the child also had to be seen as a good Catholic. For Dr Krystyna, it was a sacrifice of sorts; she herself had stopped attending church after she had begun her medical studies. She and her son became regular churchgoers. She even cultivated the friendship of a young priest, who became a frequent visitor to the house. For Ania's sake, she set up a shrine in the living room for the Madonna and Child. Ania adored baby Jesus and dreamt about becoming an angel or a saint. She was enamoured by everything to do with the Church and became excessively pious.

Playing with other children in the yard Ania was beginning to pick up from her playmates anti-Semitic phrases: 'The Jews are vermin!', 'They have killed Jesus.'

Mother and son did not know what they could do to protect her from the vile things she was hearing in the yard. To teach Ania to question the guttersniping anti-Semitism may not have been a wise thing to do. It was to the child's advantage to 'blend' into the environment. They put their hope in the young priest they had befriended, without revealing Ania's secret. He listened to Dr Krystyna's concern about the lack of charity in the hearts of so many Poles and replied:

'But it's a fact. The Jews were responsible for the death of Jesus!'

She tried to implant in Ania some positive ideas about the Jews and hoped that after the war, if her family survived, Ania's proper education would eradicate the moral deformation she had acquired.

In spite of the hardships of life in occupied Warsaw, Ania lacked for nothing and had a happy, healthy childhood. With time, the visits of 'her mother' from the countryside became less frequent. They were a happy family; Dr Krystyna was her real mother and Zb. was her adoring big brother.

At the end of the war, in 1945, when Ania was about nine years old, Zb.'s mother made some half-hearted inquiries for ways of searching for Ania's surviving relatives. Without names or certainty as to where they came from, it proved futile. To her shame, she had to admit she felt relief! Parting from Ania would have broken her heart.

The new socialist Poland helped Ania to settle into a new school routine. She replaced her worship of Jesus with an adoration of Stalin, the Wise Leader, and started composing odes to him and to universal peace. She joined the Young Communist League and wore the red scarf with enthusiasm.

Around 1950, rumours reached her that some foreign-looking Jews came into the neighbourhood to make inquiries about a young girl named Anabela Rubin. Neighbours were questioned and Dr Krystyna, after many sleepless nights, decided to send Ania to the countryside to her fictitious mother.

Years passed, and Ania, the sweet, adorable little girl, was transformed into a temperamental teenager, her periods were painful and she was prone to tears. She found fault with Dr Krystyna, she was old-fashioned and her brother was patronising. Dr Krystyna diagnosed Ania's emotional tumult a result of hormonal storms.

After a lapse of time, the search for the Jewish girl named Anabela Rubin was renewed. This time, it took on a more concrete form, backed up by the Red Cross and a New York-based Jewish organisation, aided by a friendly Swiss diplomat in Warsaw.

In New York, a Jew named Abraham Rabinowicz was sparing neither money nor effort to trace 'their' Anabela, who was the only surviving member of his once large family. He was an uncle of Ania's biological mother who had reached New York just before the outbreak of the war. He had begun his search for the child soon after the end of the war.

Dr Krystyna was facing the prospect of separation from Ania once more. In desperation, she even considered moving to another city. Her son intervened and said 'No!' She had done it once before but now providence, or whatever it may be called, was catching up with Ania's Jewish destiny.

The hardest part was telling Ania the truth. She was at a vulnerable stage of adolescence, prone to moody introspection and a dreamer expecting something extraordinary to happen in her life, but never the revelation that she was a Jew.

After being told the truth of her origin, she locked herself in her room for two days, refusing to eat or speak to anybody. She felt robbed and cheated by those she loved, and soon after she ran away and spent a week on the move, not telling them where or with whom she sheltered. She returned home a changed girl, subdued, and began to take an interest in Jews. She hung around the places where they congregated, near the prayer house and charity soup kitchens set up for the elderly Jews. Like a detective, she was on the lookout for clues. In spite of her resolve to get close to them, she found them loathsome, particularly the bearded ones who resembled the photograph sent by the supposed 'uncle' from New York.

Whatever the claims of those people in New York, she was sure she couldn't be Jewish. There must have been a mix-up in the hospital maternity ward; a Christian baby must have got mixed up with a Jewish one. Such things were known to happen – that would explain everything!

A letter from New York supplied details about the family. Her mother, born Sonia Rabinowicz, had married a young Jew named Arthur Rubin. Sonia gave birth to a baby girl, not in a hospital but at home; not in Warsaw but in Otwock, in a summer retreat for the wealthy. The letter provided more information about Ania's family background. Sonia had met her future husband, also a Polish Jew, in France where both were medical students. They were married in 1935 and Anabela was born in the spring of 1938. Her father Arthur was a good-looking and charming man, the son of a well-to-do leather goods merchant from Lwow.

Included in the letters from New York were two pre-war snaps of Ania's parents, a formal wedding photograph and one of her mother aged 18. There was no denying it: Ania/Anabela was the spitting image of her biological mother! Ania felt sorry for her Jewish parents, but loved her Christian family. She had been baptised and raised as a Catholic and wished to remain one.

Dr Krystyna was heartbroken about Ania's dilemma and her own situation. In her distress she asked her son, the girl's adored 'big brother', to deal with her.

He contacted the priest who had instructed Ania when she was being prepared for her confirmation, and asked for help. Father Xavery was sympathetic.

'Dear child,' he addressed her softly and quoted St Paul: 'By the grace of God, I am what I am! The Holy Spirit moves us towards that which God intends us to be, setting before us new horizons and new tasks.'

'I want to die!' Ania sobbed.

'It's not up to us to make such decisions.'

He pointed out that she, like Christ, was born a Jew and had a Jewish mother. When the Second Coming took place, when all the Jews would embrace the true faith, she would be singled out as someone who had already done it. Perhaps Christ had chosen her for a 'special mission'.

He made the sign of the cross over her and blessed her. She grabbed his hand and kissed it.

Dr Krystyna was not at all happy with the priest's words of comfort. This was not what she had wished him to say. She went to consult a visiting rabbi in Warsaw. He listened and, after a long spell of silence, as if he was consulting an invisible judge, he declared:

'There is justice in heaven, if not on this earth.'

His long white beard shook when he spoke. 'The wish of the girl's dead parents has to be carried out! In view of the extent of the catastrophe that has befallen the Jewish people, Ania's survival is a miracle that revealed a divine purpose. You and your son, righteous gentiles, were instrumental in preserving a Jewish life. Jewish sacred books teach "He who saves one life saves the whole world." '

The Rabbi looked at Dr Krystyna with compassion and blessed the gentile woman who had risked her life to save the child. He promised to say a prayer for Ania's well-being.

The heartbreak of separation had begun. On the evening before her departure, while packing, Ania and Dr Krystyna were both tearful. Suddenly Ania dropped what she was doing and exclaimed;

'How strange! I have two mothers! One Jewish and dead, and the other Polish and very much alive!' They hugged and cried.

At the Warsaw airport, before boarding the flight for New York, Zb. made her promise to write to them immediately on her arrival. Her last words were, 'I'll come back to you soon!'

While putting away Ania's photographs Dr Krystyna uttered a deep sigh.

'Ania must have grown into a beautiful woman,' I said – for the sake of saying something.

'We never heard from her.' Zb. said.

Their letters from Warsaw were being returned, stamped 'Unknown at this Address'. Further inquiries about Ania/Anabela's whereabouts led nowhere. The old uncle had died and the family had moved.

'And later she probably married and changed her name, which would have made it even more difficult to trace her,' Dr Krystyna speculated.

'Whatever she chose to do, I hope she has never given up skiing,' Zb. added, lifting the gloom.

Dr Krystyna reminded herself of her duties as hostess and I was urged to have a second helping of her delicious home-baked cake that tasted exactly like the ones my own mother used to make.

'Perhaps it's all for the best,' she said with a sigh when getting up to collect the plates.

THE NUPTIALS OF EROS AND MARS

They say that Mars and Eros, the gods of war and sex, are accomplices, competing with each other in wreaking vengeance on humanity, sometimes together, sometimes separately. This time it was not to wreck my life, but to repair it.

Perhaps 'Our Ania' had had a hand in it. Everything conspired to throw Zb. and me together. The German occupation and the entanglement of the Jews and the Poles had created a powerful emotional bond. The war made us feel like veterans, united by our losses.

A brief encounter like ours might have ended as a short-lived fling, the kind that often flourishes in ski resorts and lasts as long as the winter snow.

By contrast, a love affair begins the process of reinventing the ways we perceive the world and ourselves. Against my will, without words, our eyes declared our love. It had exploded, as it often does, at the wrong time and in the wrong place. One moment, the routine of life flows contained within its perimeters in an orderly way, and at the next moment, an explosion of emotion shatters the comfortable framework.

It seemed unbelievable to both of us that we had been absent from each other's lives and were to part so soon. When lovers steal time, they are like thieves trying to get away with as much emotional loot as can be carried off. He wanted to know everything about my life, about my ancestors, parents, brother, sister and Kasia.

At times, his bed was the place where I was settling the score of the Polish-Jewish 'rupture', lashing out at anti-Semitism and the role of the Catholic Church.

'There weren't enough Poles like your mother and you!' I lamented. Far too many of his compatriots had actively assisted in delivering the Jews to the Gestapo. He valiantly tried to defend the reputation of Poland, the only country that had not produced a Quisling-like collaborator. The Poles had been fighting on every front and dying for the liberation of other countries. I felt sorry for him. One sunny day in Zakopane, a skier intrigued by a woman wrapped like a mummy chooses her as the object of his frivolous attention and a week later he is nursing her Jewish sorrow.

During our nuptials, the dead mingled with the living and after making love my sobs often punctured our slumber. Zb. was determined to purge me of my grief.

That night, I dreamt that my parents visited me and found me in bed with Zb. My mother looked at both of us in silence, then turned to Father and said, 'She is in good hands, we can leave.'

When I woke up, I was startled by the dream. I would have thought that she would have strongly disapproved for two reasons. First, he was not a Jew. Secondly, she regarded people following blind impulse as fools! In our family the supreme example of this kind of foolishness was Sabina, our excessively romantic aunt who had deserted her husband to follow a lover. 'Beware,' Mother warned. 'When you lay a finger on someone's shoulder, you never know what the consequences may be.'

My situation reminded me of Ruth, an Israeli friend, who would have understood what was taking place between the skier and myself.

Ruth was born in Poland and during the war, at the age of six, her mother had managed to push her out of the train destined for Auschwitz. For some weeks the girl had to fend for herself until a peasant family took her in. After the war, at the age of eleven, her family in Israel traced her and brought her to Palestine.

The child with dark, exotic looks had grown into a ravishing beauty. At puberty, the hormonal disturbances as well as the nightmare memories of her past had turned her into a rebellious teenager. At 16, she ran away from the relatives who had provided a caring home. The stunningly attractive teenager, with a husky voice and alluring personality, lived precariously and dangerously, moving through the streets of Tel Aviv wrapped in a haze of mystery and sex appeal. Men's eyes devoured her. She married the first man who declared love. But her wild spirit could not cope with domestic constraints and she walked out on her new husband.

Again she drifted aimlessly, hanging out at the beaches and spending time avidly reading any book she could lay her hands on. Eventually, a handsome, sexy lifeguard, a man of few words, picked her up. Of Moroccan origin, with a bronzed body, his skin always oiled, his curly dark hair pomaded, he resembled a Greek god. Strolling together, he and Ruth were the most handsome couple on the beach. He was a strong swimmer and an equally strong lover and they would meet a few times a week and make love, always during siesta time.

'I never wanted to stay the night. Not once!'

Even in her recollection, Ruth made a point of emphasising the significance of the above fact. For her, the importance of the relationship lay not so much in the act of making love, satisfying as it was, but in what happened to her afterwards. Each orgasm would unlock a torrent of sobs and she would cry without restraint.

'I simply sobbed my heart out,' she said, as if it was the most natural part of lovemaking. The 'life-saver' lover most likely attributed her dramatic climaxes to his sexual prowess. But she knew better. He was saving her life and didn't even know it! Her lover through his lovemaking had become her Wailing Wall. The essential thing in their relationship was that he never questioned what made her so inconsolable. He just held her in his strong arms and rocked her like a baby until she fell asleep, exhausted. The beachcomber's mattress, with its messy sheets, offered Ruth a home for her grief and trauma.

After a year she felt healed without recourse to psychiatric intervention, but through the strong arms of the simple man with a powerful sex drive and a matching absence of curiosity. When she no longer needed to cry, she left the lifeguard and the Tel Aviv beach and moved to a kibbutz where another kind of healing took place. Soon after, she married an intelligent, loving man, had children and shared with him a life filled with meaning and contentment.

Zb. liked Ruth's story and it had become part of our intimacy.

'The man who gave me Poland', with the gesture of handing over the keys to his apartment, had offered a home not only to my troubled soul but also to the abandoned dead that inhabited it.

THE MINISTRY OF CULTURE

I began to say goodbye to Poland in a variety of ways. Looking through the window of Zb.'s flat and watching the street life below, every detail of daily life took on an inordinate significance, even a mother pulling a child on a sleigh. A streetwise urchin, who was scooping up as much coal as he could carry from what spilled out of the horsedrawn wagon, symbolised the cunning and endurance of children.

Across the road a grocery shop was taking delivery from a van unloading trays of fresh bread and rolls. I hungered to bite into a roll, like I used to have for breakfast at home, shaped like two half moons joined together and sprinkled with poppy seeds. They were for me what madeleines were for Proust.

That in turn gave me the idea of preparing a surprise breakfast for the man who so generously offered me Poland. I went down and joined the queue, and listened to people grumbling about the poor quality of the sausages, the empty shelves and other shortages. I felt sorry for them, and the comparison with the supermarket in London where I did my shopping, bursting with a variety of goods, invited disquieting thoughts. Did it have to be like this? I managed to get the rolls, butter, milk and tea.

After the shopping, I crossed the road and my attention was drawn to a wrought-iron gate leading into an eighteenth-century palace that was still in a state of disrepair. The war had left the stuccoed walls blistered and peeling, exposing chipped, raw bricks. On closer inspection, I noticed a large brass plaque above the gate, identifying the building as the seat of the Ministry of Arts and Culture. The pillars on both sides of the gate displayed smaller plaques listing the individual institutes of higher education housed in the building: the School of Music, the School of Fine Arts, the Theatre School and the *Film School*. Most of them were actually located in Lodz, but their offices were in Warsaw.

My eyes were fixed on the Film School plaque. The question 'How do you become a student here?' and Andrzej and Cezary's reply, 'Speak to the Dean!' kept repeating inside my head as in an echo chamber.

I entered with the shopping bag and asked to see the Principal of the Film School. The secretary, an elderly woman, looked annoyed by my request.

'Professor Teoplitz?' she announced. 'He is too busy to receive anyone. He has just returned after four weeks of absence abroad. Have you got an appointment?'

'No,' I hesitantly replied.

'Nobody can see him without a prior appointment.' She went back to typing, expecting me to leave.

'I live in England and unfortunately I have to leave in two days' time.'

The mention of England made her curious. She took off her glasses to take a better look at me, and reluctantly raised herself from the chair. Everything about her betrayed a bureaucratic malice.

'I know he is not seeing anyone today,' she said, vanishing into a long corridor. While waiting I was looking at the painted ceiling. The Baroque Muses of Music and Dancing were floating on clouds held up by angels. The interior of the palace, unlike the exterior, was kept in immaculate condition and furnished with antiques and valuable paintings – it resembled a museum.

She returned with pursed lips, still looking resentful, and ushered me into Professor Teoplitz's office.

The room serving as his office was elegant but dimly lit. Professor Teoplitz was behind a huge desk buried under piles of books, files and papers. Of heavy build and elegantly dressed, he struck me as a friendly, fatherly looking man. The bold tie and smoke-tinted glasses afforded him a fashionable look.

'The secretary did not think I should break the rules for you.'

He appeared to be amused by my audacity. Asked what brought me, I repeated the question I had already asked his students. Was there any chance of being accepted as a student at the Film School?

Instead of giving an answer, he regarded me for a while with the same amused expression that had greeted me in the first place.

'Look at that.' He guided my attention to a massive pile of letters and applications sitting at the end of his desk. In a magisterial tone of voice, he explained that they were from applicants wishing to enrol in the school. Mostly from Western Europe, from countries without state-run film schools, including England; some even from Scandinavia. The bombardment of applications was a result of the growing reputation of the new wave of Polish films abroad; the Lodz Film School was the place where the filmmakers trained.

'Poland is a socialist state that provides free, state-sponsored education. Wouldn't you say it stands to reason that a poor country like Poland should not spend its scarce government money on students from rich capitalist countries?'

I nodded in agreement. I was staggered to hear that to train a film student was as expensive as training a fighter pilot. A fortune!

He took off his glasses and fixed me with a penetrating look. The prolonged pause made me realise what an idiotic idea it had been to bother him in the first place. I was wasting both his and my time.

After the silence, which I took as a sign of the termination of the interview, his tone became more hopeful. The school, he continued, always kept places reserved for foreign students, so far only from friendly socialist countries, like Bulgaria, and from the Third World. However, in some cases it would be possible to make an exception for a Western applicant. For instance, if I had a father who was a distinguished Communist activist or had received Lenin's Order of Merit, or, for that matter, any other similar Communist Party distinction, then I could receive special consideration. His friendly smile was meant as an encouragement to produce a father with the required Communist high status.

Though he meant well, by invoking the Kremlin-approved distinction he had touched on a sore nerve. I had never forgiven the Soviet Union for the secretly signed Soviet-Nazi pact before the outbreak of war in September 1939 and the way they connived in the partition of Poland between them.

In my family the first victim of the pact was my cousin Mundek, a devout Communist, who hung himself when he heard the news. My brother's Siberian experience had added to the simmering anger.

'If you must know, my father earned a political distinction: unfortunately, not from Lenin or Stalin, but from Hitler. It was the Auschwitz order of martyrdom!' I could not resist a jibe at the Professor.

'And my brother got his education in Stalin's gulag in Siberia.'

Having discharged my resentment I thanked him for his time and said goodbye. I was furious with myself. It served me right! The interview was a reminder that I had to learn to curb my impulsiveness. I was already on my way out when the secretary came running after me. 'The Professor wants you back,' she announced, looking sour.

I offered my apologies to him, embarrassed by my explosion. He, too, looked upset. He invited me to sit down and switched to fluent English. Like most Poles educated before the war, his tongue strained to achieve an exaggerated approximation of a classy accent.

'Personally, I would like to open the doors of the school to a number of students from the West,' he declared. Politically it was not a popular idea, not yet anyway, but it may be worth a try. And with a broad smile that made his face resemble a benevolent parent about to scold an unruly child, he pointed again to the pile of applications on his desk.

'Take a good look at the pile of applications. They wrote and waited for an answer but you barged in without an appointment!' Apparently, to become a filmmaker this kind of nerve was a desirable character trait.

'All the same, I wouldn't like to raise your hopes unnecessarily.'

The Ministry of Education had a policy of only considering candidates who already had either an academic or an artistic accomplishment. Amongst the current accepted candidates were two qualified medical doctors, an architect, a published writer and a mathematician.

'I am an artist,' I informed him. 'And in April I am holding an exhibition of my paintings and drawings in a prestigious London West End gallery.'

'What a fortunate coincidence,' he replied with a smile 'In April I am invited to London for a conference of the International Archive Society of which I am President.'

The conversation continued in the spirit of friends arranging a time and place for a future meeting. Nevertheless, he was at pains to emphasise that beyond the promise of visiting my exhibition, he couldn't guarantee any official commitment. At the end of the interview he swore me to absolute secrecy. I was not to repeat it to anyone as it could harm him and ruin my chances. I solemnly promised.

Before my departure he threw a question at me, for which I was not prepared. 'If you are an exhibiting painter, why films?'

I had never bothered to put into words the frustration I felt when painting. Stories would explode inside my head that I failed to integrate into my paintings. My artistic inspiration and passion did not fit into the scope of easel paintings that was too restrictive and too static. The epic narrative paintings of the Renaissance period would have been ideal for my artistic temperament. Narrative art had become outdated and the prevailing trends favoured abstract painting or surrealism, which were not my favourite genres of painting either. However much expression and emotion went into my pictures, I was always left feeling dissatisfied.

'I need to marry my images to movement and make them talk, laugh and cry!'

I wasn't sure if this made sense to him, but he nodded without asking for further explanation.

Professor Teoplitz saw me out, watched by the surprised secretary, for such gestures of courtesy were accorded only to 'important' visitors. She even forced a friendly goodbye, overriding her bureaucratic 'no admittance' stance. I sent her a look of victory. Breaking barriers always gives me profound satisfaction. Put me in an out-of-bounds situation, either as a Jew, a woman or a foreigner, and I'm likely to go into battle!

Outdoors, the sunny, crisp frost pinched my cheeks and sobered me up. The sense of satisfaction derived from accomplishing the unexpected soon evaporated. It was lunacy! I lived in London. I was married with a young child. There was the Iron Curtain. In two days' time I'll be on a plane leaving Poland.

I returned to Zb.'s flat and set the table for the intended surprise breakfast. The accumulation of the morning's impressions – the fresh rolls, the visit to the Film School and waiting for Zb.'s arrival – had put me in a spin. My aspirations were expanding and at the same time shrinking.

When he arrived, he looked at the table and said: 'This is how I would like it to be forever!' I was sorry I couldn't share the secret of my conversation with Teoplitz.

'I have a special gift for you,' Zb. said. He opened it to reveal a cut-up fragment of a Holy Scroll parchment that he had found in the flea market. The Nazis used them for boot lining, and what had been intended as sacred had over time become valued merchandise in markets or second-hand shops.

'I want you to take it back to London as a token of our shared Polish-Jewish inheritance. Let me know what's written in it!' were Zb.'s parting words.

5
After the Pilgrimage

AFTER THE PILGRIMAGE

Poland was receding from view. Cruising at great height, I was assailed by many unanswerable questions. Was there a purpose in my survival, or was it sheer blind luck, without meaning? Survivors of catastrophes, I was told, often question their right to exist.

When he was five, my son asked, 'Mum, where do the dead go?' At a loss as to how to answer, I did what most adults do and pointed to the sky. I wasn't sure about the traffic of dead souls in England, but in Poland they stayed put, waiting to be released from oblivion, like my dead family who must have been waiting for that phone call from my husband about the Polish film that had set me on the journey. It had taken me a long time to understand that unappeased spirits could turn into raging furies.

The thought of the impending reunion with my husband concentrated my mind on the aspects of love and unfaithfulness. I began to ruminate over books, plays and films dealing with the amorous adventures of married women, their virtues and betrayals. Which of them could possibly come to my rescue?

Tolstoy's ravishing and aristocratic Anna Karenina was not a helpful model. Chekhov would have been kinder. I turned to the French, the reputed masters of marital infidelity. Gustav Flaubert's *Madame Bovary* offered a lesson in the disaster awaiting any respectable middle-class woman consumed by passion. Only George Sand was closer to my spirit. She wore trousers, was a mother, had love affairs and definitely knew more about love and unfaithfulness than I did. Openly critical of marriage, she had extramarital affairs. In a letter to a friend, she declared: 'Life is the most beautiful thing in the world when one is in love and the most detestable when one stops loving.'*

---

* From *In Her Own Words*, by George Sand, edited by Joseph Barry (Garden City, New York: Anchor Press/Doubleday, 1979).

I summoned memories of films that had once made me swoon or cry. The great love stories of the screen, which had shaped my teenage ideals about glamour and romance, depicted women who loved adventurously and dangerously. They were either ruined by love or brought utter ruin upon their lovers. This was not an alternative I wished to contemplate.

My encounter in the Tatra Mountains with the skier brought to mind the English film *Brief Encounter*, the touching story of a married suburban woman who meets a man at a provincial railway station, and their relationship develops into a tender but unconsummated love. Shot in black and white, the characters represented level-headed adults torn between their love and family obligation. In this case, the lover chose a decent way out by deciding to go overseas before her passions could wreck their family life. Englishmen who opted for the gentlemanly role of a 'love fugitive' could, as members of the British Empire, still take advantage of the many opportunities offered by at least three English-speaking continents!

There the comparison with my own 'brief encounter' ended. Being divorced, Zb.'s marital status made him a free man but the politics of the Cold War made him a captive of the regime. For lovers like him, married or single, getting out of the country would be a prolonged and difficult undertaking.

There are so many ways to describe a 'new-born' love that leaves us naked, needy and vulnerable. Even after parting, my skin remembered his touch and my lips had the imprint of all the spoken and the unspoken words between us. I had never felt like this before.

I traced the progression of my sexuality since puberty. The outbreak of the war revealed my mother's anxiety over my pubescent shape. In the bathroom, looking at my growing breasts, she exclaimed: 'Thank God your breasts are not fully developed. In times of war, it's better this way.' Only months before they had become a point of contention between us. I had set my eyes on a bra that I desperately wanted displayed in a shop window, made of shining pink satin, trimmed with lace and tiny rosette buds. At the gym, when we undressed, the more developed girls displayed such bras like trophies.

Before my departure from home, Mother handed me a cotton vest, which would have flattened my chest even more. I refused to wear it. Mother's dread of rape was palpable and I shall never know if it was from personal experience or passed on from generation to generation, an inherited collective memory.

Much later I understood that sexual awakening in wartime could be dangerous and I resolutely guarded my virginity. The fear of getting pregnant inhibited any manifestation of erotic urges. While keeping my legs closed, my head was exploding with wild dreams about love with a capital 'L' and my lips thirsted for the taste of kisses and other imagined erotic pleasures.

Separated from maternal supervision at an early age, the customary restrictions imposed by mothers on daughters passed me by. As a result, my perception of becoming a woman was a self-manufactured construct. In the passage from girlhood to womanhood, I must have missed a vital stage. Biologically I was a full-grown woman; my body had acquired the necessary curves and bulges, yet despite growing older and being sexually active, I stayed at heart a girl.

My husband observed this girl-wife persona early in our marriage and once, in exasperation, complained: 'Don't you know what a woman is or does?' The question stunned me. It forced me to acknowledge that I indeed had a blurred self-image and had no idea how to *be* or *act* as a married woman. In Zb.'s arms, my sense of self as a mature woman beckoned with new possibilities.

Floating through clouds, it was easy to spin fantasies about fitting both men into my life. I anticipated that the encounter with Zb. was bound to bring some dislocation into my life, but I hoped that my marital stability would not be shattered. I did feel a deep affection for my husband, and the blot of my unfaithfulness buzzed inside my head like a noisy wasp ready to sting.

The safety-belt announcement signalled the approach to Heathrow. The descending plane broke through the cloud barrier, revealing England's green patchwork. A painter I knew who was besotted with the variety of shades of green in the English landscape once observed, 'An inch of green is greener in England.' He was right; the English land coming into view was a juicy green even in winter. I felt an upsurge of affection for my adopted country. It was a relief to be in a country where two political parties fought out their differences in Parliament. England meant safety.

The reunion with my English family was just as emotional as my parting from my dead Polish family. I clasped my son with a bear-like hug, loving him not only for myself, but also for the family of which he had been deprived. Dressed up in his grey school uniform, he was already representing a miniature model of an English gent: in long grey trousers, a blazer and school tie. Yet hidden under this newly acquired exterior was a vulnerable little boy. I bent down to do up his shoelaces and an instant association forced itself upon me: a heap of children's shoes on display at the Auschwitz Museum. I drew him to me with a fiercely possessive love.

The initial anxiety about the reunion with my husband vanished as soon as we embraced. I was genuinely happy to see him, and to be held in his arms. After the 'sh-sh-sz-s' tones of Polish, the cadences of the tight-lipped English language had a calming effect. His dry, English sense of humour never failed to make me laugh. To my surprise, I discovered it was not so difficult to love two men at the same time, particularly with one at a safe distance.

WELCOME HOME

After Poland, London was like an Aladdin's cave. The staggering abundance and variety of consumer goods displayed in the shops provoked a contradictory response. The well-stocked supermarket shelves bulging with goods, the capitalist proof of success, was seductive. Yet I couldn't help feeling uneasy. Did one really need imports of out-of-season fruits and vegetables from far-away countries? It seemed a travesty of common sense and perhaps indicative of capitalist malaise.

'Why not take it as a reassuring aspect of democracy and of free choice?' my husband suggested.

I couldn't help thinking of the endless queues in Poland, where the most basic articles of consumer goods were in short supply, if available at all. Zb. regarded the inefficiency of the socialist economic system as a means of humiliating its citizens. When asked what I could send him from London, his only request was for a typewriter ribbon, an item in chronically short supply. At his university, colleagues would often remove them from each other's typewriters and cover up the act of theft by replacing them with old ones.

Zb. was never far from my mind. My friend Basil, a boastful womaniser and a man well-versed in conducting extramarital affairs, gave the following advice:

'A brief encounter means brief! Prolong it and it will sag like a punctured balloon.'

My affair with Zb. had, in a perverse way, injected a new emotional charge into our marriage. It is said that marital infidelity can be a balm to an ailing marriage: couples ruthlessly cannibalise the 'third party' in order to repair a run-down relationship. Nevertheless, I felt compelled to come clean about Zb. It took place in bed and after an ominous silence, to my utter surprise R. made his own confession. While I was away, he had met someone and had had an affair. I was more unsettled by this revelation than I had expected to be. I felt terribly jealous! My husband was the linchpin of my stability. He reassured me that it was only a passing fling: he loved me and nobody could ever replace me. With that we fell asleep in each other's arms.

Our separate affairs added a new dimension to our perception of each other. We were coming to grips with our changing selves and needs. Professionally, R. was moving into a new phase. New opportunities during the property boom made his practice as a chartered surveyor too restrictive. In partnership with some architects and with loans from the City, they set out to develop old bomb sites, seeing themselves as the new master-builders. They were rebuilding war-damaged cities in England and abroad.

Money, more than infidelity, was responsible for a radical shift in our relationship. R.'s preoccupation with success and a lifestyle fit for a gentleman meant little to me. My indifference to wealth was a legacy of the war. Having witnessed the dispossession of my family, I was cured of any serious attachment to material possessions. If it had happened once, as it did to my family, it could happen again, anywhere.

Amazingly, my take-it-or-leave-it attitude proved to be of immense help to R.'s professional life. By nature a cautious man, it made him bolder when negotiating high-risk deals. In one crucial situation, on the verge of a deal that would either make a killing or bring ruin, I urged him to go for it. If the worst came to the worst, I consoled him, we could always go and live cheaply in some Mediterranean country. I cherished an Arcadian vision of leading a simple life, going 'native' on some island in Spain or Greece. A corollary of this imagined idyll was a friendly environment for our child to grow up in. In short, my paradise was at the end of a cheap one-way boat ticket.

R.'s deal, however, had turned him into a well-to-do man. When he bought a Rolls-Royce as a surprise for me, I failed to express the expected enthusiasm. I forgot the psychological significance of cars as masculine sex symbols and mentioned my preference for the old Rover. It was an unforgivable blunder.

'How can anyone object to the good things in life?' My husband couldn't hide his anger.

'I love the good things in life!' I protested.

'So what's the problem?'

I wasn't sure myself, until the echoes of my mother's voice expressing fear of envy reached me: 'Too ostentatious! It doesn't bode well.'

As a child, I was forbidden to use my new bicycle in our yard so as not to invite envy from the poor children. I had to wait for the summer holidays to ride my bike freely in the countryside.

My husband sensed that with my homecoming a process of 'reviewing' my life had begun and that the experiences in Poland were a frame of reference. Nothing and nobody was the same. My pilgrimage had been effective in that it had forced me to see places, events and people in a new light, including his parents.

My in-laws never inquired about my family background or what happened to them. They treated me as if ghosts had sired me. After my return from Poland, my grudge towards them increased. Young couples often forget that, by mating, they not only unite two individuals but also merge family histories and genetic inheritance. When R. and I met, our different backgrounds were no barrier to our loving – if anything, we liked the challenge – but my recent stay in Poland had made me acutely aware of those barriers.

It took on a serious turn when our son's education came into consideration. According to my husband, to secure the child's future, he would have to be sent to prep. school as a boarder.

'At the age of seven?'

'It begins in the cradle,' he reminded me.

I had forgotten that he had entered our son's name at a number of public schools before he was a year old. My husband, loving father that he was, like many other sensible people set out to provide for our son the best education and advantages that money could buy. R. was an 'old boy' of a good public school in London, which in itself was a recommendation for our son's future suitability.

I was learning about Anglo-Saxon class snobbery and the rituals connected with early grooming for class stratification.

'Sending young children away from home at such a tender age is outrageous!'

In Poland, only orphans or handicapped children from the poorest families would be sent away from home. To a foreigner like me, the idiosyncratic ways of educating children to conform to English upper-class aspirations were incomprehensible. These exchanges led invariably to fierce quarrels.

R., on the other hand, had a clear vision of both his and his son's future. It stretched before him like an open and well-marked road.

By contrast, my own sense of the future was impaired. I had never developed a mental blueprint for growing into maturity or old age. The Holocaust had deprived me of this. Having never seen my parents or any of my extended family grow old I would look to strangers on whom I modelled myself.

In the end I had to concede that I was hardly the most reliable person to veto such a promising prospect for our son's future. I was, after all, a foreigner with anarchic leanings, an artist and not the most practical of mothers.

Finally, he presented me with a persuasive argument.

'Think of all the foreigners who send their sons, at great expense, to be educated in private English schools. Why not reserve judgement until you have visited one or two?'

Betteshanger in Kent was indeed impressive and appealing. Housed in a spacious, baronial-style mansion, the imposing, mock Gothic building was set in a large, well-kept park, surrounded by countryside with gently rolling hills. The school's educational facilities were of the highest standard. The gym, a swimming pool and many creative activities, including a theatre, took care of physical and artistic development. The children looked relaxed and happy. A nurse was a full-time member of staff.

After meeting the headmaster and other members of staff, I was impressed by the liberal spirit that guided their attitude towards the children's education and their social requirements. The headmaster, a charming, fatherly man, declared his enthusiasm for the newly emerged State of Israel. They had other Jewish children, and a few Hindu and Muslim pupils as well. The religious needs of all of their charges were taken care of and racial and religious tolerance was thoroughly observed by the school.

My resistance vanished. As for our son, he had already been brainwashed by everybody into believing what a splendid idea it was. He was an only child and a boarding school would provide new playmates and a structured life. The loneliness of a child without siblings would be solved. My son's immediate future was settled and, inadvertently, it helped to decide mine as well.

EXHIBITION

The crocuses in London parks began to push their heads above the ground, fooled by warm weather. So did the bold-coloured tulips standing erect, like guards.

In my studio, my paintings and drawings were waiting to be sent out, to face the eyes of people who would either like them or criticise.

As a figurative painter, my models were the source of my stimulation, chosen from amongst friends, male and female, or a succession of resident foreign au pairs. Some were country girls, others from well-to-do urban homes who had come to learn or improve their English or to earn money.

Like Kika from Barcelona, from an upper-middle-class family. The elegant young girl, strikingly good-looking, who smelt of expensive Spanish and French eau de toilette, joined our household. There was something old-fashioned and Victorian in her demeanour. At mealtimes she spoke only when spoken to.

Once, during one of our dinner parties, Basil, the one-time advisor on infidelity and aspiring documentary filmmaker, was holding forth about the current season of Bunuel's films at the National Film Theatre. Kika was quiet but attentive, and around coffee time she joined in.

'*Bunu-el?*' she announced. 'Bunuel is my uncle.' She pronounced the name by correctly placing the accent on the last syllable.

The great film director was her mother's brother whom she had never met, nor had she seen any of his films. In Franco's Spain they were banned and he was declared *persona non grata*, accused of propagating Communist and anti-clerical views. His openly anti-Franco stand was enough to condemn him. Our admiration for her celebrated uncle pleased her, but her polite manners kept under wraps any excessive expression.

Basil could hardly contain his excitement and offered to take Kika to see her uncle's films. Soon after, a phone call from Bunuel summoned Kika to Paris to spend a week with him. It was to be her first visit to Paris and an important family reunion. We gave her a week off and assured her that it would be fine if she wished to stay longer. I was thrilled for her sake and a bit jealous. To our utter surprise, she returned before the week was up.

'Kika, why?'

Uncle Bunuel was very nice to her, she reported, but in truth, she wanted to see Paris as an ordinary tourist. Instead, Uncle Bunuel, proud of his beautiful niece, chose to introduce her to his friends, amongst them Picasso, Braque, Matisse and other luminaries of the Paris art and intellectual scenes. According to Kika, the elderly gentlemen were a jolly lot, excessively drinking and smoking and noisily arguing about politics, art and women. To her, they were just a group of old cronies who smelled of tobacco and were lost in reminiscences about the Paris of their youth. Not in the least cowed by the reputations of the illustrious artists, she simply decided to cut her visit short, using the excuse that she had to get back to London. Kika was too polite to say that she was bored.

Life was so unfair! I would have given anything to have an uncle like Bunuel and have the chance to mix with the giants of the Paris art world.

By contrast, Luisa 'La Portuguesa' from the Azores was from a humble home. She came to London to learn English, but in her case economic necessity dominated and she used to send most of her earnings to her mother. Luisa was a bright 23-year-old with smiling dark eyes. She gave the impression of a kitten waiting to be stroked. The combination of charm, good looks and oozing sex appeal often exposed her to the hazards of predatory men. Her flaring nostrils and generous lips bore the imprint of a possible African ancestry, but her long, silky black hair made one think of Asian women. She often sang the *Fado*, the Portuguese love songs, while doing her domestic chores or looking after our son.

Luisa was a keen sitter with no inhibitions about posing, even in the nude, and once seated in the studio an extraordinary transformation would take place. The stillness of the pose, accompanied by silence, would profoundly affect her mood. First her eyes would mist over, a signal that she was on the verge of tears. When it happened the first time, I was alarmed. Was she in pain, or perhaps in the grip of the menstrual blues? I offered to break off, but she insisted that we carry on. In time I got used to those dramatic changes and would carry on painting, accepting the tears rolling down her cheeks that she did not bother to wipe. On such occasions the scene in the studio acquired an aura of veneration, as if being painted aroused in Luisa some soul-stirring spiritual experience. She made me think of women's faces seen in Catholic churches, shedding tears of adoration and expectancy in front of icons. I sensed it was best not to probe into her emotional turmoil. Luisa's wordless sorrow flowed through my brush and onto my paintings. At the end of the painting sessions, Luisa would revert back to her cheerful self and I could hear her usual chatter, laughter and songs.

Under our roof, Luisa's life and my art had become entwined. She stayed with us for several years, becoming part of the family. When she become pregnant, my husband blamed me for Luisa's situation. This took place long before single motherhood had become accepted. Her lover, an artist she met through me, panicked and ducked his responsibilities. She gave birth to a baby girl and named the baby Mira. Eventually she found a man who married her in order to protect her from being deported. Obtaining a British passport allowed her to stay in England.

The painting of Luisa had an important place in the catalogue of the Brook Street Gallery exhibition. *Luisa Mending* had the place of honour, displayed in the gallery's large window facing the main street. It depicted her with a slightly tilted head, mending a piece of white linen.

The composition was inspired by Cézanne's portrait, *An Old Woman With a Rosary*, on display at the National Gallery. This early Cézanne, like some of Rembrandt's paintings, was, for me, an icon that paid homage to old age. The sombre tonality of the painting, dominated by cobalt blue, affected me the same way Luisa's silent tears had. Perhaps the image reminded me of my mother and Kasia, the two women I had often seen seated in a similar posture while mending socks.

For a time I was under the mistaken impression that the sitter of Cézanne's picture was his mother. In fact, it was a nun who had suffered a crisis brought on by a loss of faith and had run away from her convent. Cézanne found her wandering confused on the road, so he took her home, where she became a devoted member of his household.

The first visitor to arrive for the formal opening of the exhibition was Josef Herman, who was familiar with most of my work as some had been painted under his tutelage. His approval meant a lot to me. He was a substitute father figure, sharing with my father not only the same name and similar coloured eyes, but also generosity of spirit. Both were free with their praise and encouragement. When Josef gave me a congratulatory hug, my throat tightened.

Mary was another early visitor and it was a strange sensation to see her away from the analyst's chair and the mauve mohair blanket. I observed her, with a glass of wine in her hand, spending a considerable time in front of each painting. This was the first time she had had the opportunity to see my work and, as a gesture of approval, she purchased a small oil painting, *Fishermen Mending Nets*, from my Ibiza period. Hers was the first sale, the first red dot and it was an auspicious beginning as other sales followed which pleased the gallery owners. There was usually little, if any, profit from the first-time exhibitions of unknown artists. The owners were my friends and took the risk.

For the duration of the exhibition I was present in the gallery every day in order to meet visitors, potential buyers and representatives of the press, if one was lucky enough to get them inside the gallery. I was learning about the politics of the art-dealing world.

From time to time, an important collector would turn up, and such a visitor would vanish behind closed doors with the owner, where they would conduct transactions often involving the purchase of nothing less than a Braque, a Picasso or a Chagall. On the way out, he or she would look with a shrewd eye at the work of the unknown artist on display. Sometimes, if the artist were lucky, they would purchase something. For a modest investment they would occasionally pick a future winner. For the artist, such an event was the lifeline to possible renown. I was lucky: a collector bought two of my large paintings.

The most stimulating visitors were art students and other artists, my ex-Slade colleagues, a few of whom had already made reputations for themselves. Art galleries also attract bizarre characters. The eccentric middle-aged artist who smelled of turpentine and had paint marks on his shoes was a regular. The Brook Street Gallery owners regarded his behaviour as harmless. First he would inspect the paintings through his thick glasses, and then, before departing, he would let forth a diatribe against the Royal Family and the upper classes.

'The bloody lot collect pure-bred racehorses not contemporary art! They should run a circus not a country!'

On the penultimate day of the exhibition, Professor Teoplitz turned up. Seeing him on my own ground, I regarded his visit with mixed feelings. My idea of becoming a filmmaker had receded and I had already consigned the episode of my visit to the Ministry of Culture in Warsaw as a mindless whim. I must have hoped he would not keep his promise.

He wasn't alone. He had arrived accompanied by the director of the Polish Cultural Institute and a Polish art critic representing the Polish Press Agency.

The Professor took me by the arm and together we made the rounds. From his informed comments I understood that he was satisfied with what he saw and was complimentary about the quality of my paintings and large drawings.

'Many distinguished film directors drew and painted as well.' His comment led me to believe that he considered me a suitable candidate to join this select group. The press reviews, displayed on a side table, helped to reinforce the positive impressions he and his companions received. I understood that they too would have an important role in assessing my position as an artist.

In the *Arts Review*, Edward Lucie-Smith, a well-known art critic, wrote:

> The artist takes up again and again the image of a seated woman or girl. The mood is sombre. There is a relationship to the work of Herman and the influence of Cezanne is also evident...But I don't find the pictures derivative. The colour is personal...The breath and sureness crammed into spaces (of smaller oil paintings) is astonishing and the pictures must be some of the most satisfying objets de collection currently on view in London. The larger ones have a sort of gravity and weight which makes it not altogether blasphemous to summon up the image of Picasso's classical period in the 20s. This is not bravura art, but its total impact is considerable.

In *Apollo*, a glossy international magazine, Jasia Reinhard, an established critic, began her review with the following words:

> The characters and personages painted by Mira H. seem to bear on their shoulders the weight of the world. Their sturdiness and bulk is as much a part of their power as the sad gaze of experience and preoccupation is part of their presence...These seated women busily sewing, gazing, or eating, have a more universal quality. They are, so to speak, effigies of an idea as well as being identifiable characters...

Before departure, Professor Teoplitz asked for copies of the reviews to be sent to him, reverting to the formal manner of an official spokesman for the Polish People's Republic.

'We will get in touch with you in due course,' he said, and the delegation left, leaving me feeling very unsettled.

This was 1960, the year when the winds of the Cold War, usually blowing hot and cold, had of late frosted up. Khrushchev's threats, alternating with offers of peaceful co-existence, had reached their dramatic high point when at the UN Assembly session he banged his shoe on the desk, threatening to bury capitalism.

'Not a hope,' my husband said.

It was hardly the right time to consider the option of becoming a student at the Lodz Film School.

DREAMS, LEGENDS AND HISTORY

Within weeks a letter arrived with information that I was selected to attend an entrance examination at the Film School in Lodz, due to take place at the beginning of the September term. I desperately needed a session with Mary, my analyst.

'What should I do about it?'

'You alone must decide.'

Angry with myself and with her, in exasperation I cried out: 'Whoever heard of a married woman, a mother of a six-year-old-boy, going off to study in a far away country?'

The impact of feminist awakening and the shock-waves from across the Atlantic were slow to reach England. The time for the 'kitchen and bedroom' revolution, which encouraged women to seek new roles in husband–wife relationships, had not arrived yet. It was acceptable for husbands to go off to work or study far away from home, but not wives.

Besides, I was not altogether sure whether the pull that Poland was exerting was not a sign of regression. Zb., 'the man who gave me Poland', was no longer in Poland. Unhappy about our relationship, he had accepted an academic posting in, of all places, Kazakhstan. He couldn't be further away!

My husband was not enthusiastic but neither did he discourage. 'Give it a try! Even if you fail the exam, you'll never reproach me, or yourself, for having missed a chance.'

The Polish ex-lover being so far from Poland may have had a bearing on his relaxed attitude. On the way to post the letter to Professor Teoplitz, I couldn't bring myself to do it, stopped by a foreboding that my life was in some kind of jeopardy. At the same time I was fully aware that in turning away, I would probably be turning away from myself. In the end a dream decided for me.

In the dream I was walking along a narrow paved lane, laid over a luscious green lawn that led towards a row of cottages flooded in sunlight. It was somewhere in Israel and the landscape was reminiscent of a kibbutz.

Approaching me was an elderly couple. 'Husband and wife', I thought, the way one has dream-thoughts. The woman was holding onto the man's arm, the way continental couples do. Coming face to face I stepped aside to make way but they stopped to look at me and smiled. Upright and dignified, with snow-white hair, sun-tanned faces and striking blue eyes, they were a beautiful couple.

They must be tourists, I decided, having noticed a nametag on the man's jacket, the kind worn by participants of seminars or conferences: 'Johannan Ben Zakkai' was the name. They went their way but I stayed on, trying to puzzle out who they were and why they seemed familiar.

I woke up in the morning recalling the vivid dream, troubled by my inability to link the vaguely familiar historical name to a specific event or place. Not having an encyclopaedia at hand, I went to see Rabbi Hugo Gryn, who was the chief rabbi of the Reform Synagogue that my husband's family had belonged to. He was also a long-standing friend and, as always, was approachable. I knew that he would not shame me for my ignorance.

'Some dream you've dredged up from the depths of the night,' he joked, making me welcome in his office. Hugo's wit and generous spirit were recognised traits of his personality. I sometimes consulted him about family problems and he knew about my dilemma concerning the Film School. He provided the background of the character whose name in my dream had appeared affixed to a nametag on a tourist's lapel.

Johannan Ben Zakkai was enshrined in rabbinical Judaism as an influential figure. According to the legend, he had begun life as an illiterate shepherd. He married a rich merchant's daughter and, soon after, left her in order to study, thus elevating the act of leaving a matrimonial home for the sake of knowledge into a great virtue. Having studied for 24 years, he returned with thousands of disciples.

'He must have set the record for the most ancient example of the eternal student!' Hugo was known to combine erudition with a Jewish sense of humour that often livened up his sermons and his conversations.

In the annals of Jewish history, he has been recognised as one of the great teachers of his time. Living in the first century, Johannan Ben Zakkai had had the misfortune of having to deal with the Roman legions during the Jewish revolt against the Romans.

'And guess what he did?' Hugo paused – a seasoned storyteller. 'While Jerusalem was under siege by Vespian's legions, at its height he engineered his escape from the city by having himself concealed in a coffin, which his disciples carried out.'

Apparently, he foresaw the collapse of the revolt, the loss of sovereignty and the ultimate destruction of the Temple and Jerusalem. His goal was to salvage what could be saved. In the period following the destruction of the Jerusalem Temple, he built up an alternative centre of Jewish learning in Jabneh, a place on the Mediterranean coast.

'I must admit, the coffin as a vehicle for the preservation of spiritual life is a most troublesome symbol of survival.' Hugo's own survival was a testimony to the truth of his reflection. His experiences in Auschwitz, where he was deported as a youth, and his exposure to psychoanalysis made him a most original thinker and compassionate counsellor.

He soon reverted to his customary humorous way by concluding that Lodz could never be compared to Jabneh, but learning about filmmaking in order to preserve something of the destroyed Jewish world was worth the effort. My dream, he decided, was a good omen.

I posted the brown envelope, no longer wondering whether it was the right thing to do.

THE EXAMINATION

On a sunny morning in September, I was back in Poland and again at the gate of the Lodz Film School. In daylight, the entrance of the building which Father and I had once so admired looked shabby. My memory of its former condition was almost photographic and in a mental reconstruction I filled in the missing gravelled lanes and the neat flowerbeds that once surrounded an imposing forecourt. This was the first step in a spatial kind of myopia in which the extinct world of the past would often superimpose on the present.

I joined the group of nervous candidates, young men and women who had gathered in the refectory and where I encountered my first surprise. Staszek, my first contact in Poland, was also waiting to appear before the Film School commission. It transpired that he had applied to study film directing soon after our encounter in Warsaw, although the timing of his decision had no obvious connection with me. I could not rid myself of an unnerving thought that some hidden meaning was lurking in so many of the coincidences that I was constantly encountering in Poland.

When Cezary and Andrzej turned up, I had the impression that I was in the presence of characters summoned by my new destiny.

'When the story is ready, the characters will gather,' Anton Chehkov is quoted as saying. They had come to brief the new candidates on how to deal with some of the questions from the collegiate body.

'Make frequent references to Lenin's view about the importance of cinema.'

'Quote from Eisenstein's writings and mention the originality of Alexander Dovshenko.'

'Don't forget the importance of Brecht's Alienation Theatre.'

'Watch out for so and so,' they cautioned about the more severe of the professors who were conducting the interviews.

The long conference table was covered with green felt, the ubiquitous symbol of collective authority. Professor Teoplitz, who was presiding, was flanked on either side by a number of middle-aged men and a few women. His presence made me feel reassured. The set-up was formal, but some occasional banter between the professors created a relaxed atmosphere. The room was filled with clouds of smoke and the ashtrays were overflowing with cigarette ends, the nicotine crop harvested during the ongoing interviews. Teoplitz was the first to address me.

'Why would a promising painter wish to switch to films?'

I understood that, for the benefit of his colleagues, I should repeat the answer I had given at the time of our first meeting. My reply was short:

'My imagination is nomadic, it craves the opportunity to roam beyond the boundaries of a painter's studio.' The screen, I told them, was the perfect space for the marriage of my images with words, combined with movement.

Afterwards, the professors took turns in asking questions about my preferences in film, drama, music, visual arts and literature, each according to the subject he/she lectured in.

I had no difficulties explaining why Rembrandt inspired me or why in music I favoured Bruckner. I was also on safe ground on the subject of the history of art and the aesthetics of cubism.

The script-writing tutor set up an exercise that required choosing a character from any popular book for a screen adaptation. I selected Anna Karenina's love affair along the lines of the Marxist, class-based analysis, hoping it would please them. The improvised scene began with Anna Karenina all ready to run off with her lover. Just then she learns from her nanny that during the night her son had developed a high fever. The nanny herself also showed signs of being feverish. Will she stay or leave?

I concluded that without the numerous servants and the nannies who managed the rich household, Anna's love affair would perhaps have taken another turn.

'Poor Anna Karenina!' the tutor said, trying to restrain his merriment. 'Poor old Tolstoy!' Somebody else added, looking at me critically. I realised it was a foolish idea.

After each day of the exams the candidates gathered at the Honoratka cafe where we would compare notes about our performance. Half the time I was convinced that I had failed. When the results were announced and I was on the list of the accepted, I had a suspicion that I may have been treated with indulgence.

Becoming a student was a privilege. More so as at that time there was no national film school in England. In the West, only Paris had such a school.

The beginning of the school term that was to usher me back into student life was marked by a public event that took place in a municipal hall in the presence of local dignitaries and representatives from the Ministry of Culture. Amongst my future colleagues, the novices who were lined up on a stage, was a bearded Englishman wearing his Oxford University graduation gown. David was an archetypal English eccentric who had arrived in Poland in a second-hand Rolls-Royce, which had every traffic militiaman saluting, mistaking him for a diplomat. The other foreigners accepted to the school were from Bulgaria, Iraq and Mongolia.

The climax of the official ceremony, after the boring speeches praising Marx, Lenin and Gomulka, the First Secretary of the Polish Communist Party, was a collective swearing-in of loyalty to the Polish Socialist People's Republic. It also included a declaration of fraternal and eternal friendship towards the Soviet Union. The proud owner of the Oxford gown and I exchanged knowing looks which declared that as far as we were concerned, the Soviet Union and the Communist Party would have to manage without our eternal loyalty.

The Honoratka played an important role in students' lives. It offered a chance to meet established film people and writers. Though most lived in Warsaw they, too, were Honoratka regulars, Lodz being the location of the film studios and labs. It was the place where one would pick up the latest news about who was making what film, or who was encountering problems with the censor. The battle with censorship was an ongoing issue for film directors and scriptwriters.

One day the Gypsy woman caught up with me again at the Honoratka, beaming with satisfaction. 'Had I not predicted your return? Gypsy woman told the truth!'

Her fortune telling had come true! What she did not foretell was that with my penchant for crossing borders I was to rattle the Iron Curtain.

A ROOM WITH A WARDROBE

The first year spent in my native city was difficult for a variety of reasons; some anticipated, others not. I no longer had a home here and was a stranger. The question of where to live was paramount.

In principle, scholarship students like myself were automatically allotted a place at a student hostel. When I went to register, I was chased out by odours of cooked cabbage and disinfectant. Six or more women shared one large room, with communal bathrooms and toilets. Worst of all were the strict rules about visiting hours and locking-up time. Although I was prepared to rough it in Lodz, cushioned by the security of a comfortable home in London, the prospect of the hostel was depressing.

I soon learned that the Honoratka cafe was also the place to solve a variety of personal problems. Alinka, whom I had encountered during my 'pilgrimage', was there with a friend, Antoni, a Film School graduate, about to move to Warsaw to work as a cameraman with the Documentary Film Unit. He was celebrating his new posting and the chance to leave Lodz. I was invited to join their table and mentioned my visit to the students' hostel.

'You want a room?' Antoni asked and, like a conjuror, produced a bunch of keys. Detaching one, he placed it on the table. 'Gdanska 44,' he said, and pushed the key in my direction. I feared it was a drunken man's tease. He had started celebrating his new job earlier in the day and the effects of alcohol were showing in his flushed face.

'Alinka knows the room,' he mumbled. 'And the wardrobe.'

It seemed that in Poland I was destined to meet men who were dangling keys before me. I was reminded of the scene in Warsaw when Zb. offered me the keys to his apartment. In a country where getting hold of a room was an exceptional feat, to find one offered on a platter seemed to me more than sheer good luck.

The following day Alinka accompanied me to inspect the room. Before the war, it had been part of a spacious residence consisting of three large bedrooms and two sitting rooms. Under socialism it had been divided: Antoni had one room and a young family with a child occupied the rest.

It was a decent-sized room with a separate entrance. Double doors led to a balcony overlooking a concrete paved back yard. The room had seen better days. Some of the decorative features, including the cornice surrounds of the ceiling, were covered with grime and peeling paint. The parquet floor was grey from neglect and the beautiful stove covered with decorative dark-blue tiles had not been cleaned in years. A dead plant in the corner of the balcony added a telling detail to the sorry state of Antoni's tenancy.

The present co-tenants were both chemists and were greatly relieved to be getting rid of their noisy, troublesome neighbour. By law, they had no say in the matter of who could be installed in the room after Antoni's departure. He held noisy parties that had gained notoriety in student circles and earned him the reputation of an immoderate drinker, the first stage of becoming an alcoholic. From their point of view, a foreign, married woman, a non-drinker, was a change for the better.

We would be sharing some of the domestic facilities: the kitchen, the bathroom and the toilet, located in their part of the apartment. Any occupant of the room would be intruding on their privacy. I was pleased with the room and took a liking to the couple.

'About the wardrobe...,' Alinka began, but stopped short. She lit a cigarette and said in a whispering voice as if afraid to be overheard: 'It's best not to use it. Leave it as it is.'

'Why not? It's an impressive old mahogany wardrobe with three doors and the room is bare of furniture!'

I approached and opened the middle door. A musty, stale smell hit my nostrils. Alinka threw the balcony door open to air the room. Inside the wardrobe was a pile of dozens of pairs of laced-up, orthopaedic, ankle-high boots. All of the boots had the right sole raised to double thickness.

'The boots will have to go!' I said, already making mental notes on how to rearrange the room.

'Don't even think about it.' Alinka took a step back as if protecting herself from whatever was inside.

'She used to limp,' Alinka added.

'I can see they are orthopaedic boots.' I decided to have another look to see what was behind the other two doors. The upper part was stuffed with motheaten furs, old dresses, and rotting, cut-up pieces of floor rugs. The lower part had more of the boots, in different shades of leather.

'Before the war, the apartment belonged to a Jewish family,' Alinka said shutting the doors with a look of alarm.

'Why hasn't anyone thrown out this junk?'

'Because, *she* doesn't allow it. Two previous tenants have tried and had nasty things happen to them. You are Jewish, your presence may comfort the owner of the wardrobe. They say she was carted off to Auschwitz before she had time to lace up her boots.'

'Charming. I was given a key to a room with a ghost then!' I tried to hide my discomfort from Alinka. She lit another cigarette, inhaled and let out the smoke in rings, her eyes focused on their dispersal.

'Do you believe in ghosts?'

'The English get a better price for a castle if it has a ghost.'

'They wouldn't if the ghosts had an Auschwitz connection.'

'Any more of the ghost stories?' I was determined not to be frightened.

'Yes,' she said. Antoni's live-in girlfriend, to prove that it was just superstitious nonsense, fed up with the useless wardrobe, had made arrangements to get rid of the contents. On that date, the brakes of Antoni's recently acquired second-hand car failed and they had an accident. He was lucky to emerge only with a dislocated shoulder but she was badly injured. After the accident his drinking became worse.

And before that, the previous tenant, also a student, fled swearing that the wardrobe was cursed. He intended to sell it and make a handsome profit. When the future owner came to collect it, he fainted and it crushed his foot. He ended up crippled for life.

'Do you believe in ghosts?' Alinka pressed on.

'No!' I declared. The ghosts I was dealing with belonged to another category – they did not interfere with car brakes. They were on a mission to take care of the world of the living. In the absence of prophets, they keep vigil and when necessary sound the alarm to wake us up to the damage we do to life.

I was prepared to share the room with the ghost of the limping woman who had been carted off to Auschwitz. But after moving in I took steps to protect myself, *just in case.* I invited a local rabbi into the room to conduct the Kadish – the prayer for the dead woman who limped.

The collection of her orthopaedic boots stayed intact, as relics of her unrecorded life, but not forgotten. During the time I spent in the room as a film student, she never bothered me.

THE CEMETERY COMES BACK TO LIFE

This time I was determined to locate Mother's grave. I arrived in a taxi at the cemetery and knocked on the keeper's door. Instead of the keeper that I had met before, an unfriendly stranger faced me. He looked more like a bouncer confronting an intruder. The hefty fellow, with watery blue eyes, ran his fingers through his greasy blond hair and declared that if I was from the press, he had nothing to say; he had enough problems with the police who kept asking him questions. He was about to turn on his heels when a bill pushed into his hand changed his attitude.

'The previous keeper is dead,' he said.

He must have told the story about the former keeper's death so often that it sounded like a recitation, interspersed with frequent expletives. He had died some months earlier in suspicious circumstances, apparently a victim of murder. He had disturbed a gang of night robbers who specialised in stealing valuable marble from the headstones of the buried. It was profitable: recycled, it could be sold as almost new. According to unconfirmed rumours, the thieves had also stolen his illegal hoard of dollars.

A death in a cemetery, a violent death at that, had a grain of the macabre. The man who promised to lead me to Mother's grave had gone to his own, taking with him the invaluable information he possessed about the Jewish cemetery and particularly the ghetto section. It was a great loss for the occasional Jewish visitors from abroad, like myself, who came to search for family graves. The keeper being new was not entirely familiar with the layout of the vast section of the ghetto part of the cemetery. He was sorry – in a month or two he would have learned his way around.

I decided to venture out on my own, armed only with a vague description provided by someone who was in the ghetto.

'Search close to the wall. Look out for an oak tree.'

The area resembled an overgrown steppe: tall grasses, now gone to seed, were towered over by spiky thistles, nature's own barbed wire. The dry autumn weather had distilled an intoxicating scent from the abundance of wild flowers and plants. Occasionally a bird flew from under my feet, startled by the noise of crushed thistles. Wading through undergrowth that reached up to my shoulders, my progress was painfully slow. The ghetto section of the cemetery was a haven for wild life. I was stepping over fertile ground where nature was relentlessly recycling death into life. I soon lost my bearings and, disorientated, I tripped and fell into a hole as deep as a crater, almost blinded by a spiked thorn that jabbed into my eye. I might even have stomped over Mother's grave without realising it. I took it as a warning and made my retreat.

Trying to find my way back, I came across what I first mistook for a Gypsy caravan. On closer inspection, I realised it was a film production van, and I recognised the ubiquitous light meter in the hands of the cameraman. The director was wearing a black leather jacket, tight riding breeches and officers' high boots – obviously the fashion with the film fraternity – and was discussing the story with the actors. The cameraman kept looking up at the sky and complaining about the clouds that had hidden the sun. In time, I, too, would learn about the hazards of the enforced idleness when shooting outdoors, waiting for the clouds to disperse.

The accidentally encountered film crew gave me an opportunity to watch a film in the making. The director was briefing the two actors playing the leading roles:

'We are shooting an unusual kind of a Romeo and Juliet love story but with a difference. Our Romeo is an elderly confused Jew, and his Juliet happens to be an old maid suffering from a religious delusion-mania. Our Verona has no balcony, only a barn in a Polish village. The encounter between the two takes place during the German occupation and after the war, in a Poland liberated by the Russians who...'

He never finished the sentence – they would have understood that he meant the early years of Moscow-imposed Communism.

The script was based on a real-life story, first reported in the Polish press in 1947. It concerned an unusual court case against a citizen Wieslawa F., accused of holding captive Jacob C., a Jew on the run from the Nazis. She was an unmarried peasant woman who lived alone with two dogs, cats and a goat. For her, the war brought a miracle in the person of the fugitive Jew and when she found him hiding in her barn, she believed that Christ himself had appeared in disguise. This Christ was covered in lice and his skin was festering from neglected cuts. She nursed him back to health, and managed somehow to hide him from the Nazis and, just as important, from her neighbours. At the end of the war, when the 'ungodly' Communists took over, she decided that the time of danger for her Jew/Christ was not yet over.

The hour of her downfall arrived when her next-door neighbour, who nursed a grudge against her, tipped off the authorities that she was hoarding an undeclared crop of potatoes and livestock, a punishable offence. Raiding citizen Wieslawa's barn they found the Jew, terrified and raising his hands in surrender, expecting to be shot. Only then did Jacob discover that the war had ended two years previously!

During the trial, the judge was lenient towards Citizen Wieslawa F. She was declared mentally disturbed and sentenced to be sent to an institution.

As soon as the sun came out, at the director's command 'Action! Camera, Sound rolling!' everybody sprang into action. From the held-up clapboard I learned the title: *Christ in the Barn*.

The actor playing the Jew had difficulties with the ill-fitting, glued-on beard. And the goat supposedly led by the actress playing the old peasant woman was leading her. The scene of the first encounter between the Jew and the woman had to be repeated. After the fourth take, the day's shooting was over. The crew got busy wrapping up the equipment.

My failed attempt to find Mother's grave had provided an opportunity to watch the toilsome process of filmmaking. The cemetery, as the location for the film *Christ in the Barn*, had been injected with a spark of life. The reality of celluloid was working to rescue the story of another Polish Jew on the run.

THE FIRST STEPS IN FILMMAKING

The Film School's curriculum, as well as listing a variety of theoretical subjects relevant to cinematography, provided the chance to make three short films each year. A close link with the Theatre School offered a pool of aspiring actors on whom one could test one's directorial skills.

The projection theatre was at the centre of our immersion in the film culture. Classical and contemporary films were part of the non-stop film projections, often running late into the night. Students would drop in whenever they could and we got used to watching films from the middle or from the end, and then back to the beginning. Films were our staple diet; we breathed, ate, watched and talked them, the ones that inspired us and the ones that we, ourselves, were hoping to make.

Most film directors nurse a special tenderness for their first film, as was the case with my *Black Pompeii*.

As a novice searching for suitable documentary subject matter, predictably, I focused on socially deprived people. To my surprise,

Professor J. Bossak, the tutor of documentary films, expressed serious reservations.

'Think of something more personal,' he suggested.

He was a natural-born teacher and he would always search for a kernel of merit, even in the most half-baked idea. His directness and warmth earned him the students' affection and respect.

My next proposal was indeed very personal, and very short: 'Black Pompeii – a lament for the dying Lodz Jewish cemetery. Four pall-bearers clad in black, carry a coffin. To be shot in winter. For sound effects, use liturgical music.'

'Why "Black Pompeii?"' He was intrigued by the title.

In my mind I had twinned Lodz with ancient Pompeii, the Roman town destroyed by volcanic eruptions in 79 AD. Blackness, soot and ashes were the link between victims of the Lodz ghetto and Pompeii.

I had visited the ruins of Pompeii while on my honeymoon and the artefacts displayed at the Naples Museum had left an unsettling impression. Trapped beneath the flow of lava, the victims of Pompeii's volcanic eruptions had become nature's raw material, creating out of death, in its most perverse way, an art form. Men, women and children and domestic animals were transformed into sculptures of alarming power, their gestures of anguish preserved for posterity. The solidified lava had become their shroud of eternity.

Pompeii made me think of the Lodz ghetto population, caught in the panic of deportations, herded into gas chambers and reduced to ashes.

Professor Bossak's response was direct.

'I don't see a film in it yet. You're using too many words. You're a painter, do a story-board.' I received from him a priceless lesson on how to switch from thinking in words to moving pictures.

Black Pompeii, a ten-minute film, begins with the cemetery's crumbling brick wall from which dripping wet letters sprout like ivy as a background to the title.

The action involves four pall-bearers clad in black with a coffin emerging from a cemetery enveloped in a thick mist. Their walk takes them first past the ruins of the marble mausoleums, which the Lodz magnates had built for themselves and their families. The camera pans over a landscape filled with fractured black marble columns sticking out from the earth like rotten, loose teeth. The pall-bearers become entangled in the thickets that have grown over the collapsed, ruined headstones of the poor: congested in death as in life.

In this desolate landscape they move like restless sleepers unable to wake up from a nightmare. There is no visible end, no burial for the four men carrying the burden of the dead. They are more like ghosts condemned to eternal wandering through the dying cemetery.

I was lucky in the cameraman with whom I was teamed up. Krzysztof Malkiewicz was already in his third year of studies. He approached the project with empathy and devotion, shooting the film with the inventiveness and care of a veteran craftsman on a high commission. Through his attention to detail, Krzysztof was preserving for posterity, at least on film, a lost folk art. He used special lighting effects to enhance the traditional Jewish motives carved in tombstones. The Tree of Life broken in half: candles symbolising the flicker of an extinguished life. The Lions of Judah, the guardians of the Torah, chiselled in stone by anonymous artisans.

After viewing the final cut, Professor Bossak observed that with *Black Pompeii* I had given my parents a symbolic funeral. How amazing that this had not occurred to me before!

'That's what good filmmaking should do. It should always carry more meaning than intended,' he added.

For the next production of a short film I turned for inspiration to art.

The Holy Family is an animated film in which instead of using graphics or drawings, I made use of reproductions of Russian icons and medieval Christian iconography, taken from art books. The story of the Jewish Holy Family in Auschwitz is narrated through the use of animated icons, images of the Holy Family. The tone of the film is set by the sound effects that include sacral music mixed with the words '*Jude raus! ["Jews out!"] Jude raus! Jude, Jude, Jude...!*' shouted the way the Nazis used to and carried by an echo. In the five-minute film shot in colour, I had metaphorically transposed the drama of the Crucifixion into the contemporary Jewish catastrophe.

The storyline included three key sequences: first the brutal separation of the Holy Family, depicting the moment when the infant Jesus is torn from Mary's arms. This is followed by the Crucifixion, depicting how crucified Jesus is pulled off the Cross leaving a bleeding empty space. The *pietà* sequence includes shots of Jesus being snapped from Mary's arms, and the emptiness, like a blood-red shadow, suggests an oozing pain and agony.

The ultimate destruction of the Holy Family takes place in close-up. The torn fragments of the Holy Family are arranged as in collage and set on fire. The cut out glossy reproductions curl and twist, as the recognisable Holy faces slowly burn and turn into ashes. The flames almost lick the camera lens, smudging the screen with smoke.

At festivals, the *Holy Family* film was praised for its originality and impact. The fact that it was purchased by a distributor increased my confidence. I had, after all, managed to relocate my talent from painting to the screen.

The next hurdle was to prove myself when working with actors.

Homecoming, my first short feature, was based on the experience of the unhappy visit to our apartment. As an author-director, writing the script, I was exploring the extent to which one could tamper with autobiographical facts when filtered through cinematic imagination. Film directors exercise a unique privilege of being able, on the screen, to manipulate the flow of time. In *Homecoming*, being a film about the dramatisation of memory, I made use of the technique of flashback, interweaving the past with the present.

Homecoming achieved a coherence that was absent in real life. The film made the rounds of international film festivals where it received favourable press reviews as an example of an original way of handling parallel realities. So far I was proving myself a filmmaker.

My early 'Polish films' were, like my life, zigzagging between past and present, between a celebration of life and a devotion to the dead. Poland was the territory where Europe's Jewish catastrophe had left most of the traces.

COMMUTING DURING THE COLD WAR

The experience of having one foot in England and the other in Poland during four years of film studies was both enriching and disturbing. The frequent journeys between capitalist England and Communist Poland which involved crossing the Iron Curtain called for a balancing act.

With each departure from Poland I was aware of leaving behind a world filled with appalling contradictions. Though it was a country vibrating with intellectual and artistic vigour it presented a sad monochrome world filled with intolerable anomalies. Office typewriters and photocopying machines carried crude identification numbers slapped on with thick paint. Under guard at all times, the socialist state's exclusive control of its property symbolised a rampant bureaucratic paranoia about citizens' access to even this most commonplace technology. Everything was done to prevent the circulation of possible criticism of the regime.

In the early 1960s, at the height of the Cold War, commuting across the Iron Curtain was unheard of unless you were a diplomat or a high-ranking official. But that's exactly what I did, until someone at the Polish Security Office took notice.

At school my hectic lifestyle earned me the nickname 'Mira of the crazy documents' which, in Polish, has a humorous ring. My commuting style apparently broke the guidelines set by the Polish Foreign Office that regulated foreign-student travel to and from Poland. Officially, such visas were valid for one year and only for a single entry and exit. Passports had to be surrendered and would be returned at the end of the academic year, after one had presented the index book to the authorities, as proof that the workload had been fulfilled.

At the end of the first autumn term I realised I was in deep trouble. I had to be home for my son's major school breaks at least three or four times a year. At the Honoratka cafe, where my dilemma was discussed, someone suggested a solution: get yourself a medical certificate recommending home leave on health grounds.

Dr K., an Honoratka regular and a declared cinema aficionado with a reputation of obliging his friends' requests, checked me into his hospital. This was the first step to legitimising my request to take leave on health grounds. After my admission, I developed a temperature due to lax hygiene conditions, which made me into a bona fide patient. Dr K. could write out a medical certificate with a clear conscience recommending weeks-long convalescence at home. I realised that if I wanted to continue with my studies, I had to eliminate the problem of entering the country on a student visa, with its imposed restrictions. I need to be free to make use of frequent exits and entries to Poland. I fell back on the use of short-term tourist visas for each journey. The Polish consular personnel in London became accustomed to my regular visits. Obtaining entry and exit visas had become so routine for me that for a long time nobody questioned it. Bending the rules when crossing frontiers, real or metaphorical, gave me the same kind of satisfaction I had derived during the war.

My frequent transitions from Lodz to London and back were beginning to exhibit an effortless smoothness. The possession of a British passport added to my sense of security, despite the original warning issued by the British Foreign Office. After three years I was beginning to take my crossings for granted. I had failed to anticipate the complications ahead of me.

COME AND SPY FOR US

On arrival home for the Easter break, just as I felt secure in my commuting routine, my husband greeted me with some startling information. During my absence, someone from MI5 had left a message that on my return they would like me to get in touch with them. Had I kept up with Cold War spy thrillers I might not have been so surprised.

'Do I have to comply with their request?'

'Only if you want to.'

I had a choice in the matter, my husband assured me. He knew about such things. During the war he had been attached to an intelligence unit in the Middle East on account of his knowledge of French.

'Well?' he asked.

I was too curious to let such an opportunity pass. After all, for a film director, every experience should be grist to the cinematic mill. I even suspected I knew the reason for their interest in me.

On my last journey to Poland, instead of flying, I went by train; travelling first class and no longer dreading the confrontation with German train guards. Halfway into the journey, just past East Berlin, the train had an unscheduled and prolonged stop. Going in search of a dining car I discovered that it had been detached before entering the Eastern Zone.

The compartment next to mine was occupied by a group of jolly Russians. The two women and a man who spoke excellent English dealt with my inquiry about the missing buffet car with customary Russian hospitality. They invited me to share their food as they were travelling with a well-stocked hamper filled with Russian caviar, sausages, sandwiches and vodka. We chatted about this and that and I learnt from the man, who seemed to be their spokesman, that they were diplomats who were returning to Moscow having just completed a stint at the Russian Embassy in London. In their compartment I noticed a naval officer's uniform hanging near the window. After the train pulled into Warsaw we parted company.

A month later, when the back issue of the *Sunday Observer* arrived from England, I learned who one of the Russians I had met on the train was. Splashed on the front page was the news about the current spy scandal involving British MP John Profumo and two call girls, Christine Keeler and Mandy Rice Davies. Implicated in the affair was none other than the charming and attractive Captain E. Ivanov whose photograph also made the front page. It showed him wearing a naval officer's uniform. I may have been the last English-speaking person to meet him after his getaway from London. How exciting!

The arranged interview with MI5 was conducted at home in the presence of my husband. Two chaps, looking uncannily like their Ealing Comedy counterparts, arrived wearing raincoats, discreet ties, grey suits and meticulously polished black shoes. One of them made the formal introductions whilst our housekeeper, Edna, brought in a trolley with refreshments.

I broke the ice by saying that I could guess why they wished to talk to me. The man who was doing all the talking seemed more than a little surprised by my statement.

'In that case, it will make our task that much easier,' he said, pulling from his briefcase a photograph which he offered for my inspection.

'What do you know about this man?'

To my disappointment, the face before me was not of the Russian spy. The man in question was a Polish journalist I had met at the Honoratka cafe. We had shared the same table on a number of occasions, but in truth I hardly knew anything about him except for his profession. One day he mentioned that he was being posted to London. The occasion called for a display of Anglo-Polish hospitality and I extended an invitation for him to call on us in London, which he did.

'Recently, I invited him to dinner together with some other friends.'

'We know that,' said the man who did the talking as he consulted his notebook. He flipped through the pages and read out the names of the other guests. One of them was Gerry, a writer from Canada, whom I always teased about his loyalty to the Communist Party.

'Your friend,' the MI5 agent corrected me, 'is no longer a Communist.'

I was shocked. Not only did they know whom we entertained, but they also had detailed information about the political profiles of our guests! They had been keeping tabs on our life! Whereas I would have expected this in Poland, it came as a shock to discover such things on our own doorstep. In indignation, I looked at my husband, but he was busy scrutinising his nails. Why had he not warned me?

'I thought this was a free country!' I protested.

'So it is. And to protect your freedom we need your co-operation. For instance, the Polish gentleman in question may not be who he says he is.'

He went on to explain how the Eastern Bloc consular staff often incorporated journalists who were on the payroll of their Secret Service. Many of them were fronting for what in popular terms was called the Soviet Union's 'dirty tricks' department.

'People like you can help us to separate the wheat from the chaff.'

His appeal to my patriotic reflexes, to rush to the defence of England, amused me. People like *me*? If only they knew! I began to feel sorry for poor England and MI5, if it depended on the help of the likes of me, an unreliable, chaotic chatterbox. In the family I had a reputation for blurting out any morsel of family gossip I had heard. Sooner or later, the MI5 visit itself would become a dinner-table anecdote.

'What we have in mind,' he continued, taking a sip of tea, 'is something quite simple.'

So I was *not* expected to deliver top-secret documents concerning the Warsaw Pact's nuclear silos to someone in Poland. While there, I had been prudent enough to stop using my camera, just in case a beautiful landscape I admired was hiding such an objective.

'You speak the language,' he continued. 'You meet all sorts of people. All you'll need to do is just keep your eyes and ears open when you are in Poland. Every little bit helps...'

'Sorry, Her Majesty's Secret Service will have to manage without me.'

A silence settled on the room. I was looking at one of my paintings of Luisa in sombre blues. How did I get from that to MI5 trying to recruit me? The Cold War, the witch-hunts, the spying scandals on both sides of the ideological war-zone had created a climate of hysteria and I, a freewheeling commuter tearing through the Iron Curtain, must have inadvertently touched on a high-tension spy wire.

I stood up and they understood the tea session was over. Both men also rose and began to button and unbutton their jackets, a nervous gesture men often use when at a loss. It bought them extra time.

The 'talker' pulled out his card, jotted down an additional phone number, and handed it to me.

'If you change your mind, here is the number to call.' At the door he added:

'By the way, if you encounter any problems with Polish Security, please let us know immediately.'

Glad to be rid of them, I paid scant attention to his last words. I dismissed the London MI5 episode as nothing more than fodder for a future film script about spying.

'YOU MUST MEET SO AND SO'

During my London Christmas break Alex Jacobs, an enthusiastic supporter of budding filmmakers, proposed that we join him at a Christmas party at Doris Lessing's home. The occasion, he decided, would be a good opportunity for a filmmaker to meet a distinguished writer. He could never resist the urge to introduce people he felt should meet.

'I don't know her! We cannot just be foisted on her.'

'She keeps open house and I'll let her know about it.'

That was how my husband and I found ourselves at a gathering where we hardly knew anybody.

After the introduction to our hostess, Alex looked disappointed.

'I have told her you are a promising filmmaker!' he scolded me. According to him, I failed to engage her in a meaningful conversation beyond the hand-shaking ritual and the customary pleasantries.

What could one say to a writer one admired? To mention casually that I had stayed awake all night reading *The Golden Notebooks*, shaken by the book's impact, might have embarrassed the author. I mumbled my tribute as politely as I could.

She certainly looked the part of a writer of distinction. An unfashionable but classic hairstyle with a bun fixed at the back of her head added an ageless touch. Her features could have fitted into any century.

At the Christmas party, chance brought me together with another pair of writers for whom my connection to Poland was of interest. Perhaps it was not so much blind chance as the fact that I had never learned how to eat standing up whilst balancing a drink in one hand and a plate of food in the other that placed me next to an attractive young woman with thick glasses. We fell into a conversation and she was amused to discover that I knew neither my hostess nor any of her other guests.

'A gatecrasher?' Her wry humour appealed to me.

American-born Ruth Fainlight was a published poet whose reputation was growing on both sides of the Atlantic. We soon established that we both had a son, and had shared the experience of having lived for a while in Spain. Much later into the friendship, the fact that we were both Jewish became an additional bond. Her husband, the writer Alan Sillitoe, on hearing about my studies in Poland, was keen to introduce me to his Polish translator of *Saturday Night and Sunday Morning* who was currently visiting London. I was thrilled to hear that his books, including *The Loneliness of the Long Distance Runner*, were being translated into Polish.

Jadwiga Milnikiel, the translator, was a middle-aged, attractive woman, ash-blonde with blue eyes, radiating natural warmth enhanced by a voice infused with cheerfulness and laughter.

Jadwiga was no stranger to London having spent eight years with her husband, Polish Ambassador Jan Milnikiel, accredited to the Court of St James's. They stayed from 1953 to 1961; his tour of duty lasted long enough to have bestowed on him the honour of the doyen of the Corps Diplomatique.

Back in Poland, her position as an ex-ambassador's wife and her connections with people in high places, including the Polish Ministry of Culture, had helped to overcome the censors' initial objections to the books she wished to translate. She had chosen Sillitoe for his anarchic and rebellious spirit.

'The hero of *The Loneliness of the Long Distance Runner*,' she said, 'should shake up our own fucked up Young Communist League.'

Jadwiga enjoyed poking fun at the anomalies in the Polish political system, in spite of being part of the establishment class, the *nomenklatura*. Her own life before she reached the position of 'Mme Ambassador' included the experiences of being overrun by the Soviets after the war broke out. She and her family had been deported into 'deepest Russia'. Upon their release, she had joined the newly formed Polish army, and like many others was evacuated from the Soviet Union via Persia, Palestine and from there to Egypt, where she met her future husband, also in the Polish army.

Alan Sillitoe, a passionate collector of old maps, unrolled a map of the Soviet Union and the Middle East and traced the route Jadwiga's life had taken between 1939 and 1945.

Her liveliness and warmth were infectious. She had the gift of forming instant friendships, and by the time the evening came to an end it felt as if I had known her for a long time. And when parting, she said, 'When you return to Poland, you must come and stay with us in Warsaw.' I knew she meant it.

EUROPE: THEIRS AND OURS

In Warsaw, Jadwiga received me with a 'Make yourself at home' welcome. The Milnikiels lived in Warsaw's fashionable district where many of the Party and government members had their residences. It was a spacious, open-plan villa with an attic room that served as Jadwiga's study and guest bedroom. The household included the ex-ambassadorial couple, their two young sons born in England, Jadwiga's mother and a resident maid, a village girl who reminded me of Kasia. Later, a maiden aunt came to live with them as well.

Their home was filled with souvenirs of their time in London. In the sitting room, on the piano were displayed formal photographs of Jan and Jadwiga, seen with the great and mighty. The place of honour was given to the Queen, in an ornate frame, seen welcoming them. Standing next to Her Majesty were signed photographs of other royal persons, alongside a collection of photographs of current and ex-Prime Ministers, including Churchill. On the walls were smiling faces of artists of international repute, who had enjoyed their hospitality and had become their friends.

Jan Milnikiel was the son of a miner from Silesia. His status as an authentic working-class man was crucial to his diplomatic career as the representative of the Polish People's Republic. Academic accomplishments, a degree in geology and engineering, had added to his impeccable socialist pedigree.

The Melnikiels practised an almost archaic style of Slavonic hospitality. After a few visits I was accepted as one of the family. Their home offered me an opportunity to escape from Lodz as often as I could, providing a respite from the ghosts of the past. The family was unashamedly Anglophile, and finding myself in a household filled with the English teatime rituals forced me to admit how much I was missing England.

Jadwiga's attic studio was filled with books in Polish and English. The titles of the books revealed the wide range of her intellectual interests: literature, history and social sciences.

She was a wonderful dinner-party companion, telling jokes about herself and the many pompous people that she encountered as a diplomat's wife. Once, a stiff-shirted diplomat at a reception had asked her what she liked best in life.

'I love eating, drinking, talking and fucking!' she claimed to have replied.

It was a mystery how someone with her temperament had managed for so many years to fit into the protocol-confined lifestyle of a diplomat's wife. Perhaps allowances were made for the new class of Soviet orbit diplomats.

Ironically, after the prolonged tour of duty in the West, including Sweden and Canada, their English-born children had to learn Polish, and the parents had to learn to adjust to the daily reality of life in socialist Poland.

By the time I was entrusted with a key to their house, giving me the freedom to turn up at any time, the ex-ambassador took me aside for an important talk. Jan, a man towering in height, was looking down on me like a schoolmaster facing a pupil. Pouring a large whisky for himself and me, he declared: 'There are three things you must never do in Poland! Rule one, never bring into the country any literature or magazines published by exiles in opposition.' I knew he meant *Kultura*, a quarterly magazine printed in Paris that published contributions from the best and most talented Polish writers and academics in exile. It was in great demand amongst the Polish intelligentsia and anyone frequently crossing the Iron Curtain was likely to be approached about such a favour.

I had to suppress a desire to laugh in view of the fact that the latest issue of *Kultura* was on display on the coffee table for all to see. Realising that I was looking at it, he smiled, and with a wink explained that he had to read 'this stuff' as part of his job. He was in charge of the Western desk at the Polish Foreign Office. The contrast between his words and his expression betrayed his awareness about the irony in the situation.

'Rule two, never change money on the black market.'

Before continuing with the third warning, he lit a Marlboro cigarette and inhaled deeply. He was a heavy smoker; his rasping voice and shortness of breath were already showing the symptoms of the emphysema that would kill him.

'And last but not least, never go with a man to a hotel! If you're fool enough to fuck around, you've got a home here! And if you break any of these rules, it will be *my task to read your file* anyway, damn it!'

Jadwiga and Jan were critical of the Soviet-style practice of censorship and were democrats at heart, but Jan, as a high-ranking official, had to do more of the play-acting. In their house I was often unintentionally privy to conversations that touched on sensitive political issues. Their neighbours, high Party officials, would drop in, bringing with them the latest news about the infighting within the Party's hierarchy or rumours about scandals brewing in the Kremlin. Nobody paid much attention to my presence, though they knew I was from 'the West'.

The most passionate discussions concerned the Polish-Soviet relationship and the future of Europe. The preoccupation with the Russians was likely to crop up in any conversation. Three hundred years of exposure to Russian domination had cast a long shadow over Polish national consciousness. Poland's present political situation and its future were closely tied up with the temperament of the Russian people and their leaders. It seemed to be the perennial, unresolved issue on which the survival of Poland's independence hinged.

'The Americans have got it all wrong,' one of their friends argued. 'Not Communism, but Russia's autocracy and unreconstructed imperialism is the major threat to the West.' It was a very provocative statement to be made in the house of an official representing the Polish Foreign Office, given that its official foreign policy was pro-Soviet.

'Russia is like a tug-boat which keeps dragging Central Europe into its Asian orbit,' somebody else added.

I myself disliked the label of East European and would correct, with irritation, anyone failing to locate Poland within the heart of Europe.

I recalled that above Zb.'s desk hung a map of 'his Europe', on which he had marked the boundaries of his freedom of movement. As a European, his life was hemmed in between East Germany and the Soviet Union. Even within the Soviet Union, Poles were restricted as to where they could travel.

The earnest conversations about the fate of Europe conducted within the Milnikiels' circle of friends would be meaningless in London. To my husband and our English friends, Europe meant Western Europe only. On either side a parallel mental Iron Curtain controlled the concept of Europe as a geographic and cultural entity.

Watching television in London it was plain to see that the political perspective was transatlantic with Washington at its centre. The English language was the bridge over which economic and cultural traffic rolled.

One evening in London, while my family watched the news, my son asked, 'Will you vote for John F. Kennedy?' The extensive coverage of the US presidential elections in the English media confused the child, making it difficult to comprehend that Kennedy was not part of English life.

For the Poles, the political point of gravity was Moscow, a fact much resented. In Jadwiga's house I would often encounter some high-placed party apparatchik who, having returned from a recent official trip to Moscow, would pour scorn on the conditions of life in Russia. The Poles liked nothing better than to swap impressions and experiences reaffirming the inferior standard of living of their Soviet comrades. Unlike Western visitors who were lodged in the best hotels, citizens of the 'fraternal' socialist countries were put up in hotels used by the natives. Having a bath could be a serious matter as the plugs rarely fitted. It was mind-boggling! The same country that had sent sputniks into outer space and manufactured sophisticated military hardware was incapable of supplying bath plugs or other items for domestic use. Like most Poles, this particular visitor to Moscow both mocked and feared the Russians.

The concerns voiced at the Milnikiels' in the 1960s about the shape and future of Europe, even after the fall of the Berlin Wall, still carry echoes into the present time. Even today, with NATO's protective wings spread over Central and Eastern Europe, Poland remains hemmed-in between a post-Communist, dangerously unstable Russia and its German neighbour, now territorially united, and once again politically and economically powerful.

The legacy of Hitler and Stalin hangs over Poland like a poisonous cloud.

ANOTHER INVITATION TO COME AND SPY FOR US

Already in my third year of studies, returning from London to Lodz, I took my passport to have it stamped as I had done countless times. Registering with the appropriate authorities at the Komisariat had to be done with each arrival. I presented myself in the morning to the official I always dealt with, a friendly militiaman whom I had even used as an extra in my previous film. I was in a hurry to get to the school and had even kept the taxi waiting. I knew that the formality would not take long, the militiaman always stamped my passport without delay. On this occasion he took longer than usual.

'Just a small formality,' he assured me as he walked off with my passport in hand. After a while he returned and announced that his boss wished to see me. I followed him to the second floor, protesting that I had not eaten breakfast, had a taxi waiting and was expected at the school for a dubbing session.

'Don't worry. We dismissed him and will get you another as soon as the boss has had a chance to talk to you.'

The boss's office, it turned out, consisted of three men sitting behind a long table, facing me. The man in the middle was inspecting my passport and shaking his head ominously, signalling his disapproval. I was getting very nervous. The feeling in the room revived memories of the wartime Soviet interrogations.

'You have broken the regulations of foreign students' terms of residence in Poland,' he said in a grave voice.

I explained the reason why I did it. I had to be back home when my son had his school holidays. Using tourist visas instead of the one-year visa issued to students was the only way I could continue the studies.

'It costs a fortune to fly as often as you do.'

'My husband can afford it.'

I calculated that the man's yearly wages were a fraction of what I would spend in travel expenses in one term alone.

'What do you know about Mr Zb.?' one of them asked, flipping through his file, on which I noticed was attached a passport-size photograph of Zb.

'Ah, I am very fond of him. And he gave me back Poland!'

'He did what?' The three men exchanged anxious looks. 'What else did he give you? Any documents? Photographs?'

'Just love! He is the man who gave me Poland,' I said, amused by the impact of the phrase. They looked at each other like doctors in a consultation dealing with an insane patient. One of the men who had kept silent up till now joined in. His voice was rather cultivated.

'And your husband, does he know about this generous Pole who so carelessly gives away Poland to foreigners?'

'He not only knows, he collected the stamps from the letters Zb. was sending from Kazakhstan.' Their faces betrayed the unspoken censure of my English husband's tolerance: *A Polish husband would have known what to do with such a wife.*

'We have information that your husband is working for the British Secret Service.'

This was laughable! During the war, R.'s duty involved frequenting Baghdad brothels reporting on what kind of military information the whores were picking up from the troops who visited them. In the family, his military past was a source of merciless teasing.

'You are making a film about the Soviet army, have obtained uniforms from a Soviet garrison...In Poland, you have access to people in high places.' His eyes were drilling into mine.

The interrogation was taking a serious turn and I was getting very frightened. In a flash the words of the MI5 agent came back to me, and with it the ridiculous idea that the Secret Service chaps, the world over, formed an international fraternity! The British lot, having failed to recruit me, had tipped off their Polish counterpart: 'She is yours now, you try her!'

'I wish to contact the British Consul and inform them that I have been detained,' I demanded.

'Oh no!' The chief interrogator protested, 'This is only a friendly chat.'

I mentioned that I had an important appointment at the school that I could not miss.

'Don't worry, we have informed the school that you will be late.' And in a tone of reconciliation, added. 'Poles abroad were also questioned by *your* MI5.'

He produced from his briefcase the copy of the *Observer*, the newspaper that carried an interview I had given about the Film School, praising the prevailing liberal climate.

'This shows your friendliness towards the country of your birth.'

I knew what was coming. He was going to appeal to my friendly feelings for Poland and ask for my help.

'You know so many important people in England,' he continued.

When I heard him use that phrase I had to repress a desire to laugh. The Secret Service chaps in London had used identical words! Could it be that *they* of the international spy fraternity were learning their lines from the same script?

I sat it out with a stony face. Having failed to blackmail me over Zb., they changed the tone and thanked me for my 'co-operation'. My stamped passport was handed back to me; my ordeal was over.

'By the way, treat this *chat* as strictly confidential.'

Out in the street, instead of going to the school, I took a taxi to the railway station and went to Warsaw. I found Jan Milnikiel at home. To calm my agitation, he poured me a double whisky and listened to my report about what took place. I kept quiet about the London visit, however.

'Why are you so upset? It took them nearly three years before they got on to you. Now they will leave you in peace.'

'Do they try it with everybody?'

He nodded. 'Sometimes they even succeed,' he added. We never talked about it again.

Back in Lodz, I immediately sought out my colleague from Iceland, to find out how 'they' had dealt with him.

'Oh, every time I am drunk I am picked up by the militia who haul me before this guy who expects me to say "yes" and to sign something. They tried to blackmail me by threatening to inform my wife about my regular Polish girlfriend who is expecting our child. I told him to go to hell! My wife has a lover and she in turn is expecting his child. Idiots! They know nothing about Scandinavian-style open marriages.'

I decided in the future not to miss any spy films.

SHAKESPEARE IN ENGLAND AND IN POLAND

Shakespeare had become a bridge between my life in England and Poland. In the room dominated by the wardrobe containing the dead woman's orthopaedic boots, I had pinned on the wall the following quote from *The Tempest*: 'We are such stuff, as dreams are made on, and our little life is rounded with a sleep.' It was a sentimental reminder that at the Jaszunska Gymnasium, before the outbreak of the war, for the end of the school term we had performed *The Tempest*.

The magical element of *The Tempest* entered my life again when Betteshanger, my son's prep school in Kent planned their end-of-term performance. In between the Jaszunska Gymnasium in Lodz and the Betteshanger performance of *The Tempest*, millions of men had blown each other up, causing millions of deaths. And millions of words had been written about the Second World War and the Holocaust.

An Ariel played by a boy with bony limbs, before his voice had broken, was an altogether different Ariel to our acrobatic Evunia, the smallest girl in our class. Running, jumping and floating through the air – our somersaulting Evunia would always land on her feet. And how would a boyish Caliban compare with my own performance?

Marianna Lipszyc, our housemother, was a remarkable woman. An inspired educator and a professed humanist, in her tutorials she held up her favourite cultural heroes for us to admire, amongst them Mahatma Gandhi, Helen Keller and Zamenhoff, the father of Esperanto. She used every opportunity to prove to us people's inherent potential for good. There was also another side to her: theatre was her obsession and Shakespeare was her god.

The impetus to make a film about Betteshanger, my son's school, was to offer up a hymn to the preciousness of the young boys' lives – a memento of the period before boyish charm fades and the approach of manhood clips the wings of youthful flight. And indirectly, also to pay homage to the likes of Marianna and her pupils, of whom only two survived.

As a painter turned filmmaker and as a mother, I wished to use the camera as a substitute for the painter's brush. Renoir painted portraits of his children, as did Rembrandt, who immortalised his son Titus in a number of paintings.

It was to be my first independently produced documentary. Though it would be shot in England, Professor Bossak agreed to accept it as part of my second-year film quota.

The film *End of Term* covered the regular end-of-term school activities, the preparations for the forthcoming exams, including the rehearsals of *The Tempest*, culminating with the crescendo of the performance day.

In Lodz, before the war, Marianna did her best to introduce Shakespeare to the pubescent Polish-Jewish girls as a giant of European literature. Why she chose *The Tempest* and not something in a lighter vein such as *A Midsummer Night's Dream*, will remain a mystery. Like everything else she did, she used the occasion to teach us what the language of poetry and theatre was capable of. The Polish translation was just about adequate to the task.

Unlike Marianna, the Kent school headmaster who directed the play had no difficulties in conveying to his junior actors the essence of Shakespearean English.

This time, the guide to my understanding of *The Tempest*, the pastoral drama, wasn't Marianna, but Shakespeare's original text and the historical background to the Bard's plays. It was for me a revelation that a real-life event may have influenced the play. Apparently, a group of would-be colonists undertaking a perilous journey to the New World had been shipwrecked in Bermuda. Shakespeare seemed to have become preoccupied with the morality of the prospect of early colonisation.

It vindicated my school friend Marysia, who played Prospero and whose Communist older brother held the view that the play was anti-colonial in intent!

With the production of *End of Term* in Kent I was thrown in at the deep end, having combined the function of the director/producer and art director. Two talented camera operators supported me: Bryan

Probyn, a much-experienced feature cameraman, and Peter Suschitzki, a much younger man. He and his girlfriend disapproved of my choice of the subject matter: filming privileged children in a private school was not altogether 'politically correct'! Irrespective of their personal preferences, both did justice to the technical and artistic requirements of the film. The camera had to be as mobile and agile as the boys were, moving in and out of the classrooms and dormitories. Some sequences conveyed a mood of quiet concentration, observing the boys when writing letters home or cramming for exams. Others were dynamic, keeping up with the rhythm of the gym activities, boys showing off on the cricket field or gathering in the dining room to celebrate somebody's birthday. The bulk of the film concentrated on the *The Tempest* rehearsals.

The culmination of the three weeks of shooting included the end-of-term performance followed by the school fete.

To my delight, *End of Term* made the rounds of international film festivals and was bought and televised by Granada TV.

The wonder was how an alien like myself had managed to get under the skin of English boarding-school life and capture its wistfulness. The rituals of privileged boys living between home and school, between departures and arrivals, exposing them to repeated separations and reunions, touched on a sensitive nerve.

During the filming, and after, I was never far from our Jaszunska Gymnasium version of the play. More so as in the background of our 'Polish Tempest' were the rumblings of the war and our rehearsals coincided with Hitler's entry into Prague (15 March 1939). It marked the beginning of 'the war of nerves'. But none of this had distracted us from the preparation for the play.

The build-up of international tension eased somewhat in April after the signing of the Mutual Assistance Pact between Poland, Britain and France. Now Poland had powerful allies and Hitler would never dare to touch Danzig, the free Baltic city that he was claiming. We basked in a new sense of security. The mighty British Empire and France were with us!

We were rehearsing with renewed enthusiasm, putting on an end-of-term play always aroused excitement at our school. The choice of the play was in the hands of Marianna, but everything else was left to the girls' initiative, offering an outlet for pupils' artistic aspirations.

Hitler or no Hitler, we immersed ourselves in our Shakespearean adventure of survival on the magical island. I secretly coveted the role of Miranda, believing that even my name suggested my suitability.

To my chagrin, I was chosen to play Caliban, the deformed, native inhabitant of the enchanted isle.

Kasia was given the task of concocting Caliban's costume. She made use of large safety pins to hold together a used potato sack in which she cut openings for the head and arms. Underneath it, I was to wear my brother's discarded brown sweater. She added pincushions to raise the height of one shoulder. The overall effect resembled the Hunchback of Notre Dame from the film that was currently showing in the Lodz cinemas. As a finishing touch, she plaited straw into my hair that made me look like a scarecrow. At the dress rehearsals and the make-up sessions, with the help of soot and the costume, my external transformation into blackness, slavery and savagery was complete.

Never having seen a black man, a black Caliban conjured up images of the negroes in American films. On the Hollywood screen they were portrayed as friendly, round-faced folk whose fleshy lips were always smiling. There was nothing savage in the way they served and looked after the white people. On the contrary, they were always presented as devoted guardians of the white people's children.

I did have an idea, though, about slavery, shaped by the Jewish Passover celebrations. When the family gathered round a festive table, we would take turns reading from the Hagaddah about the Exodus from Egypt. The text had a clear message. It commanded the Jews to remember that we ourselves had once been slaves! Each generation was obliged to relate to it as if it had happened in their lifetime.

Identifying with Caliban's slavery complicated matters. I found his grovelling upsetting to the extent that I even had problems learning the lines.

'*Do not torment me!*'

Much as I sympathised with Caliban's lot, the Caliban in me who was forced to fetch logs and water resented having to beg Prospero for mercy. Was I not the rightful owner of the island? How dare Prospero treat me as a slave!

'Prospero was not a megalomaniac ruler but a Christian civiliser in possession of a powerful source of knowledge!' Marianna tried to shift my interpretation.

My friend Esta, one of the trio of our close-knit group, who was cast to play Miranda, could always be relied upon to take issue with any reference to Christianity. A daughter of a learned Talmudist, she was the only one among us who could quote from the original Hebrew texts. She took issue with the concept of Christianity's notions of forgiveness, insisting that it was borrowed from Judaism. Esta used every opportunity to reinstate Judaism as the matrix of ethics, reminding us that Rabbi Hillel taught the tenet 'Love thy neighbour as thyself' before Jesus' time.*

Esta, as Miranda, was draped in a lacy curtain and garlanded with flowers. Holding the magic book, her physical stillness was a natural asset. Even her strictly orthodox father would have approved, as not an inch of her body was visible; she was swathed in the curtain as if it was a tent.

Marysia, also part of our pack, was cast as Prospero on account of her commanding height. She had another interpretation: a Marxist one instilled by her Communist older brother. According to him, Caliban was simply a victim of European colonialism. For some strange reason the costume chosen for her made her look like a cardinal or a chief rabbi.

'A Jewish Prospero, then,' Esta quipped.

Evunia played Ariel because she was one of the smallest girls in the class. The role of the airy spirit fitted her like a glove, and, being acrobatic, she also knew how to walk on her hands.

The performance was a great success with parents and official visitors. The end-of-term school calendar culminated with a grand social event: a ball in which formal dress was compulsory. Traditionally it always opened with a polonaise, led by the teachers.

The presence of boys, invited from a fraternal gymnasium, had turned the occasion into a keenly anticipated attraction. This was the season for the older girls to go boy-crazy and incited speculation about who would pair off with whom, who would get the most attractive or the most distinguished boy? Any kind of boy – whether suffering from acne, already shaving, or with a voice at the breaking stage – when dressed in a formal dark suit and white shirt with bow tie, could generate dreams of romance and love.

No trace is left of the formal photograph taken for *The Tempest* production. I, in my Caliban costume, was seated in the second row next to Marysia/Prospero with Esta/Miranda to my left. Marianna, who normally never used cosmetics of any kind, had even donned a dash of pink lipstick for the occasion. No record survived of the teachers, girls or boys who had danced the polonaise in Lodz in the summer of 1939.

---

* Hillel the Elder, first century BC: one of the party of the Pharisees, his teachings of goodwill and gentleness were echoed a generation later by Christ.

LESSON II: THE LITERACY TEST

Preparing my diploma film, *Lesson II*, part of the graduation, my colleagues were taking bets. Would I pull it off or fall flat on my face?

Lesson II was to be a war epic about Soviet prisoners of war. The male students made a list of the factors against me: I was a woman with no experience of soldiering or battle. And even more important, I had never encountered German or Soviet soldiers in person, only in films. They were genuinely concerned and voiced serious doubts about the undertaking.

They pointed out that to avoid stereotypes, film directors must be familiar with every detail of battle conditions – be it in victory or defeat. One must be able to differentiate the soldiers' ranks, the way they march, roll cigarettes, eat, sleep and defecate. Many of my male colleagues were doing military reserve duty and I would often see them appear within the school grounds wearing military uniforms.

'We speak from experience,' they assured me.

Nobody at the school knew about my war biography. I had good reason not to spread information about my encounters with the Soviets. It suited me to be taken for someone who had spent the war years in England.

And wishing me well, some suggested I should consider something more suitable for a woman; for instance, a story about lovers in a car chase or better still a domestic drama. Everybody knew that sex, suspense and a beautiful landscape were important ingredients for the success of any film.

I obstinately stayed with my project. *Lesson II* was inspired by Curzio Malaparte's story 'Red Dogs' from his book *Kaput*. Malaparte had put his finger on the pulse of the new and alarming aspect of an all-out war in which intelligence and literacy were the prime targets for annihilation!

A well-connected Italian aristocrat, Malaparte was an author and a journalist. During the Second World War he had enjoyed special privileges allowing him access to the German High Command. After the invasion of the Soviet Union he was permitted to visit the Eastern Front.

The story 'Red Dogs' describes how a group of Soviet prisoners of war are brought to a Ukrainian village, under the charge of German officers stationed in the Ukraine who, bored and malicious, devise a special way to humiliate the prisoners. The 'literacy lesson' is the result. Assembled in what used to be a Soviet schoolyard they are put through a 'literacy test'. As with the Jews, deception is an important tool in manipulating the prisoners of war. Promised that the fluent readers would fare better than the failures, the once brave Russian soldiers, like schoolboys, are reduced to a state of jittery nervousness. The stakes are high and everybody is motivated to pass, some even cheating where possible. Education being such a vital part of *Homo Sovieticus*, the majority of them pass and feel sorry for their few comrades who fail and face an uncertain fate. The cruel twist is that the poor readers are spared and the literate are shot.

The anonymous group of prisoners in 'Red Dogs', in my script, leapt from the pages as individual characters. Some of the observations were based on my own encounters with a variety of uniformed Germans and Soviets during the war.

Lesson II offered me an opportunity to transpose to the military sphere the infamous 'selection process' practised on Jews in concentration camps. The spectre of the columns of men in uniform facing an enemy also in uniform whose finger was pointing either to the *right* or *left*, indicating life or death, was for me the most alarming aspect of the Nazi legacy.

Once in production, when I tried to recruit an assistant none of the prospective school candidates wished to be associated with a film facing so many pitfalls. In the end, I had to bribe a colleague with a promise of an invitation to London. By contrast, my assigned cameraman, Erol Ferudin, was most supportive. He was born in Lodz to an ethnically mixed family: a Polish mother, and a Turkish father whose bakery used to be famous in pre-war Lodz. Erol's presence introduced a sentimental element as I remembered shopping in his father's store with my parents.

We spent days researching at the Warsaw Documentation Archive, viewing miles of German and Soviet newsreel footage (Erol spoke Russian and I German). I made notes and sketched details of Soviet and German military uniforms and other artefacts connected with the German offensive along the Eastern Front. It was a crash-course in barrack room and battlefield conditions.

Considering the Film School facilities, *Lesson II* was an unusually huge production. In my adaptation of Malaparte's story I changed the season from autumn to a snow-bound winter, and the Ukrainian mud-sunken village landscape to an army garrison, affording the camera visually striking contrasts.

We had twelve shooting days and 100 extras provided by the Polish army. My production manager had managed to obtain Soviet uniforms from a local Russian garrison commander who would have been shocked to discover that he was helping a director holding a British passport. I was pleased with the weather forecast: severe frost and heavy snowfalls, though the actors and extras cursed it. Throughout the production the temperature often reached 15 degrees Celsius below zero. During rehearsals the recruits giggled at the sight of their female 'citizen film director' dressed like an Eskimo.

After shooting ended I learned about a betting fever that had spread amongst the theatre school students who were assigned to the production. Who was going to bed me first? With whom would I end up having an affair? At least it was a reversal of the conventional situation – that is, the male director who has affairs with his female stars!

The finished film – far from bringing shame – `earned praise for everyone involved, and the certificate of distinction at international film festivals.

An ingrained obsession with war, with conflict and oppression, would continue to hold me in its grip and help mould my future films.

PERSONA NON GRATA

By 1965, my half-here and half-there life was nearing its end. I had vacated my room in Lodz and I began to say goodbye to friends and ghosts. The reckless commuting years were coming to an end. My diploma film was done – all I needed for my diploma was to prepare a written thesis: 'The Language of Dreams and Film – A Comparative Study.' And I had a whole year to do it in London.

The proposed subject matter involved a process of deconstructing dream sequences used by famous directors in their films and comparing the film version with the original dreams that had inspired them. It was a quest to establish how the dreamer perceives dreams and how they compare when translated into film language.

For instance, when someone relates a dream in which they describe the action of walking in a field, how exactly did they see themselves? Does the subject see himself from afar, in the cinematic language of a long shot, or was it in close-up? Or in a wide angle that included the surrounding landscape? Was he advancing towards 'a camera' or away from it? When conversation took place, did the person see himself talking?

Similarities abound, in spite of the wilder and more chaotic nature of dreams. The cinema had created the technology that had enhanced the potential screen language for dreaming with one's eyes open.

While in analysis with Mary, I had kept a diary of dreams and had accumulated enough of my own to include them in the thesis.

'Well,' my husband said, 'Now that you are back and finished with Poland, what are your plans? Back to painting perhaps?'

The period of adjusting to a life at home was also a time of taking stock. Poland, after all, had not swallowed me up. It had enriched me in many ways and provided a tool for artistic self-realisation.

It also brought me closer to self-knowledge, about the demons that lurk deep in my soul, waiting for a chance to surface. There was no way of getting away from the fact that my creativity was rooted in events that took place in the country of my birth, the country where the Germans had placed their most infamous death camps. One must never forget that Poland was the land over which two homicidal political systems laid to waste a fragile democratic tradition, and in the process wiped out hundreds of years of Polish-Jewish culture. After so many years the trauma of the Holocaust still affects the offspring of the victims and, in different ways, the descendants of the perpetrators.

Immediately before my departure for London, I was staying *chez* Melnikiel, who had become my second family. Four years previously, I had met the man who offered to 'give me back Poland', but it was Jadwiga and her husband Jan who gave me the opportunity to feel 'at home' in Poland.

Just before booking my flight home, the ex-ambassador took me aside and from the way he was puffing the cigarette I could see he was agitated. The scene reminded me of the time Jan took on the role of guide through the Communist ideological minefield, by laying down the law about the dos and don'ts at the beginning of my stay in Poland.

Standing by the mantelpiece, his favourite position when exercising ambassadorial authority, he began: 'You must have noticed that our friends rarely mention Jews or Israel?'

I had indeed observed a marked change in the atmosphere at their social gatherings. Amongst their close friends were 'closet' Jews who were keeping their origins hidden. High-up party officials, for political expediency, were cutting themselves off from the past. The undercurrent of tension was tangible.

'Frankly,' Jan added as an afterthought, 'One can understand their position after the nastiness of 1958.' The nastiness Jan mentioned had a name, which I avoided using in their presence: anti-Semitism. And it still forced many Jews to depart.

Jan and Jadwiga's sympathy for Israel was no secret. During the war, both of them had spent time in Palestine with the Polish army. The pioneering spirit of the Jews had won their admiration and many Palestinian Jews became close friends.

The Milnikiels' sympathy for Israel placed them in a bind. In his official capacity, he was forced to toe the anti-Zionist Soviet line. Though the Soviets had originally supported the creation of the State of Israel, soon after they switched sides and became staunch allies of the Arab states. In times of international crisis, the Soviet anti-Zionist propaganda was adopted by the Soviet satellite states.

Jan spoke with bitterness about his compatriots who were also only too eager to embrace the Soviet-inspired anti-Jewish policies. He acknowledged with sadness how the native anti-Semitism needed little kindling from the outside to spread.

My own experience of anti-Semitism in Poland was minimal. People like the Milnikiels, Zb., his mother, and others like them, including my Film School colleagues, shielded me from its impact. But it was impossible not to be aware of its extent.

'Once you're back in London, don't communicate with your friends,' Jan carried on with his instructions. 'It may cause them serious problems!'

'Not even with you?'

He was nervously fishing for another cigarette before making an affirmative nod. It was best not to do it directly! Jadwiga would arrange a third-party contact through a Swiss diplomat. I understood that future contact with me could carry serious consequences for everyone concerned. In his official capacity at the Foreign Office, Jan was privy to top-secret information. I did not even dare to guess what kind of danger signals he had picked up.

During the commuting years, in my bravura, I had broken the visa rules too many times. I was married to a man who had once served in the British intelligence service. I had refused to spy for Poland, and I had close contact with my family in Israel.

After Jan's warnings, my imminent departure gave me nightmares. My passport could be impounded, preventing me from leaving Poland. Such occurrences were known to happen. I recalled my husband's warning that my British passport might not be able to protect me.

Perhaps the Milnikiels shared a similar anxiety when they decided to see me off at the Warsaw airport. Jan, towering over a chaotic crowd of passengers, kept his hand on my shoulder, steering me towards passport control. At the barrier he delivered the last command.

'Don't return to Poland, not in the foreseeable future!'

I was about to protest 'What about my thesis, my diploma?', but Jan silenced me with a 'No buts, do as I say' expression. At this sad parting we kissed and hugged with heavy hearts. Would we see each other again? They watched me as I passed through the exit gate with my British passport in hand, which smoothed the way like a magic wand.

My heart was pounding when I faced the customs officials known to take a sadistic pleasure in intimidating departing passengers. In my case, the search was even more detailed, and every item of my luggage was carefully examined. They were paying special attention to pockets, the seams of my dresses, every bulging object, including large metal buttons. I watched amused as they tried to unscrew a bulky round-shaped pendant, part of a decorative bracelet I was wearing. I realised they must have been looking for concealed spy gadgets.

In anger and pain, I was ready to cut loose from a nation that did not want me. But I had not anticipated a situation in which the Polish authorities would not let go of me, even in my absence.

Through Jadwiga's third-party contact, I discovered that the Polish authorities' interest in my activities continued unabated. Though I had kept the pledge given to Jan Milnikiel and refrained from communicating with friends, some of my friends were nevertheless harassed by the Secret Service. Periodically, they were grilled about their supposedly 'secret' contacts with me. During the interrogations, it was hinted that I was a dangerous spy in the pay of the Americans and the British!

This was intensified after the Six Day War broke out in the Middle East in 1967. Moscow's war on Zionism took on a crude form, with repercussions for the remaining Polish Jews. Israel, supported by America, was victorious and the Arabs, backed by the Soviet Union, were the losers. In the anti-Zionist propaganda unleashed by the Kremlin the Jews were used as convenient scapegoats. The Cold War turned colder.

The Soviet Bloc's ideological offensive resulted in yet another mass exodus of Polish Jews. During the 'cultural' purges that followed, the Lodz Film School lost a few of its prestigious professors, amongst them Teoplitz and Bossak.

Back home in London, I was busy setting up the production of *Passport*, a film made possible by a grant from the British Film Institute. The half-hour feature film was a result of my anxiety regarding having a passport. Poland had sensitised me to the practical and psychological significance in the possession of this often life-saving document. Dilys Powell, the renowned film critic of the *Sunday Times*, wrote in her review that the film was 'disturbing in its Kafka-esque fashion...'.

The Polish authorities had not given up keeping track of my professional activities. My filmmaking activities did not escape attacks in the Polish press, and after directing a BBC play, *A Boat to Addis-Ababa*, their attacks sharpened. The film was based on a short story published in Poland!

The time of the play's action was the Warsaw ghetto uprising. It dealt with Poles, known as 'Greasers', who were either blackmailing Jews who managed to run away or 'selling' them to the Gestapo.

After the transmission of the TV play, in the Polish press it earned me the description of a 'Jewish viper' that the Motherland had clasped to its bosom. I was declared *persona non grata*, and prevented from obtaining the official graduation document. I was also barred from visiting the country for 14 years. My mother's grave, which I had finally managed to locate, was again left unattended.

'Your Poland!' My English husband, who couldn't hide his contempt, also implied a degree of disgust at my complicated feelings for my country.

Eventually, my hurt feelings and revulsion towards Poland turned to pity. Poor Poland, I thought! In spite of its long history of having faced neighbours who had tried to wipe it off the map of Europe, twice already, on regaining its independence, for many Poles, anti-Semitic activities had became central to it's political and social life.

'Why don't you write Poland off? England is your home, and English is your language now. Turn your back on that wretched country!'

If only it were that simple.

I love England with a sober affection, but for Poland I feel tenderness. I discovered that my Polishness was as much part of my psyche as my Jewishness and it could not be separated. When in despair, to console myself I think about the proportionately large number of Poles who have risked their lives to save Jews. They are honoured as Righteous Gentiles at the Yaad V'shem gardens, with trees planted in their name which had grown into a small forest. Such women and men were heroes and represent every strata of Polish society.

Soon after the Solidarity period and the changes in the political climate, my ban from visiting Poland was lifted and I managed to get a visa to Poland to shoot the film *Loving the Dead* (Channel 4). The film posed the question of how the Poles co-exist with the Jewish ghosts.

In the note for the catalogue of the London Film Festival the writer Gil Elliot wrote the following:

> ...the protagonist and director went to the country of her birth, to find out how the Poles in present day Poland live with the shadow cast over them by the millions of Jews murdered in their country during World War II...A powerful film and a record of Europe revisited like a home shrunken with time...This is a personal record that brings Poland and Europe together, gathering in on us like the dark wind in Rilke's 'Diuno Elegies'. More than a documentary, a feature film with her life at the centre and around that core, the dedicated camera eye of an artist, unblinking; lightning on truth. A masterly achievement.

Epilogue

'Film is light.' That's how Frederico Fellini once defined the essence of cinematography.

I was eager to join the fraternity of filmmakers, our modern alchemists, who, by filtering light through optic lenses and chemical processes, manage to distil reality into sheer illusion. In film the language of images precedes thought. When the cinema goes dark and the projector's beam alights, the screen comes alive with stories illustrated with the hieroglyphs of the mind. Miraculously, most of humankind has learned to decode them, and an almost unique universal literacy spans the globe.

During my work as an independent filmmaker a triptych of films dealing with conflict and oppression took me on a global spin. In the faraway places, in South Africa, the Middle East, India and elsewhere, I was asked what inspired me. I mentioned my parents' Lodz ghetto experiences, and my father's fate in Auschwitz as the propelling engine in my various explorations of people's capacity for dehumanising each other regardless of national or continental boundaries.

In South Africa *Maids and Madams* (Channel 4) dealt with apartheid from the perspective of black and white women's racial confrontation. It explored the encounters of a most intimate and domestic kind that transpired under the roof of the Madams' home.

Observing apartheid in action gave me an insight into how easy it is to dehumanise people and deprive them of basic rights, another milestone in my ongoing journey to understanding the Lodz ghetto. Any black person looking at me would see in me a representative of the system. I found myself in a truly anomalous situation. As a Jew, some years earlier I would have been condemned to death on account of my race but in South Africa I was perceived as a white woman with all the privileges claimed by the whites.

Talking to the Enemy (Channel 4) examined the national clash between the Israelis and Palestinians, the tragedy of two peoples claiming the same land. Once more I touched on risky subject matter. My sympathies were divided equally between Israel, where I had family, and the Palestinians. My commissioning editor questioned whether a film director in my position could be objective. In the end, when the film was shown in England and other English-speaking countries, I proved that it was possible. By and large the Jewish view was that the film favoured the Palestinians and the Arabs claimed that it favoured Israel – a good indication that indeed the scales of objectivity were kept in balance.

The background to filming in India was through my social connection with people rooted in the Anglo-Indian history. It was my friendship with Raj Mulk Anand, an Indian writer whose first book about the Untouchables was published in London in the late 1930s, that inspired me. *Caste at Birth* (Channel 4) a film about the Untouchables, was a result of this relationship.

I kept meeting the author in the house of a friend during his frequent visits to London.

'You have made a film about South Africa, you have made a film about the Israeli-Palestinian conflict. Don't you think you should come to India and make a film about the oppression of the Untouchables?' Raj Mulk Anand addressed this reproach to me in the late 1970s. It took a few years before I finally realised his wish.

Each of the above films earned international recognition and numerous prestigious awards. In their wake, as well as international distribution, their success brought many invitations to participate at international film festivals.

Film festivals enrich filmmakers' perception of their own work by offering a platform for meeting other film directors. The direct contacts with live audiences occasion often riveting question and answer sessions, but most importantly they provide grounds for extraordinary encounters and reunions. Such a reunion occurred at the New York Jewish Film Festival, held at the Lincoln Center in 1997, after the film *Loving the Dead* was screened.

The end of the screening was greeted with a dead silence. Such silences in a cinema speak volumes. When the lights came on the audience was reluctant to clap in case a noisy reaction would be an affront to the sombre mood. After the usual question time at the end of the projection, the pressure of time schedules forced me to move to the lounge where I could continue talking with people keen to discuss the film.

In the group of people was a grey-haired elderly woman supporting herself on a stick who pressed a coin into my hand.

'I want you to keep it! And when you look at it, think about the people through whose hands it passed,' she said.

I had seen such coins displayed in Holocaust museums. Made of tin, it was in circulation in the Lodz ghetto and was known as an

'RM' or 'Rumki', a reference to Rumkowski, the issuer of the coin and the Elder of the Ghetto. The printing of the ghetto's own currency proved to be a folly. It had isolated the Jews even more from the rest of occupied Poland.

'Feel its weight!' she said.

It felt light in my hand, too light for 'serious' money.

'This could buy a slice of bread,' she added.

The possession of such 'Rumkis', she explained, was often a matter of life and death. My parents would have handled such coins that now had a museum value. Before I could ask for her name, she made her way towards the exit and vanished.

The group of people shrank to a few individuals keen to talk about the merit of the film and about my work as a woman film director. Many of the questions were of a personal nature, about my life. Being used to questions from the audience I had learned to glide over them as sincerely as possible but to keep it short.

I noticed a short, plump woman hanging back from the group, yet keeping her eyes on me. She wore a cream-coloured anorak and was muffled up in a woollen scarf. Her round face and grey eyes conveyed a hidden amusement derived from what I was saying. Each time I looked in her direction, intending to encourage her to come closer, she withdrew even more into the corner. But her eyes never left me. When most of the people dispersed she finally addressed me.

'Where were you at the end of the war?'

'In Jerusalem.'

Her voice, coarsened by a Brooklyn Jewish accent, sounded familiar. In an instant I recalled the girl from Grodno. Standing still, my mind was racing and I could hear the sounds of her practising the piano. I could discern traces of her mother, Sonia, whose dimpled face was always flushed from the kitchen heat, peeping out from behind her middle-aged Americanised daughter's presence. And her father, Melczer, the dentist who was fixing gold crowns in the mouths of the high-ranking Soviet officers...

'Ilonka?!'

We fell into each other's arms, both tearful.

It was a raw, wet New York autumn day and outside the Lincoln Center the wind tossed the trees. In the cafe across the road we looked at each other silently, touching hands. The reunion after so many years created a mental whirlwind for both of us. We had found each other in the New World, but the memories of the Old

World were heavy, crushing the fragile sense of togetherness. So much had happened to both of us that it was difficult for us to connect – too much joy, too much sadness.

'What about Sonia, Melczer and the other members of your family?' Before I managed to finish the question she cut me short.

'All dead. I am the only survivor.' After a short pause she added, 'Do you remember Kostia?'

How could I forget the sledge journey with Kostia through the snow-covered fields and the frostbitten trek towards the Lithuanian border.

'Kostia saved my life. He hid me.'

What happened after I left and Kostia returned with the story of my arrest?

'Mother felt guilty for letting you leave. So did father. I wept for days. I blamed her for entrusting you into Kostia's care. You were in such a hurry to get away,' Ilonka mused. 'Like an animal sensing danger.'

In Grodno, she and I used to whisper late into the night and our imagination was inflamed with teenage dreams, now we were two middle-aged women facing each other, waiting to learn something about our lives. When the waitress brought the refreshments, Ilonka searched for her small, plastic pill-container and was popping multicoloured pills into her mouth.

'Cortisone, for inflammation of muscles, a very painful condition,' she explained. The cortisone made her even larger than she was before. She was also taking pills for high blood pressure.

'You look good.' Her eyes were scrutinising my face for wrinkles. Her own showed the ravages of age and hard times.

She offered a brief review of her own mundane life in America, where she had landed in 1953 and married a good but simple man, also a survivor from Grodno. They had two children, a daughter and a son. The son was doing well. The daughter, a lesbian, was drifting, trying her luck as a pop singer. Ilonka had a part-time job in an insurance office as an accountant. Her husband was suffering from a mild form of Parkinson's. He was now retired and needed a lot of attention.

'Tell me about yourself.' Ilonka waited but I was tongue-tied. The disparity of our situations pained and burdened me. How could I tell her that in New York, which had kept her grounded, I was flying, carried on a wave of media attention? I was a film director from London, with desirable New York connections to people on the cultural forefront. My time was filled with press interviews and parties. I was feeling full of vigour, having fulfilled some of my aspirations. Ilonka's body had expanded in size but her spirit had shrivelled. It was not fair how fate had treated her! She was so promising and talented. Had our reunion deepened her sense of loss, and reminded her of the high cost of her own survival?

I told her that I had been married but was now divorced with one son who was married with two children. I told her about my brother's time in Siberia and that he and my sister lived in Israel where they had a reasonably good life. Did she feel jealous of my good fortune?

'What about the piano playing? Your writing?' I asked, changing the subject. She had neither the conditions nor the time for such things, she said. Even her desire to study English literature had never been fulfilled.

Ilonka kept her eyes on her watch, anxious not to miss the last train to New Jersey. We parted, both of us saddened by the exchange.

At night, my thoughts were preoccupied with Ilonka. I was and was not surprised that we met in New York, a city of immigrants. Hadn't we planned in the long winter of 1940 to meet at the end of the war, in Warsaw or Paris? We had even set the date: the first Sunday in May.

Her juvenile, short poem that she had composed as a gift for my departure surfaced from under the layer of dust that gathered in my memory. I phoned her and recited it.

> My friendship rolls like a tear.
> My dreams fly like birds,
> Circling the earth.
> In a heap of words,
> Solid as rocks.
> Listen and look out for them!

She did not remember she had written it. Ilonka's hard life and the desertion by her Muse made me cry.

Index

Compiled by Stephanie Johnson

Printed and bound by CPI Group (UK) Ltd, Croydon, CR0 4YY

13/04/2025

14656490-0005